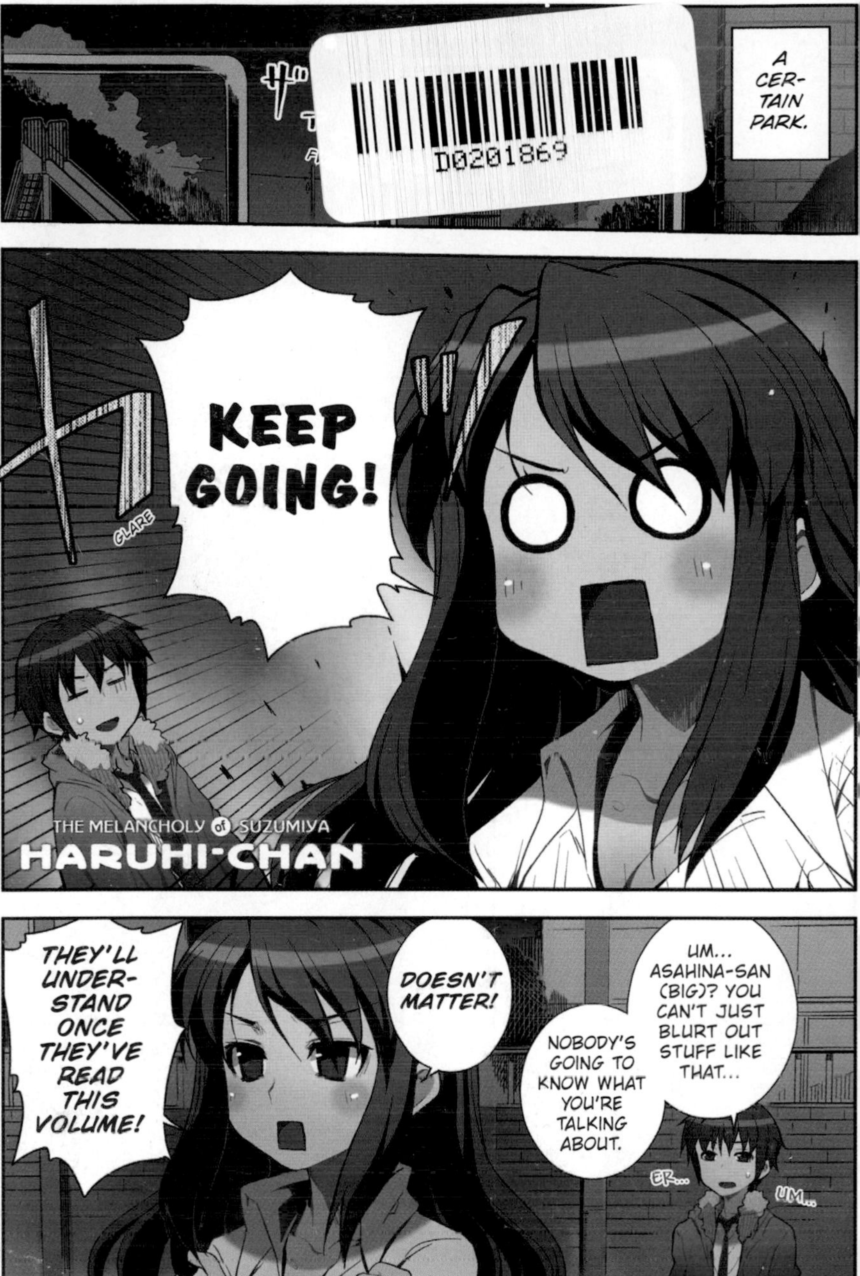
A CERTAIN PARK.
KEEP GOING!
GLARE
THE MELANCHOLY of SUZUMIYA
HARUHI-CHAN
UM... ASAHINA-SAN (BIG)? YOU CAN'T JUST BLURT OUT STUFF LIKE THAT...
NOBODY'S GOING TO KNOW WHAT YOU'RE TALKING ABOUT.
UM...
ER...
DOESN'T MATTER!
THEY'LL UNDERSTAND ONCE THEY'VE READ THIS VOLUME!

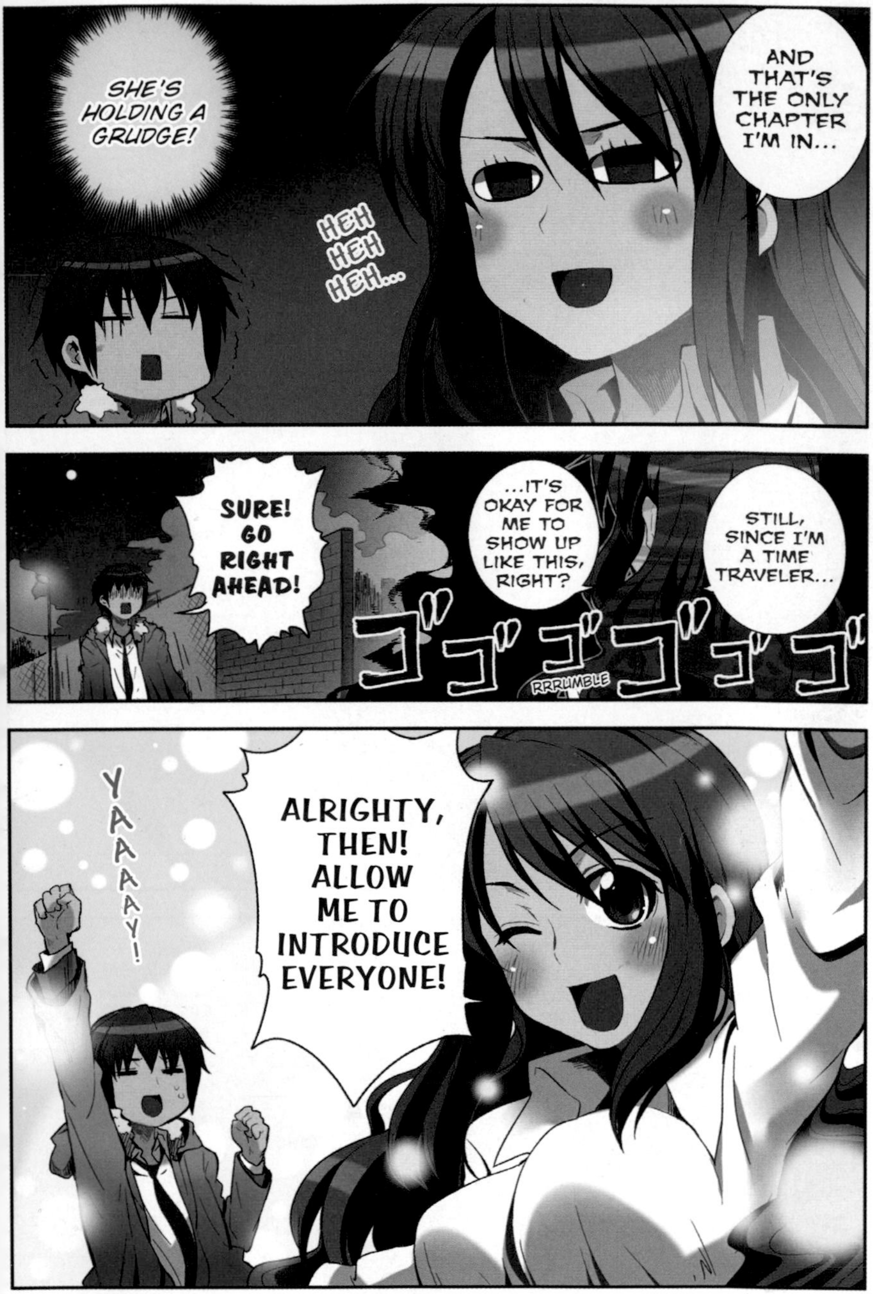
AND THAT'S THE ONLY CHAPTER I'M IN...
HEH HEH HEH...
SHE'S HOLDING A GRUDGE!
STILL, SINCE I'M A TIME TRAVELER...
...IT'S OKAY FOR ME TO SHOW UP LIKE THIS, RIGHT?
ゴゴゴゴゴゴ
RRRUMBLE
SURE! GO RIGHT AHEAD!
ALRIGHTY, THEN! ALLOW ME TO INTRODUCE EVERYONE!
YAAAAY!

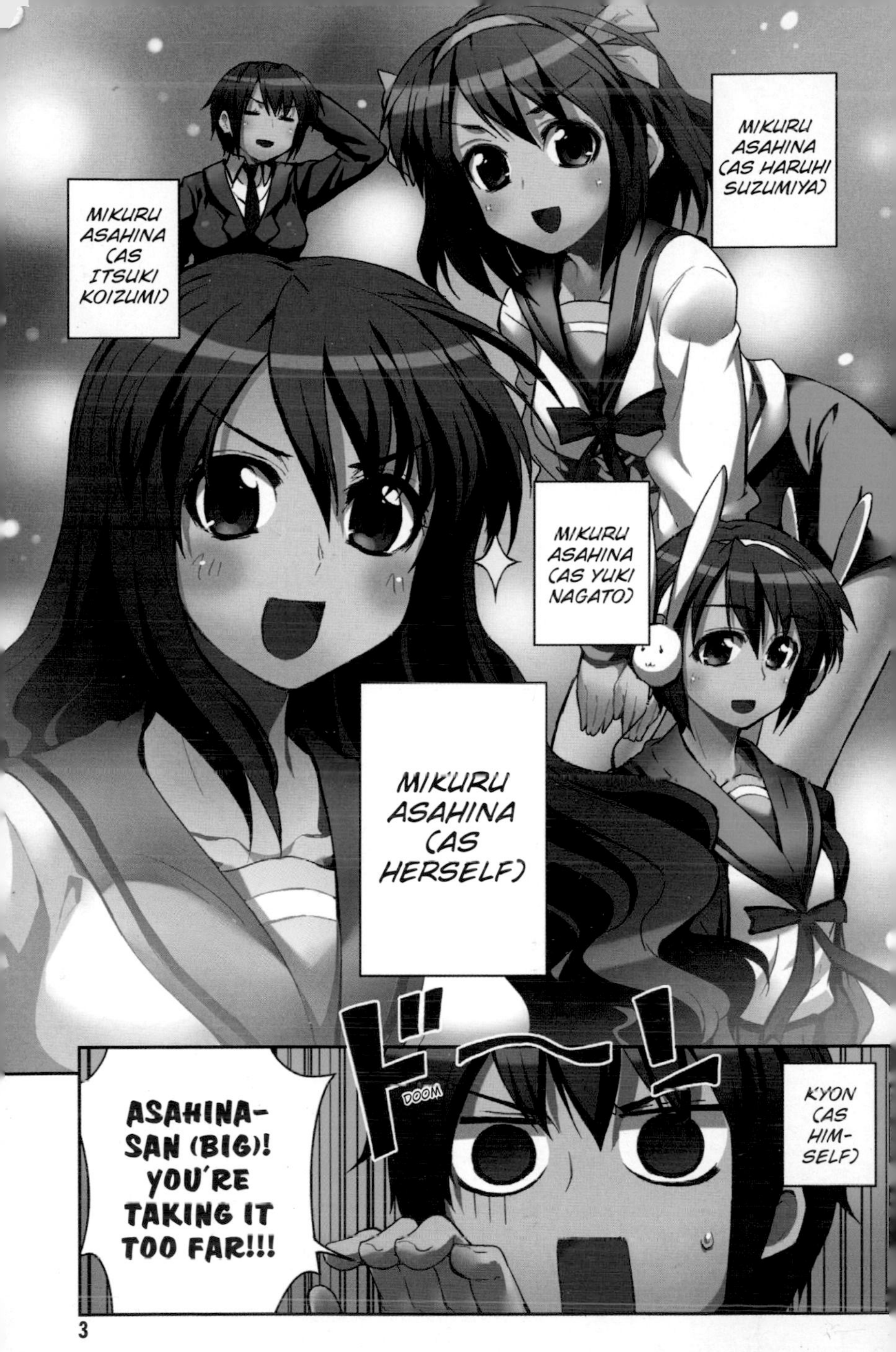
MIKURU ASAHINA (AS HARUHI SUZUMIYA)
MIKURU ASAHINA (AS ITSUKI KOIZUMI)
MIKURU ASAHINA (AS YUKI NAGATO)
MIKURU ASAHINA (AS HERSELF)
KYON (AS HIM-SELF)
ドー!!
DOOM
ASAHINA-SAN (BIG)! YOU'RE TAKING IT TOO FAR!!!

The Melancholy of Suzumiya
Haruhi-chan
03

INDEX

THE MELANCHOLY of SUZUMIYA HARUHI-CHAN 03

The Untold Adventures of the SOS Brigade

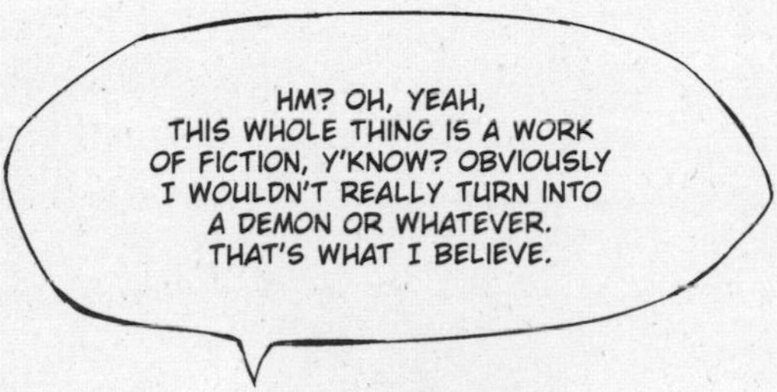
HM? OH, YEAH, THIS WHOLE THING IS A WORK OF FICTION, Y'KNOW? OBVIOUSLY I WOULDN'T REALLY TURN INTO A DEMON OR WHATEVER. THAT'S WHAT I BELIEVE.
HA HA HA...

STORY: **NAGARU TANIGAWA** ART: **PUYO** CHARACTERS: NOIZI ITO

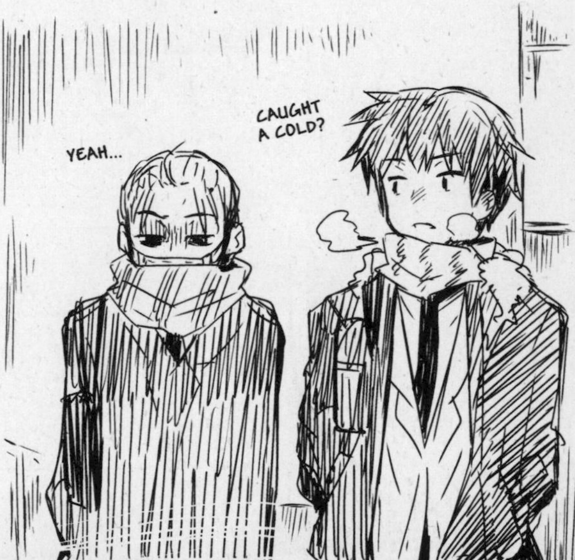
CAUGHT A COLD?
YEAH...

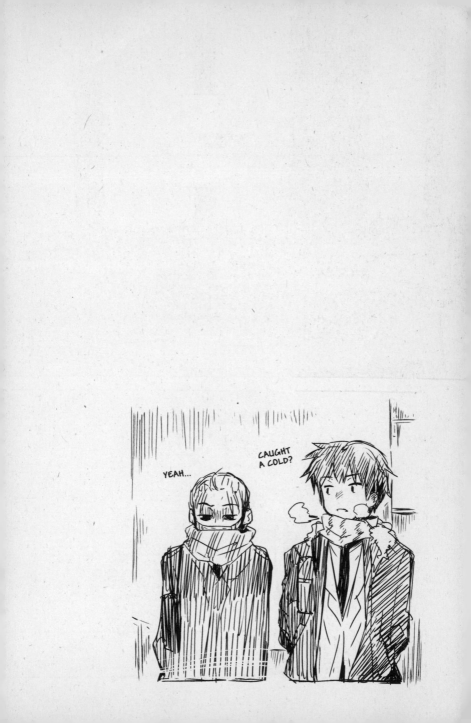

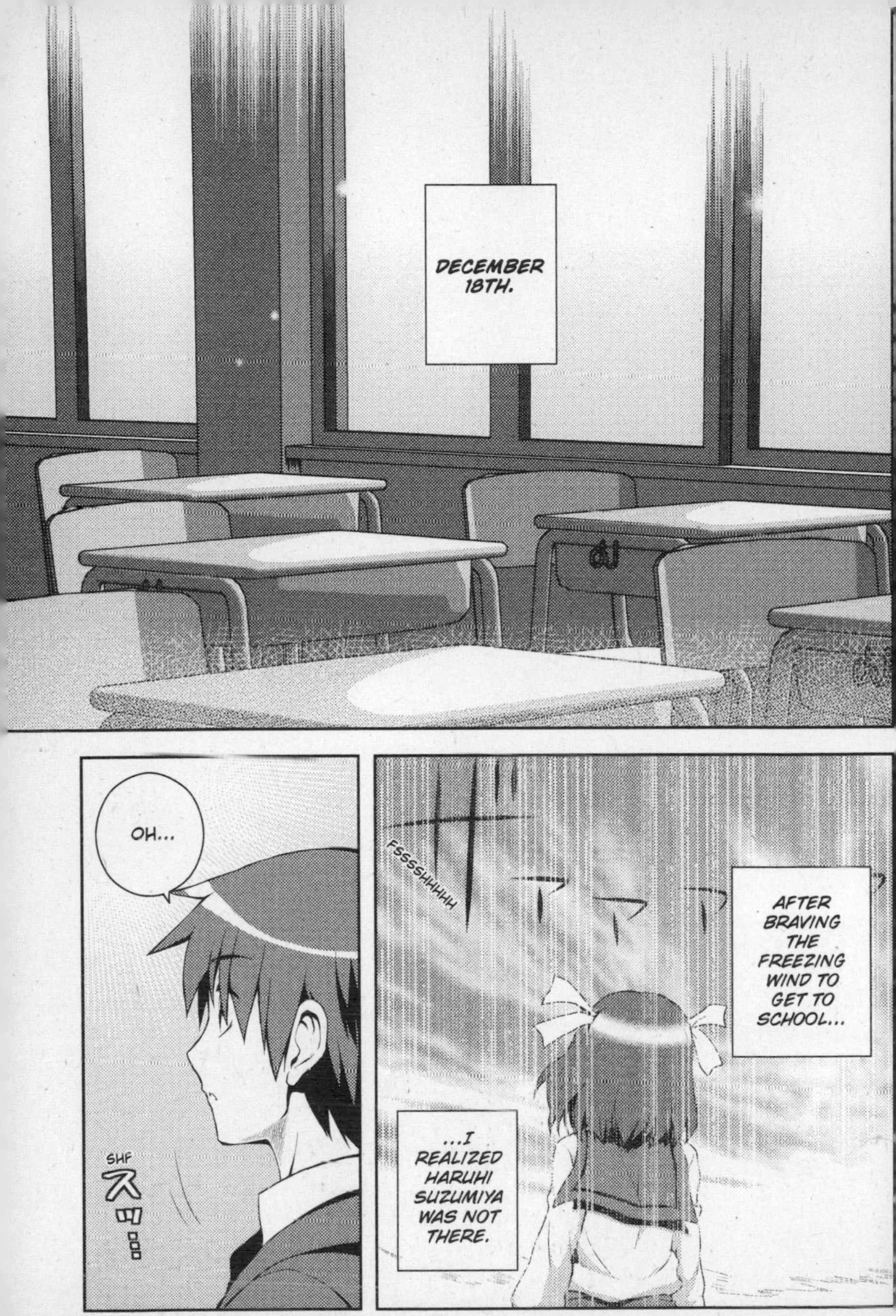
DECEMBER 18TH.
AFTER BRAVING THE FREEZING WIND TO GET TO SCHOOL...
FSSSSHHHHH
...I REALIZED HARUHI SUZUMIYA WAS NOT THERE.
OH...
SHF
スッ...

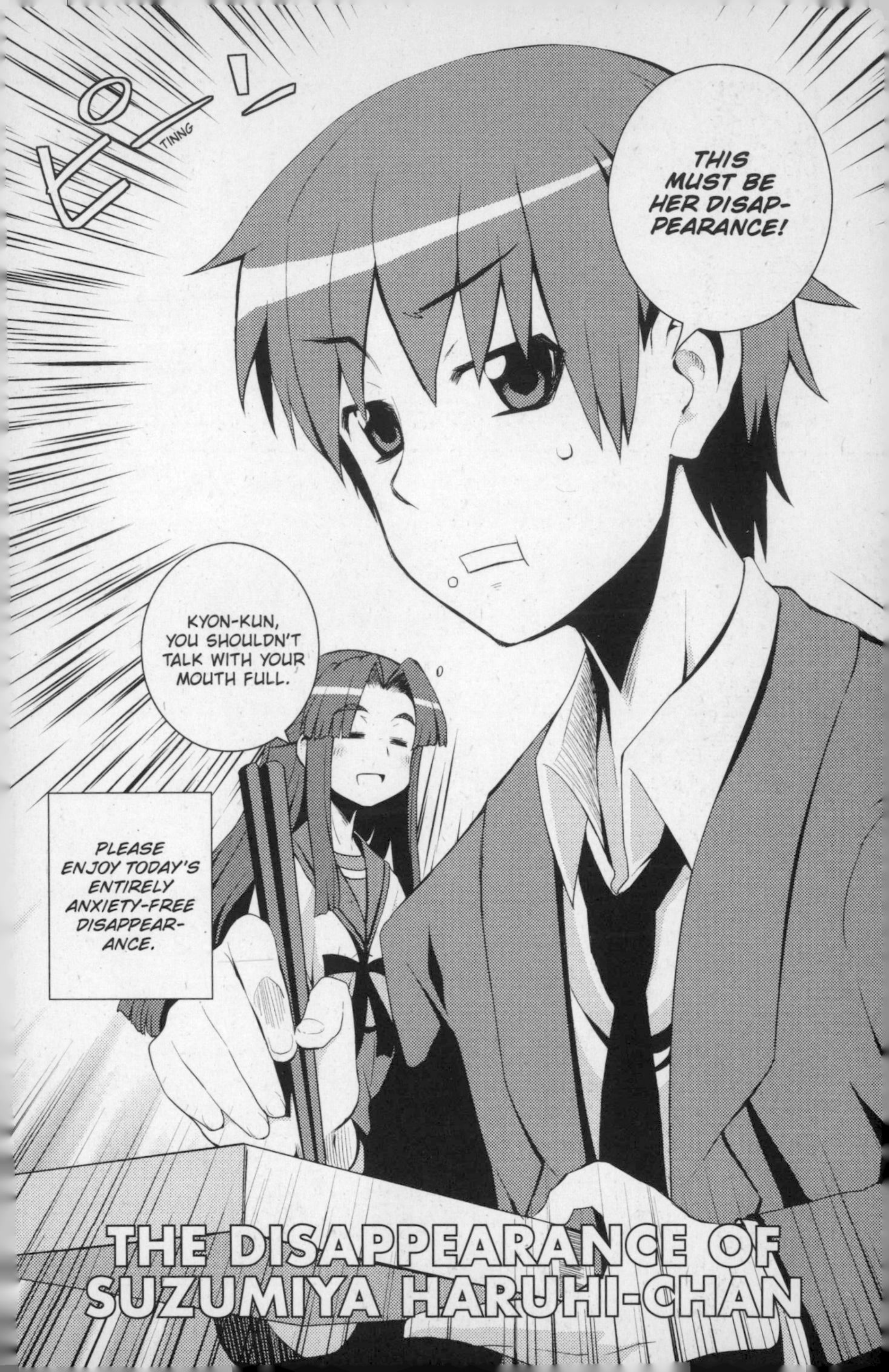
THIS MUST BE HER DISAPPEARANCE!
TINNG
KYON-KUN, YOU SHOULDN'T TALK WITH YOUR MOUTH FULL.
PLEASE ENJOY TODAY'S ENTIRELY ANXIETY-FREE DISAPPEARANCE.
THE DISAPPEARANCE OF SUZUMIYA HARUHI-CHAN

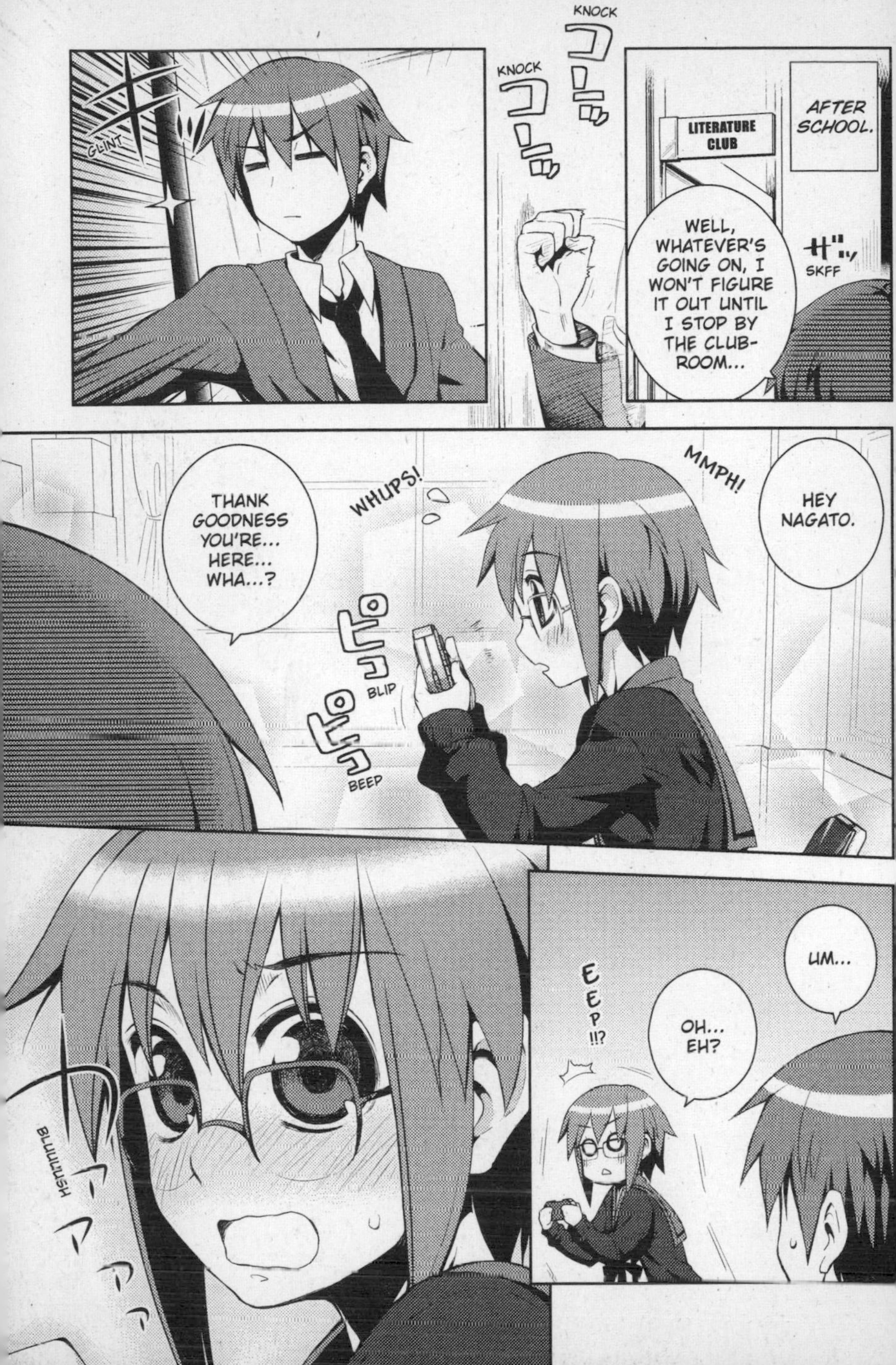
AFTER SCHOOL.
LITERATURE CLUB
WELL, WHATEVER'S GOING ON, I WON'T FIGURE IT OUT UNTIL I STOP BY THE CLUB-ROOM...
SKFF
KNOCK
KNOCK
GLINT
HEY NAGATO.
MMPH!
WHUPS!
BLIP
BEEP
THANK GOODNESS YOU'RE... HERE... WHA...?
UM...
OH... EH?
EEP!!?
BLUUUSH

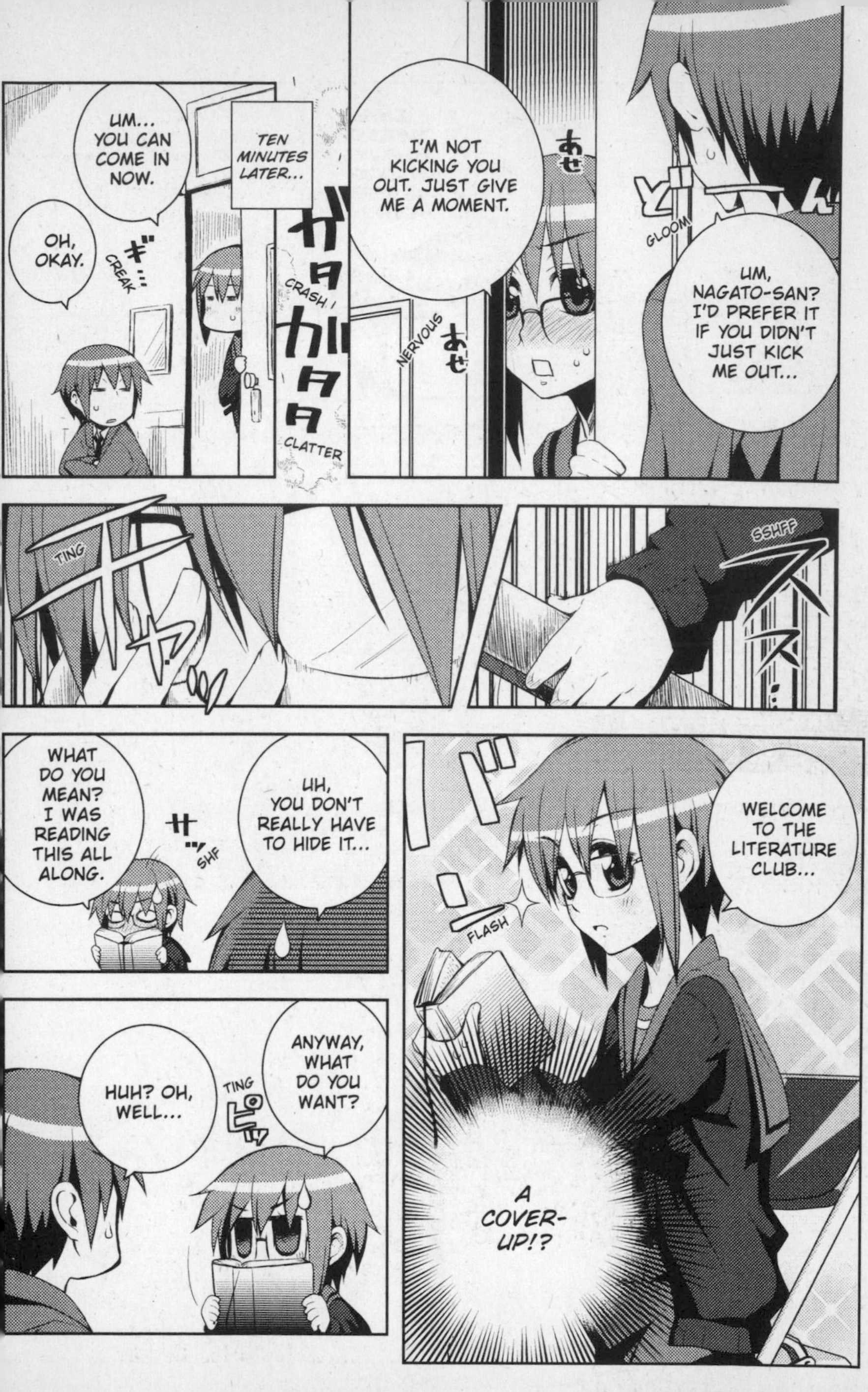
GLOOM
UM, NAGATO-SAN? I'D PREFER IT IF YOU DIDN'T JUST KICK ME OUT...
I'M NOT KICKING YOU OUT. JUST GIVE ME A MOMENT.
NERVOUS
CRASH
CLATTER
TEN MINUTES LATER...
UM... YOU CAN COME IN NOW.
CREAK
OH, OKAY.
SSHFF
TING
WELCOME TO THE LITERATURE CLUB...
FLASH
A COVER-UP!?
UH, YOU DON'T REALLY HAVE TO HIDE IT...
SHF
WHAT DO YOU MEAN? I WAS READING THIS ALL ALONG.
ANYWAY, WHAT DO YOU WANT?
TING
HUH? OH, WELL...

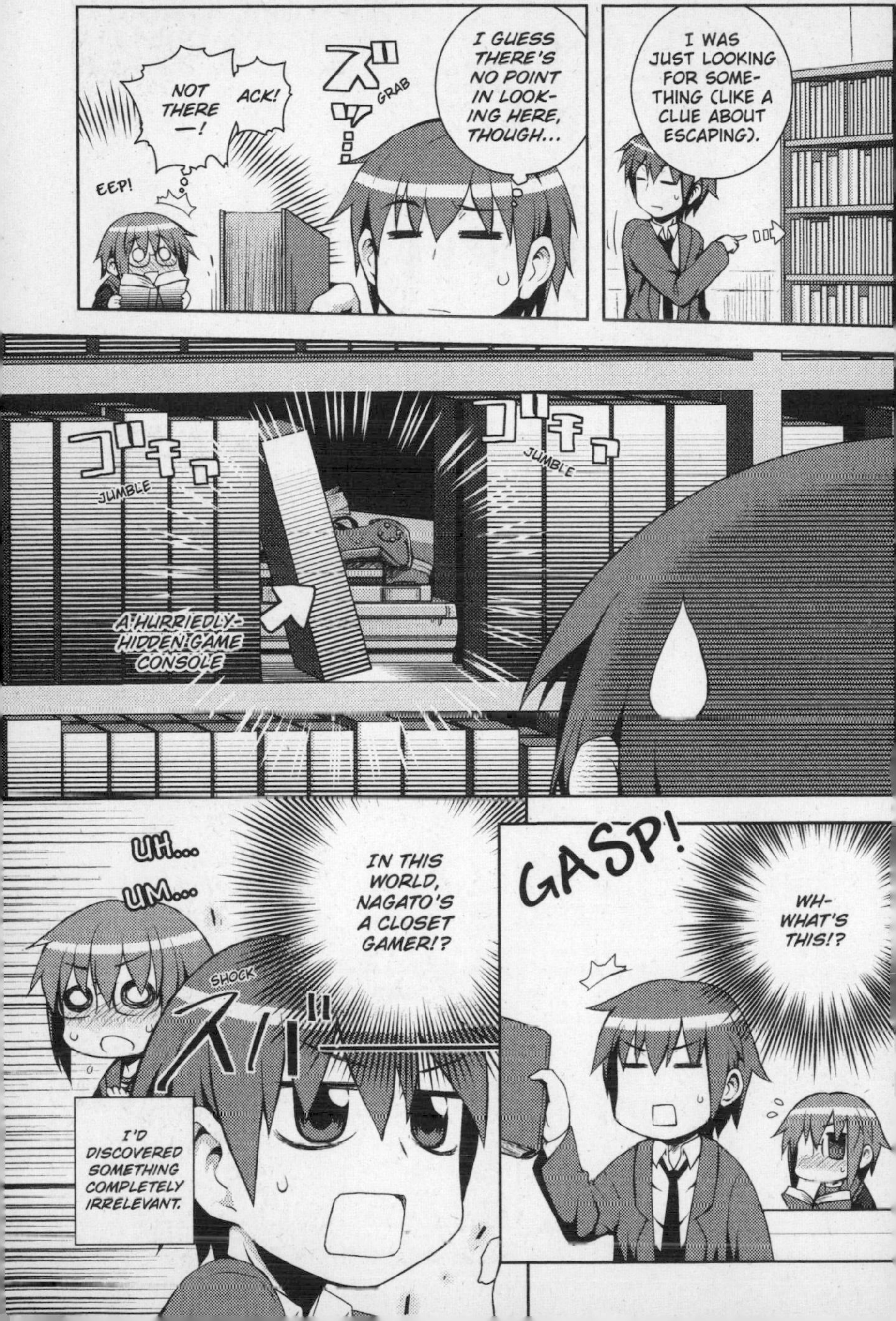
I WAS JUST LOOKING FOR SOMETHING (LIKE A CLUE ABOUT ESCAPING).
I GUESS THERE'S NO POINT IN LOOKING HERE, THOUGH...
GRAB
ACK!
NOT THERE—!
EEP!
JUMBLE
JUMBLE
A HURRIEDLY-HIDDEN GAME CONSOLE
GASP!
WH-WHAT'S THIS!?
IN THIS WORLD, NAGATO'S A CLOSET GAMER!?
UH...
UM...
SHOCK
I'D DISCOVERED SOMETHING COMPLETELY IRRELEVANT.

INTERLUDE: THE DISAPPEARANCE OF MIKURU-CHAN

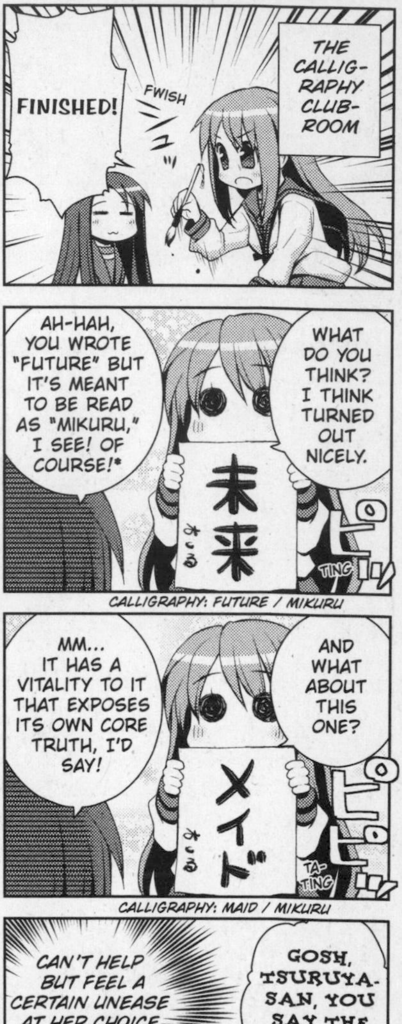
THE CALLIGRAPHY CLUBROOM
FWISH
FINISHED!
WHAT DO YOU THINK? I THINK TURNED OUT NICELY.
AH-HAH, YOU WROTE "FUTURE" BUT IT'S MEANT TO BE READ AS "MIKURU," I SEE! OF COURSE!*
未来
みくる
TING
CALLIGRAPHY: FUTURE / MIKURU
AND WHAT ABOUT THIS ONE?
MM... IT HAS A VITALITY TO IT THAT EXPOSES ITS OWN CORE TRUTH, I'D SAY!
メイド
みくる
TA-TING
CALLIGRAPHY: MAID / MIKURU
GOSH, TSURUYA-SAN, YOU SAY THE NICEST THINGS!
CAN'T HELP BUT FEEL A CERTAIN UNEASE AT HER CHOICE OF WORDS, THOUGH...
TEE HEE!

*THE TWO KANJI MIKURU HAS WRITTEN ARE USUALLY READ "MIRAI," WHICH MEANS "FUTURE," BUT THEY CAN ALSO BE READ "MIKURU."

INTERLUDE: THE DISAPPEARANCE OF TSURUYA-SAN

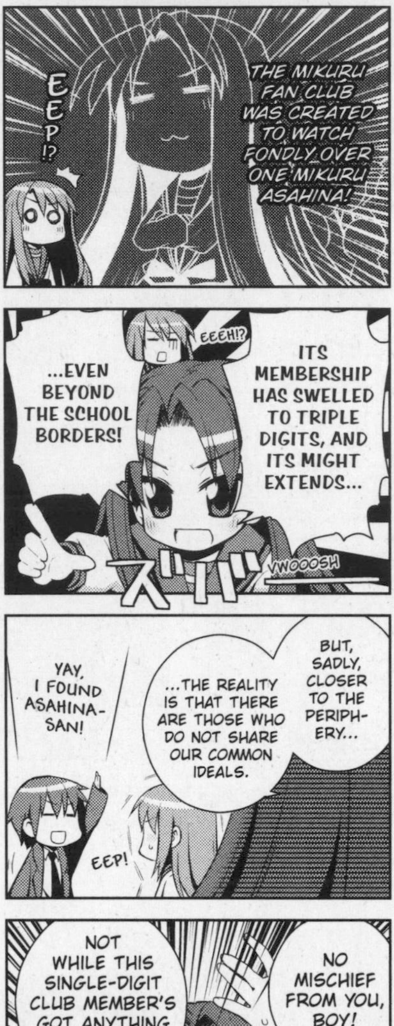
THE MIKURU FAN CLUB WAS CREATED TO WATCH FONDLY OVER ONE MIKURU ASAHINA!
EEP!?
ITS MEMBERSHIP HAS SWELLED TO TRIPLE DIGITS, AND ITS MIGHT EXTENDS...
...EVEN BEYOND THE SCHOOL BORDERS!
EEEH!?
VWOOOSH
BUT, SADLY, CLOSER TO THE PERIPHERY...
...THE REALITY IS THAT THERE ARE THOSE WHO DO NOT SHARE OUR COMMON IDEALS.
YAY, I FOUND ASAHINA-SAN!
EEP!
NO MISCHIEF FROM YOU, BOY!
NOT WHILE THIS SINGLE-DIGIT CLUB MEMBER'S GOT ANYTHING TO SAY ABOUT IT!
Mikuru Fan Club
AAAAAGH!!
HONYA!?

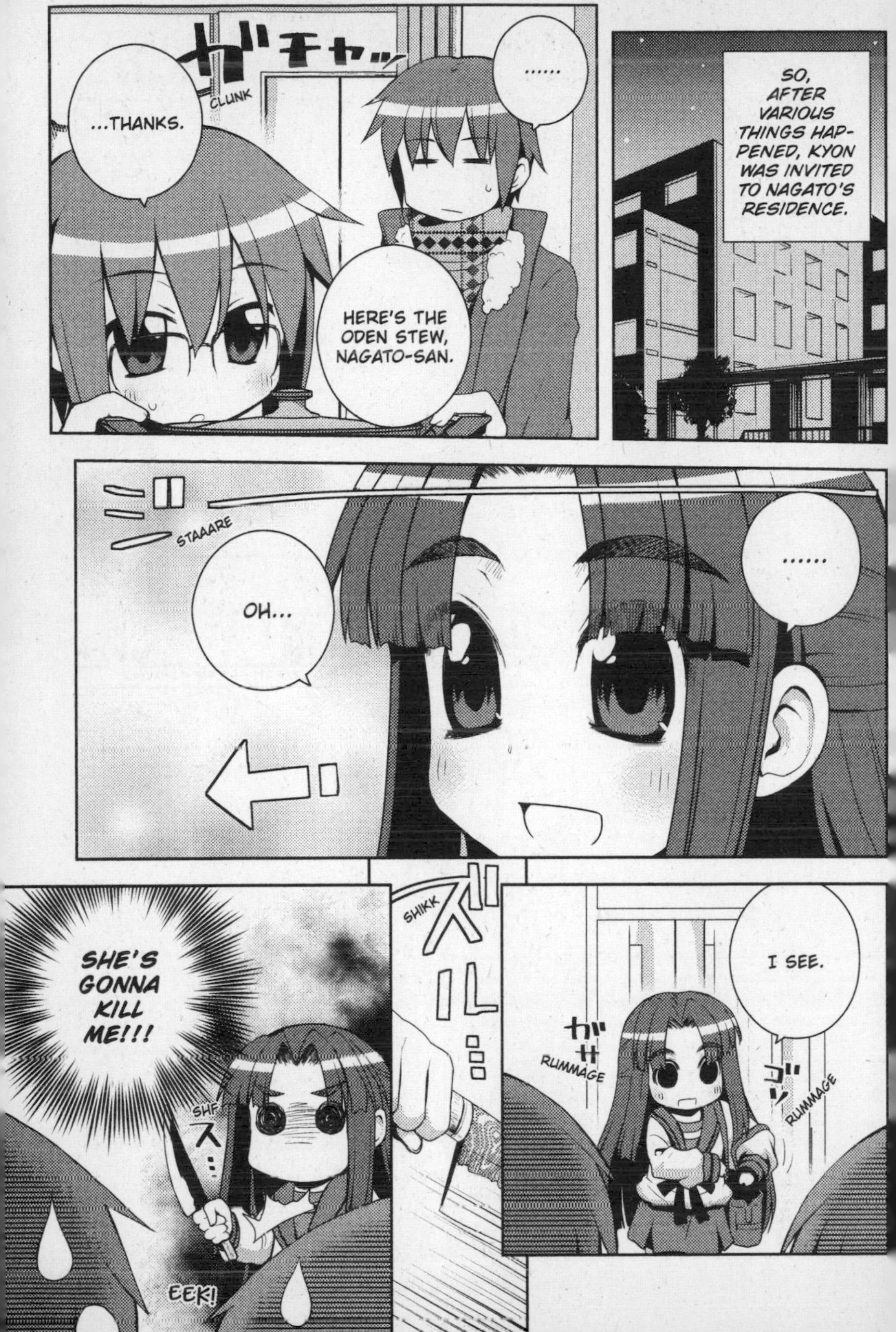
SO, AFTER VARIOUS THINGS HAP-PENED, KYON WAS INVITED TO NAGATO'S RESIDENCE.
......
ガチャッ
CLUNK
...THANKS.
HERE'S THE ODEN STEW, NAGATO-SAN.
......
OH...
ジー
STAARE
I SEE.
ゴソ
RUMMAGE
ガサ
RUMMAGE
ズル
SHIKK
SHE'S GONNA KILL ME!!!
ス
SHF
EEK!

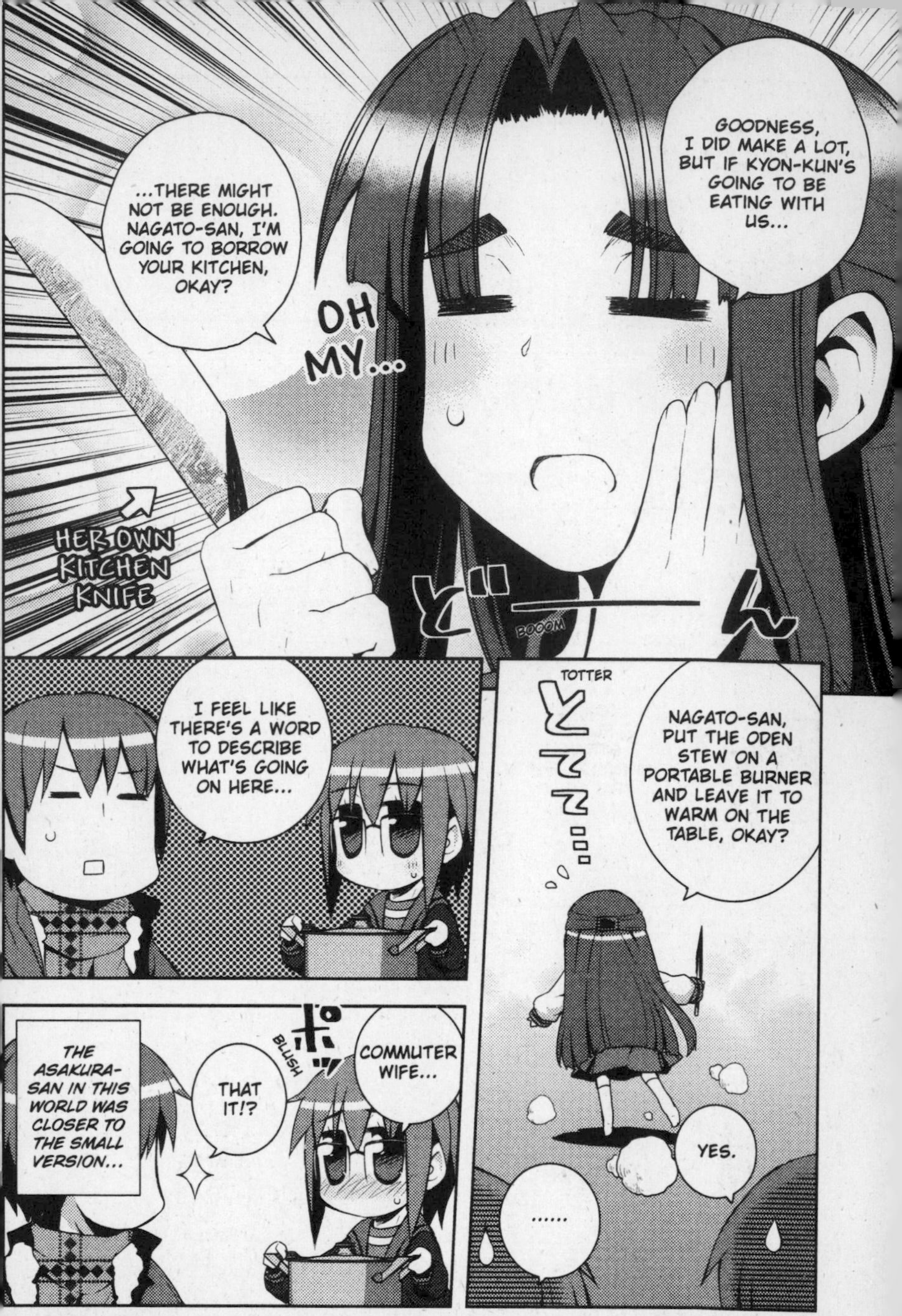
GOODNESS, I DID MAKE A LOT, BUT IF KYON-KUN'S GOING TO BE EATING WITH US...
OH MY...
...THERE MIGHT NOT BE ENOUGH. NAGATO-SAN, I'M GOING TO BORROW YOUR KITCHEN, OKAY?
HER OWN KITCHEN KNIFE
どーーん
BOOOM
TOTTER
とてて...
NAGATO-SAN, PUT THE ODEN STEW ON A PORTABLE BURNER AND LEAVE IT TO WARM ON THE TABLE, OKAY?
YES.
......
I FEEL LIKE THERE'S A WORD TO DESCRIBE WHAT'S GOING ON HERE...
COMMUTER WIFE...
ポッ
BLUSH
THAT IT!?
THE ASAKURA-SAN IN THIS WORLD WAS CLOSER TO THE SMALL VERSION...

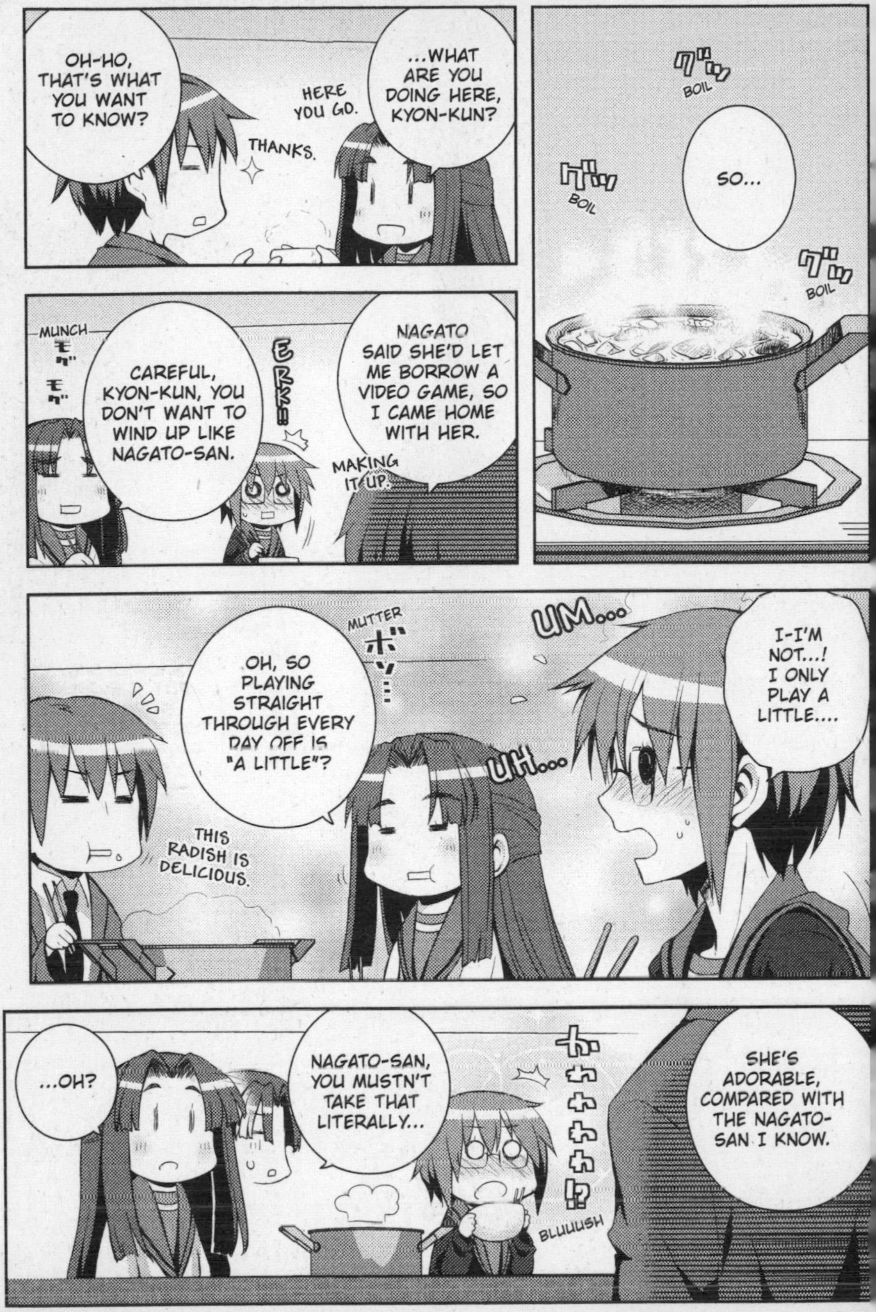
BOIL
BOIL
SO...
BOIL
...WHAT ARE YOU DOING HERE, KYON-KUN?
HERE YOU GO.
THANKS.
OH-HO, THAT'S WHAT YOU WANT TO KNOW?
NAGATO SAID SHE'D LET ME BORROW A VIDEO GAME, SO I CAME HOME WITH HER.
MAKING IT UP.
ERK!!
CAREFUL, KYON-KUN, YOU DON'T WANT TO WIND UP LIKE NAGATO-SAN.
MUNCH
I-I'M NOT...! I ONLY PLAY A LITTLE....
UM...
UH...
MUTTER
OH, SO PLAYING STRAIGHT THROUGH EVERY DAY OFF IS "A LITTLE"?
THIS RADISH IS DELICIOUS.
SHE'S ADORABLE, COMPARED WITH THE NAGATO-SAN I KNOW.
BLUUUSH
NAGATO-SAN, YOU MUSTN'T TAKE THAT LITERALLY...
...OH?

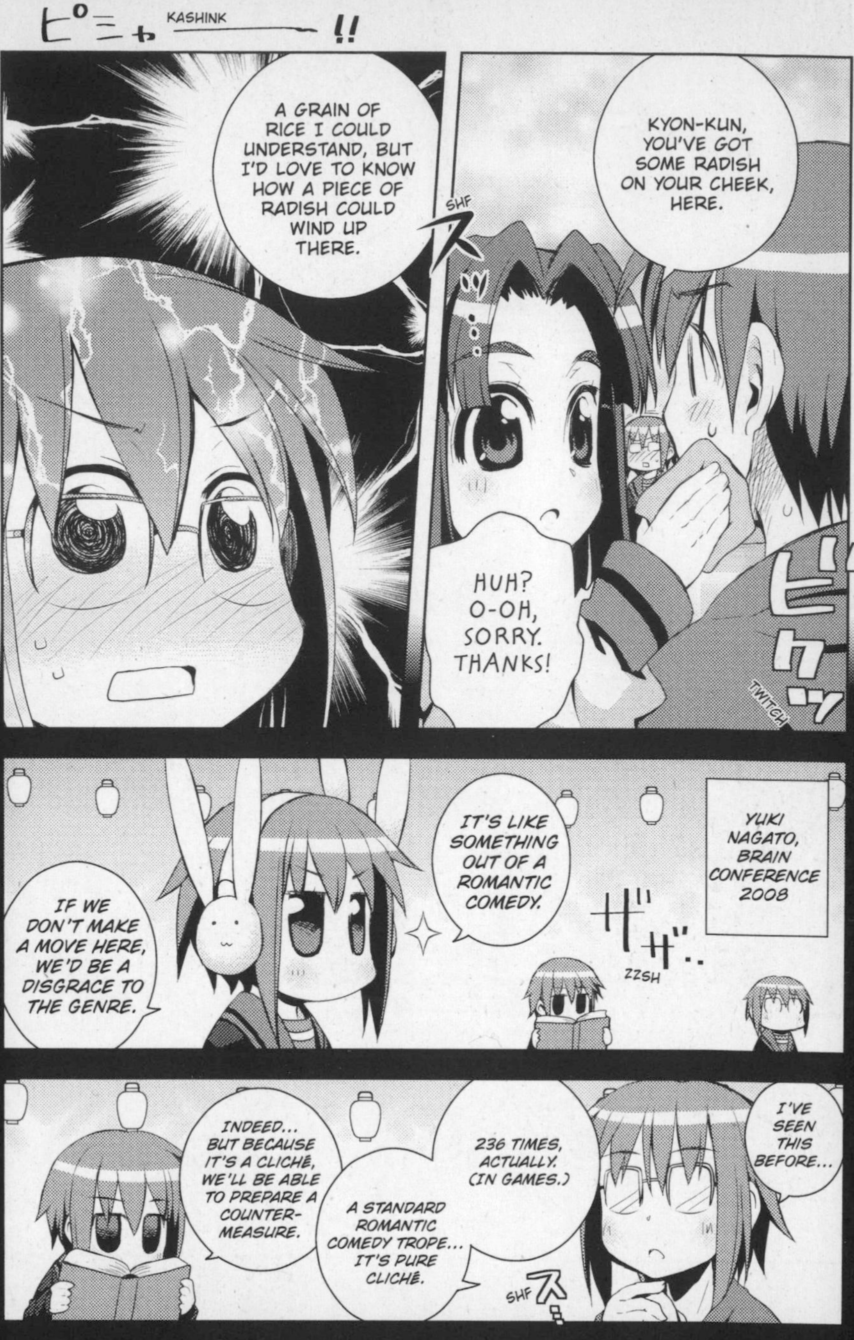
KYON-KUN, YOU'VE GOT SOME RADISH ON YOUR CHEEK, HERE.
SHF
HUH? O-OH, SORRY. THANKS!
TWITCH
KASHINK
A GRAIN OF RICE I COULD UNDERSTAND, BUT I'D LOVE TO KNOW HOW A PIECE OF RADISH COULD WIND UP THERE.
YUKI NAGATO, BRAIN CONFERENCE 2008
ZZSH
IT'S LIKE SOMETHING OUT OF A ROMANTIC COMEDY.
IF WE DON'T MAKE A MOVE HERE, WE'D BE A DISGRACE TO THE GENRE.
I'VE SEEN THIS BEFORE...
SHF
236 TIMES, ACTUALLY. (IN GAMES.)
A STANDARD ROMANTIC COMEDY TROPE... IT'S PURE CLICHÉ.
INDEED... BUT BECAUSE IT'S A CLICHÉ, WE'LL BE ABLE TO PREPARE A COUNTER-MEASURE.

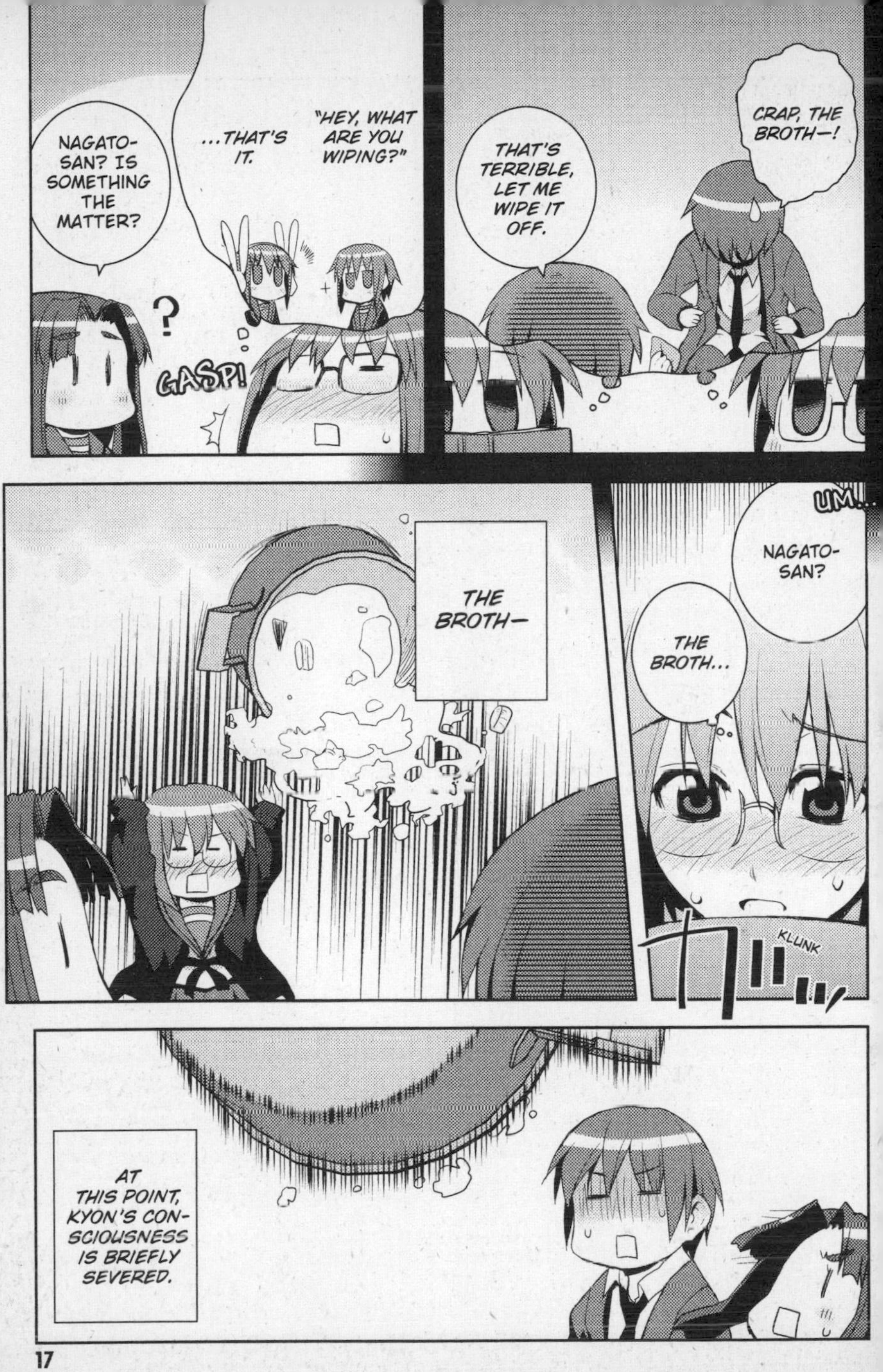
CRAP, THE BROTH—!
THAT'S TERRIBLE, LET ME WIPE IT OFF.
"HEY, WHAT ARE YOU WIPING?"
...THAT'S IT.
NAGATO-SAN? IS SOMETHING THE MATTER?
GASP!
UM...
NAGATO-SAN?
THE BROTH...
KLUNK
THE BROTH—
AT THIS POINT, KYON'S CON-SCIOUSNESS IS BRIEFLY SEVERED.

INTERLUDE: THE DISAPPEARANCE OF HARUHI-CHAN

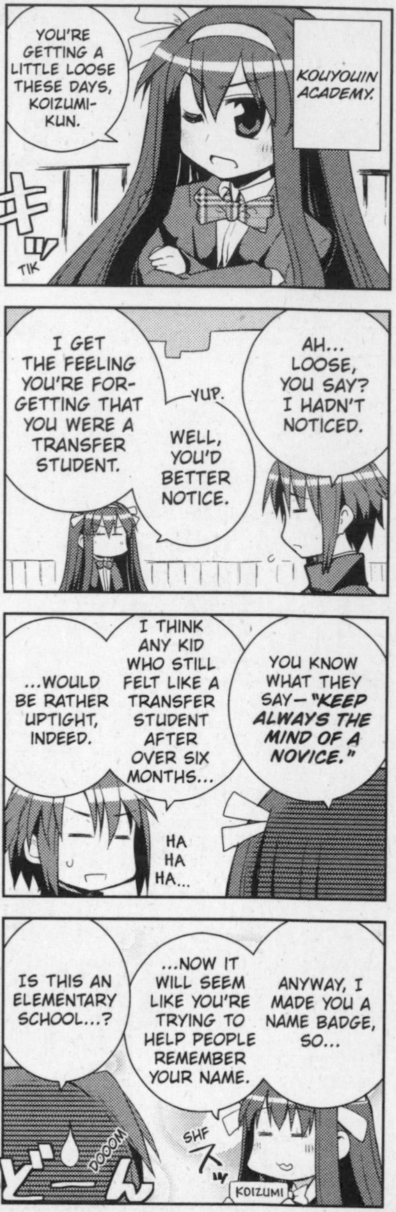
KOUYOUIN ACADEMY.
YOU'RE GETTING A LITTLE LOOSE THESE DAYS, KOIZUMI-KUN.
TIK
AH... LOOSE, YOU SAY? I HADN'T NOTICED.
WELL, YOU'D BETTER NOTICE.
YUP.
I GET THE FEELING YOU'RE FOR-GETTING THAT YOU WERE A TRANSFER STUDENT.
YOU KNOW WHAT THEY SAY— "KEEP ALWAYS THE MIND OF A NOVICE."
I THINK ANY KID WHO STILL FELT LIKE A TRANSFER STUDENT AFTER OVER SIX MONTHS...
...WOULD BE RATHER UPTIGHT, INDEED.
HA HA HA...
ANYWAY, I MADE YOU A NAME BADGE, SO...
...NOW IT WILL SEEM LIKE YOU'RE TRYING TO HELP PEOPLE REMEMBER YOUR NAME.
IS THIS AN ELEMENTARY SCHOOL...?
SHF
KOIZUMI
DOOOM

INTERLUDE: THE DISAPPEARANCE OF ITSUKI KOIZUMI

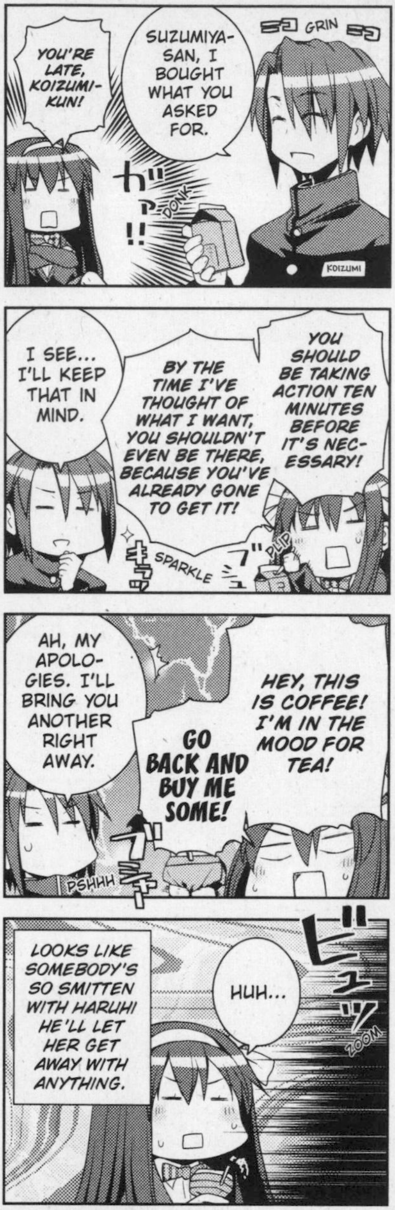
GRIN
SUZUMIYA-SAN, I BOUGHT WHAT YOU ASKED FOR.
YOU'RE LATE, KOIZUMI-KUN!
DONK
KOIZUMI
YOU SHOULD BE TAKING ACTION TEN MINUTES BEFORE IT'S NEC-ESSARY!
BY THE TIME I'VE THOUGHT OF WHAT I WANT, YOU SHOULDN'T EVEN BE THERE, BECAUSE YOU'VE ALREADY GONE TO GET IT!
PLIP
I SEE... I'LL KEEP THAT IN MIND.
SPARKLE
HEY, THIS IS COFFEE! I'M IN THE MOOD FOR TEA!
GO BACK AND BUY ME SOME!
AH, MY APOLOGIES. I'LL BRING YOU ANOTHER RIGHT AWAY.
PSHHH
ZOOM
HUH...
LOOKS LIKE SOMEBODY'S SO SMITTEN WITH HARUHI HE'LL LET HER GET AWAY WITH ANYTHING.

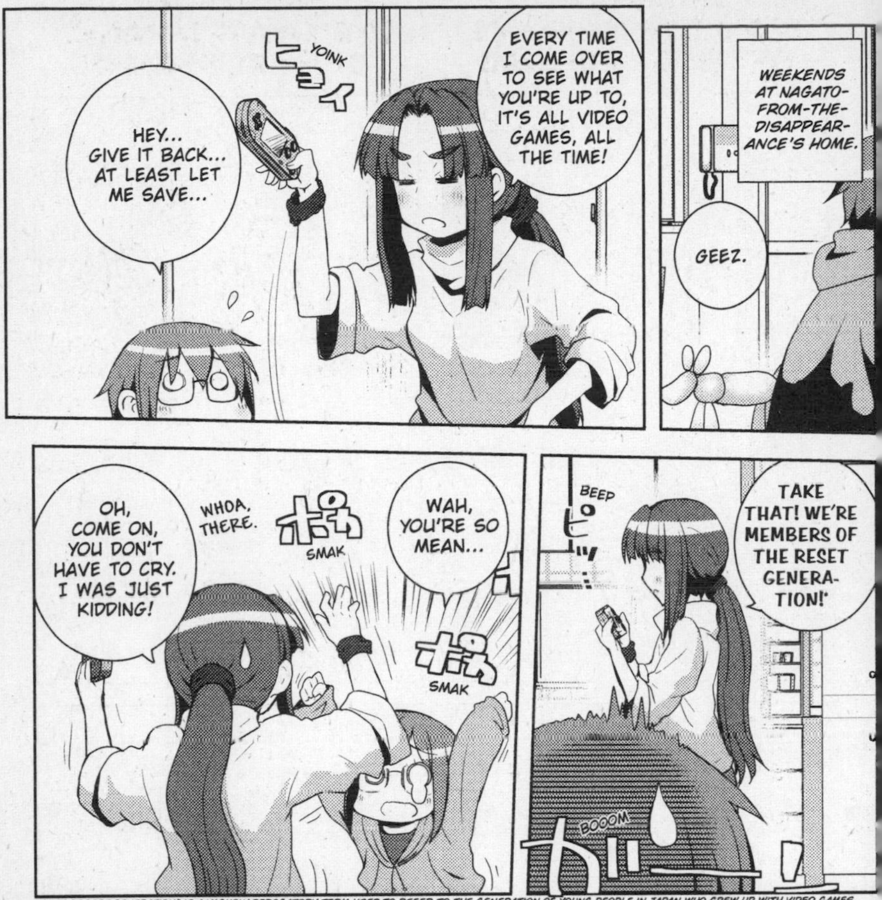
WEEKENDS AT NAGATO-FROM-THE-DISAPPEARANCE'S HOME.
GEEZ.
EVERY TIME I COME OVER TO SEE WHAT YOU'RE UP TO, IT'S ALL VIDEO GAMES, ALL THE TIME!
YOINK
HEY... GIVE IT BACK... AT LEAST LET ME SAVE...
TAKE THAT! WE'RE MEMBERS OF THE RESET GENERATION!*
BEEP
BOOOM
WAH, YOU'RE SO MEAN...
SMAK
WHOA, THERE.
OH, COME ON, YOU DON'T HAVE TO CRY. I WAS JUST KIDDING!
SMAK

*THE "RESET GENERATION" IS A VAGUELY DEROGATORY TERM USED TO REFER TO THE GENERATION OF YOUNG PEOPLE IN JAPAN WHO GREW UP WITH VIDEO GAMES, AND THUS AT SOME LEVEL OSTENSIBLY BELIEVE THAT THEY CAN PUSH THE "RESET BUTTON" TO UNDO WHATEVER PROBLEMS THEIR IRRESPONSIBILITY CAUSES.

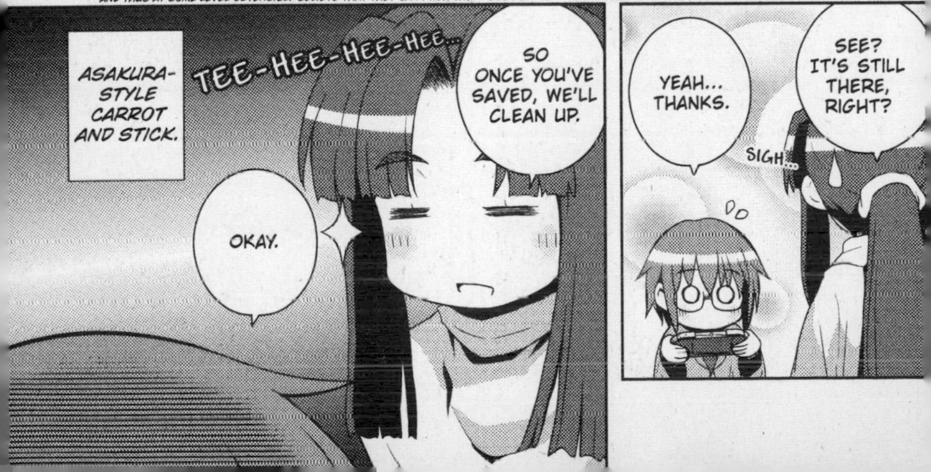
SEE? IT'S STILL THERE, RIGHT?
YEAH... THANKS.
SIGH...
SO ONCE YOU'VE SAVED, WE'LL CLEAN UP.
TEE-HEE-HEE-HEE...
ASAKURA-STYLE CARROT AND STICK.
OKAY.

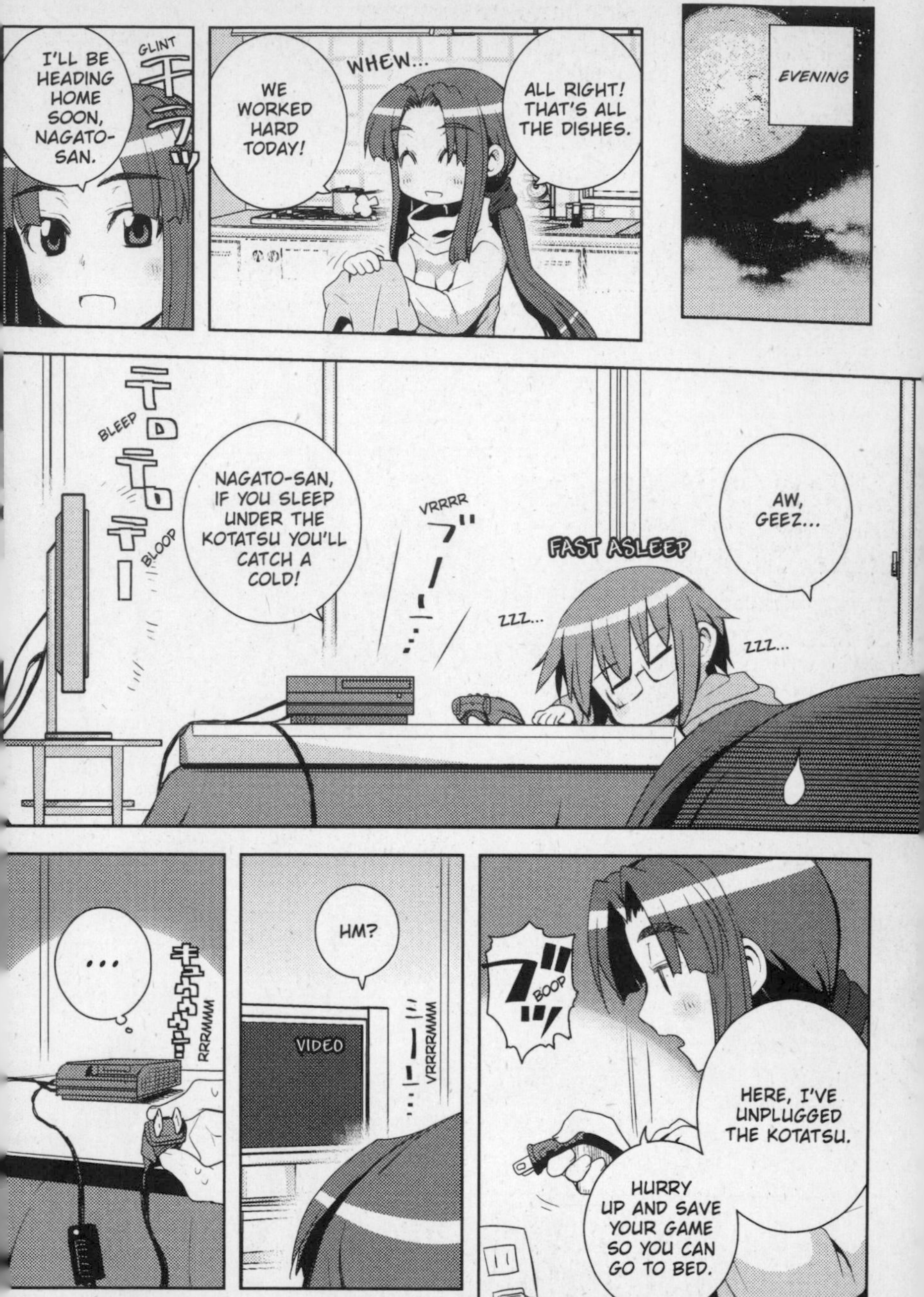
EVENING
ALL RIGHT! THAT'S ALL THE DISHES.
WHEW...
WE WORKED HARD TODAY!
GLINT
I'LL BE HEADING HOME SOON, NAGATO-SAN.
AW, GEEZ...
ZZZ...
FAST ASLEEP
ZZZ...
VRRRR
NAGATO-SAN, IF YOU SLEEP UNDER THE KOTATSU YOU'LL CATCH A COLD!
BLEEP
BLOOP
BOOP
HERE, I'VE UNPLUGGED THE KOTATSU.
HURRY UP AND SAVE YOUR GAME SO YOU CAN GO TO BED.
HM?
VRRRRMMM
VIDEO
...
RRRMMM

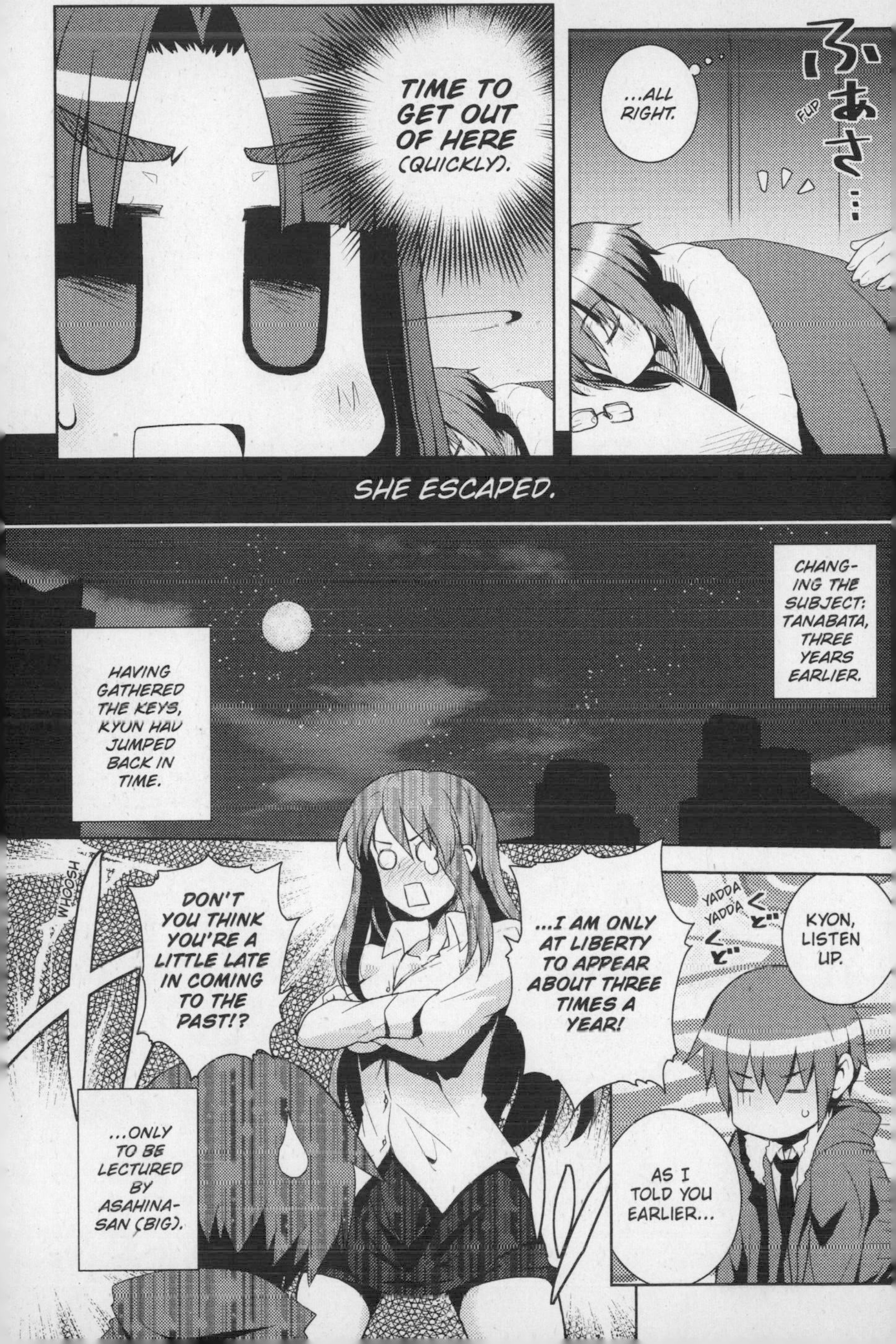
ふぁさ…
FUP
...ALL RIGHT.
TIME TO GET OUT OF HERE (QUICKLY).
SHE ESCAPED.
CHANGING THE SUBJECT: TANABATA, THREE YEARS EARLIER.
HAVING GATHERED THE KEYS, KYON HAD JUMPED BACK IN TIME.
KYON, LISTEN UP.
YADDA YADDA
くどくど
AS I TOLD YOU EARLIER...
...I AM ONLY AT LIBERTY TO APPEAR ABOUT THREE TIMES A YEAR!
DON'T YOU THINK YOU'RE A LITTLE LATE IN COMING TO THE PAST!?
WHOOSH
...ONLY TO BE LECTURED BY ASAHINA-SAN (BIG).

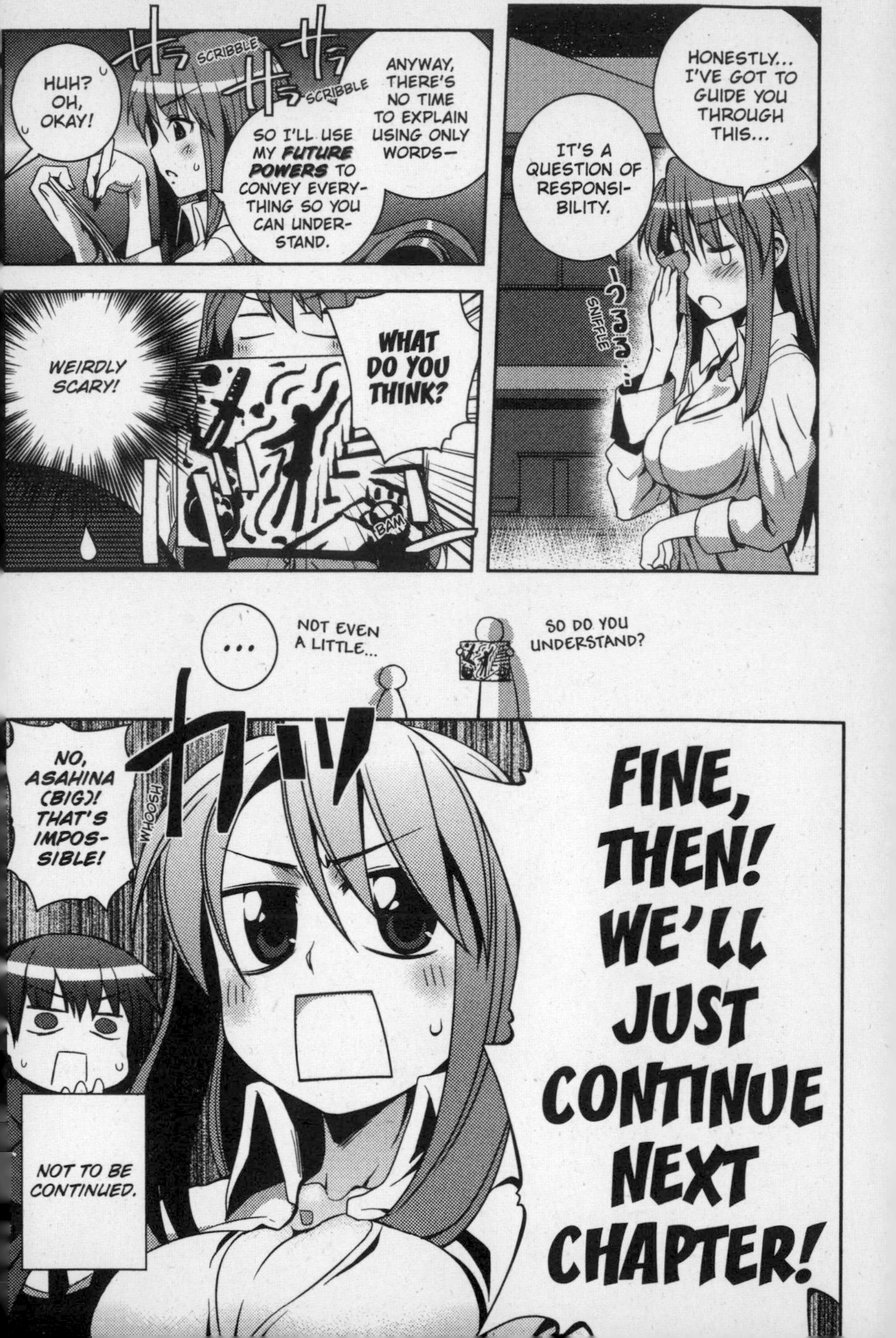
HONESTLY... I'VE GOT TO GUIDE YOU THROUGH THIS...
IT'S A QUESTION OF RESPONSIBILITY.
SNIFFLE
ANYWAY, THERE'S NO TIME TO EXPLAIN USING ONLY WORDS—
SO I'LL USE MY **FUTURE POWERS** TO CONVEY EVERYTHING SO YOU CAN UNDERSTAND.
SCRIBBLE
SCRIBBLE
HUH? OH, OKAY!
WHAT DO YOU THINK?
BAM
WEIRDLY SCARY!
SO DO YOU UNDERSTAND?
NOT EVEN A LITTLE...
...
FINE, THEN! WE'LL JUST CONTINUE NEXT CHAPTER!
WHOOSH
NO, ASAHINA (BIG)! THAT'S IMPOSSIBLE!
NOT TO BE CONTINUED.

MOM, LOOK WHAT I MADE!
WHO'RE YOU CALLING "MOM"?

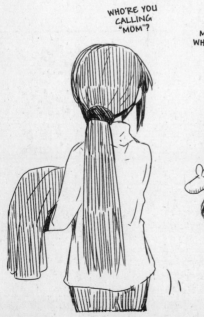

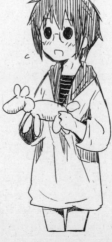

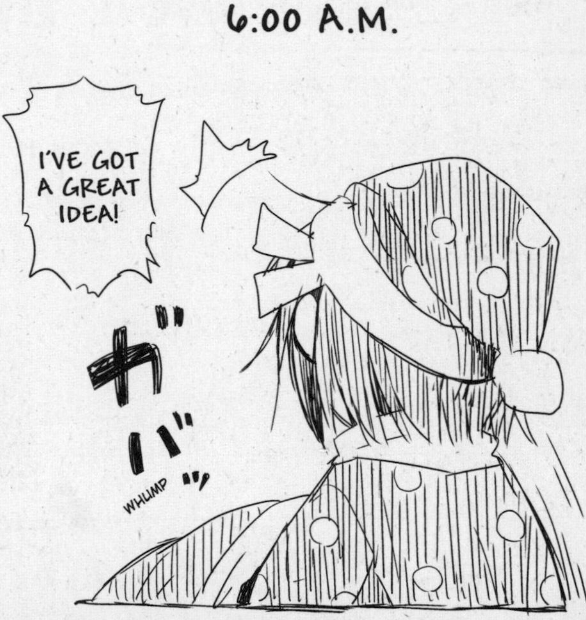
6:00 A.M.
I'VE GOT A GREAT IDEA!
ガバッ
WHUMP

8:05

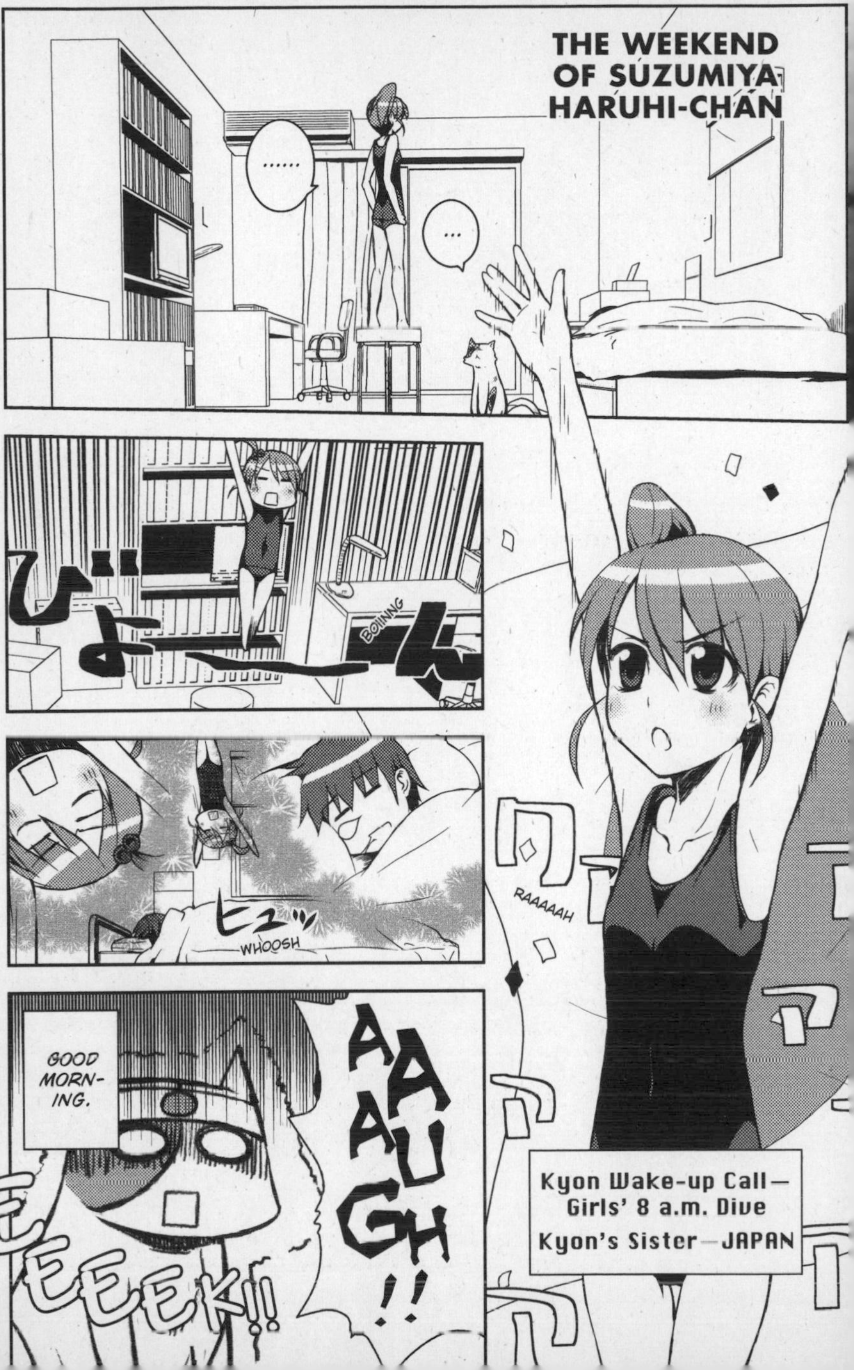
THE WEEKEND OF SUZUMIYA HARUHI-CHAN
……
…
RAAAAAH
Kyon Wake-up Call—
Girls' 8 a.m. Dive
Kyon's Sister—JAPAN
ぴょーん
BOIING
ヒュッ
WHOOSH
GOOD MORNING.
AAAAUGH!!
EEEEEK!!

9:32

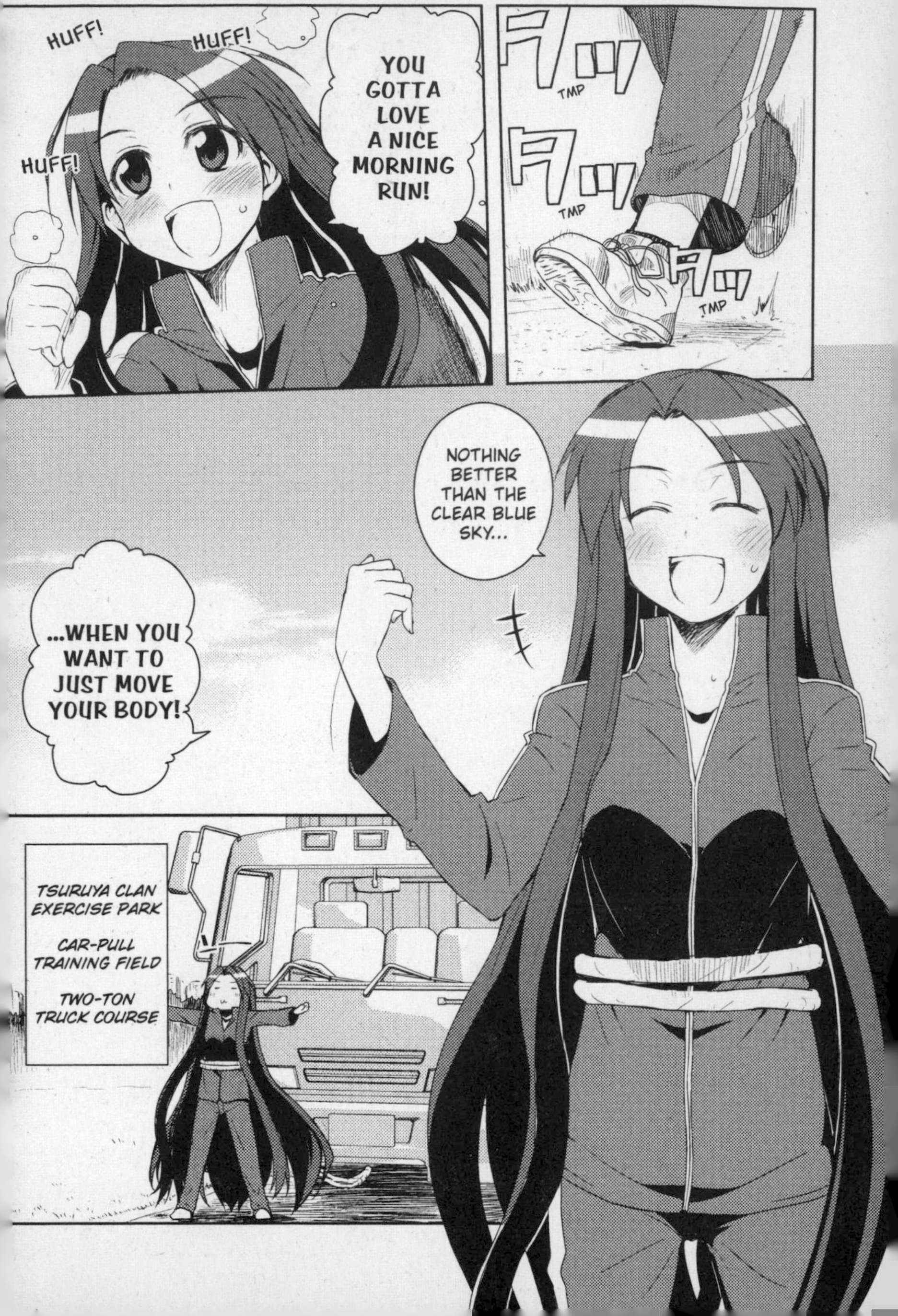
タッ
TMP
タッ
TMP
タッ
TMP
HUFF!
HUFF!
HUFF!
YOU GOTTA LOVE A NICE MORNING RUN!
NOTHING BETTER THAN THE CLEAR BLUE SKY...
...WHEN YOU WANT TO JUST MOVE YOUR BODY!
TSURUYA CLAN EXERCISE PARK
CAR-PULL TRAINING FIELD
TWO-TON TRUCK COURSE

10:20

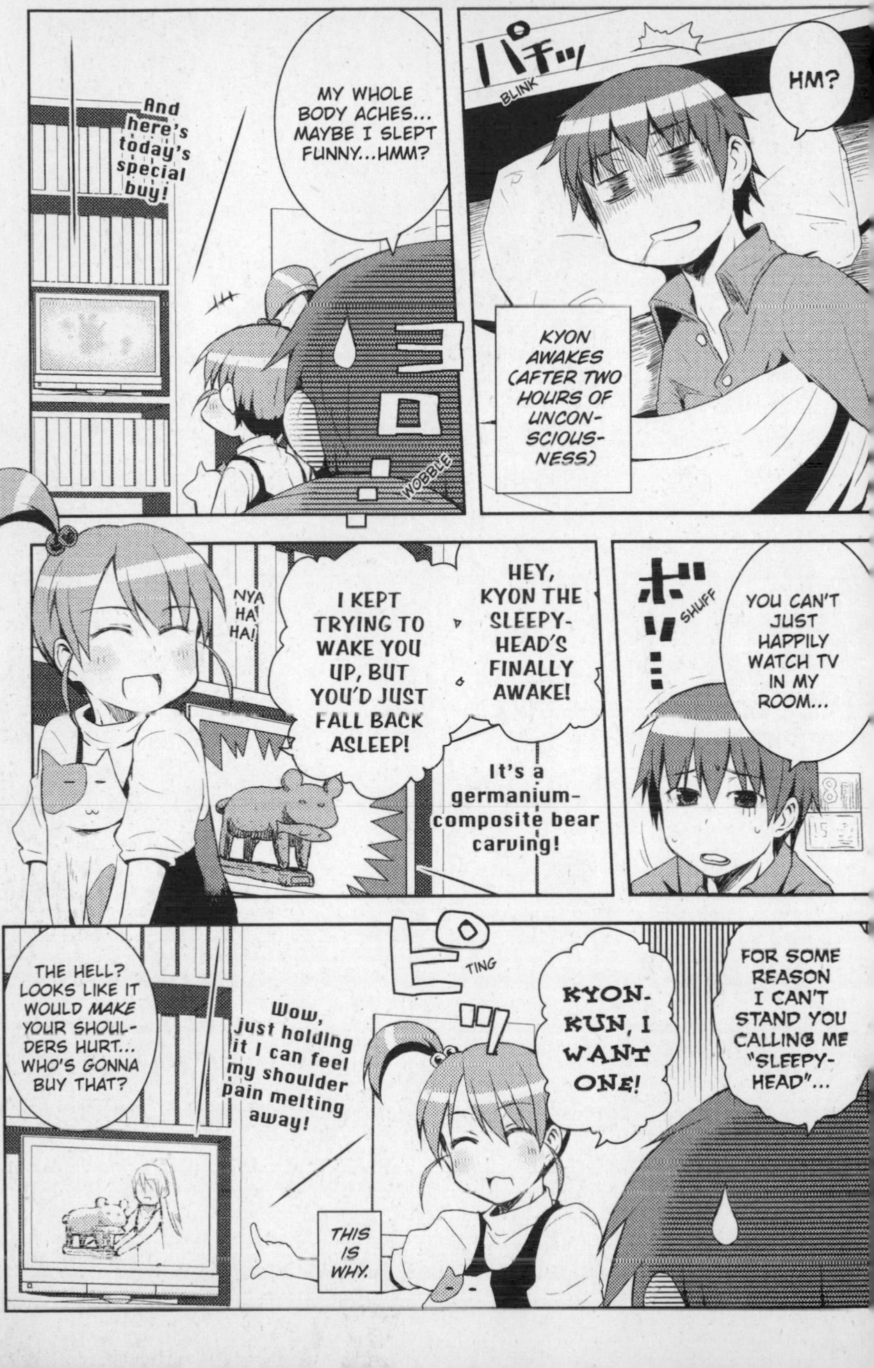
BLINK
HM?
KYON AWAKES (AFTER TWO HOURS OF UNCONSCIOUSNESS)
MY WHOLE BODY ACHES... MAYBE I SLEPT FUNNY...HMM?
And here's today's special buy!
WOBBLE
SHUFF
YOU CAN'T JUST HAPPILY WATCH TV IN MY ROOM...
HEY, KYON THE SLEEPY-HEAD'S FINALLY AWAKE!
I KEPT TRYING TO WAKE YOU UP, BUT YOU'D JUST FALL BACK ASLEEP!
NYA HA HA!
It's a germanium-composite bear carving!
FOR SOME REASON I CAN'T STAND YOU CALLING ME "SLEEPY-HEAD"...
TING
KYON-KUN, I WANT ONE!
THIS IS WHY.
THE HELL? LOOKS LIKE IT WOULD MAKE YOUR SHOULDERS HURT... WHO'S GONNA BUY THAT?
Wow, just holding it I can feel my shoulder pain melting away!

10:25

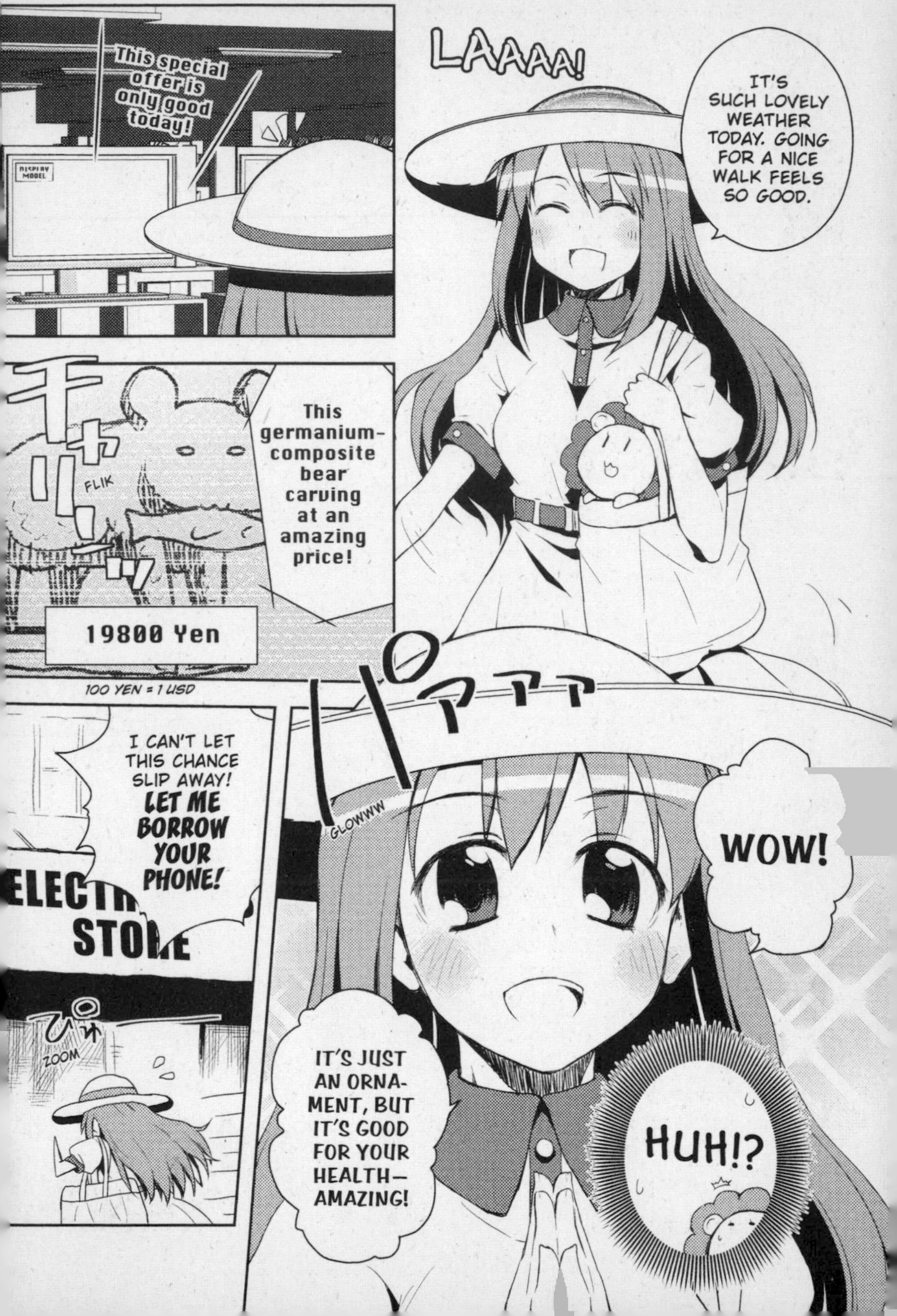
LAAAA!
IT'S SUCH LOVELY WEATHER TODAY. GOING FOR A NICE WALK FEELS SO GOOD.
This special offer is only good today!
DISPLAY MODEL
This germanium-composite bear carving at an amazing price!
FLIK
19800 Yen
100 YEN = 1 USD
パァァァ
GLOWWW
WOW!
IT'S JUST AN ORNAMENT, BUT IT'S GOOD FOR YOUR HEALTH—AMAZING!
HUH!?
I CAN'T LET THIS CHANCE SLIP AWAY! LET ME BORROW YOUR PHONE!
ELECTR
STORE
ぴゅ
ZOOM

11:45

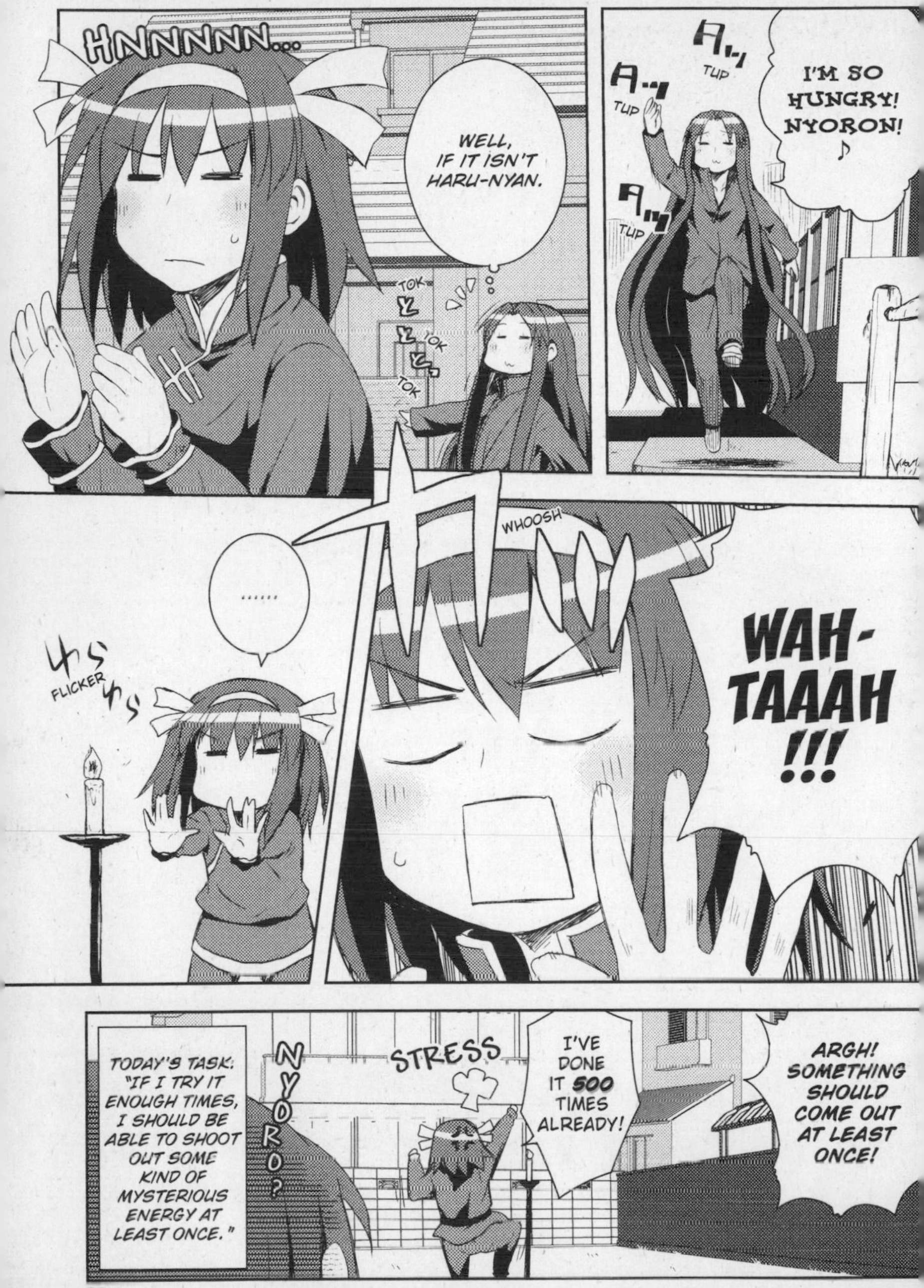
I'M SO HUNGRY! NYORON! ♪
TUP
TUP
TUP
HNNNNNN...
WELL, IF IT ISN'T HARU-NYAN.
TOK
TOK
TOK
WHOOSH
WAH-TAAAH!!!
......
ゆらゆら
FLICKER
ARGH! SOMETHING SHOULD COME OUT AT LEAST ONCE!
I'VE DONE IT 500 TIMES ALREADY!
STRESS
NYORO?
TODAY'S TASK: "IF I TRY IT ENOUGH TIMES, I SHOULD BE ABLE TO SHOOT OUT SOME KIND OF MYSTERIOUS ENERGY AT LEAST ONCE."

12:00

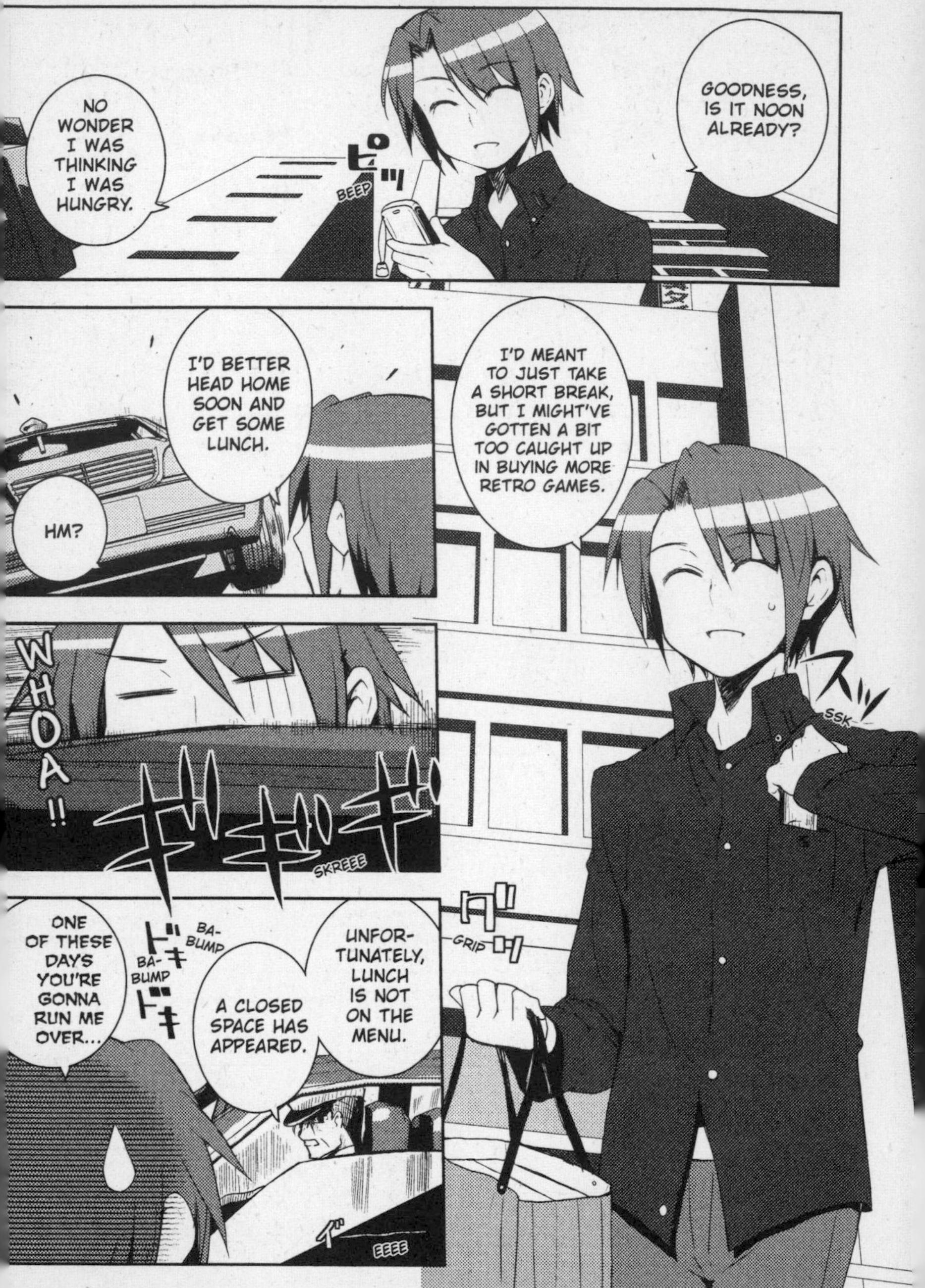
GOODNESS, IS IT NOON ALREADY?
BEEP
NO WONDER I WAS THINKING I WAS HUNGRY.
I'D MEANT TO JUST TAKE A SHORT BREAK, BUT I MIGHT'VE GOTTEN A BIT TOO CAUGHT UP IN BUYING MORE RETRO GAMES.
SSK
GRIP
I'D BETTER HEAD HOME SOON AND GET SOME LUNCH.
HM?
WHOA!!
SKREEE
UNFORTUNATELY, LUNCH IS NOT ON THE MENU.
A CLOSED SPACE HAS APPEARED.
BA-BUMP
BA-BUMP
ONE OF THESE DAYS YOU'RE GONNA RUN ME OVER...
EEEE

12:42

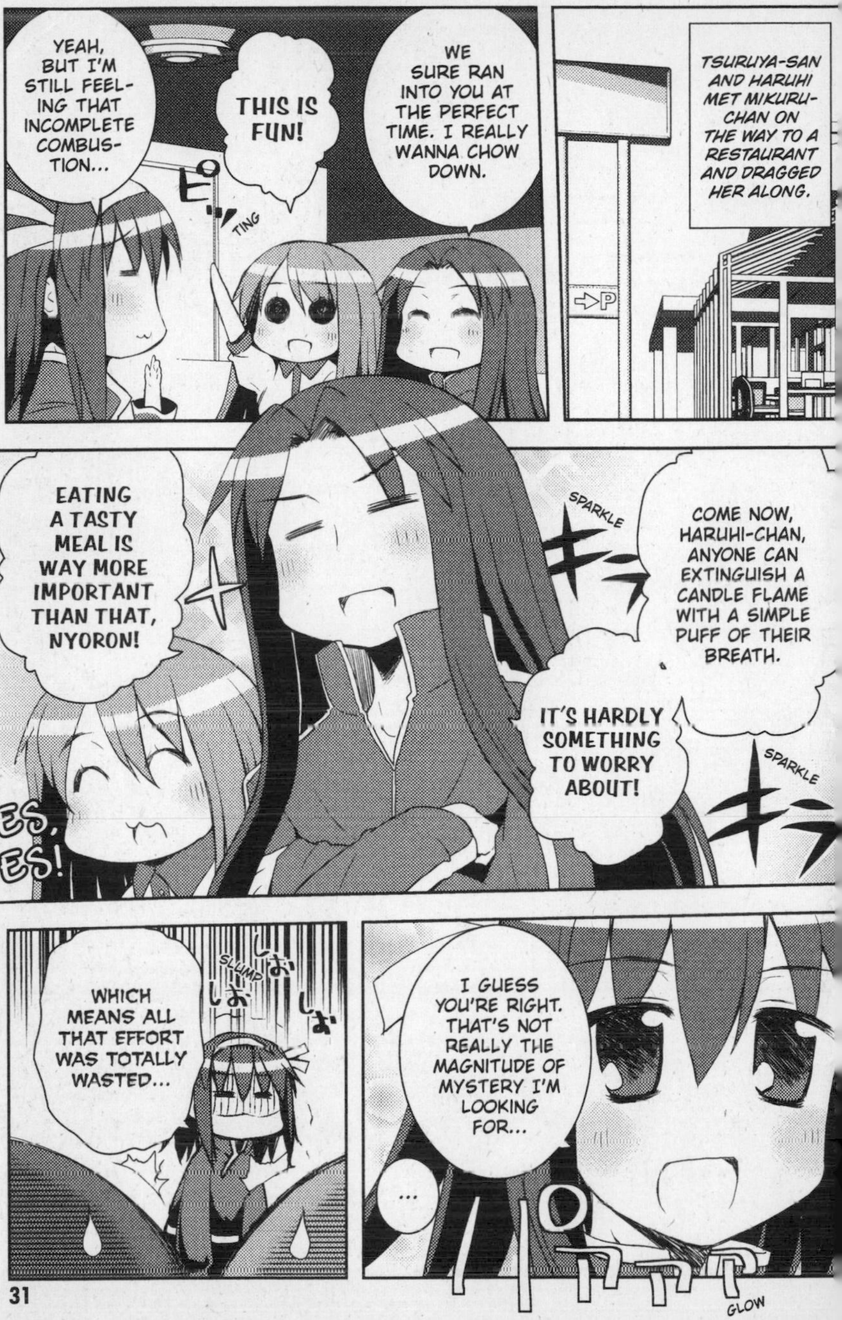
TSURUYA-SAN AND HARUHI MET MIKURU-CHAN ON THE WAY TO A RESTAURANT AND DRAGGED HER ALONG.
WE SURE RAN INTO YOU AT THE PERFECT TIME. I REALLY WANNA CHOW DOWN.
THIS IS FUN!
YEAH, BUT I'M STILL FEELING THAT INCOMPLETE COMBUSTION...
TING
SPARKLE
COME NOW, HARUHI-CHAN, ANYONE CAN EXTINGUISH A CANDLE FLAME WITH A SIMPLE PUFF OF THEIR BREATH.
IT'S HARDLY SOMETHING TO WORRY ABOUT!
SPARKLE
EATING A TASTY MEAL IS WAY MORE IMPORTANT THAN THAT, NYORON!
YES, YES!
I GUESS YOU'RE RIGHT. THAT'S NOT REALLY THE MAGNITUDE OF MYSTERY I'M LOOKING FOR...
...
GLOW
SLUMP
WHICH MEANS ALL THAT EFFORT WAS TOTALLY WASTED...

12:56

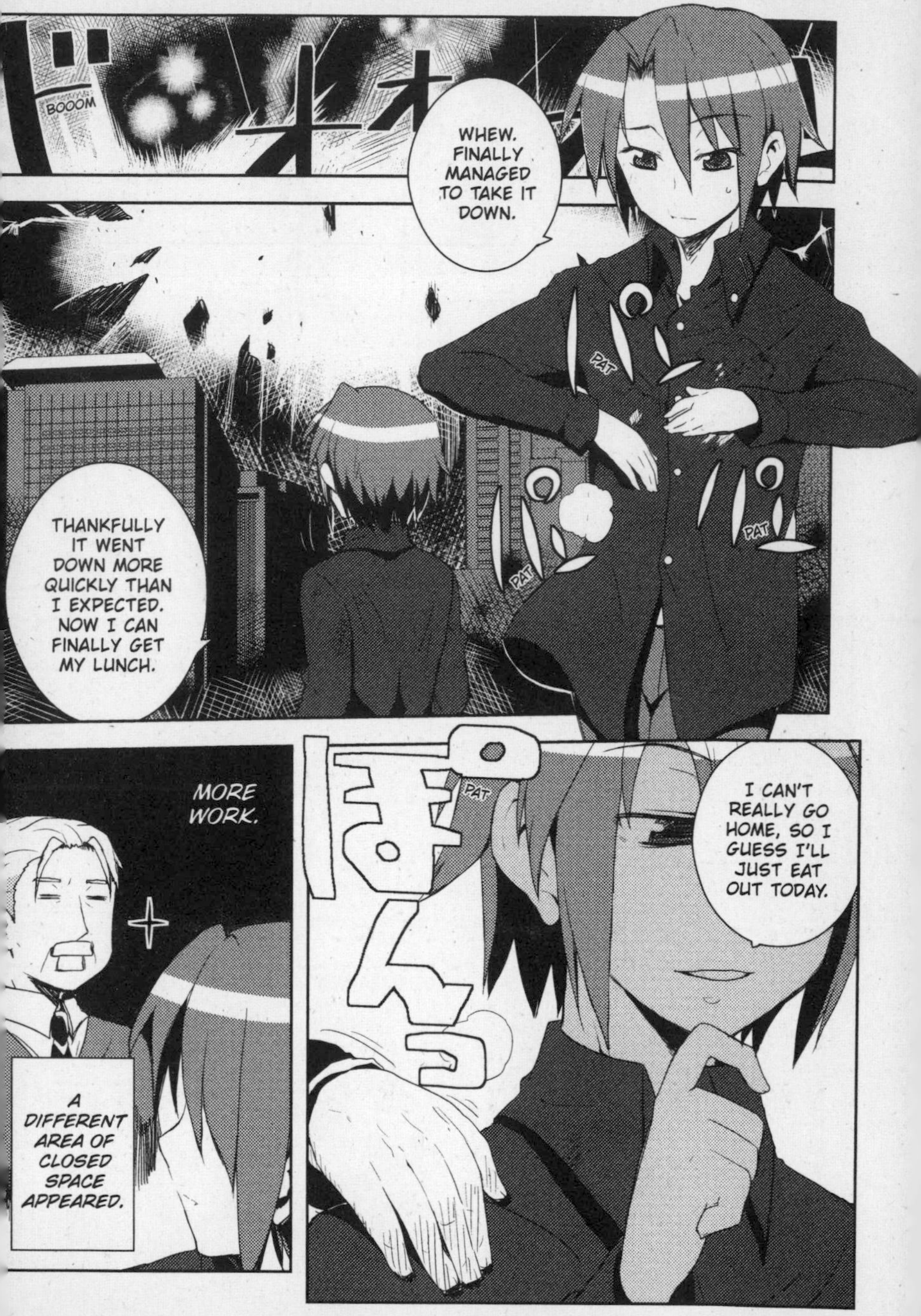
BOOOM
WHEW. FINALLY MANAGED TO TAKE IT DOWN.
PAT
PAT
PAT
THANKFULLY IT WENT DOWN MORE QUICKLY THAN I EXPECTED. NOW I CAN FINALLY GET MY LUNCH.
PAT
I CAN'T REALLY GO HOME, SO I GUESS I'LL JUST EAT OUT TODAY.
MORE WORK.
A DIFFERENT AREA OF CLOSED SPACE APPEARED.

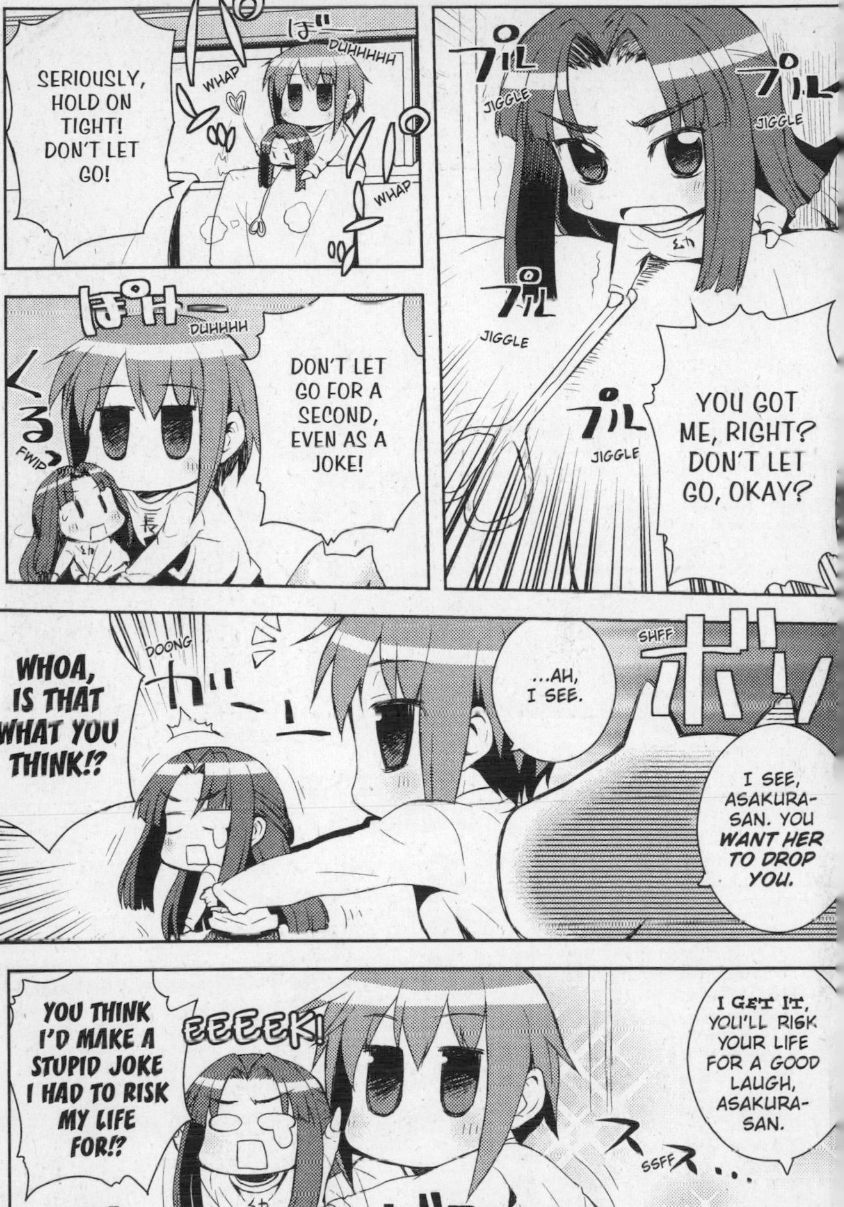
JIGGLE
JIGGLE
JIGGLE
JIGGLE
YOU GOT ME, RIGHT? DON'T LET GO, OKAY?
DUHHHHH
WHAP
WHAP
SERIOUSLY, HOLD ON TIGHT! DON'T LET GO!
DUHHHH
DON'T LET GO FOR A SECOND, EVEN AS A JOKE!
FWIP
SHFF
I SEE, ASAKURA-SAN. YOU WANT HER TO DROP YOU.
...AH, I SEE.
DOONG
WHOA, IS THAT WHAT YOU THINK!?
I GET IT, YOU'LL RISK YOUR LIFE FOR A GOOD LAUGH, ASAKURA-SAN.
SSFF...
EEEEK!
YOU THINK I'D MAKE A STUPID JOKE I HAD TO RISK MY LIFE FOR!?
FLAIL
FLAIL

14:43

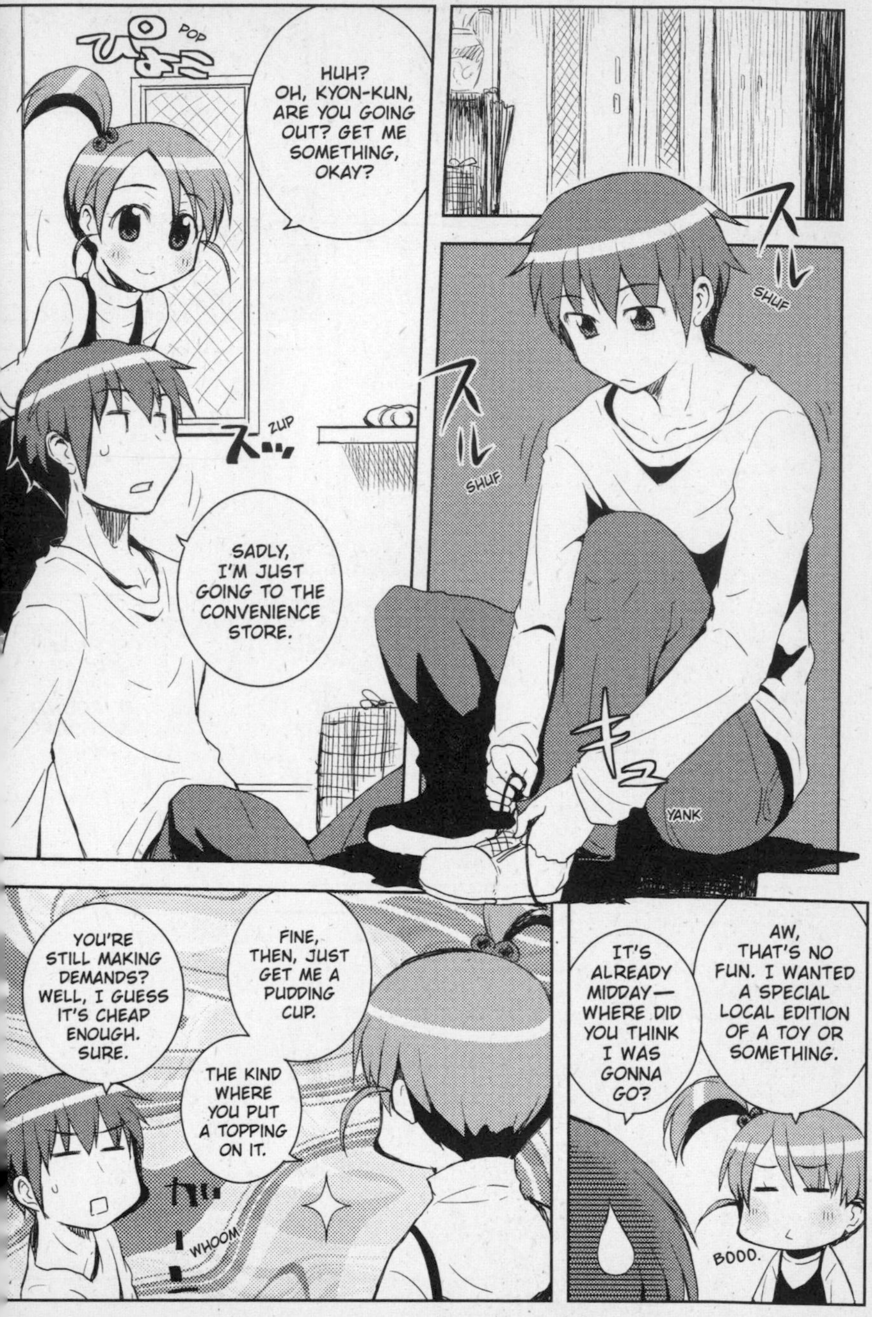
SHUF
SHUF
YANK
POP
HUH? OH, KYON-KUN, ARE YOU GOING OUT? GET ME SOMETHING, OKAY?
ZUP
SADLY, I'M JUST GOING TO THE CONVENIENCE STORE.
AW, THAT'S NO FUN. I WANTED A SPECIAL LOCAL EDITION OF A TOY OR SOMETHING.
IT'S ALREADY MIDDAY—WHERE DID YOU THINK I WAS GONNA GO?
BOOO.
FINE, THEN, JUST GET ME A PUDDING CUP.
THE KIND WHERE YOU PUT A TOPPING ON IT.
YOU'RE STILL MAKING DEMANDS? WELL, I GUESS IT'S CHEAP ENOUGH. SURE.
WHOOM

15:00

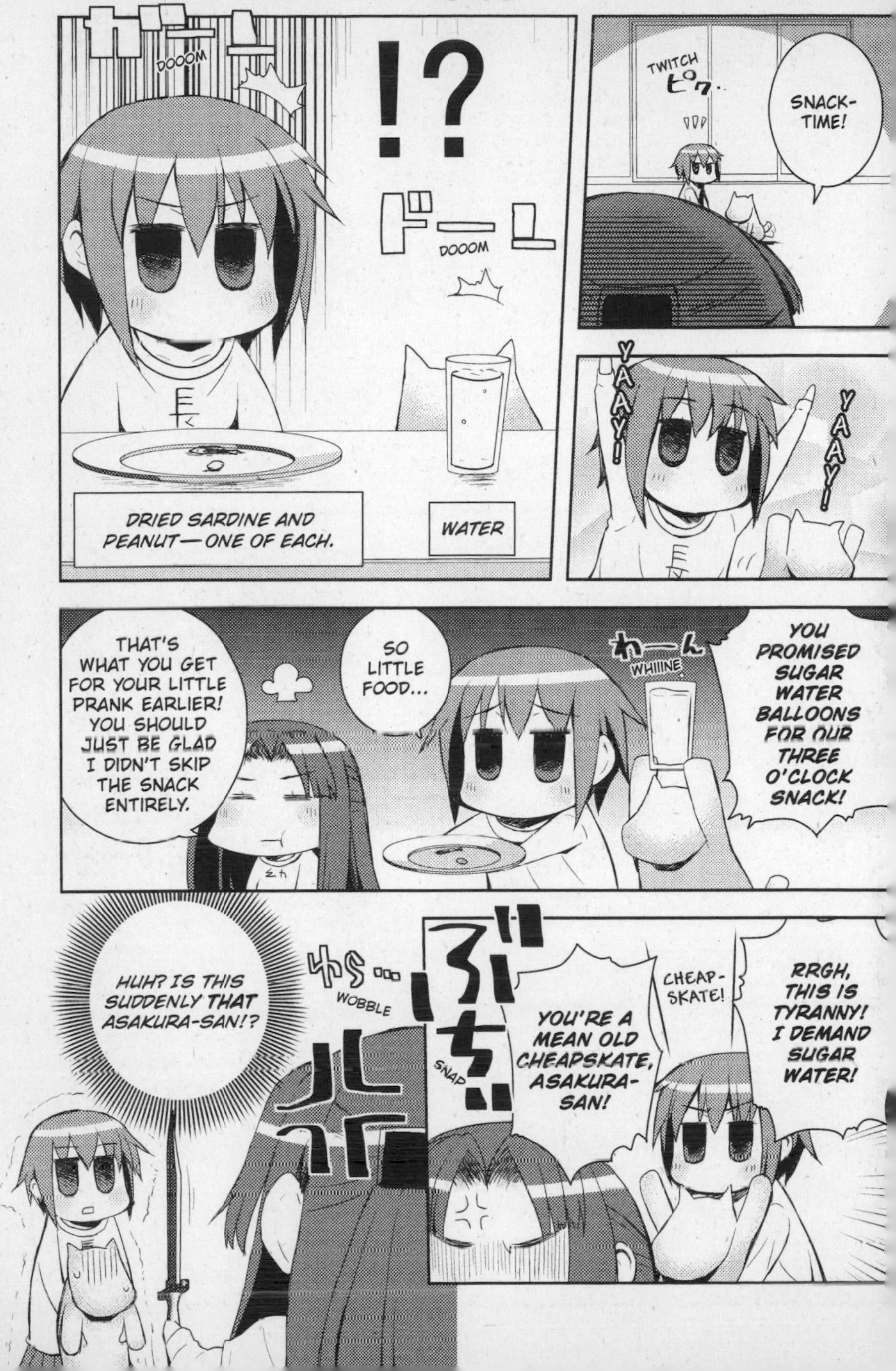
TWITCH
SNACK-TIME!
YAAAY!
YAAAY!
DOOOM
!?
DOOOM
WATER
DRIED SARDINE AND PEANUT—ONE OF EACH.
YOU PROMISED SUGAR WATER BALLOONS FOR OUR THREE O'CLOCK SNACK!
WHIIINE
SO LITTLE FOOD...
THAT'S WHAT YOU GET FOR YOUR LITTLE PRANK EARLIER! YOU SHOULD JUST BE GLAD I DIDN'T SKIP THE SNACK ENTIRELY.
RRGH, THIS IS TYRANNY! I DEMAND SUGAR WATER!
CHEAP-SKATE!
YOU'RE A MEAN OLD CHEAPSKATE, ASAKURA-SAN!
SNAP
WOBBLE
HUH? IS THIS SUDDENLY THAT ASAKURA-SAN!?

15:51

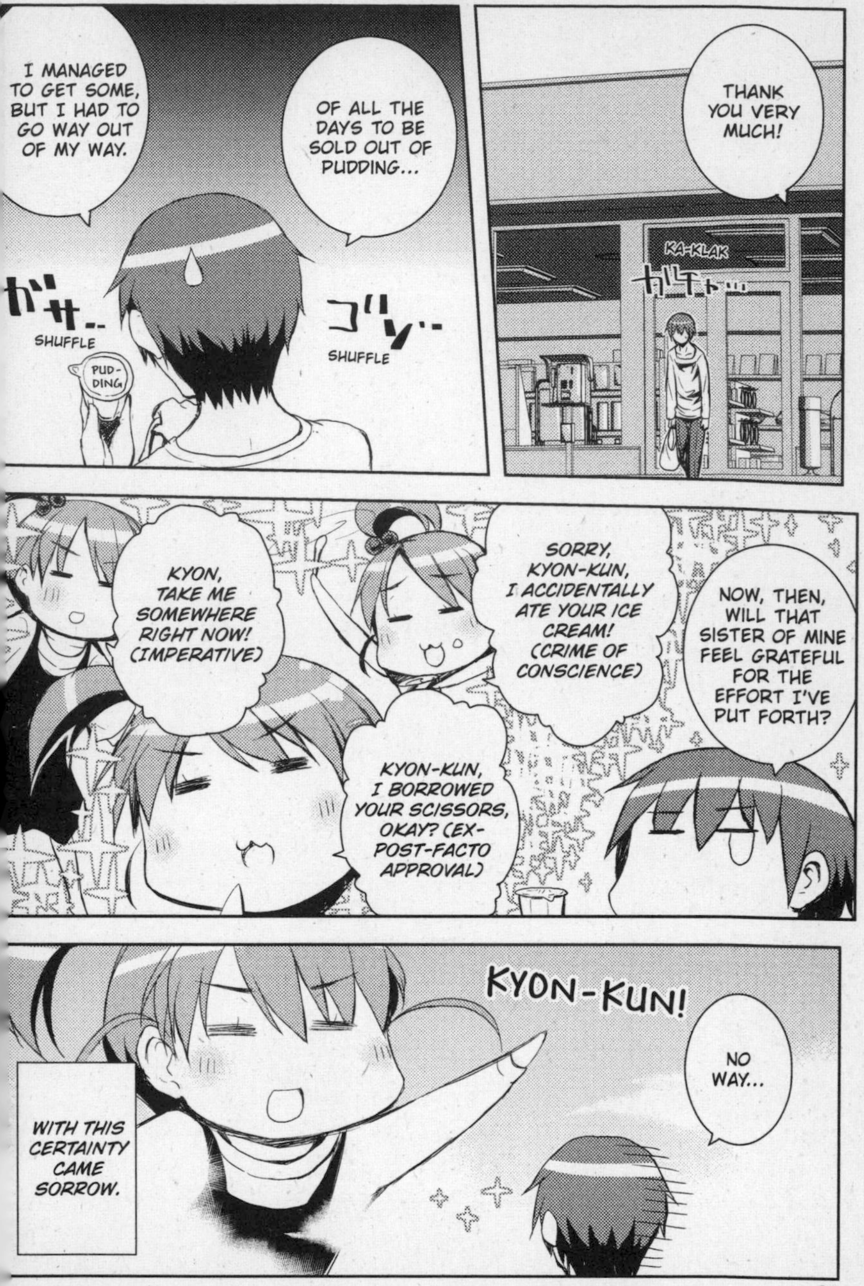
THANK YOU VERY MUCH!
KA-KLAK
OF ALL THE DAYS TO BE SOLD OUT OF PUDDING...
I MANAGED TO GET SOME, BUT I HAD TO GO WAY OUT OF MY WAY.
SHUFFLE
SHUFFLE
PUD-DING
NOW, THEN, WILL THAT SISTER OF MINE FEEL GRATEFUL FOR THE EFFORT I'VE PUT FORTH?
SORRY, KYON-KUN, I ACCIDENTALLY ATE YOUR ICE CREAM! (CRIME OF CONSCIENCE)
KYON, TAKE ME SOMEWHERE RIGHT NOW! (IMPERATIVE)
KYON-KUN, I BORROWED YOUR SCISSORS, OKAY? (EX-POST-FACTO APPROVAL)
NO WAY...
KYON-KUN!
WITH THIS CERTAINTY CAME SORROW.

15:52

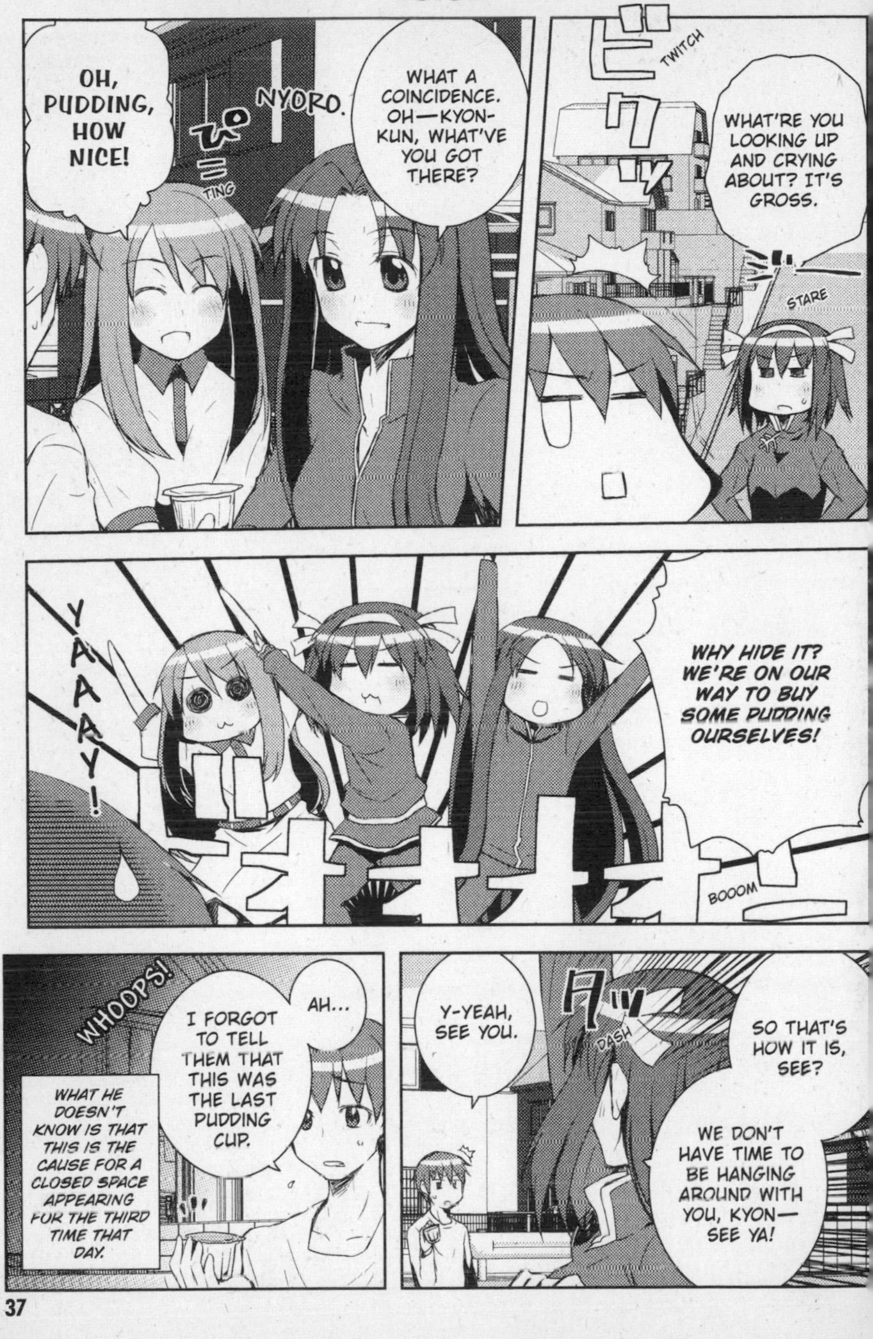
TWITCH
WHAT'RE YOU LOOKING UP AND CRYING ABOUT? IT'S GROSS.
STARE
WHAT A COINCIDENCE. OH—KYON-KUN, WHAT'VE YOU GOT THERE?
NYORO.
TING
OH, PUDDING, HOW NICE!
WHY HIDE IT? WE'RE ON OUR WAY TO BUY SOME PUDDING OURSELVES!
BOOOM
YAAAY!
SO THAT'S HOW IT IS, SEE?
WE DON'T HAVE TIME TO BE HANGING AROUND WITH YOU, KYON—SEE YA!
DASH
Y-YEAH, SEE YOU.
AH...
I FORGOT TO TELL THEM THAT THIS WAS THE LAST PUDDING CUP.
WHOOPS!
WHAT HE DOESN'T KNOW IS THAT THIS IS THE CAUSE FOR A CLOSED SPACE APPEARING FOR THE THIRD TIME THAT DAY.

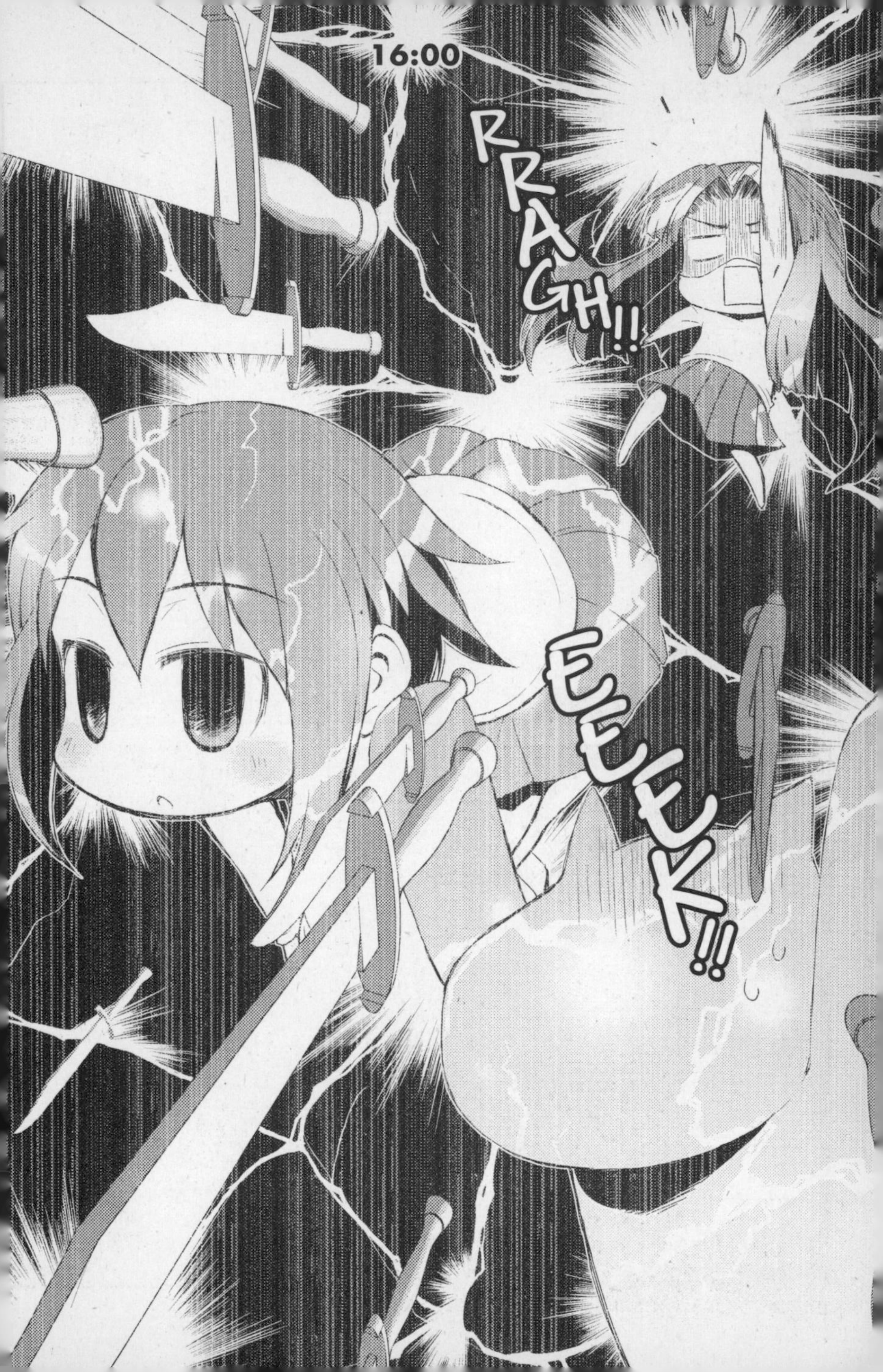
16:00
RRAGH!!
EEEEK!!

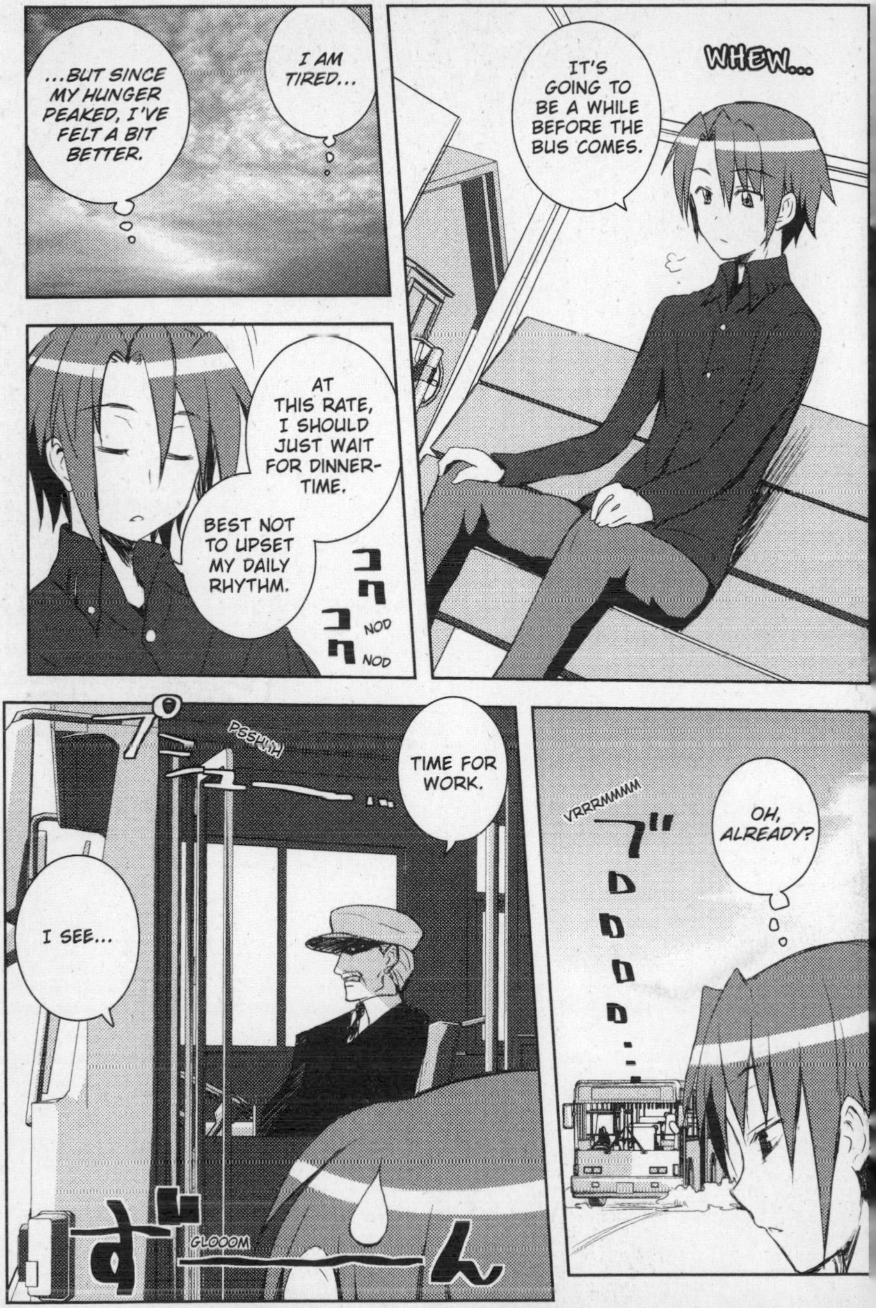
WHEW...
IT'S GOING TO BE A WHILE BEFORE THE BUS COMES.
I AM TIRED...
...BUT SINCE MY HUNGER PEAKED, I'VE FELT A BIT BETTER.
AT THIS RATE, I SHOULD JUST WAIT FOR DINNER-TIME.
BEST NOT TO UPSET MY DAILY RHYTHM.
コク NOD
コク NOD
VRRRMMMM
ブロロロ...
OH, ALREADY?
PSSHHH
TIME FOR WORK.
I SEE...
GLOOOM

17:45

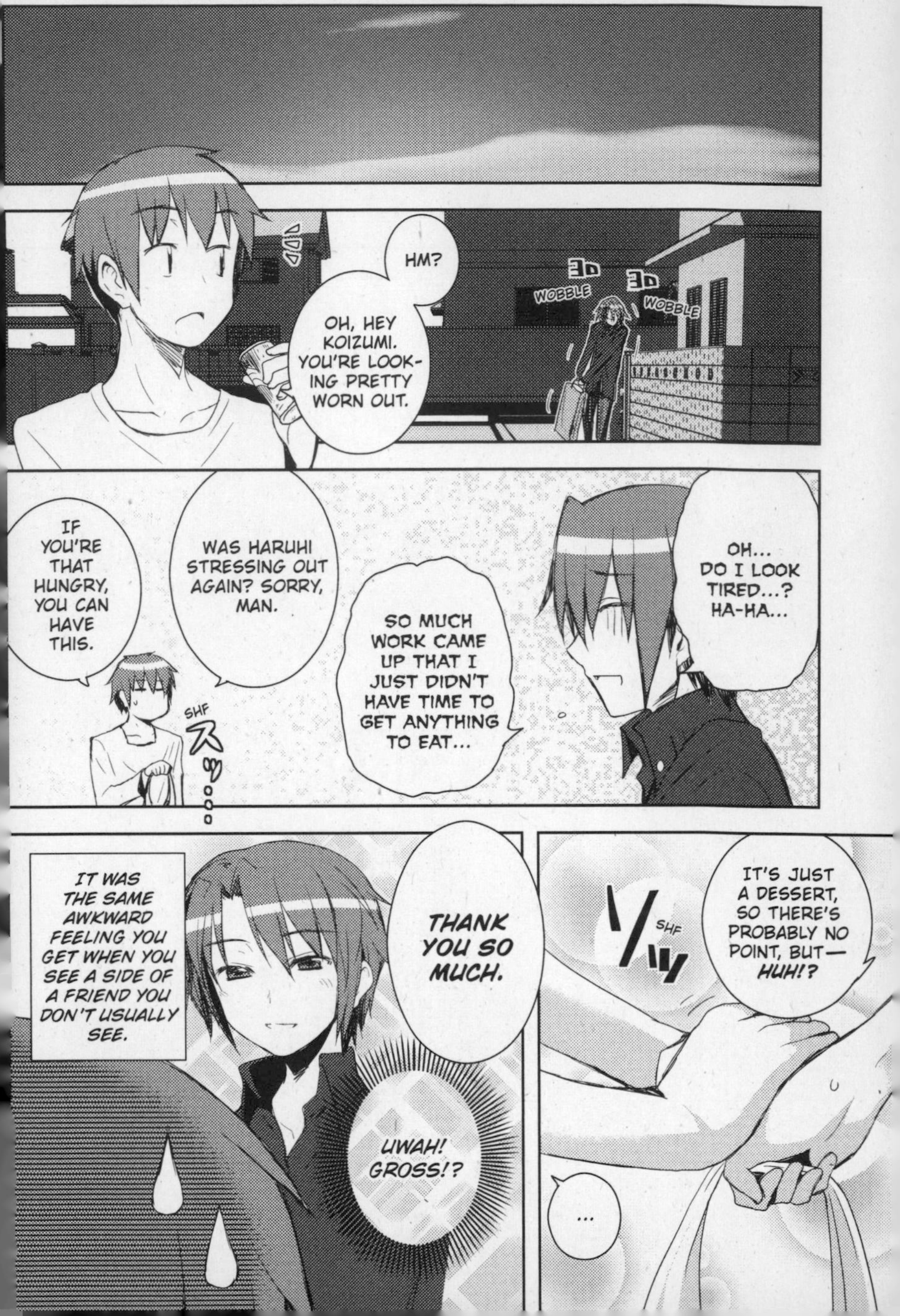
WOBBLE
WOBBLE
HM?
OH, HEY KOIZUMI. YOU'RE LOOKING PRETTY WORN OUT.
OH... DO I LOOK TIRED...? HA-HA...
SO MUCH WORK CAME UP THAT I JUST DIDN'T HAVE TIME TO GET ANYTHING TO EAT...
WAS HARUHI STRESSING OUT AGAIN? SORRY, MAN.
IF YOU'RE THAT HUNGRY, YOU CAN HAVE THIS.
SHF
IT'S JUST A DESSERT, SO THERE'S PROBABLY NO POINT, BUT—HUH!?
SHF
...
THANK YOU SO MUCH.
IT WAS THE SAME AWKWARD FEELING YOU GET WHEN YOU SEE A SIDE OF A FRIEND YOU DON'T USUALLY SEE.
UWAH! GROSS!?

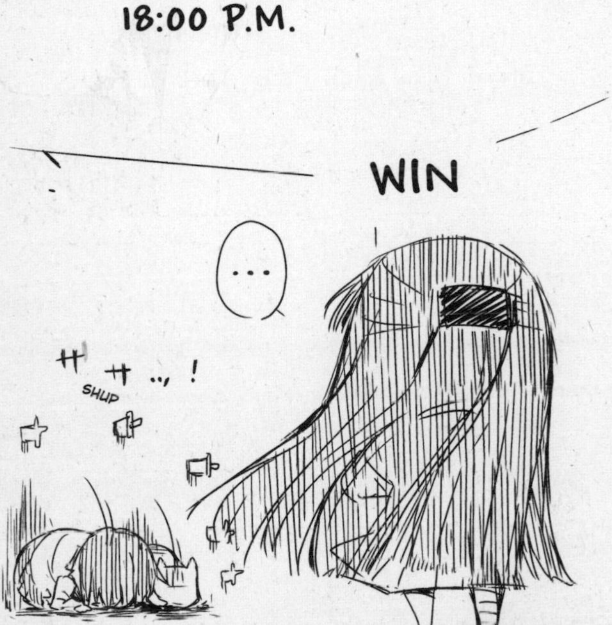
18:00 P.M.
WIN
...
SHUP

A FEW DAYS EARLIER
KUNIKIDA
TANIGUCHI, DO YOU HAVE A JOB?
YEAH, KINDA.
OH, HUH.
JOB

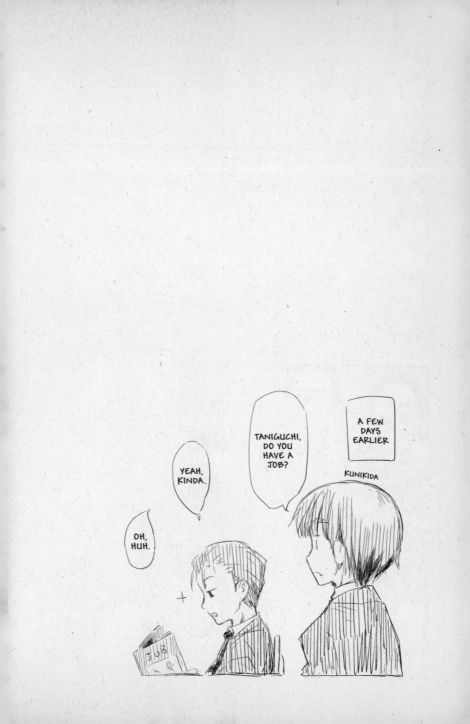

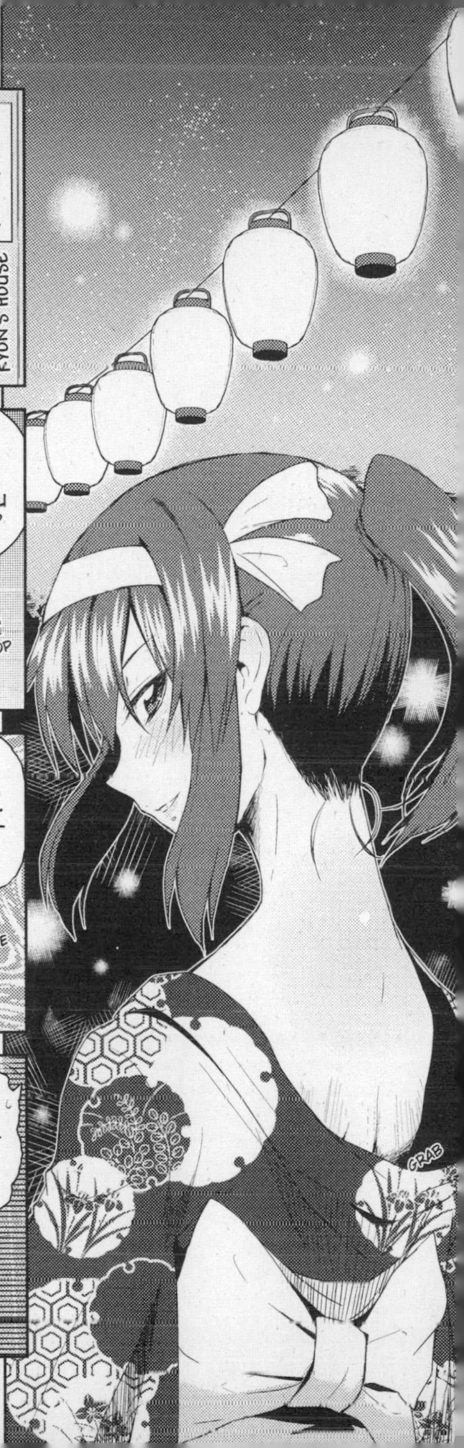
GRAB

GOING OUT

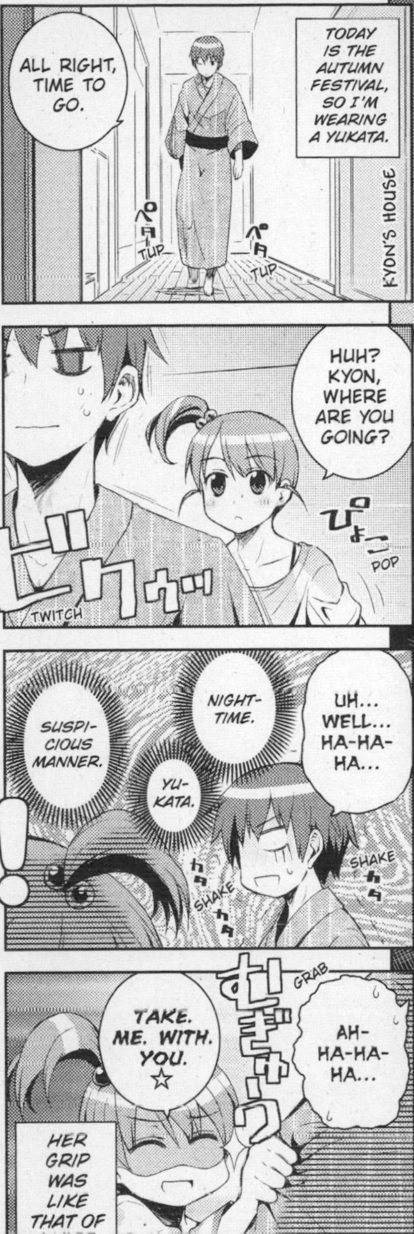
TODAY IS THE AUTUMN FESTIVAL, SO I'M WEARING A YUKATA.
KYON'S HOUSE
ALL RIGHT, TIME TO GO.
TUP
TUP
HUH? KYON, WHERE ARE YOU GOING?
POP
TWITCH
UH... WELL... HA-HA-HA...
NIGHT-TIME.
SUSPICIOUS MANNER.
YU-KATA.
SHAKE
SHAKE
!
AH-HA-HA-HA...
GRAB
TAKE. ME. WITH. YOU. ☆
HER GRIP WAS LIKE THAT OF A VISE.

●Haruhi-chan ●SOS Brigade brigade chief. Does NOT want to hold Kyon's hand. Not at all.

●Kyon ●Supposed to be the main character. Unwillingly gets along extremely well with his younger sister.

●Little Sister ●Kyon's sister. She leverages her little-sister-ness to its maximum extent. Truly, she is the Queen of Little Sisters.

LET ME EXPLAIN

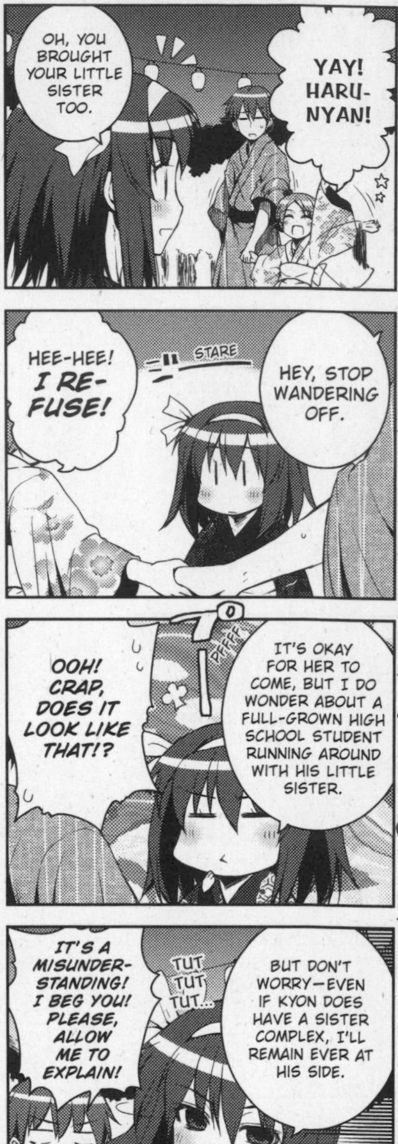
YAY! HARU-NYAN!
OH, YOU BROUGHT YOUR LITTLE SISTER TOO.
HEY, STOP WANDERING OFF.
STARE
HEE-HEE! I RE-FUSE!
IT'S OKAY FOR HER TO COME, BUT I DO WONDER ABOUT A FULL-GROWN HIGH SCHOOL STUDENT RUNNING AROUND WITH HIS LITTLE SISTER.
OOH! CRAP, DOES IT LOOK LIKE THAT!?
BUT DON'T WORRY—EVEN IF KYON DOES HAVE A SISTER COMPLEX, I'LL REMAIN EVER AT HIS SIDE.
TUT TUT TUT...
IT'S A MISUNDER-STANDING! I BEG YOU! PLEASE, ALLOW ME TO EXPLAIN!

SHRINE MAIDEN

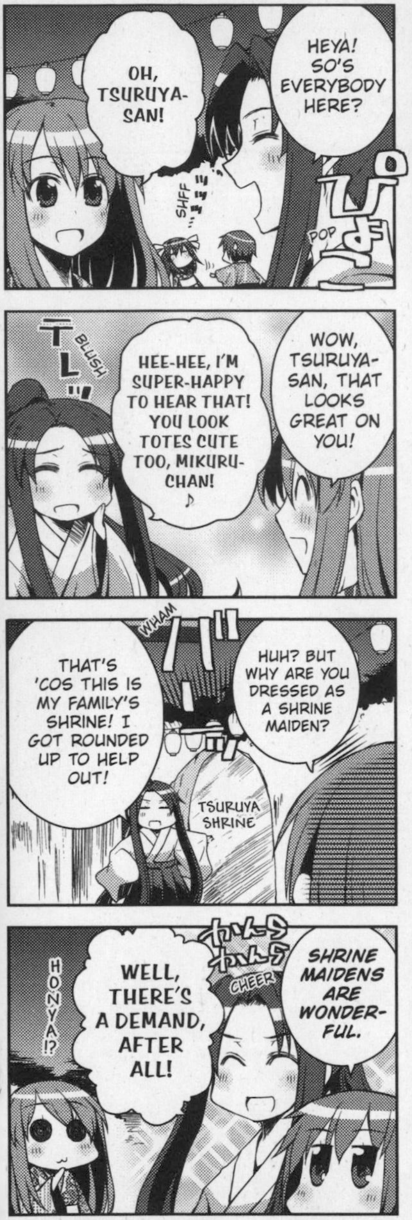
HEYA! SO'S EVERYBODY HERE?
OH, TSURUYA-SAN!
SHFF
POP
WOW, TSURUYA-SAN, THAT LOOKS GREAT ON YOU!
HEE-HEE, I'M SUPER-HAPPY TO HEAR THAT! YOU LOOK TOTES CUTE TOO, MIKURU-CHAN! ♪
BLUSH
HUH? BUT WHY ARE YOU DRESSED AS A SHRINE MAIDEN?
WHAM
THAT'S 'COS THIS IS MY FAMILY'S SHRINE! I GOT ROUNDED UP TO HELP OUT!
TSURUYA SHRINE
SHRINE MAIDENS ARE WONDERFUL.
CHEER
WELL, THERE'S A DEMAND, AFTER ALL!
HONYA!?

SPONSOR

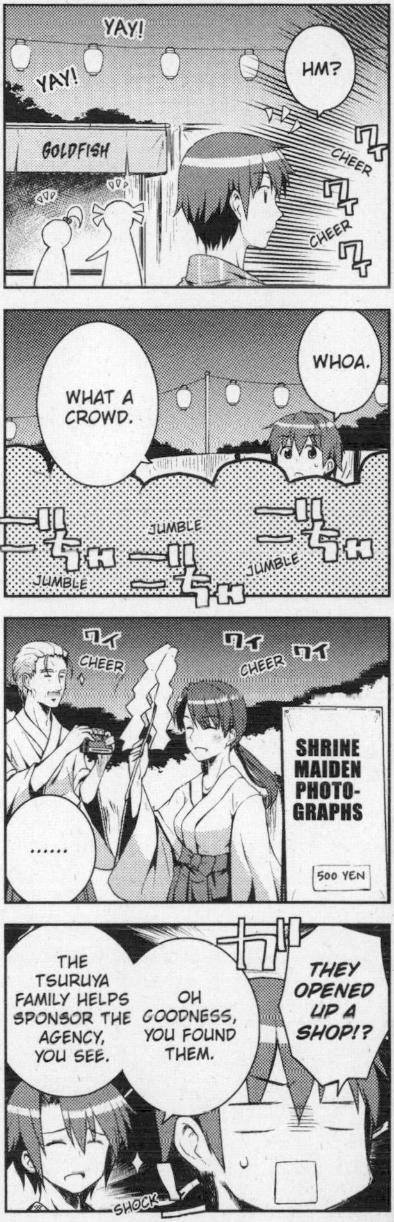
HM?
YAY!
YAY!
CHEER
CHEER
GOLDFISH
WHOA.
WHAT A CROWD.
JUMBLE
JUMBLE
JUMBLE
CHEER
CHEER
CHEER
SHRINE MAIDEN PHOTOGRAPHS
500 YEN
......
THEY OPENED UP A SHOP!?
OH GOODNESS, YOU FOUND THEM.
THE TSURUYA FAMILY HELPS SPONSOR THE AGENCY, YOU SEE.
SHOCK

EXPLANATION

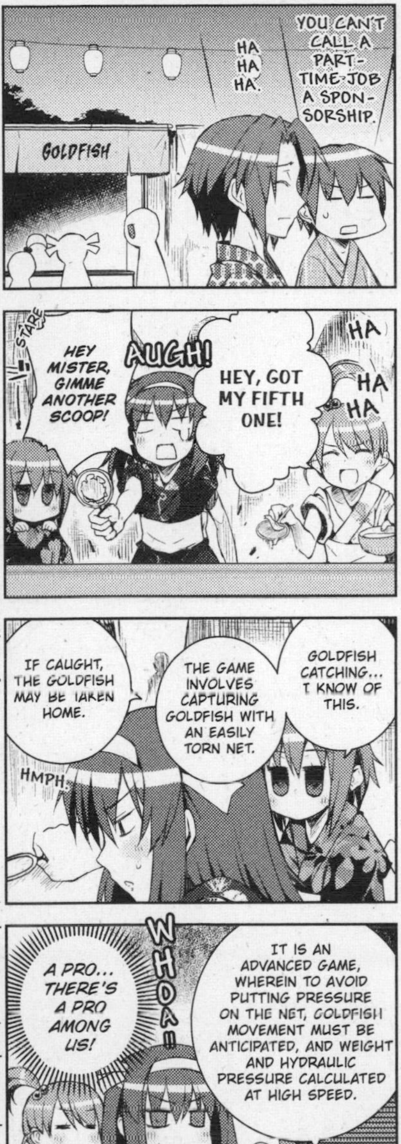
YOU CAN'T CALL A PART-TIME JOB A SPONSORSHIP.
HA HA HA.
GOLDFISH
HA HA HA
HEY, GOT MY FIFTH ONE!
AUGH!
HEY MISTER, GIMME ANOTHER SCOOP!
STARE
GOLDFISH CATCHING... I KNOW OF THIS.
THE GAME INVOLVES CAPTURING GOLDFISH WITH AN EASILY TORN NET.
IF CAUGHT, THE GOLDFISH MAY BE TAKEN HOME.
HMPH.
IT IS AN ADVANCED GAME, WHEREIN TO AVOID PUTTING PRESSURE ON THE NET, GOLDFISH MOVEMENT MUST BE ANTICIPATED, AND WEIGHT AND HYDRAULIC PRESSURE CALCULATED AT HIGH SPEED.
WHOA!!
A PRO... THERE'S A PRO AMONG US!

•Nagato •Actually an alien gamer, thus uncompromising even in the magnificent game of Goldfish Catching.

•Mori-san •A member of Koizumi's Agency. A discerning woman, she is nonetheless terrifying when angered.

•Arakawa-san •Another member of the Agency. Not that it matters, but he's dressed not as a priest but as a Shrine Maiden...?

STAINLESS STEEL

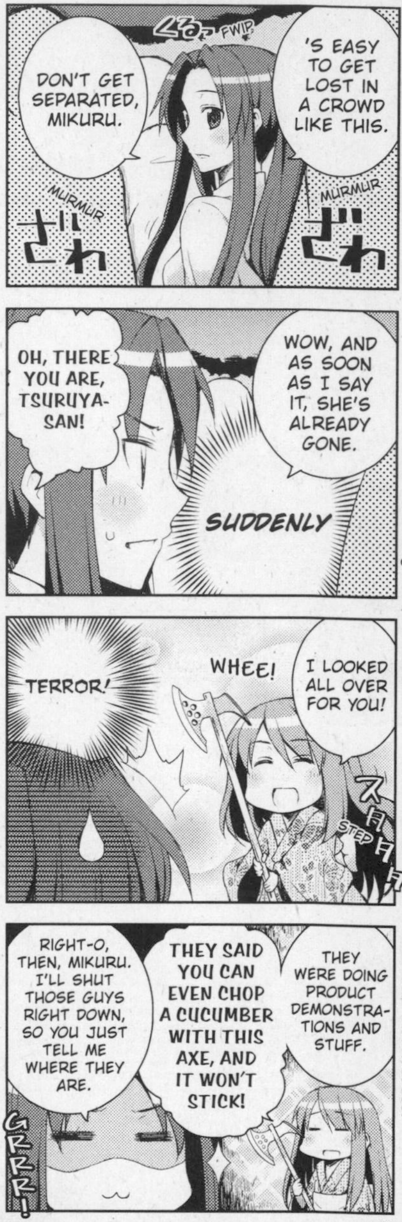
FWIP
DON'T GET SEPARATED, MIKURU.
'S EASY TO GET LOST IN A CROWD LIKE THIS.
MURMUR
MURMUR
WOW, AND AS SOON AS I SAY IT, SHE'S ALREADY GONE.
OH, THERE YOU ARE, TSURUYA-SAN!
SUDDENLY
I LOOKED ALL OVER FOR YOU!
WHEE!
TERROR!
STEP
THEY WERE DOING PRODUCT DEMONSTRATIONS AND STUFF.
THEY SAID YOU CAN EVEN CHOP A CUCUMBER WITH THIS AXE, AND IT WON'T STICK!
RIGHT-O, THEN, MIKURU. I'LL SHUT THOSE GUYS RIGHT DOWN, SO YOU JUST TELL ME WHERE THEY ARE.
GRRR!

JUST LOOKING

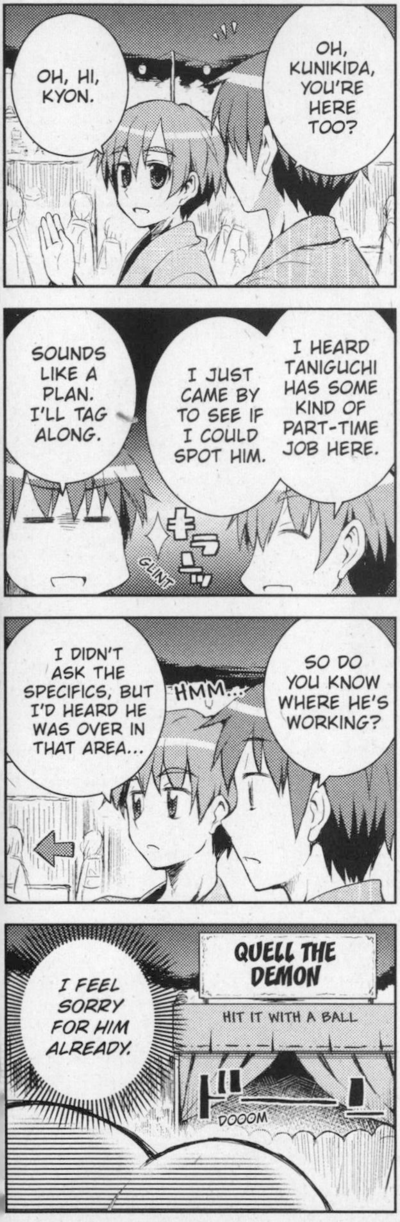
OH, KUNIKIDA, YOU'RE HERE TOO?
OH, HI, KYON.
I HEARD TANIGUCHI HAS SOME KIND OF PART-TIME JOB HERE.
I JUST CAME BY TO SEE IF I COULD SPOT HIM.
SOUNDS LIKE A PLAN. I'LL TAG ALONG.
GLINT
SO DO YOU KNOW WHERE HE'S WORKING?
HMM...
I DIDN'T ASK THE SPECIFICS, BUT I'D HEARD HE WAS OVER IN THAT AREA...
QUELL THE DEMON
HIT IT WITH A BALL
I FEEL SORRY FOR HIM ALREADY.
DOOOM

•Tsuruya-san •Even owns a shrine. Her job is to ensure the public safety of the festival.

•Mikuru-chan •Actually from the future. Loves mail-order shopping and being tricked.

•Koizumi •Enigmatic transfer student and esper. His job is quite dangerous, evidently, and its burdens never cease.

ASSAULT ON ONIGUCHI

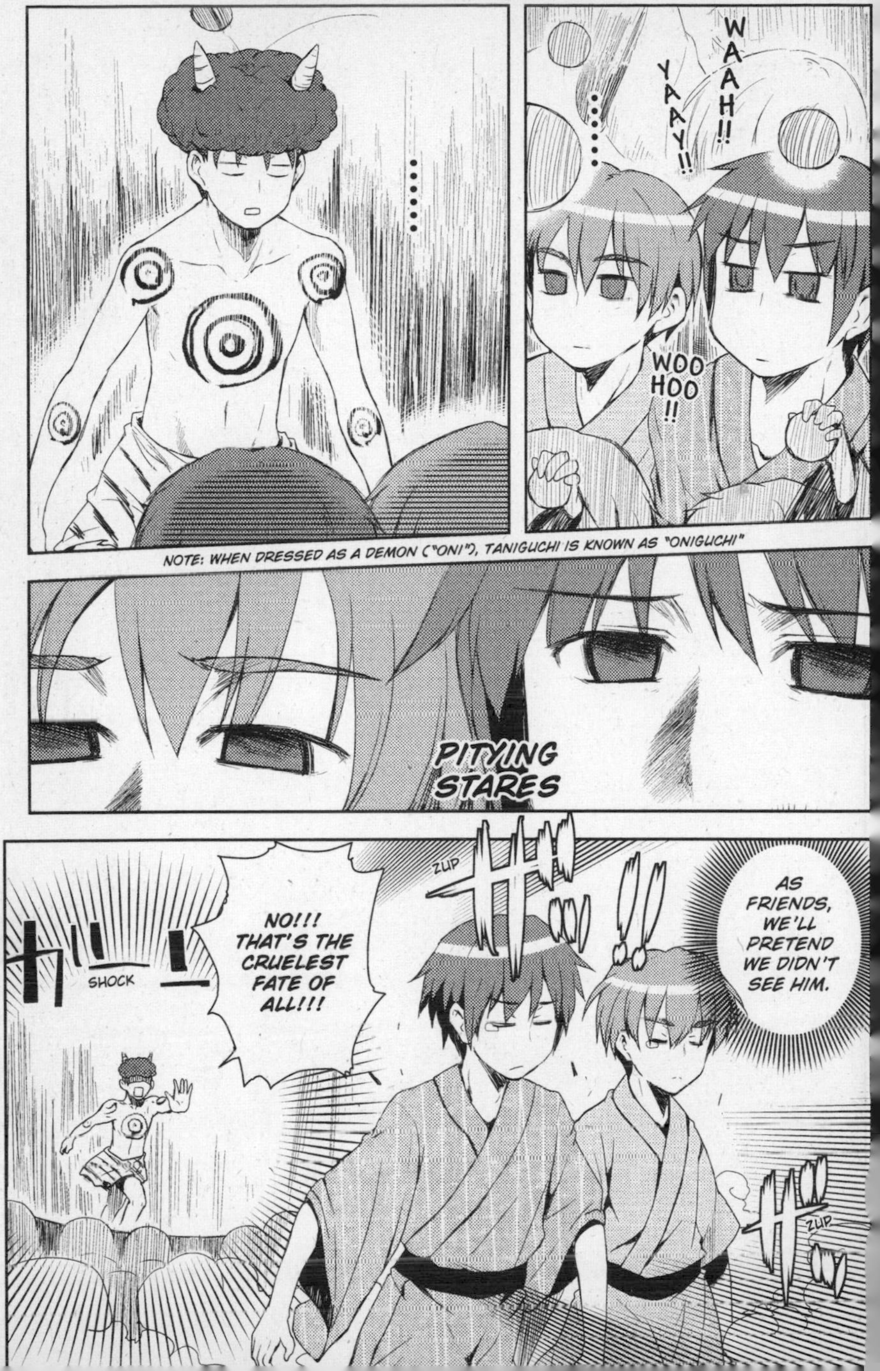
WAAAH!!
YAAAY!!
......
WOO HOO!!
......
NOTE: WHEN DRESSED AS A DEMON ("ONI"), TANIGUCHI IS KNOWN AS "ONIGUCHI"
PITYING STARES
AS FRIENDS, WE'LL PRETEND WE DIDN'T SEE HIM.
ZUP
ZUP
NO!!! THAT'S THE CRUELEST FATE OF ALL!!!
SHOCK

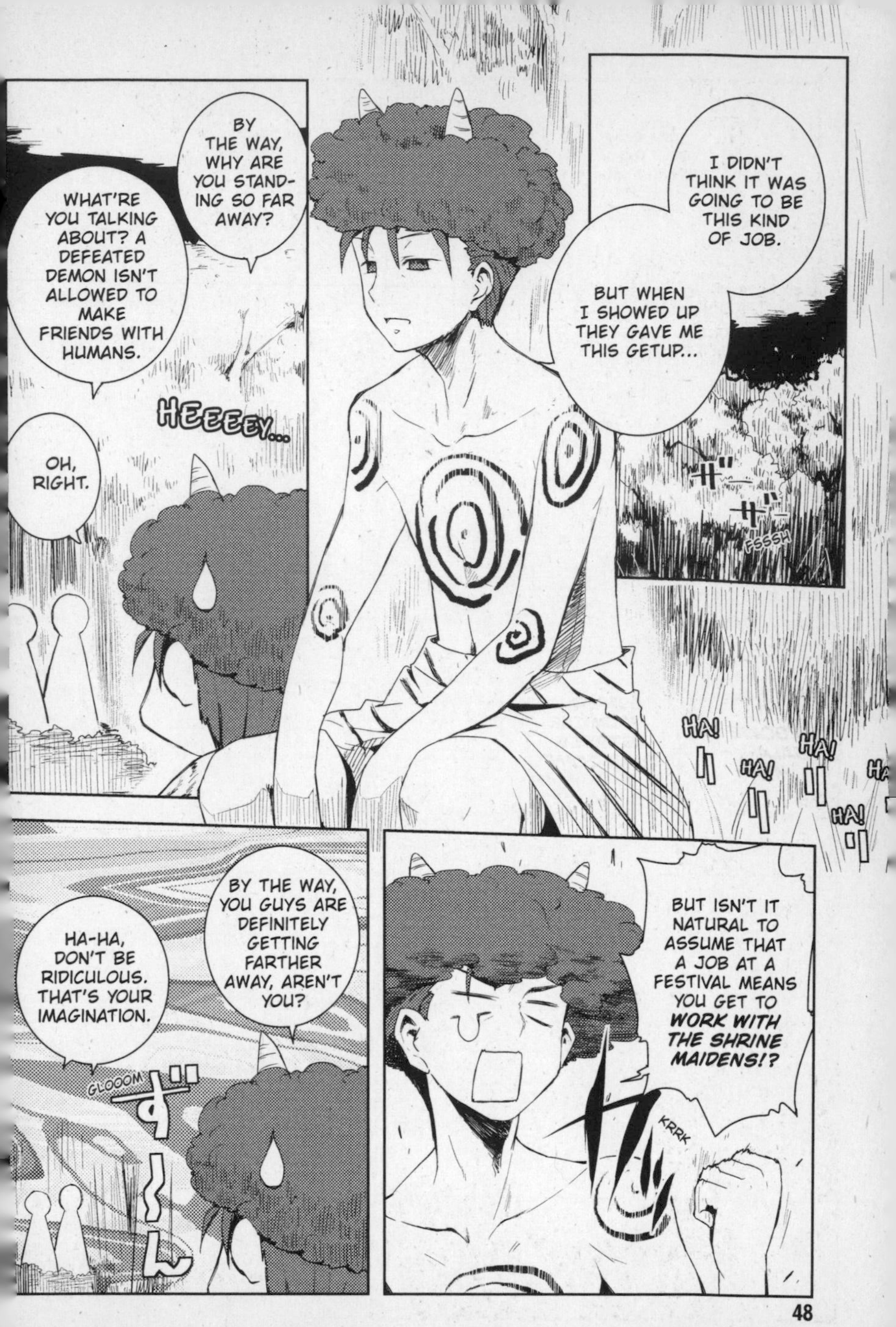

I DIDN'T THINK IT WAS GOING TO BE THIS KIND OF JOB.
BUT WHEN I SHOWED UP THEY GAVE ME THIS GETUP...
FSSSH
BY THE WAY, WHY ARE YOU STANDING SO FAR AWAY?
WHAT'RE YOU TALKING ABOUT? A DEFEATED DEMON ISN'T ALLOWED TO MAKE FRIENDS WITH HUMANS.
HEEEEEY...
OH, RIGHT.
HA! HA! HA! HA!
BUT ISN'T IT NATURAL TO ASSUME THAT A JOB AT A FESTIVAL MEANS YOU GET TO ***WORK WITH THE SHRINE MAIDENS!?***
KRRK
BY THE WAY, YOU GUYS ARE DEFINITELY GETTING FARTHER AWAY, AREN'T YOU?
HA-HA, DON'T BE RIDICULOUS. THAT'S YOUR IMAGINATION.
GLOOOM

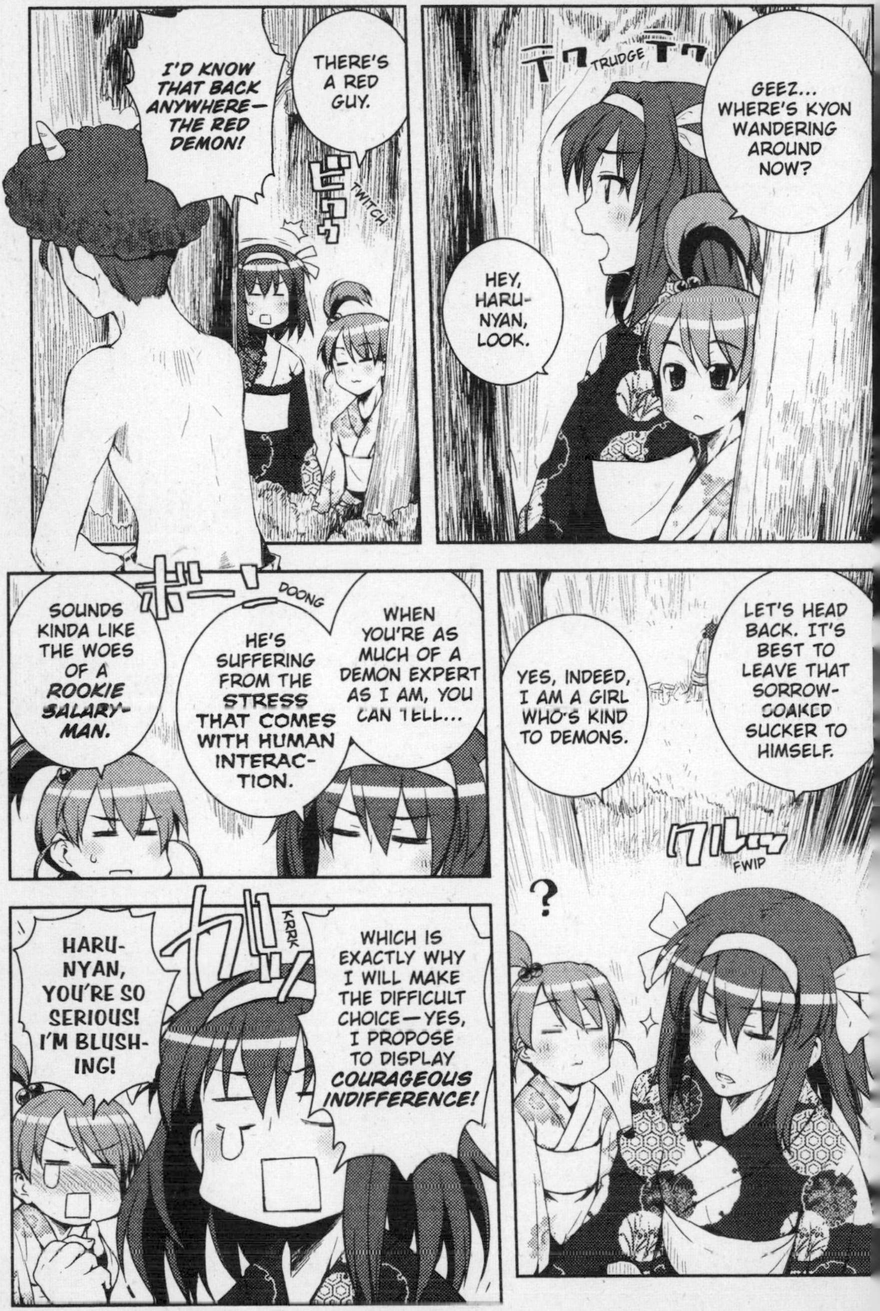
TRUDGE
GEEZ... WHERE'S KYON WANDERING AROUND NOW?
HEY, HARU-NYAN, LOOK.
THERE'S A RED GUY.
TWITCH
I'D KNOW THAT BACK ANYWHERE—THE RED DEMON!
LET'S HEAD BACK. IT'S BEST TO LEAVE THAT SORROW-SOAKED SUCKER TO HIMSELF.
YES, INDEED, I AM A GIRL WHO'S KIND TO DEMONS.
FWIP
?
DOONG
WHEN YOU'RE AS MUCH OF A DEMON EXPERT AS I AM, YOU CAN TELL...
HE'S SUFFERING FROM THE STRESS THAT COMES WITH HUMAN INTERACTION.
SOUNDS KINDA LIKE THE WOES OF A ROOKIE SALARYMAN.
KRRK
WHICH IS EXACTLY WHY I WILL MAKE THE DIFFICULT CHOICE—YES, I PROPOSE TO DISPLAY COURAGEOUS INDIFFERENCE!
HARU-NYAN, YOU'RE SO SERIOUS! I'M BLUSHING!

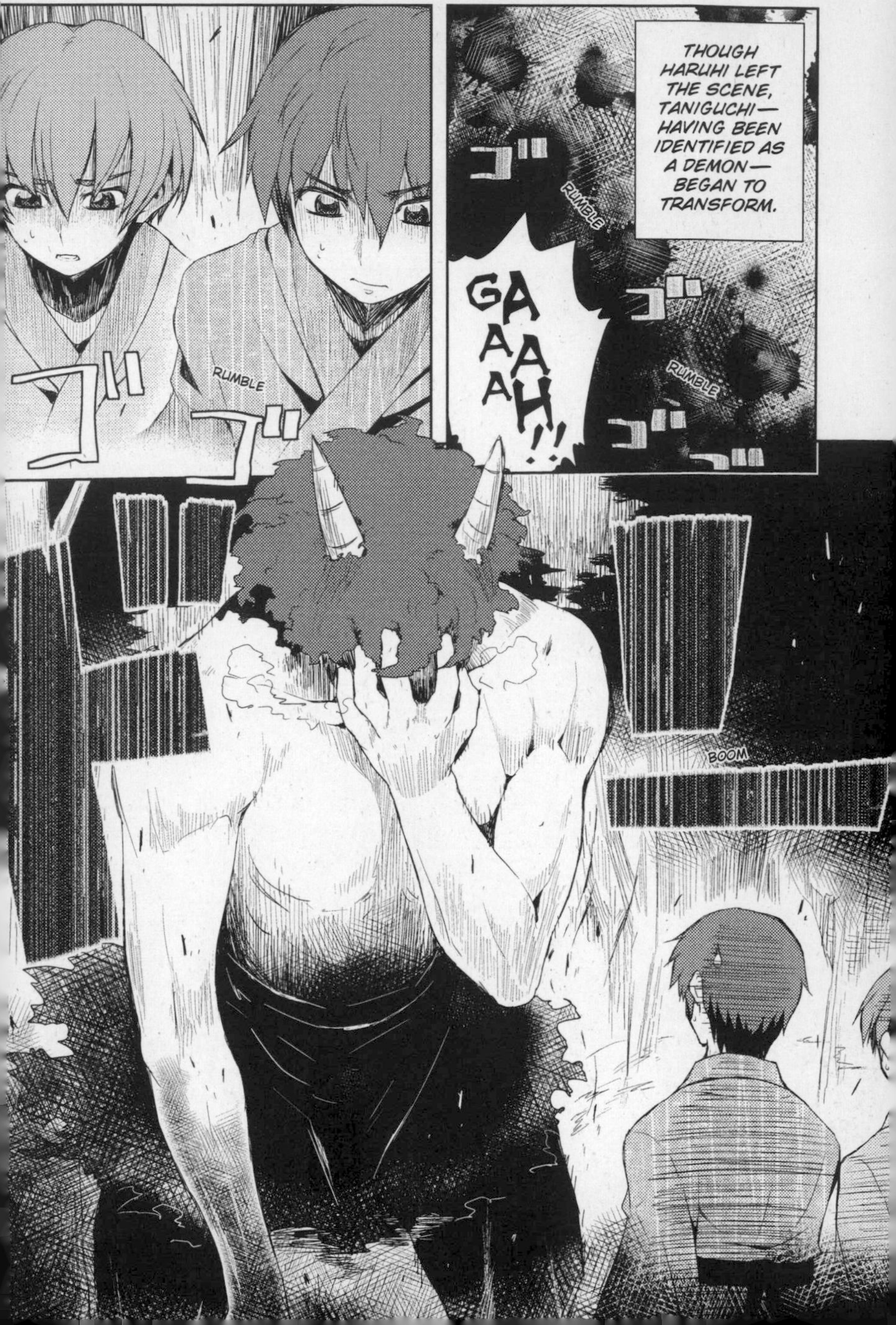
THOUGH HARUHI LEFT THE SCENE, TANIGUCHI—HAVING BEEN IDENTIFIED AS A DEMON—BEGAN TO TRANSFORM.
RUMBLE
GAAAAH!!
RUMBLE
RUMBLE
BOOM

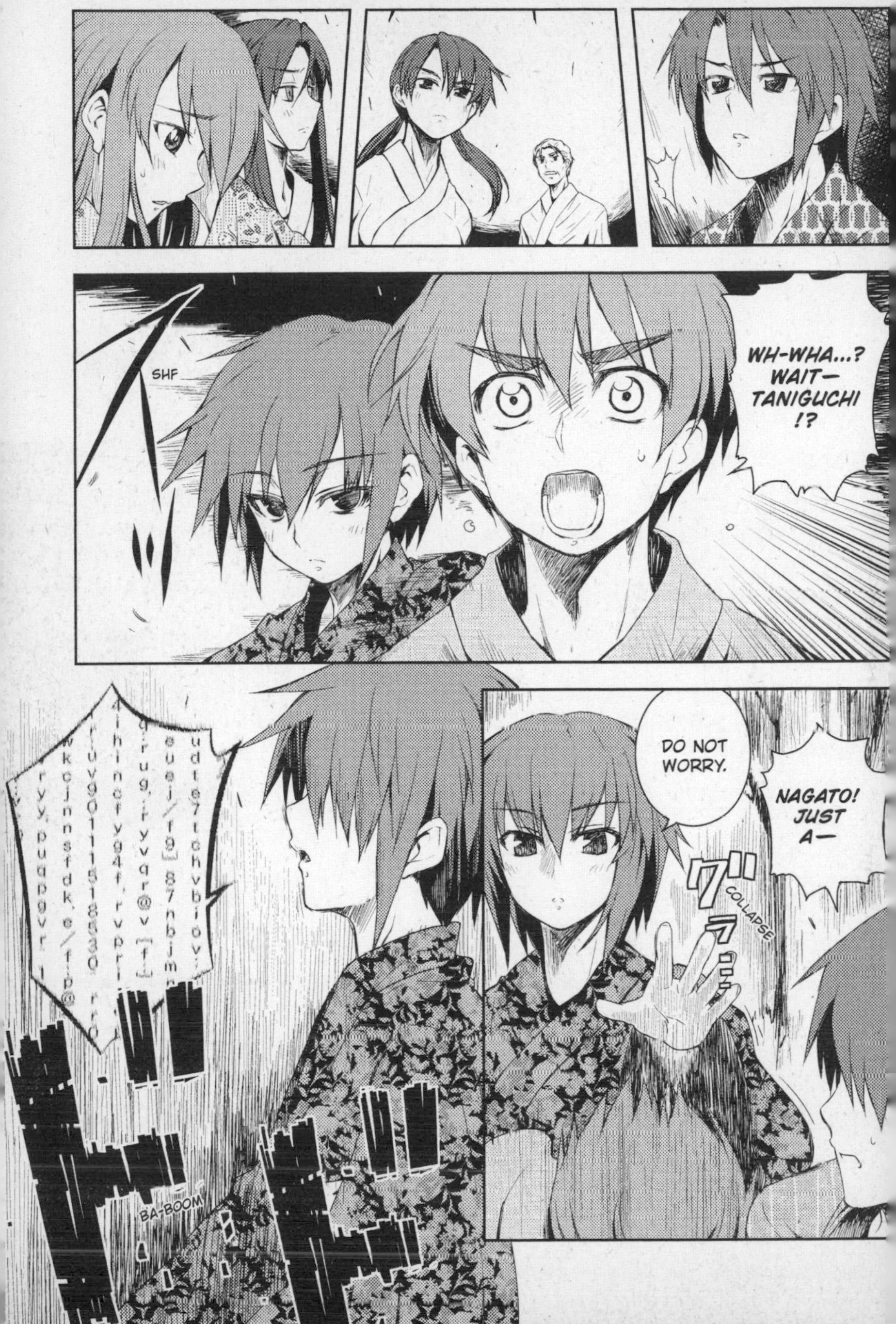
WH-WHA...? WAIT—TANIGUCHI !?
SHF
NAGATO! JUST A—
DO NOT WORRY.
COLLAPSE
BA-BOOM

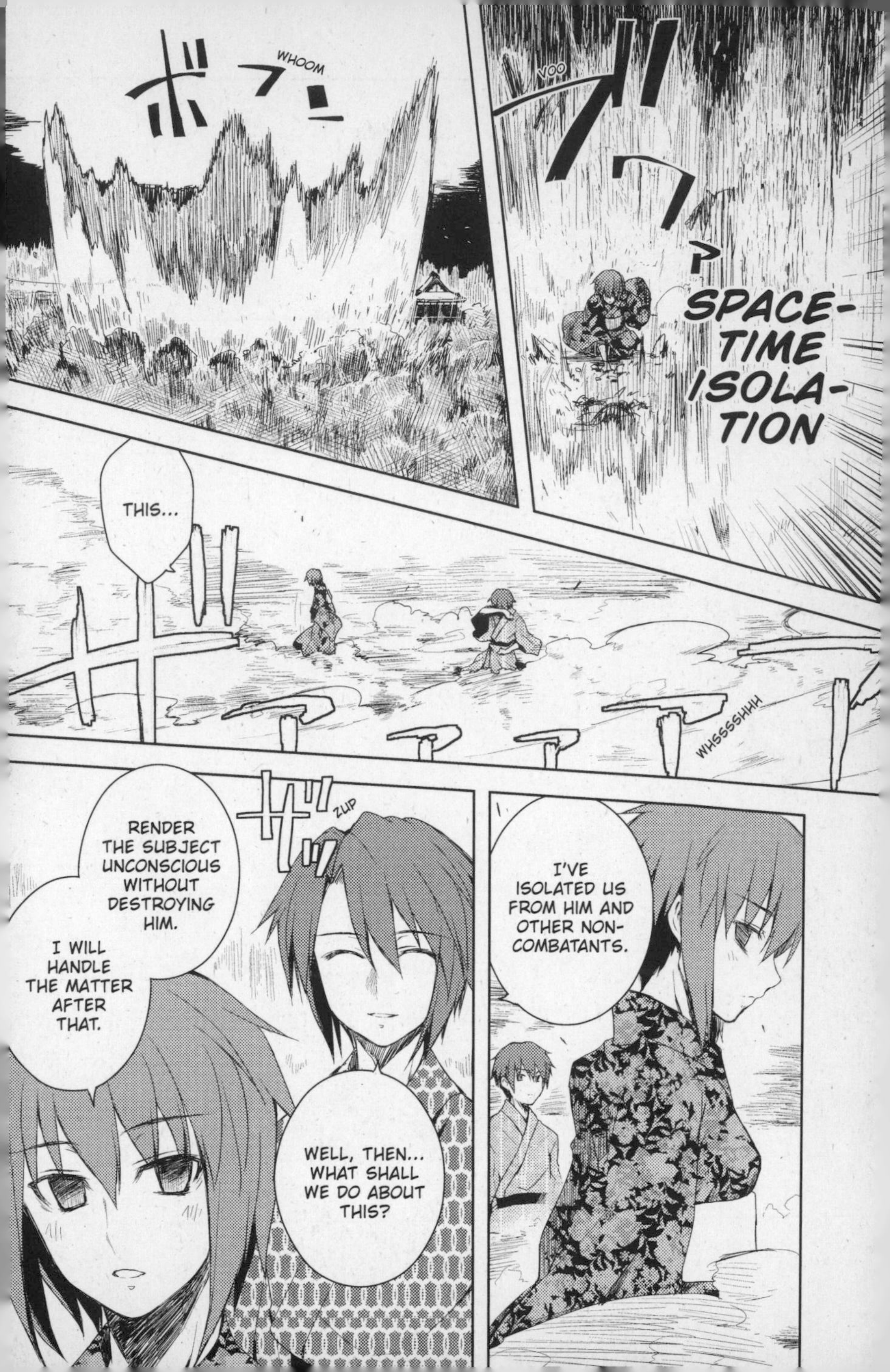
VOO
SPACE-TIME ISOLATION
WHOOM
THIS...
WHSSSSHHH
I'VE ISOLATED US FROM HIM AND OTHER NON-COMBATANTS.
ZUP
RENDER THE SUBJECT UNCONSCIOUS WITHOUT DESTROYING HIM.
I WILL HANDLE THE MATTER AFTER THAT.
WELL, THEN... WHAT SHALL WE DO ABOUT THIS?

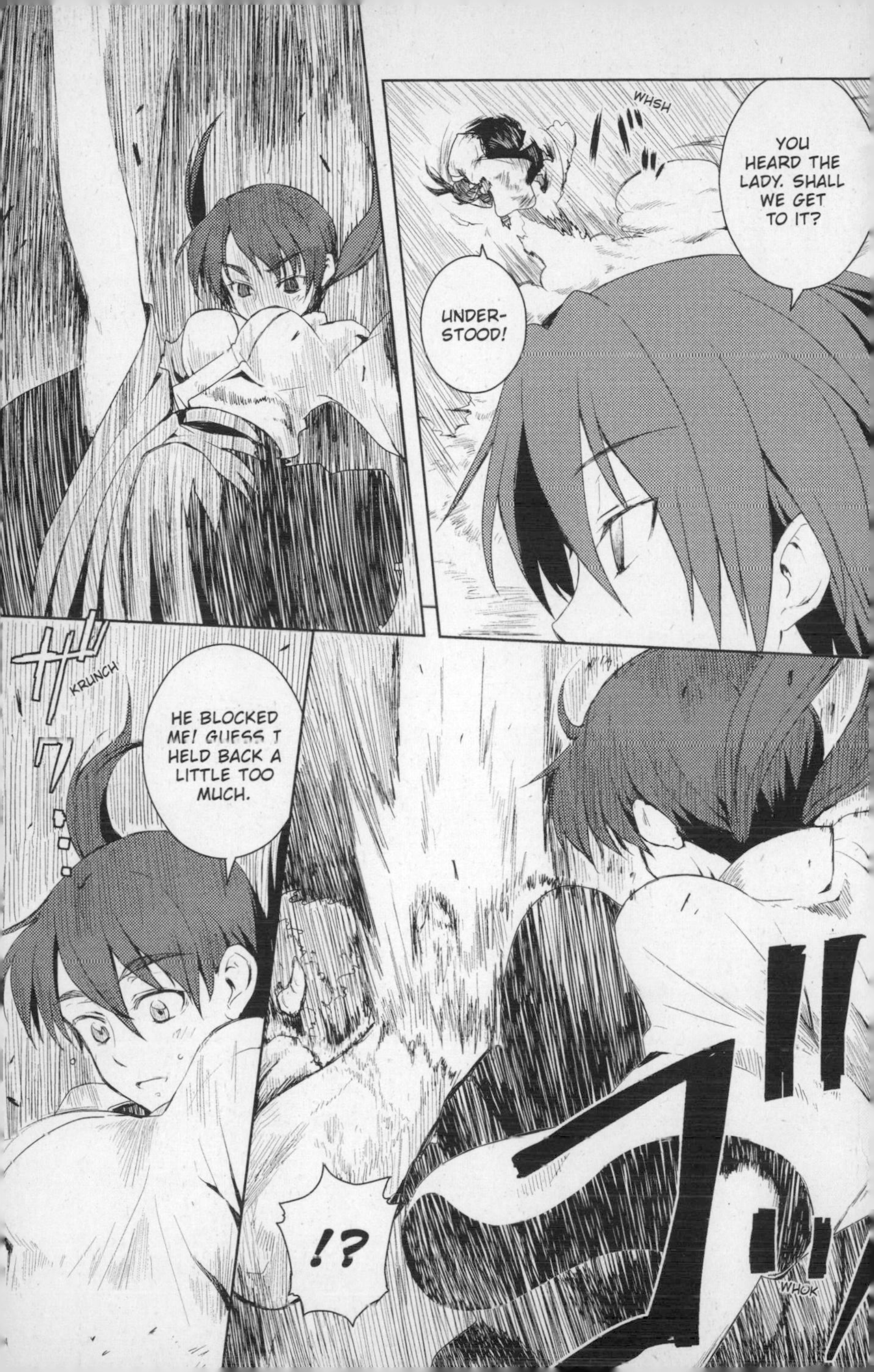
WHSH
YOU HEARD THE LADY. SHALL WE GET TO IT?
UNDER-STOOD!
!?
WHOK
KRUNCH
HE BLOCKED ME! GUESS I HELD BACK A LITTLE TOO MUCH.

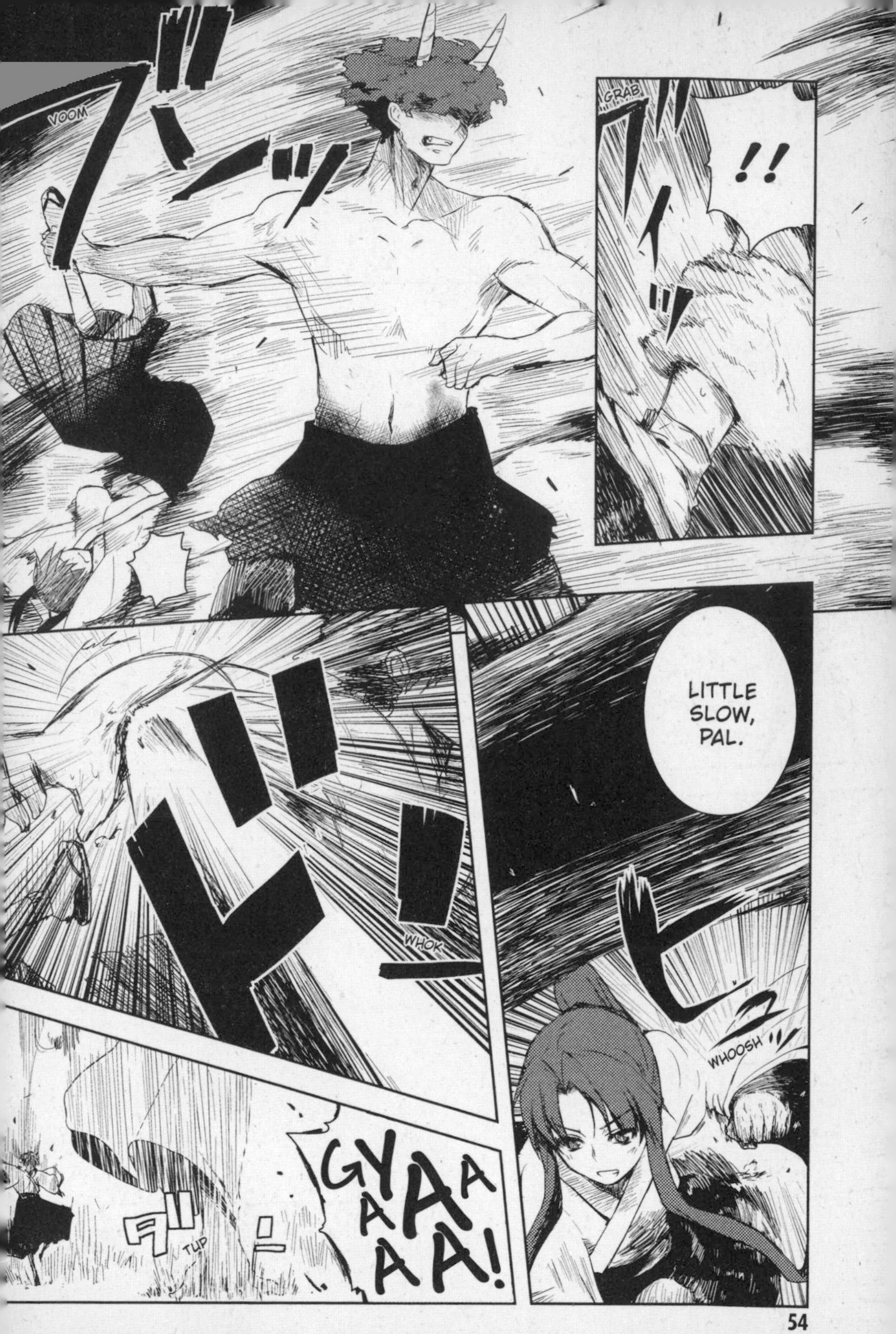
GRAB
!!
VOOM
LITTLE SLOW, PAL.
WHOOSH
WHOK
GYAAAAA!
TUP

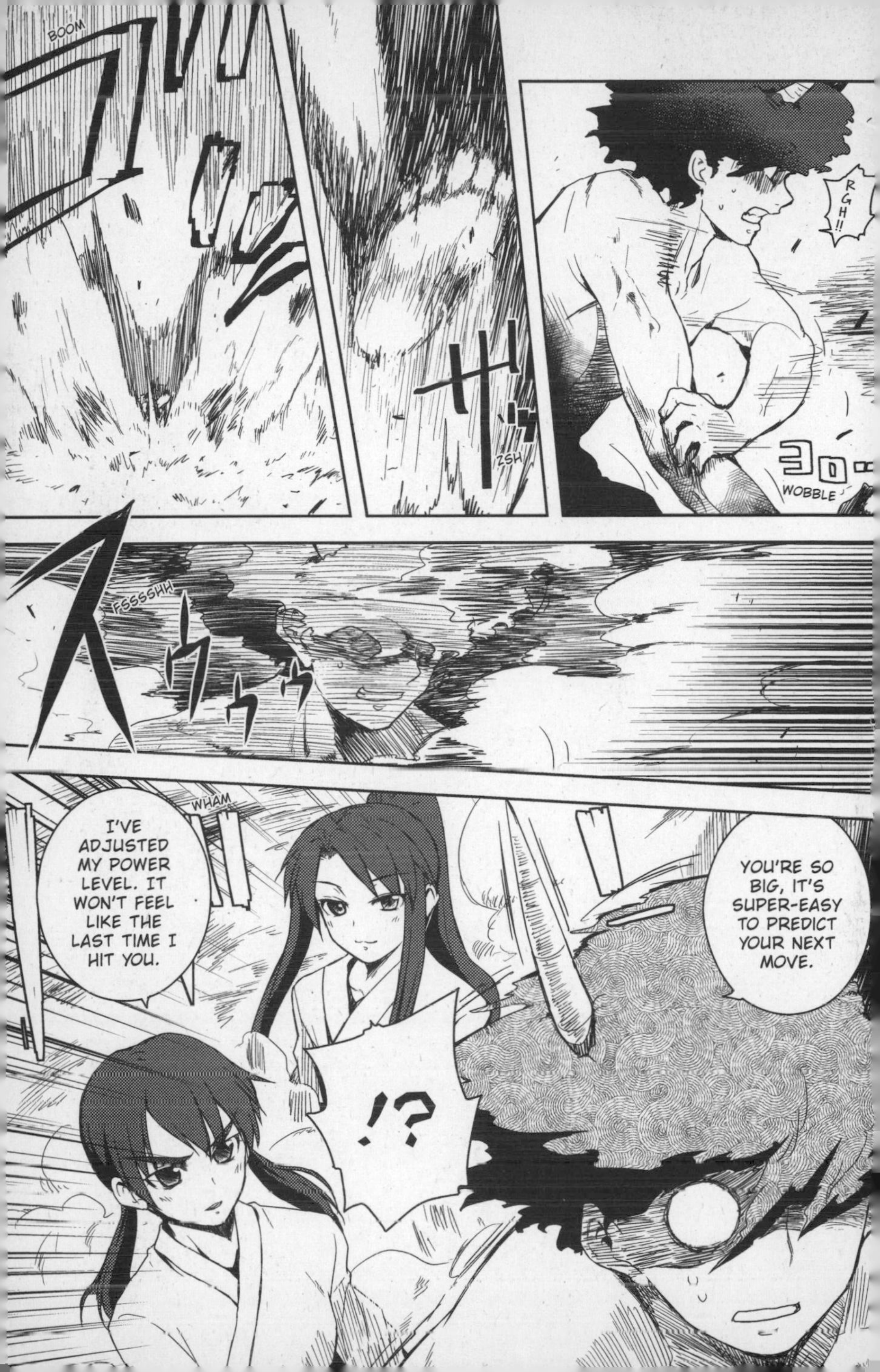
RGH!!
WOBBLE
ZSH
BOOM
FSSSSHH
YOU'RE SO BIG, IT'S SUPER-EASY TO PREDICT YOUR NEXT MOVE.
WHAM
I'VE ADJUSTED MY POWER LEVEL. IT WON'T FEEL LIKE THE LAST TIME I HIT YOU.
!?

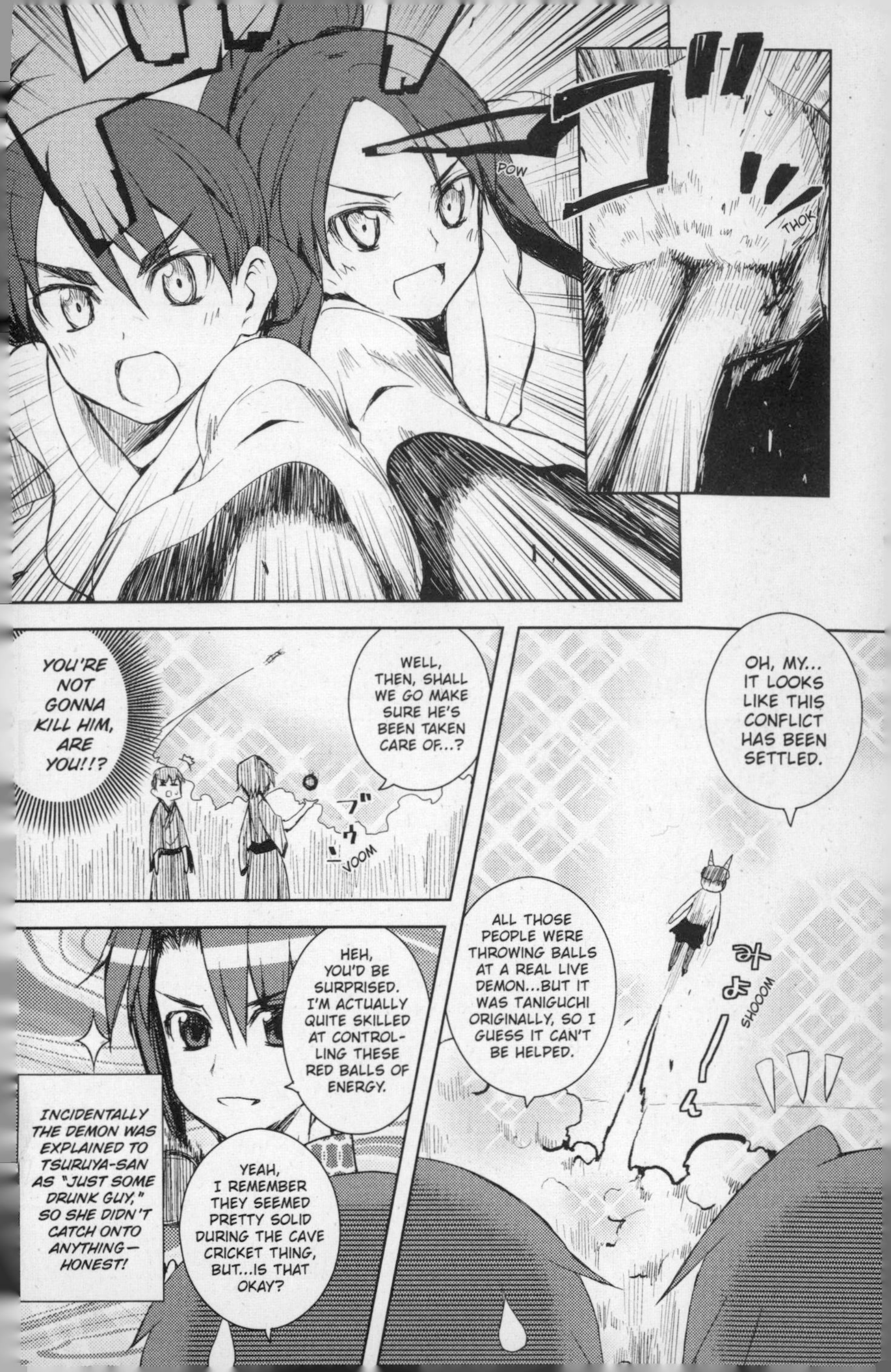
THOK
POW
OH, MY... IT LOOKS LIKE THIS CONFLICT HAS BEEN SETTLED.
ALL THOSE PEOPLE WERE THROWING BALLS AT A REAL LIVE DEMON...BUT IT WAS TANIGUCHI ORIGINALLY, SO I GUESS IT CAN'T BE HELPED.
SHOOOM
WELL, THEN, SHALL WE GO MAKE SURE HE'S BEEN TAKEN CARE OF...?
VOOM
YOU'RE NOT GONNA KILL HIM, ARE YOU!!?
HEH, YOU'D BE SURPRISED. I'M ACTUALLY QUITE SKILLED AT CONTROL-LING THESE RED BALLS OF ENERGY.
YEAH, I REMEMBER THEY SEEMED PRETTY SOLID DURING THE CAVE CRICKET THING, BUT...IS THAT OKAY?
INCIDENTALLY THE DEMON WAS EXPLAINED TO TSURUYA-SAN AS "JUST SOME DRUNK GUY," SO SHE DIDN'T CATCH ONTO ANYTHING—HONEST!

EXCURSION

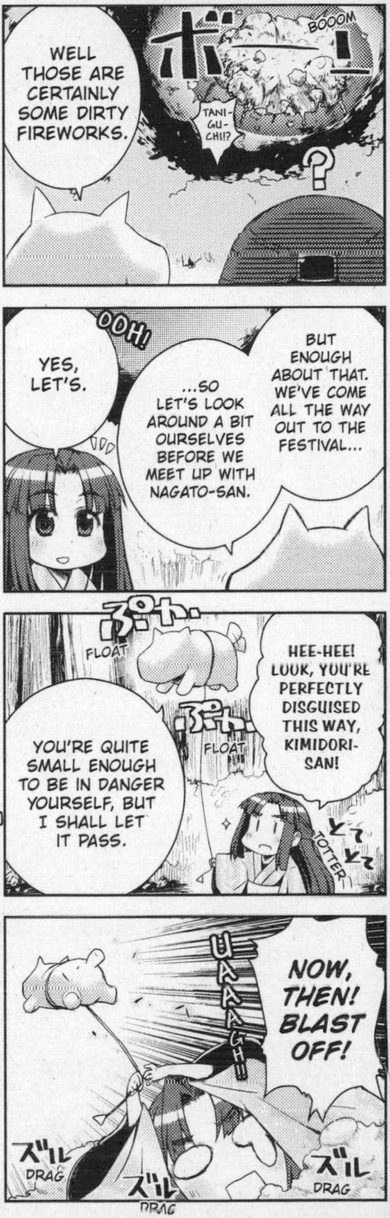
ボーン
BOOOM
TANI-GUCHI!?
?
WELL THOSE ARE CERTAINLY SOME DIRTY FIREWORKS.
BUT ENOUGH ABOUT THAT. WE'VE COME ALL THE WAY OUT TO THE FESTIVAL...
...SO LET'S LOOK AROUND A BIT OURSELVES BEFORE WE MEET UP WITH NAGATO-SAN.
OOH!
YES, LET'S.
HEE-HEE! LOOK, YOU'RE PERFECTLY DISGUISED THIS WAY, KIMIDORI-SAN!
FLOAT
FLOAT
YOU'RE QUITE SMALL ENOUGH TO BE IN DANGER YOURSELF, BUT I SHALL LET IT PASS.
TOTTER
NOW, THEN! BLAST OFF!
UAAAGH!!
DRAG
DRAG
DRAG

NATURAL ENEMY

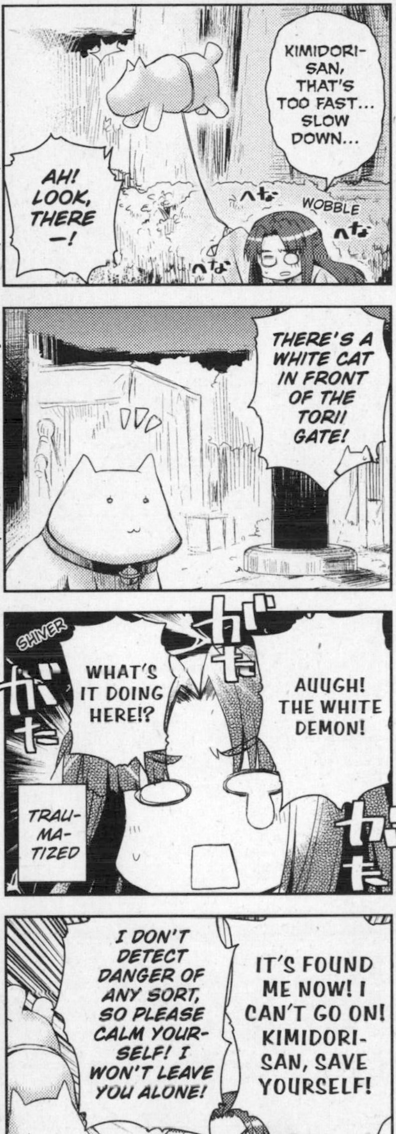
KIMIDORI-SAN, THAT'S TOO FAST... SLOW DOWN...
WOBBLE
AH! LOOK, THERE—!
THERE'S A WHITE CAT IN FRONT OF THE TORII GATE!
AUUGH! THE WHITE DEMON!
WHAT'S IT DOING HERE!?
SHIVER
TRAU-MA-TIZED
IT'S FOUND ME NOW! I CAN'T GO ON! KIMIDORI-SAN, SAVE YOURSELF!
I DON'T DETECT DANGER OF ANY SORT, SO PLEASE CALM YOURSELF! I WON'T LEAVE YOU ALONE!
BOP

•Achakura-chan •Back in action after being destroyed, crashing at Nagato's place. Snuck out to go to the festival.

•Kimidori-san •A life-form (dog) created from a balloon by Nagato. Has the perfect camouflage.

•Cat •Achakura-chan's long-time rival. See pages 38 and 56 of vol. 1.

GROWING UP

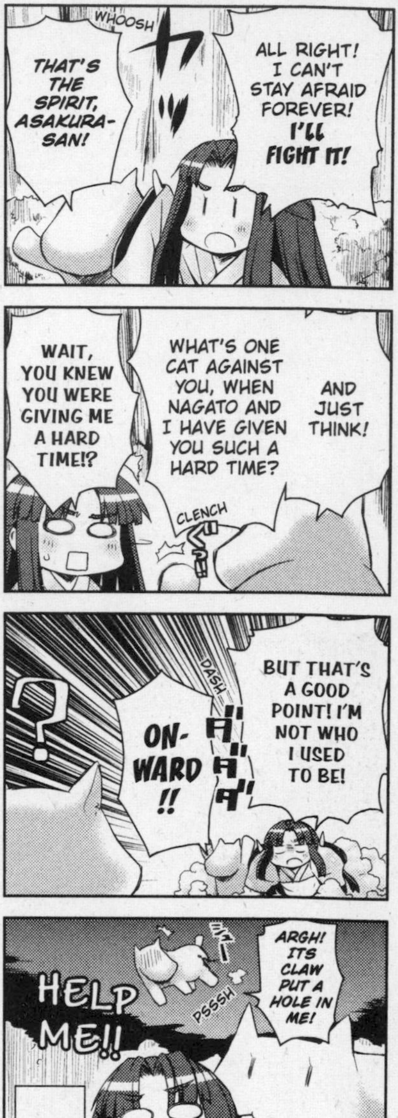
ALL RIGHT! I CAN'T STAY AFRAID FOREVER! I'LL FIGHT IT!
WHOOSH
THAT'S THE SPIRIT, ASAKURA-SAN!
AND JUST THINK!
WHAT'S ONE CAT AGAINST YOU, WHEN NAGATO AND I HAVE GIVEN YOU SUCH A HARD TIME?
WAIT, YOU KNEW YOU WERE GIVING ME A HARD TIME!?
CLENCH
BUT THAT'S A GOOD POINT! I'M NOT WHO I USED TO BE!
DASH
ON-WARD !!
?
ARGH! ITS CLAW PUT A HOLE IN ME!
PSSSH
HELP ME!!
TOTAL DEFEAT.

ASAKURA-SAN OF YORE

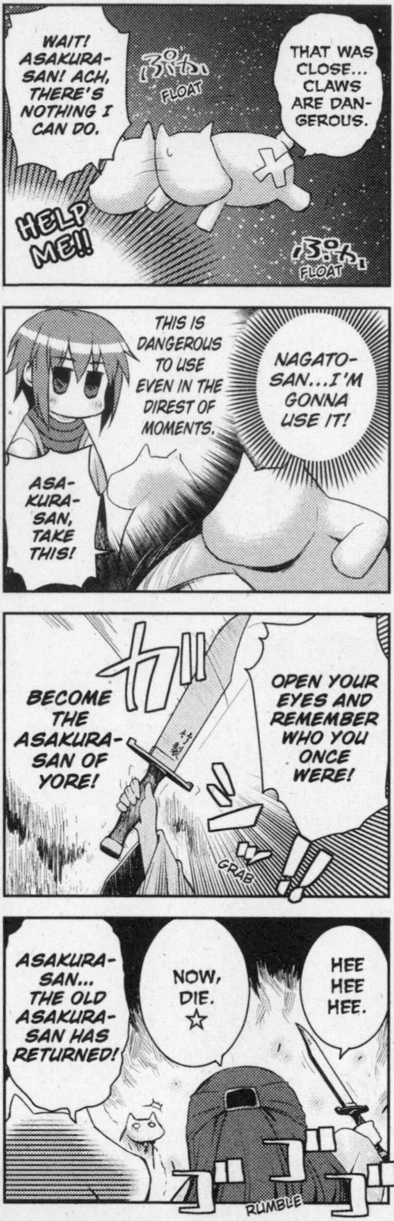
THAT WAS CLOSE... CLAWS ARE DANGEROUS.
FLOAT
WAIT! ASAKURA-SAN! ACH, THERE'S NOTHING I CAN DO.
HELP ME!!
FLOAT
NAGATO-SAN...I'M GONNA USE IT!
THIS IS DANGEROUS TO USE EVEN IN THE DIREST OF MOMENTS.
ASAKURA-SAN, TAKE THIS!
OPEN YOUR EYES AND REMEMBER WHO YOU ONCE WERE!
BECOME THE ASAKURA-SAN OF YORE!
GRAB
HEE HEE HEE.
NOW, DIE. ☆
ASAKURA-SAN... THE OLD ASAKURA-SAN HAS RETURNED!
RUMBLE

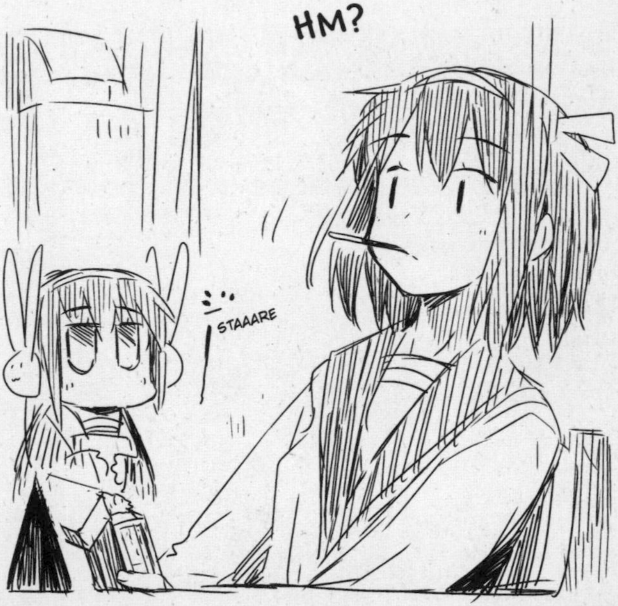
HM?
STAAARE

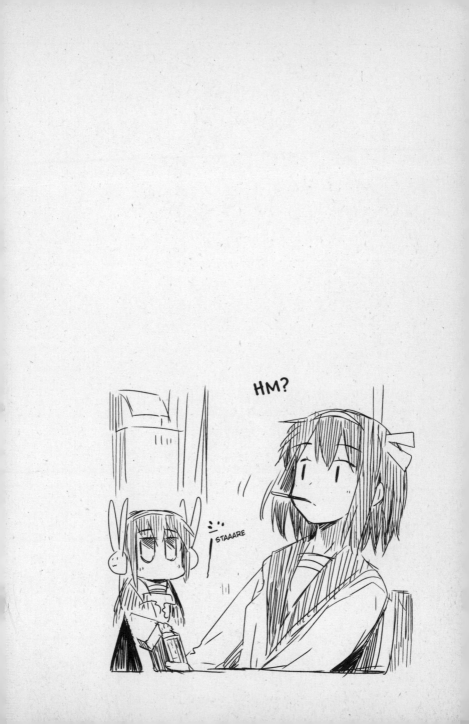

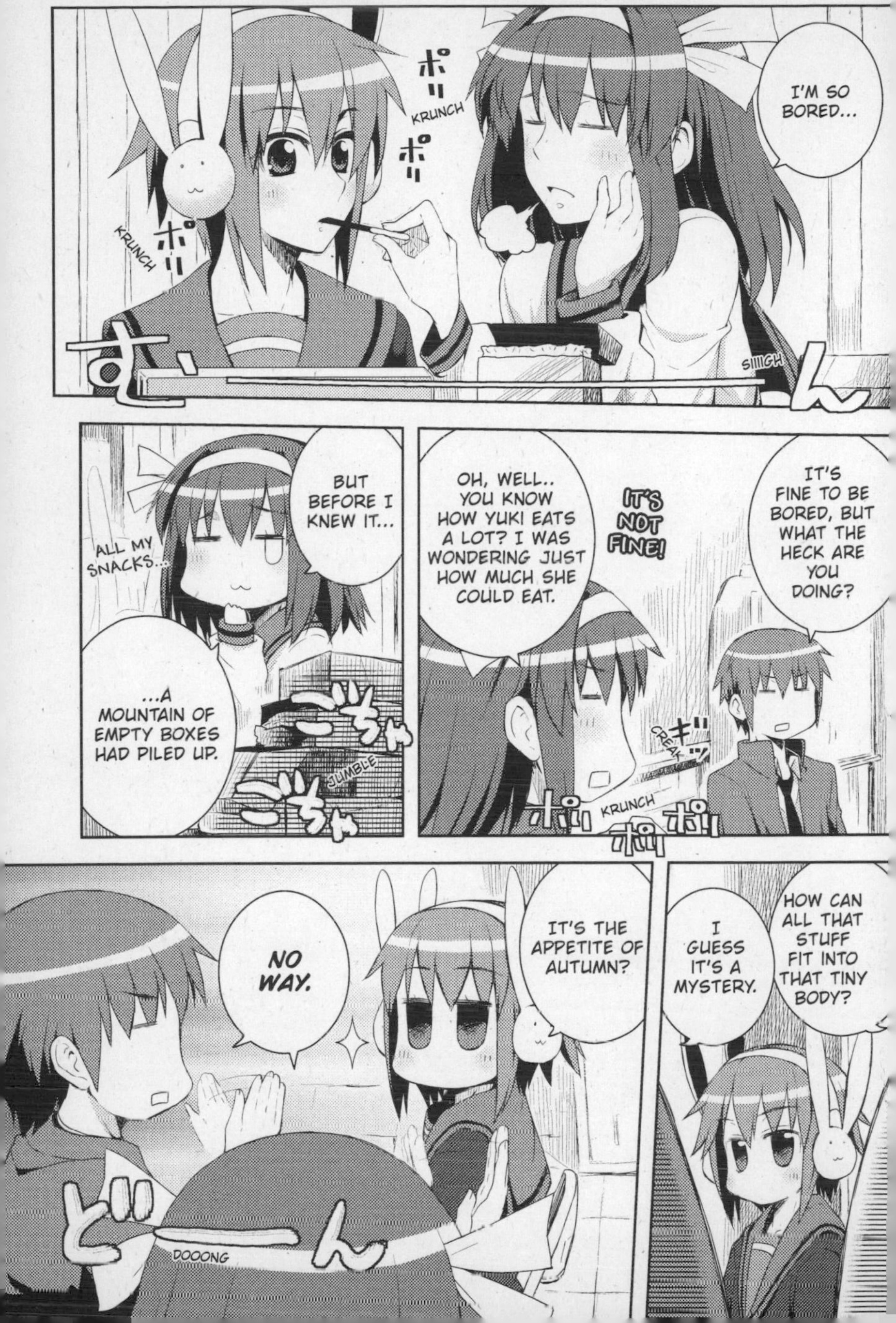
I'M SO BORED...
ポリ
KRUNCH
ポリ
ポリ
KRUNCH
SIIIGH
IT'S FINE TO BE BORED, BUT WHAT THE HECK ARE YOU DOING?
IT'S NOT FINE!
OH, WELL.. YOU KNOW HOW YUKI EATS A LOT? I WAS WONDERING JUST HOW MUCH SHE COULD EAT.
CREAK
KRUNCH
BUT BEFORE I KNEW IT...
ALL MY SNACKS...
...A MOUNTAIN OF EMPTY BOXES HAD PILED UP.
JUMBLE
HOW CAN ALL THAT STUFF FIT INTO THAT TINY BODY?
I GUESS IT'S A MYSTERY.
IT'S THE APPETITE OF AUTUMN?
NO WAY.
DOOONG

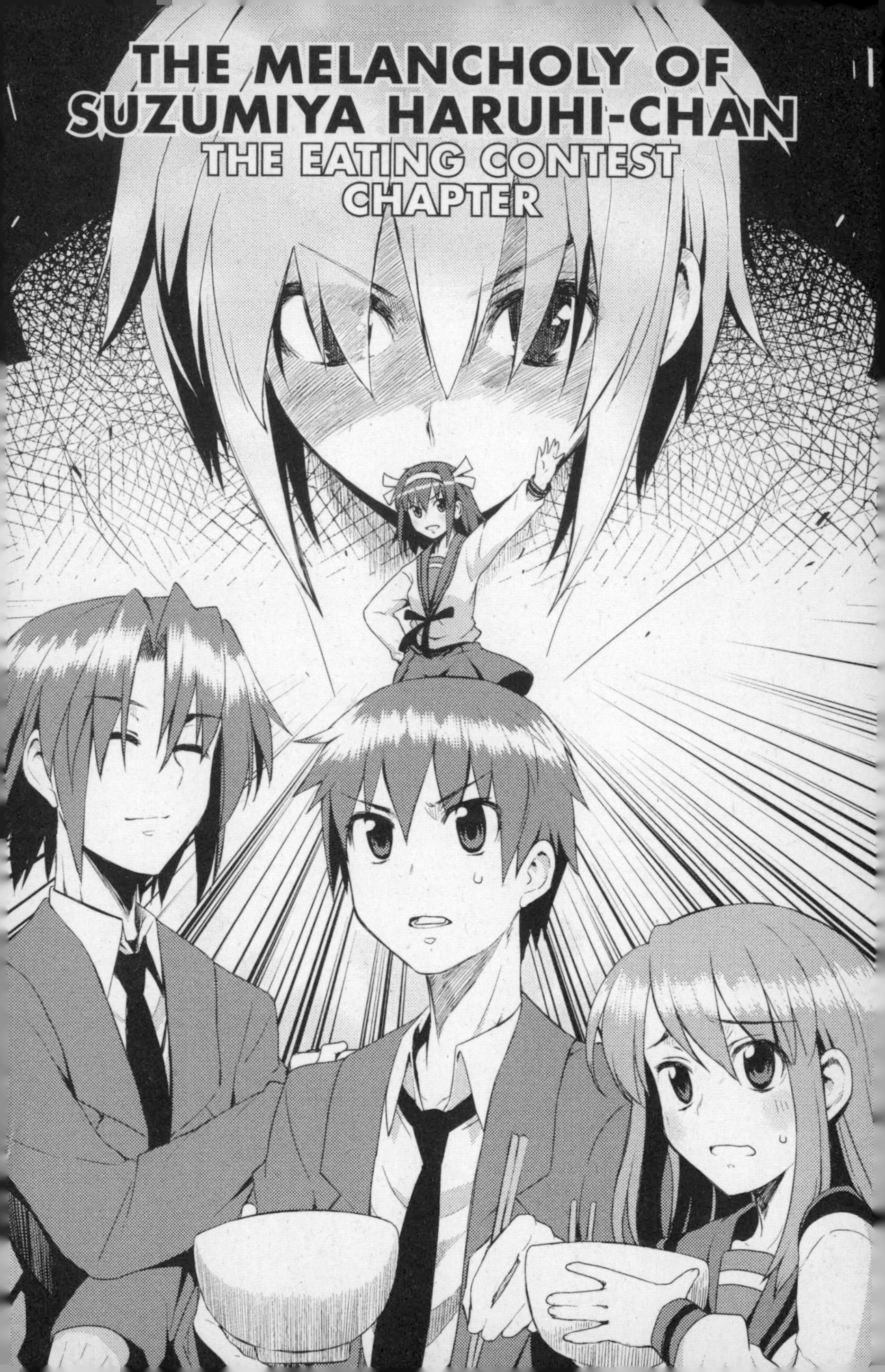
THE MELANCHOLY OF SUZUMIYA HARUHI-CHAN
THE EATING CONTEST CHAPTER

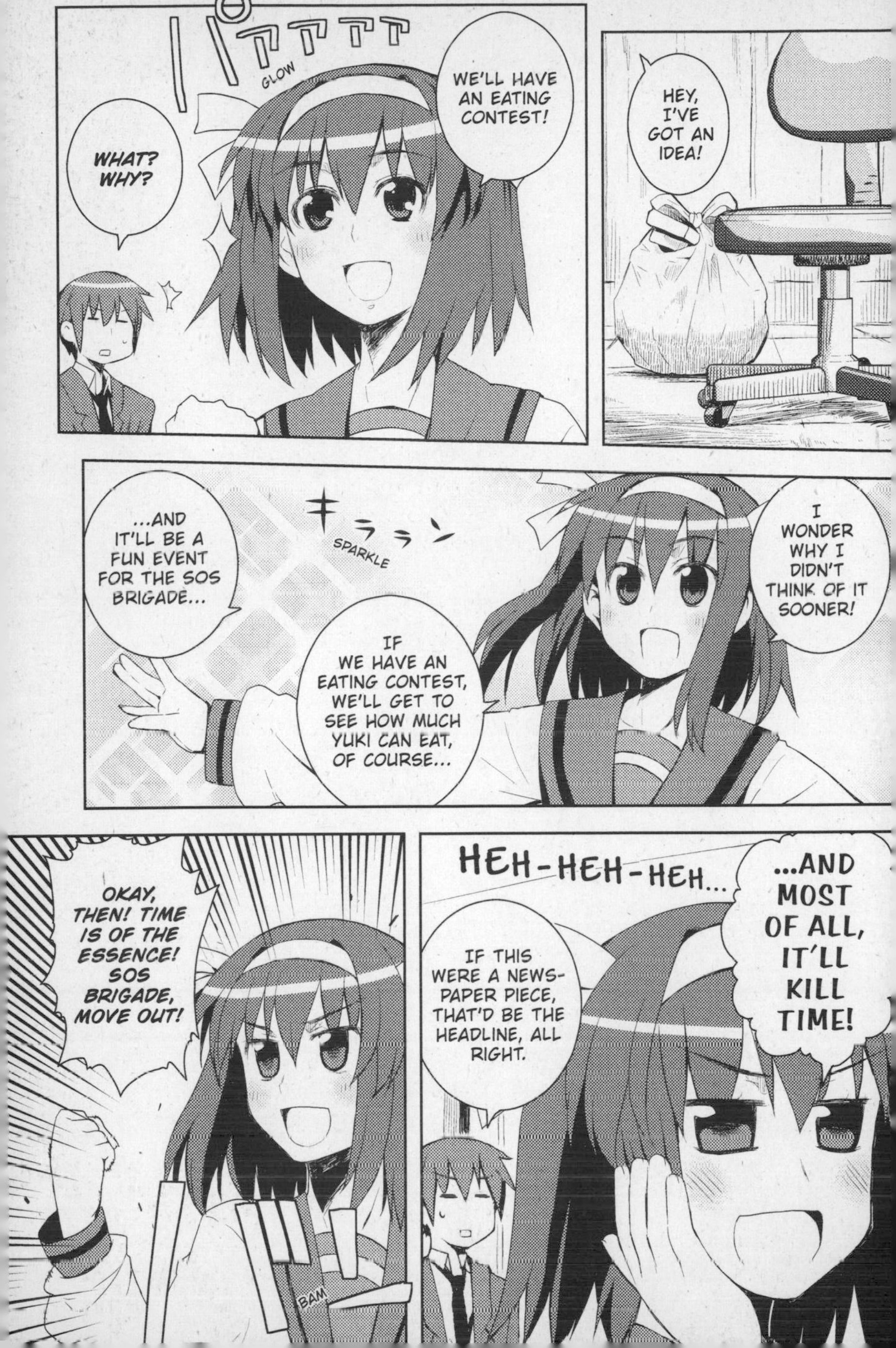
HEY, I'VE GOT AN IDEA!
WE'LL HAVE AN EATING CONTEST!
GLOW
WHAT? WHY?
I WONDER WHY I DIDN'T THINK OF IT SOONER!
SPARKLE
IF WE HAVE AN EATING CONTEST, WE'LL GET TO SEE HOW MUCH YUKI CAN EAT, OF COURSE...
...AND IT'LL BE A FUN EVENT FOR THE SOS BRIGADE...
...AND MOST OF ALL, IT'LL KILL TIME!
HEH-HEH-HEH...
IF THIS WERE A NEWS-PAPER PIECE, THAT'D BE THE HEADLINE, ALL RIGHT.
OKAY, THEN! TIME IS OF THE ESSENCE! SOS BRIGADE, MOVE OUT!
BAM

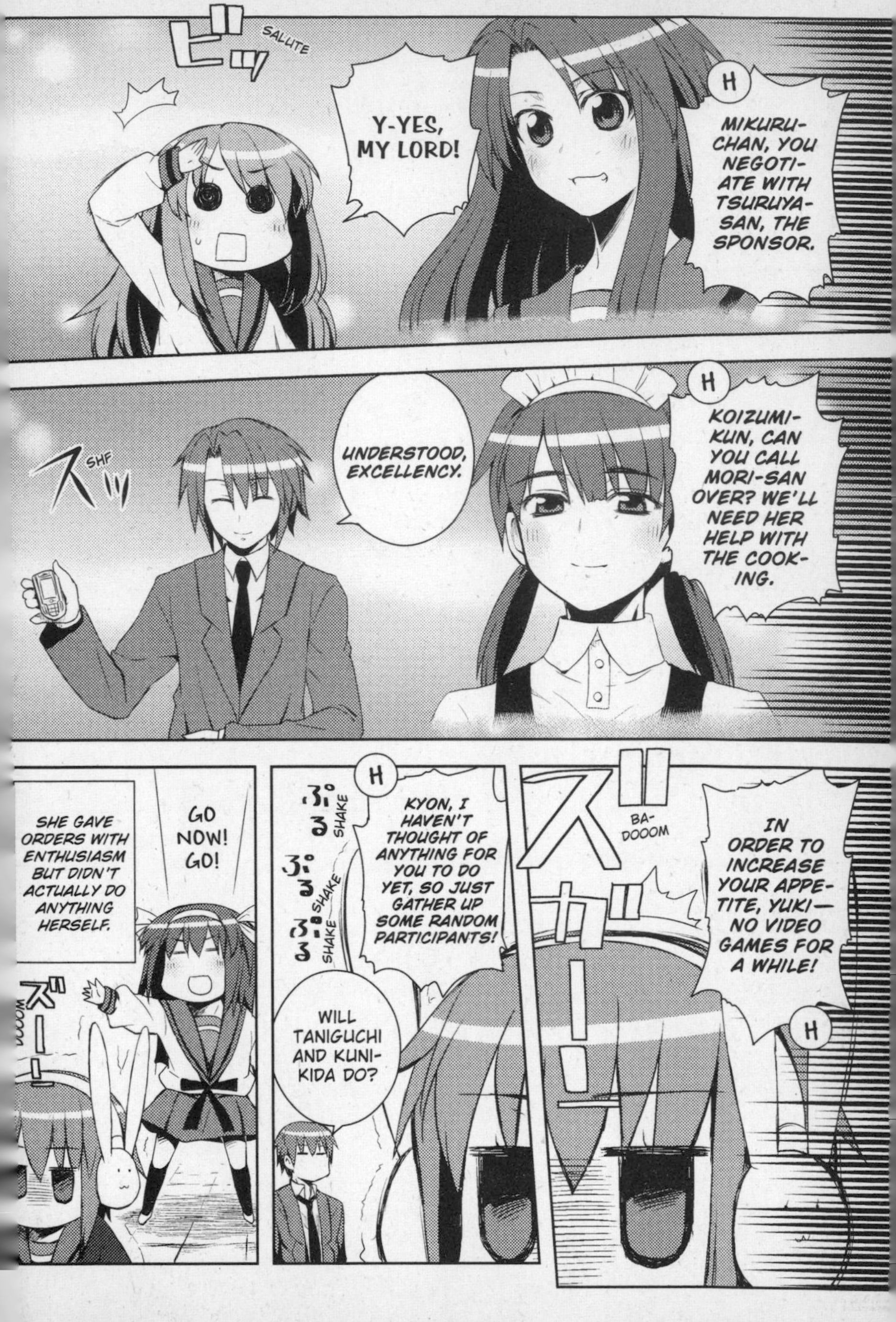
MIKURU-CHAN, YOU NEGOTIATE WITH TSURUYA-SAN, THE SPONSOR.
Y-YES, MY LORD!
ビッ SALUTE
KOIZUMI-KUN, CAN YOU CALL MORI-SAN OVER? WE'LL NEED HER HELP WITH THE COOKING.
UNDERSTOOD, EXCELLENCY.
スッ SHF
IN ORDER TO INCREASE YOUR APPETITE, YUKI— NO VIDEO GAMES FOR A WHILE!
ズガー BA-DOOOM
KYON, I HAVEN'T THOUGHT OF ANYTHING FOR YOU TO DO YET, SO JUST GATHER UP SOME RANDOM PARTICIPANTS!
ぷる SHAKE ぷる SHAKE ぷる SHAKE
WILL TANIGUCHI AND KUNIKIDA DO?
GO NOW! GO!
SHE GAVE ORDERS WITH ENTHUSIASM BUT DIDN'T ACTUALLY DO ANYTHING HERSELF.
ズーー DOOOM

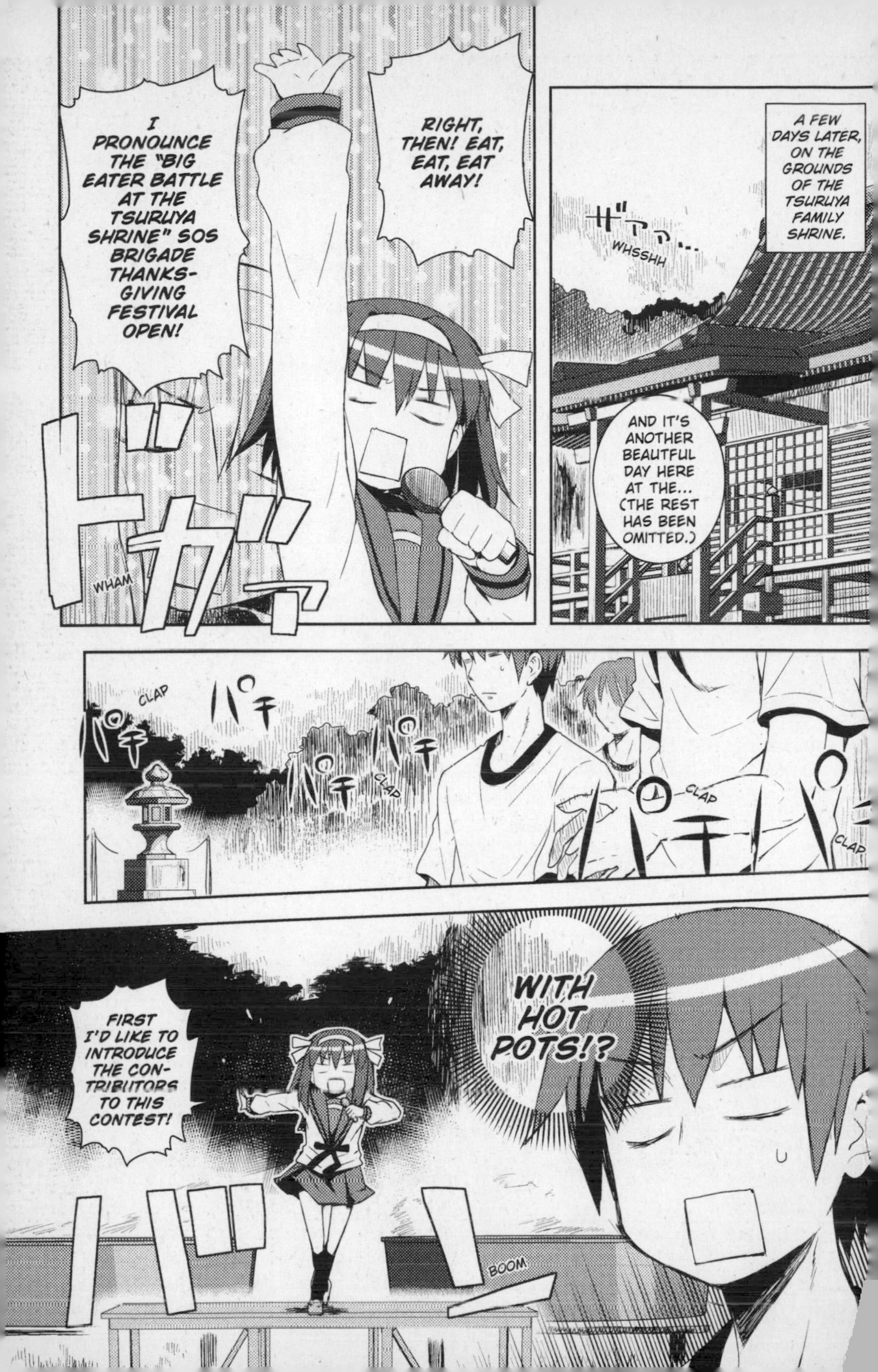
A FEW DAYS LATER, ON THE GROUNDS OF THE TSURUYA FAMILY SHRINE.
WHSSHH
AND IT'S ANOTHER BEAUTIFUL DAY HERE AT THE... (THE REST HAS BEEN OMITTED.)
RIGHT, THEN! EAT, EAT, EAT AWAY!
I PRONOUNCE THE "BIG EATER BATTLE AT THE TSURUYA SHRINE" SOS BRIGADE THANKS-GIVING FESTIVAL OPEN!
WHAM
CLAP
CLAP
CLAP
CLAP
WITH HOT POTS!?
FIRST I'D LIKE TO INTRODUCE THE CON-TRIBUTORS TO THIS CONTEST!
BOOM

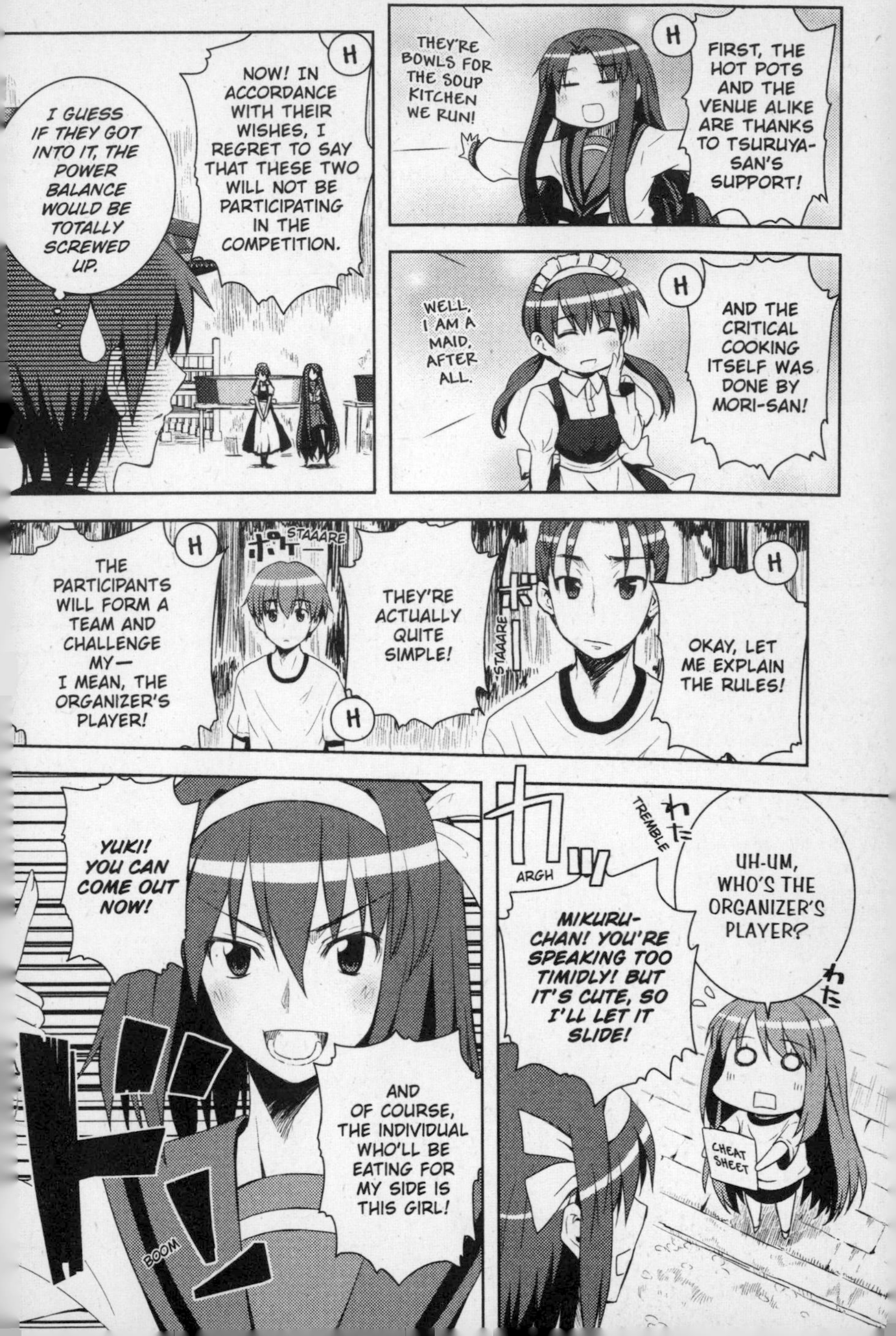
FIRST, THE HOT POTS AND THE VENUE ALIKE ARE THANKS TO TSURUYA-SAN'S SUPPORT!
THEY'RE BOWLS FOR THE SOUP KITCHEN WE RUN!
AND THE CRITICAL COOKING ITSELF WAS DONE BY MORI-SAN!
WELL, I AM A MAID, AFTER ALL.
NOW! IN ACCORDANCE WITH THEIR WISHES, I REGRET TO SAY THAT THESE TWO WILL NOT BE PARTICIPATING IN THE COMPETITION.
I GUESS IF THEY GOT INTO IT, THE POWER BALANCE WOULD BE TOTALLY SCREWED UP.
OKAY, LET ME EXPLAIN THE RULES!
STAAARE
THEY'RE ACTUALLY QUITE SIMPLE!
STAAARE
THE PARTICIPANTS WILL FORM A TEAM AND CHALLENGE MY— I MEAN, THE ORGANIZER'S PLAYER!
TREMBLE
UH-UM, WHO'S THE ORGANIZER'S PLAYER?
ARGH
MIKURU-CHAN! YOU'RE SPEAKING TOO TIMIDLY! BUT IT'S CUTE, SO I'LL LET IT SLIDE!
CHEAT SHEET
YUKI! YOU CAN COME OUT NOW!
AND OF COURSE, THE INDIVIDUAL WHO'LL BE EATING FOR MY SIDE IS THIS GIRL!
BOOM

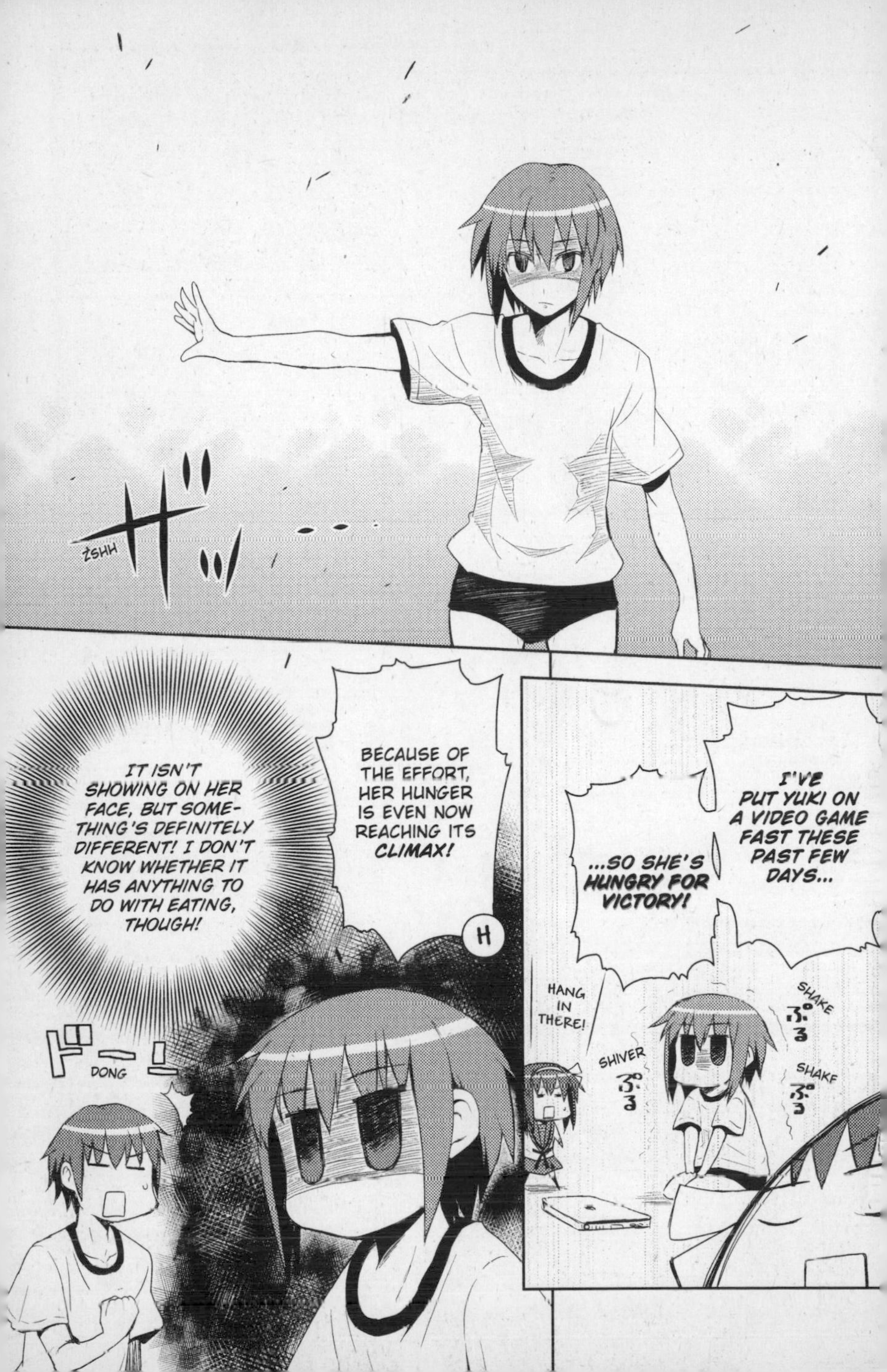
ザッ
ZSHH
I'VE PUT YUKI ON A VIDEO GAME FAST THESE PAST FEW DAYS...
...SO SHE'S HUNGRY FOR VICTORY!
SHAKE
ぷる
SHAKE
ぷる
HANG IN THERE!
SHIVER
ぷる
BECAUSE OF THE EFFORT, HER HUNGER IS EVEN NOW REACHING ITS CLIMAX!
IT ISN'T SHOWING ON HER FACE, BUT SOME-THING'S DEFINITELY DIFFERENT! I DON'T KNOW WHETHER IT HAS ANYTHING TO DO WITH EATING, THOUGH!
H
ドーン
DONG

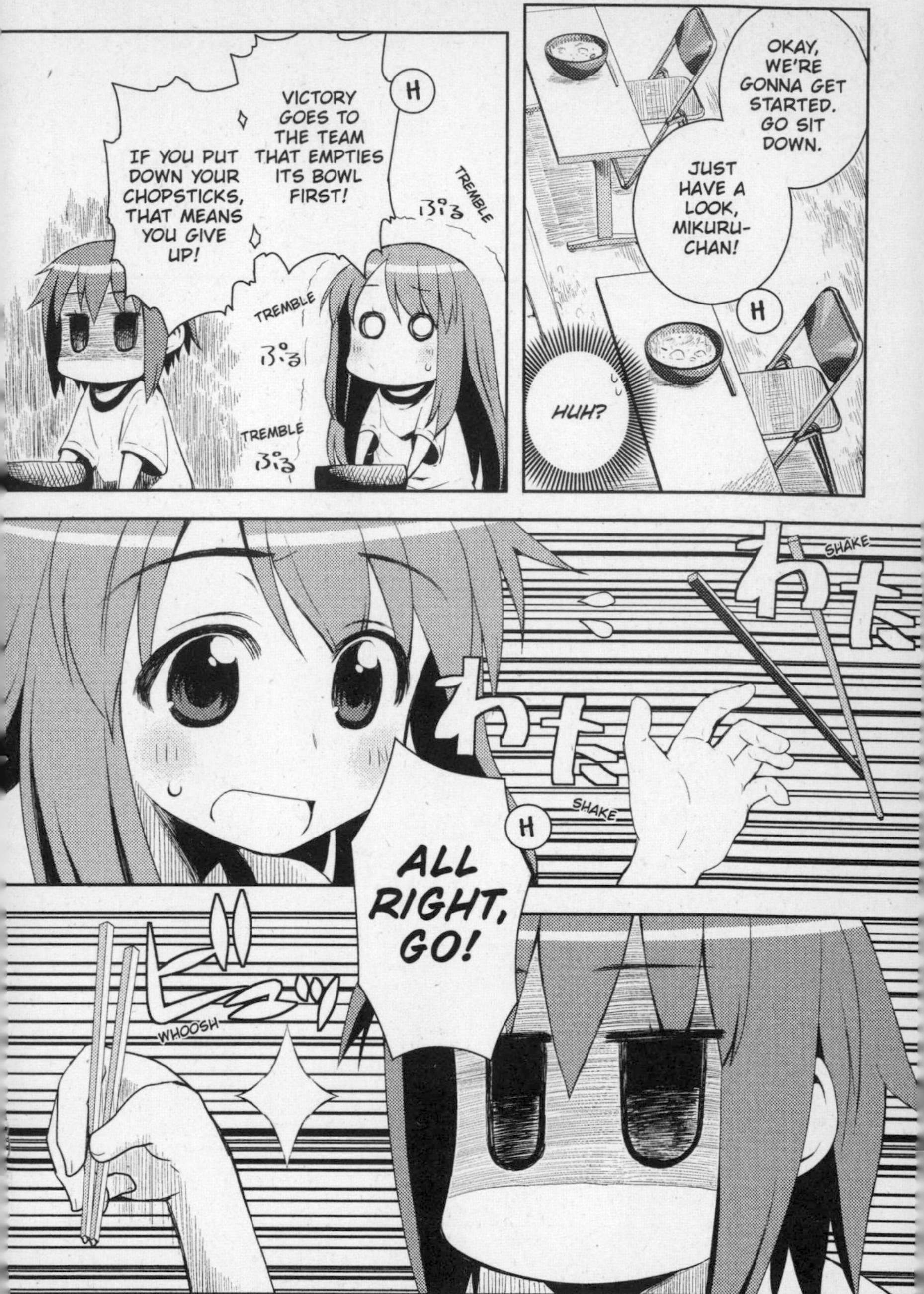
OKAY, WE'RE GONNA GET STARTED. GO SIT DOWN.
JUST HAVE A LOOK, MIKURU-CHAN!
H
HUH?
VICTORY GOES TO THE TEAM THAT EMPTIES ITS BOWL FIRST!
H
IF YOU PUT DOWN YOUR CHOPSTICKS, THAT MEANS YOU GIVE UP!
TREMBLE
ぷる
TREMBLE
ぷる
TREMBLE
ぷる
わた
SHAKE
わた
SHAKE
H
ALL RIGHT, GO!
ビュッ
WHOOSH

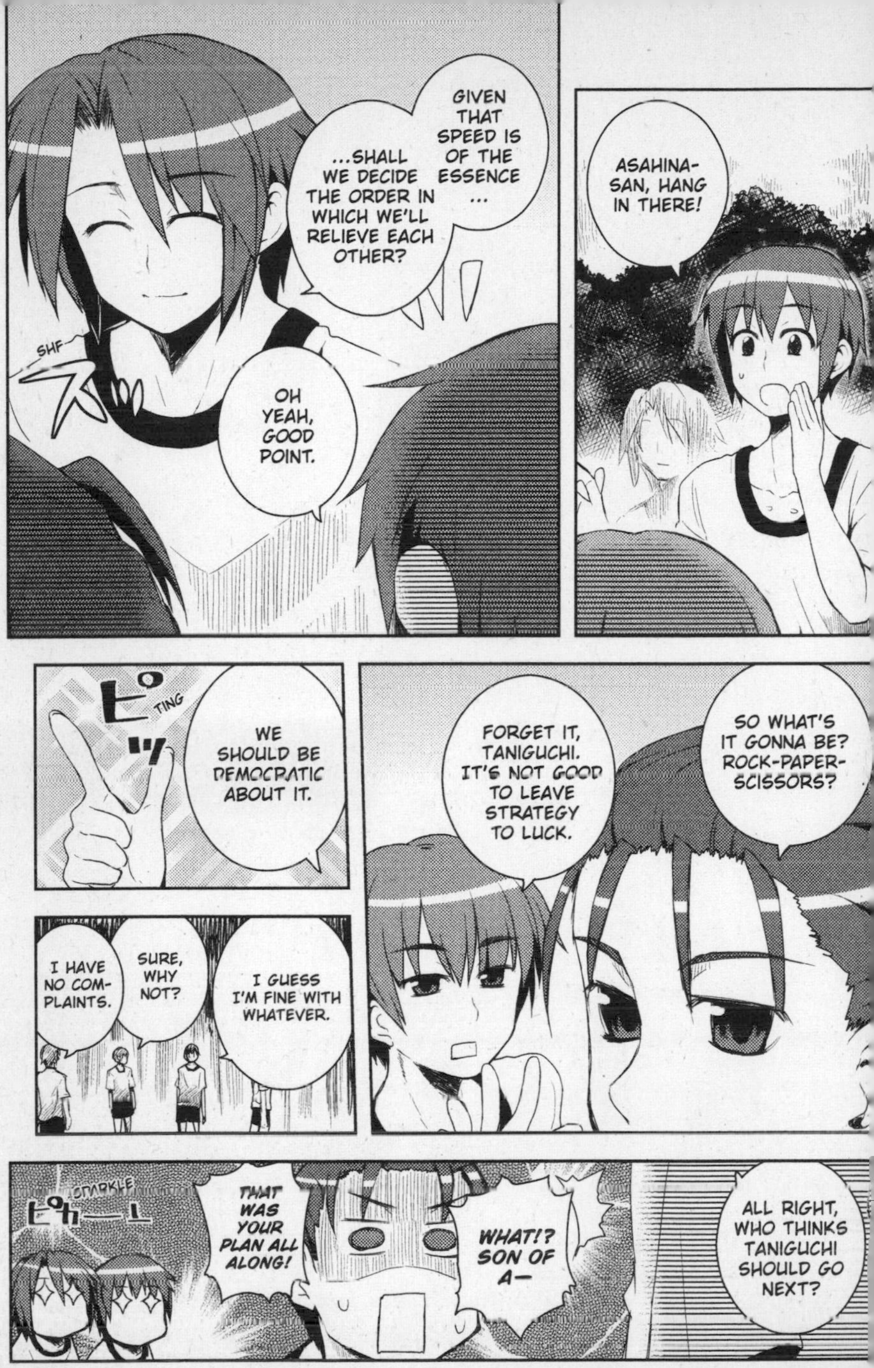
ASAHINA-SAN, HANG IN THERE!
GIVEN THAT SPEED IS OF THE ESSENCE ...
...SHALL WE DECIDE THE ORDER IN WHICH WE'LL RELIEVE EACH OTHER?
SHF
OH YEAH, GOOD POINT.
SO WHAT'S IT GONNA BE? ROCK-PAPER-SCISSORS?
FORGET IT, TANIGUCHI. IT'S NOT GOOD TO LEAVE STRATEGY TO LUCK.
WE SHOULD BE DEMOCRATIC ABOUT IT.
TING
I GUESS I'M FINE WITH WHATEVER.
SURE, WHY NOT?
I HAVE NO COMPLAINTS.
ALL RIGHT, WHO THINKS TANIGUCHI SHOULD GO NEXT?
WHAT!? SON OF A—
THAT WAS YOUR PLAN ALL ALONG!
SPARKLE

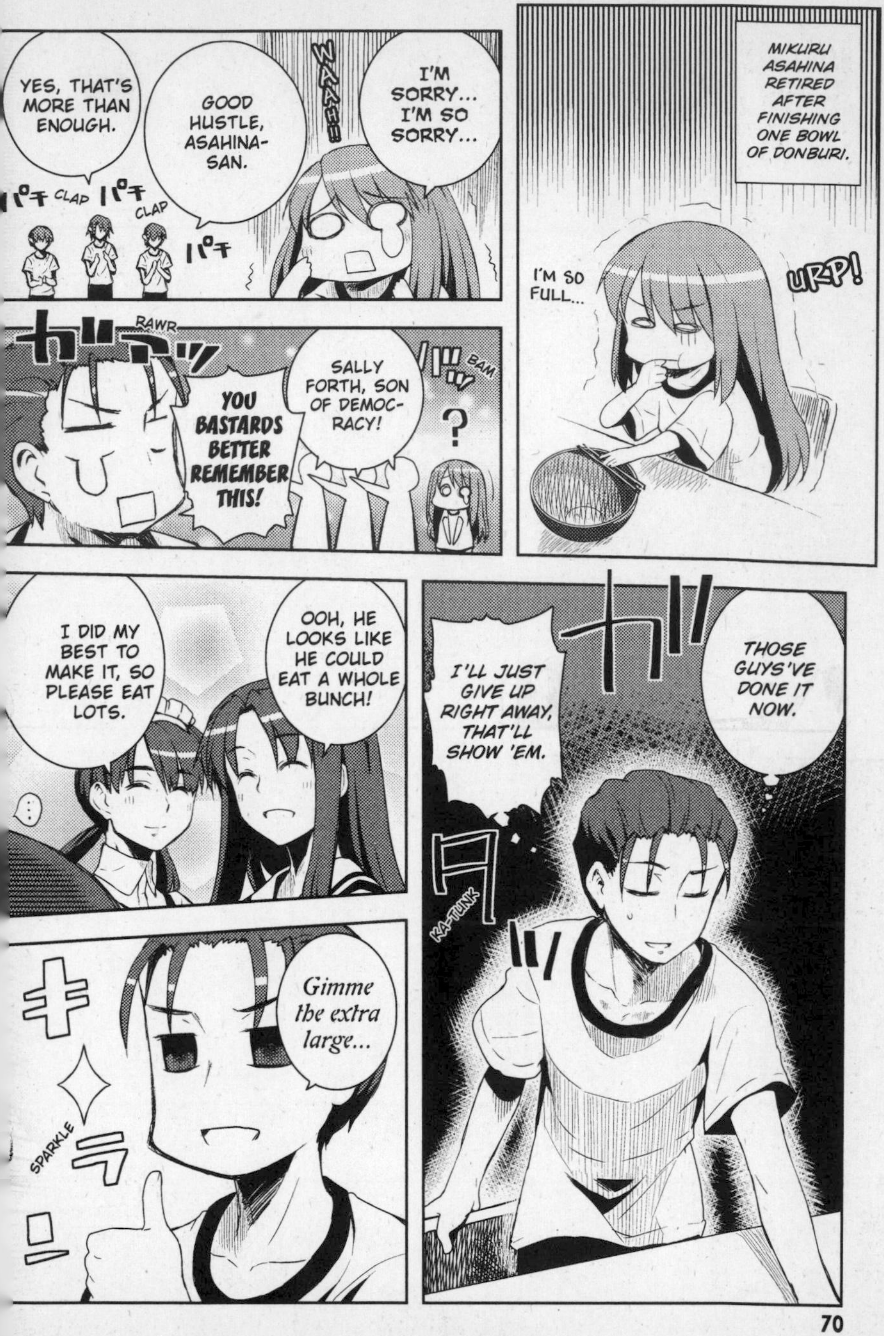
MIKURU ASAHINA RETIRED AFTER FINISHING ONE BOWL OF DONBURI.
URP!
I'M SO FULL...
I'M SORRY... I'M SO SORRY...
WAAAH!!
GOOD HUSTLE, ASAHINA-SAN.
YES, THAT'S MORE THAN ENOUGH.
パチ CLAP パチ CLAP パチ
BAM
?
SALLY FORTH, SON OF DEMOCRACY!
YOU BASTARDS BETTER REMEMBER THIS!
RAWR
THOSE GUYS'VE DONE IT NOW.
I'LL JUST GIVE UP RIGHT AWAY, THAT'LL SHOW 'EM.
KA-TUNK
OOH, HE LOOKS LIKE HE COULD EAT A WHOLE BUNCH!
I DID MY BEST TO MAKE IT, SO PLEASE EAT LOTS.
...
Gimme the extra large...
SPARKLE

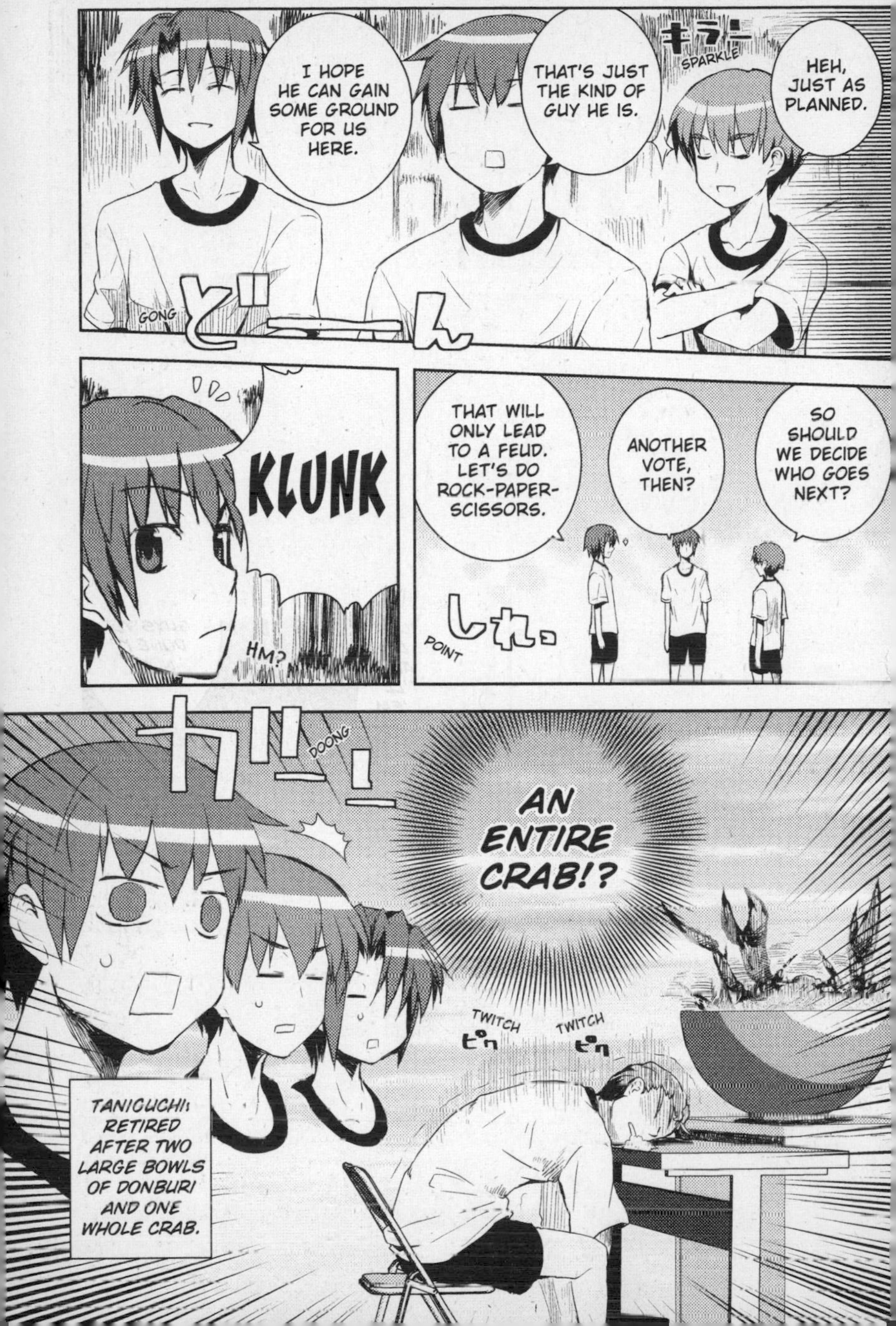
SPARKLE
HEH, JUST AS PLANNED.
THAT'S JUST THE KIND OF GUY HE IS.
I HOPE HE CAN GAIN SOME GROUND FOR US HERE.
GONG
SO SHOULD WE DECIDE WHO GOES NEXT?
ANOTHER VOTE, THEN?
THAT WILL ONLY LEAD TO A FEUD. LET'S DO ROCK-PAPER-SCISSORS.
POINT
KLUNK
HM?
AN ENTIRE CRAB!?
DOONG
TWITCH
TWITCH
TANIGUCHI: RETIRED AFTER TWO LARGE BOWLS OF DONBURI AND ONE WHOLE CRAB.

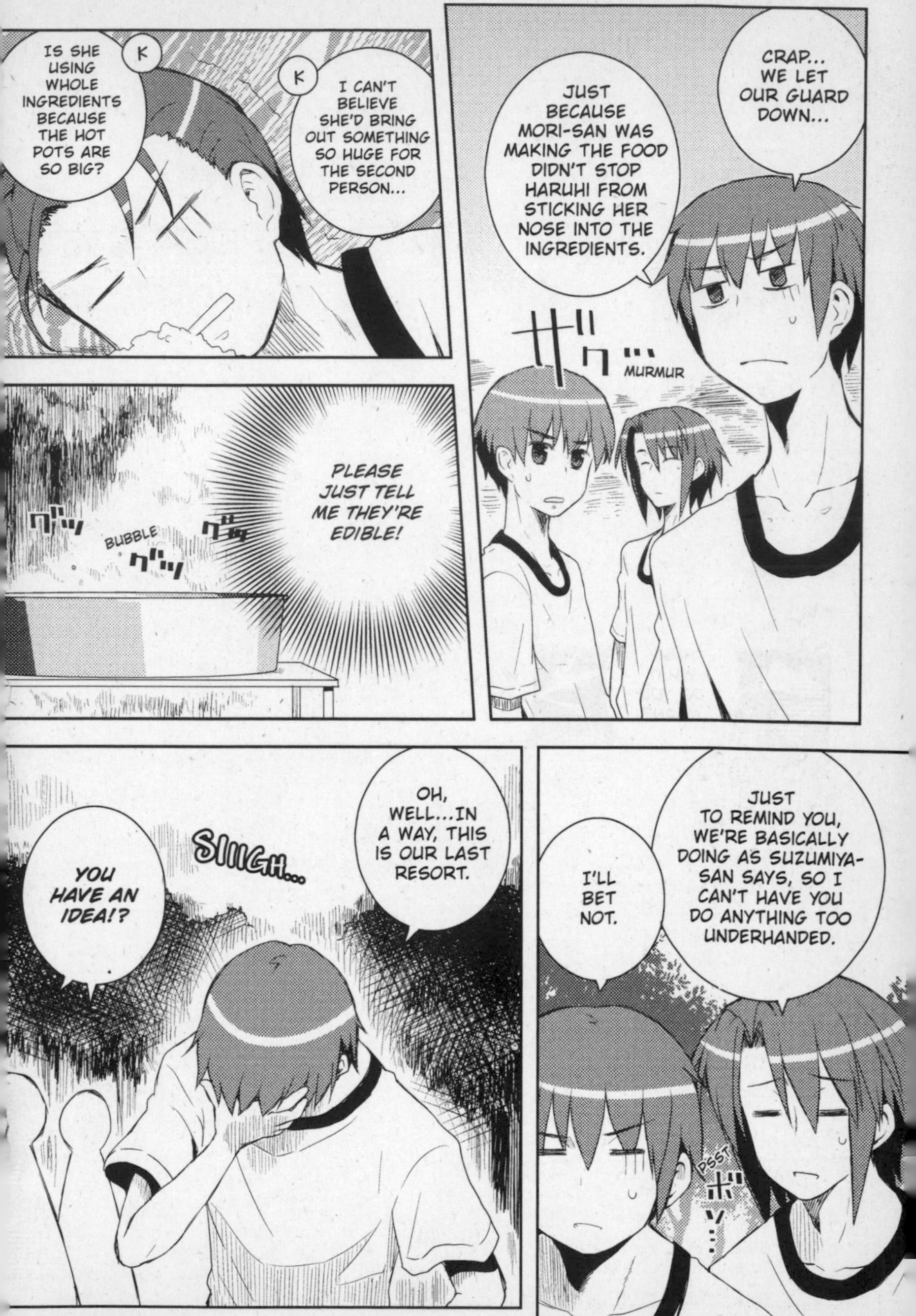
CRAP... WE LET OUR GUARD DOWN...
JUST BECAUSE MORI-SAN WAS MAKING THE FOOD DIDN'T STOP HARUHI FROM STICKING HER NOSE INTO THE INGREDIENTS.
MURMUR
K
I CAN'T BELIEVE SHE'D BRING OUT SOMETHING SO HUGE FOR THE SECOND PERSON...
K
IS SHE USING WHOLE INGREDIENTS BECAUSE THE HOT POTS ARE SO BIG?
PLEASE JUST TELL ME THEY'RE EDIBLE!
BUBBLE
JUST TO REMIND YOU, WE'RE BASICALLY DOING AS SUZUMIYA-SAN SAYS, SO I CAN'T HAVE YOU DO ANYTHING TOO UNDERHANDED.
I'LL BET NOT.
PSST
OH, WELL...IN A WAY, THIS IS OUR LAST RESORT.
SIIIGH...
YOU HAVE AN IDEA!?

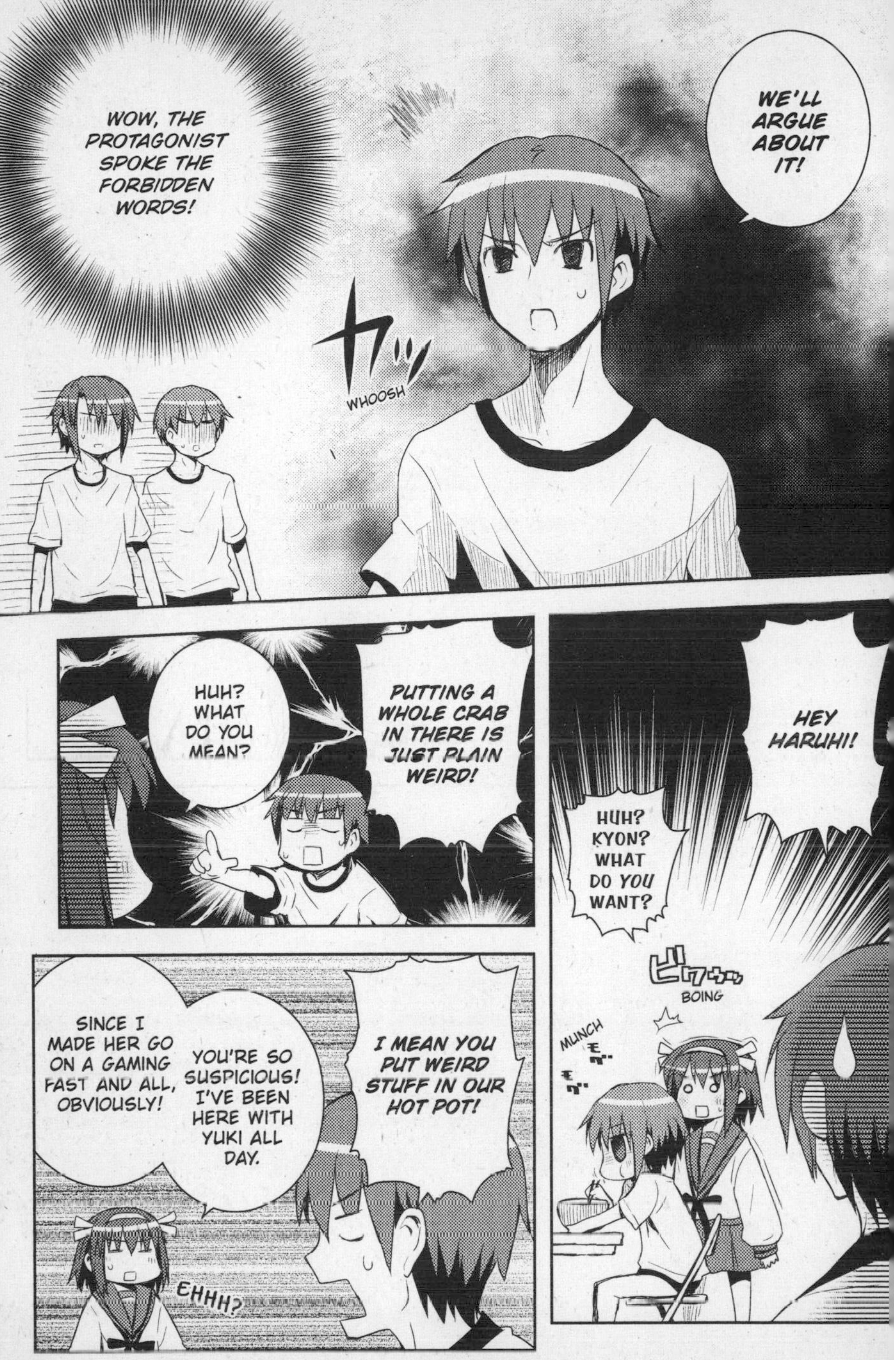
WE'LL ARGUE ABOUT IT!
WHOOSH
WOW, THE PROTAGONIST SPOKE THE FORBIDDEN WORDS!
HEY HARUHI!
HUH? KYON? WHAT DO YOU WANT?
BOING
MUNCH
PUTTING A WHOLE CRAB IN THERE IS JUST PLAIN WEIRD!
HUH? WHAT DO YOU MEAN?
I MEAN YOU PUT WEIRD STUFF IN OUR HOT POT!
YOU'RE SO SUSPICIOUS! I'VE BEEN HERE WITH YUKI ALL DAY.
SINCE I MADE HER GO ON A GAMING FAST AND ALL, OBVIOUSLY!
EHHH?

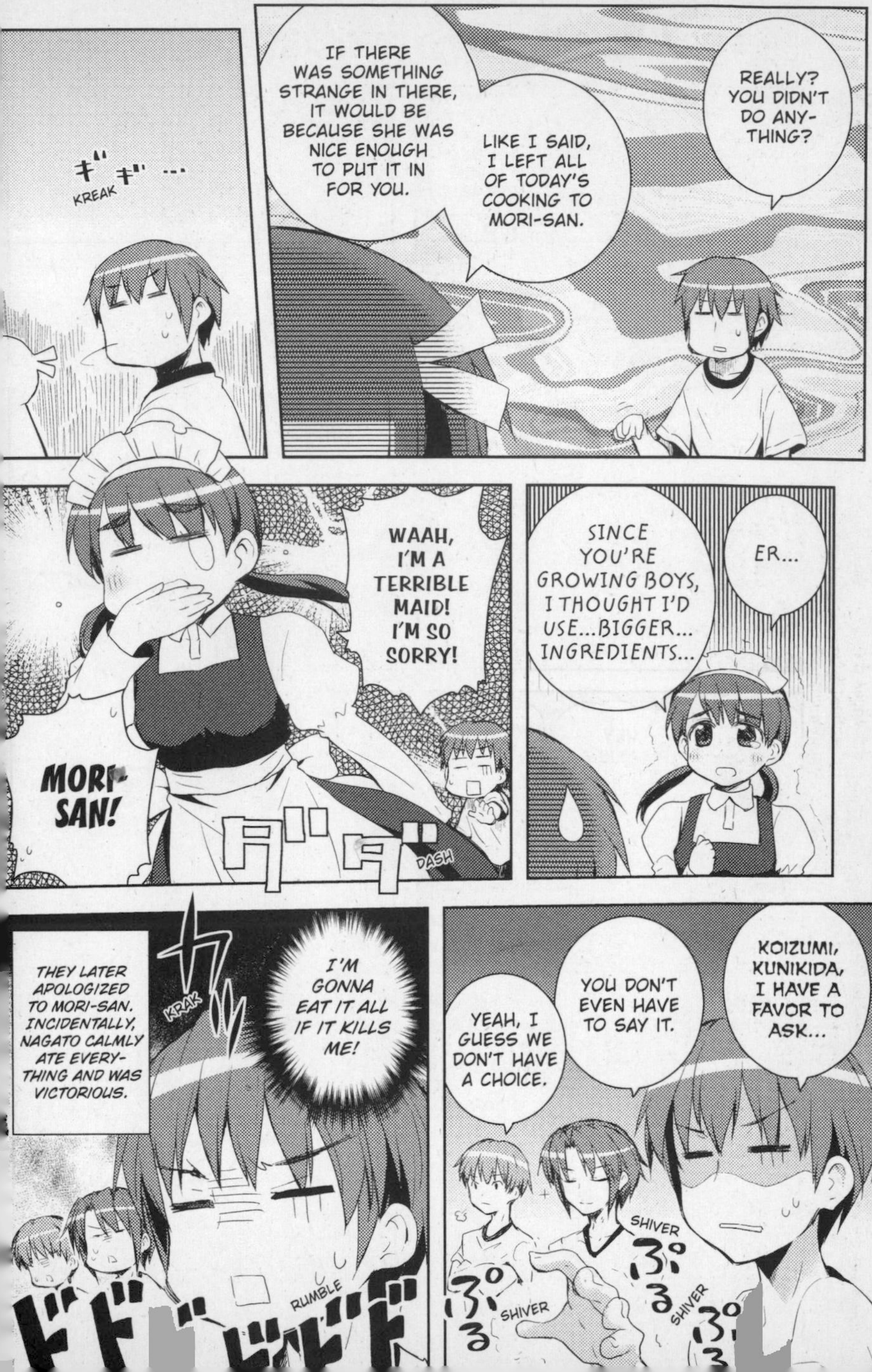
REALLY? YOU DIDN'T DO ANY-THING?
LIKE I SAID, I LEFT ALL OF TODAY'S COOKING TO MORI-SAN.
IF THERE WAS SOMETHING STRANGE IN THERE, IT WOULD BE BECAUSE SHE WAS NICE ENOUGH TO PUT IT IN FOR YOU.
ギギ…
KREAK
ER...
SINCE YOU'RE GROWING BOYS, I THOUGHT I'D USE...BIGGER... INGREDIENTS...
WAAH, I'M A TERRIBLE MAID! I'M SO SORRY!
MORI-SAN!
ダダ
DASH
KOIZUMI, KUNIKIDA, I HAVE A FAVOR TO ASK...
YOU DON'T EVEN HAVE TO SAY IT.
YEAH, I GUESS WE DON'T HAVE A CHOICE.
SHIVER
ぷる
SHIVER
ぷる
SHIVER
ぷる
I'M GONNA EAT IT ALL IF IT KILLS ME!
KRAK
THEY LATER APOLOGIZED TO MORI-SAN. INCIDENTALLY, NAGATO CALMLY ATE EVERY-THING AND WAS VICTORIOUS.
RUMBLE
ドドドドド

BEFORE THE CONTEST 1

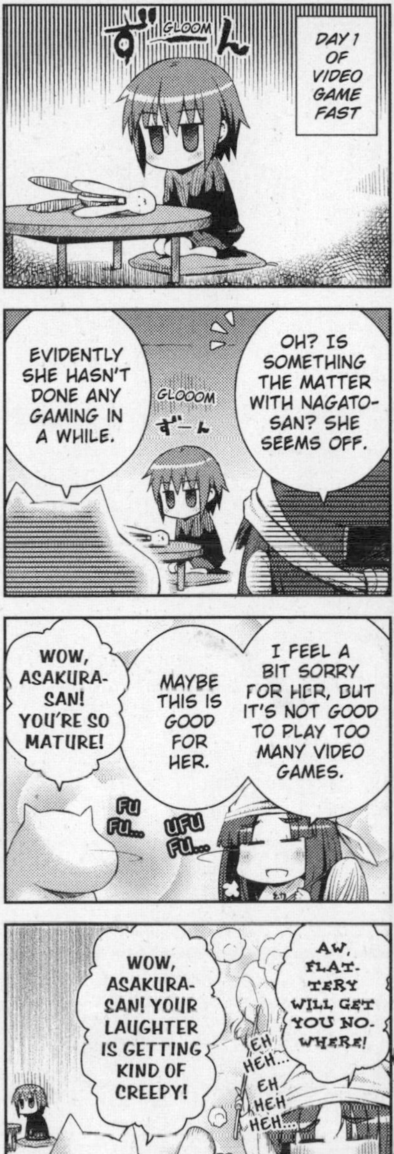
DAY 1 OF VIDEO GAME FAST
ずーん
GLOOM
OH? IS SOMETHING THE MATTER WITH NAGATO-SAN? SHE SEEMS OFF.
EVIDENTLY SHE HASN'T DONE ANY GAMING IN A WHILE.
GLOOOM
ずーん
I FEEL A BIT SORRY FOR HER, BUT IT'S NOT GOOD TO PLAY TOO MANY VIDEO GAMES.
MAYBE THIS IS GOOD FOR HER.
WOW, ASAKURA-SAN! YOU'RE SO MATURE!
UFU FU...
FU FU...
AW, FLATTERY WILL GET YOU NOWHERE!
WOW, ASAKURA-SAN! YOUR LAUGHTER IS GETTING KIND OF CREEPY!
EH HEH...
EH HEH HEH...

BEFORE THE CONTEST 2

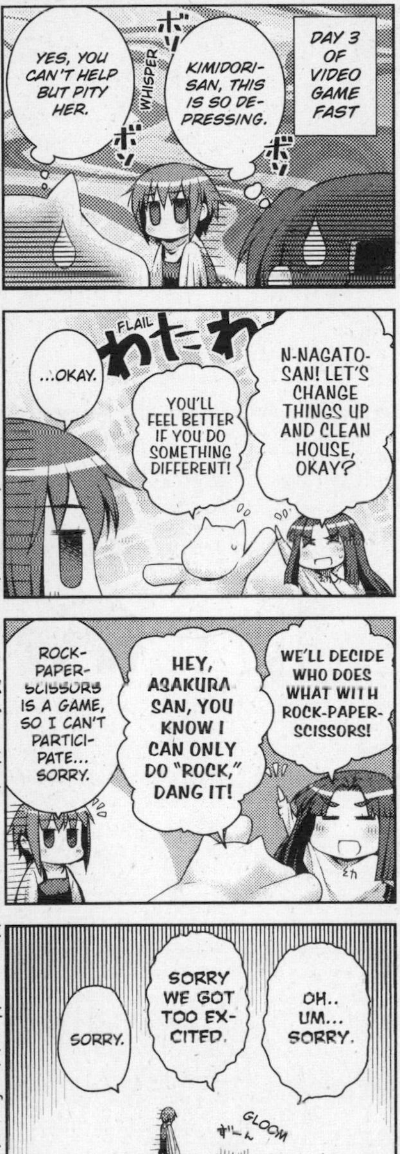
DAY 3 OF VIDEO GAME FAST
KIMIDORI-SAN, THIS IS SO DEPRESSING.
ボソ
WHISPER
ボソ
YES, YOU CAN'T HELP BUT PITY HER.
N-NAGATO-SAN! LET'S CHANGE THINGS UP AND CLEAN HOUSE, OKAY?
YOU'LL FEEL BETTER IF YOU DO SOMETHING DIFFERENT!
わたーわ
FLAIL
...OKAY.
WE'LL DECIDE WHO DOES WHAT WITH ROCK-PAPER-SCISSORS!
HEY, ASAKURA SAN, YOU KNOW I CAN ONLY DO "ROCK," DANG IT!
ROCK-PAPER-SCISSORS IS A GAME, SO I CAN'T PARTICIPATE... SORRY.
OH.. UM... SORRY.
SORRY WE GOT TOO EXCITED.
SORRY.
ずーん
GLOOM

•Achakura-san •Back in cction after being destroyed, crashing at Nagato's. A generally considerate child.

•Kimidori-san •An life-form (dog) created by Nagato from a balloon. Body is a yellow-green color.

•Nagato •Abstaining from video games in order to win the eating contest.. Makes you feel a bit bad for her, doesn't it?

BEFORE THE CONTEST 3

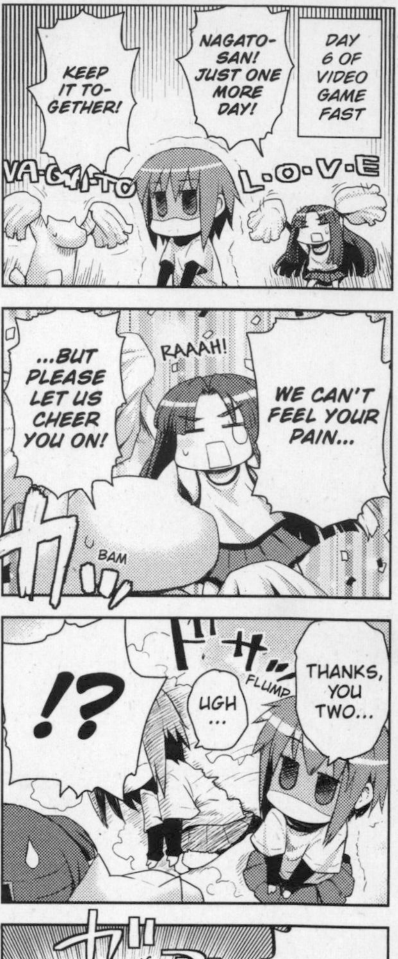
DAY 6 OF VIDEO GAME FAST
NAGATO-SAN! JUST ONE MORE DAY!
KEEP IT TO-GETHER!
L·O·V·E
WE CAN'T FEEL YOUR PAIN...
RAAAH!
...BUT PLEASE LET US CHEER YOU ON!
BAM
THANKS, YOU TWO...
FLUMP
UGH ...
!?
NAGATO-SAAAAN !!! !!! !!!
DONG

AFTER THE CONTEST

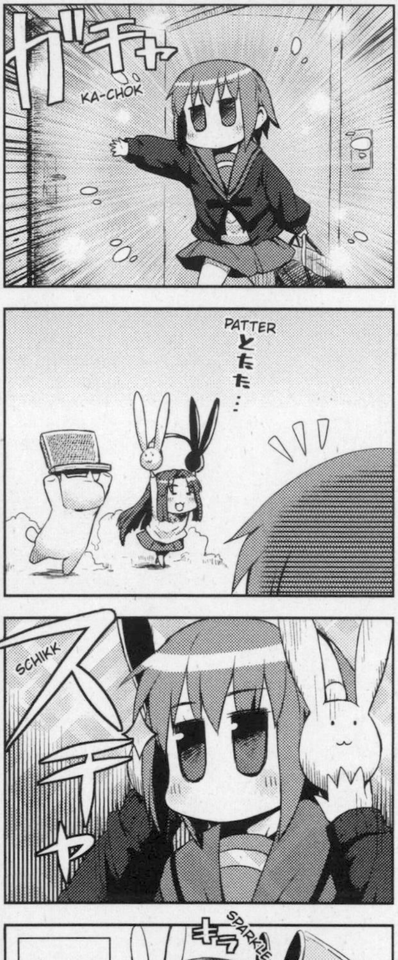
KA-CHOK
PATTER
とたた…
SCHIKK
A SMILE RETURNED TO NAGATO'S FACE.
SPARKLE
YAAAY!
SPARKLE
SPARKLE

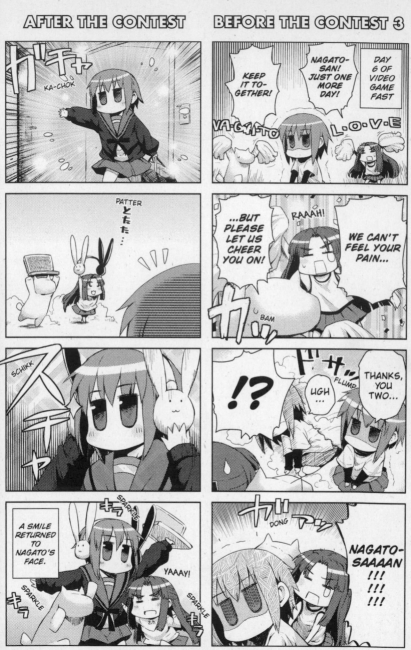

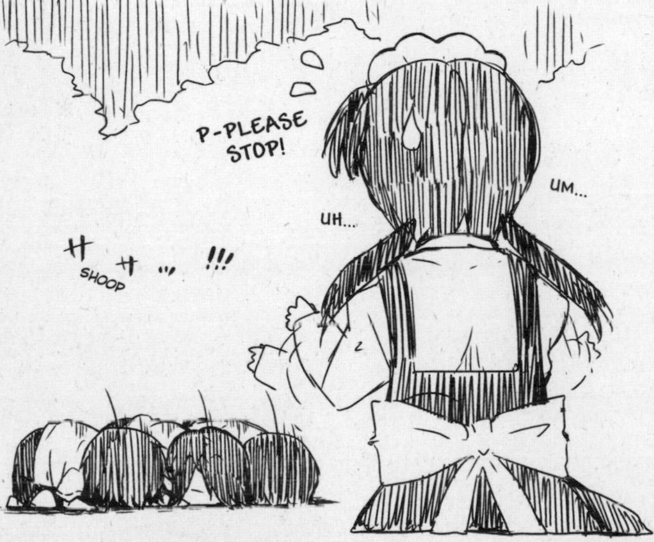
P-PLEASE STOP!
UM...
UH...
!!!
SHOOP

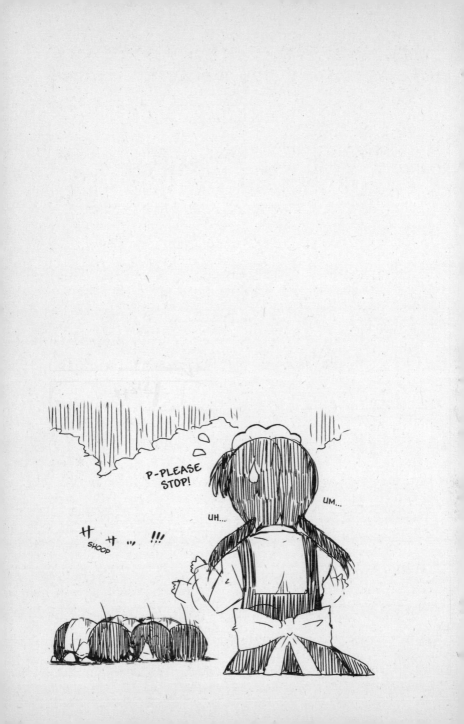

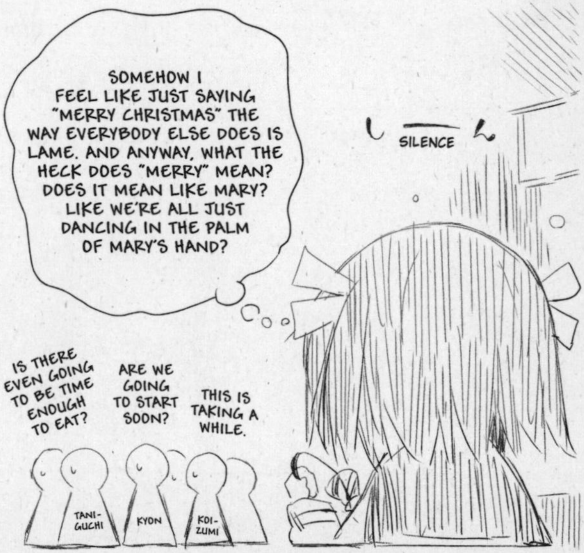
SILENCE
SOMEHOW I FEEL LIKE JUST SAYING "MERRY CHRISTMAS" THE WAY EVERYBODY ELSE DOES IS LAME. AND ANYWAY, WHAT THE HECK DOES "MERRY" MEAN? DOES IT MEAN LIKE MARY? LIKE WE'RE ALL JUST DANCING IN THE PALM OF MARY'S HAND?
THIS IS TAKING A WHILE.
ARE WE GOING TO START SOON?
IS THERE EVEN GOING TO BE TIME ENOUGH TO EAT?
KOI-ZUMI
KYON
TANI-GUCHI

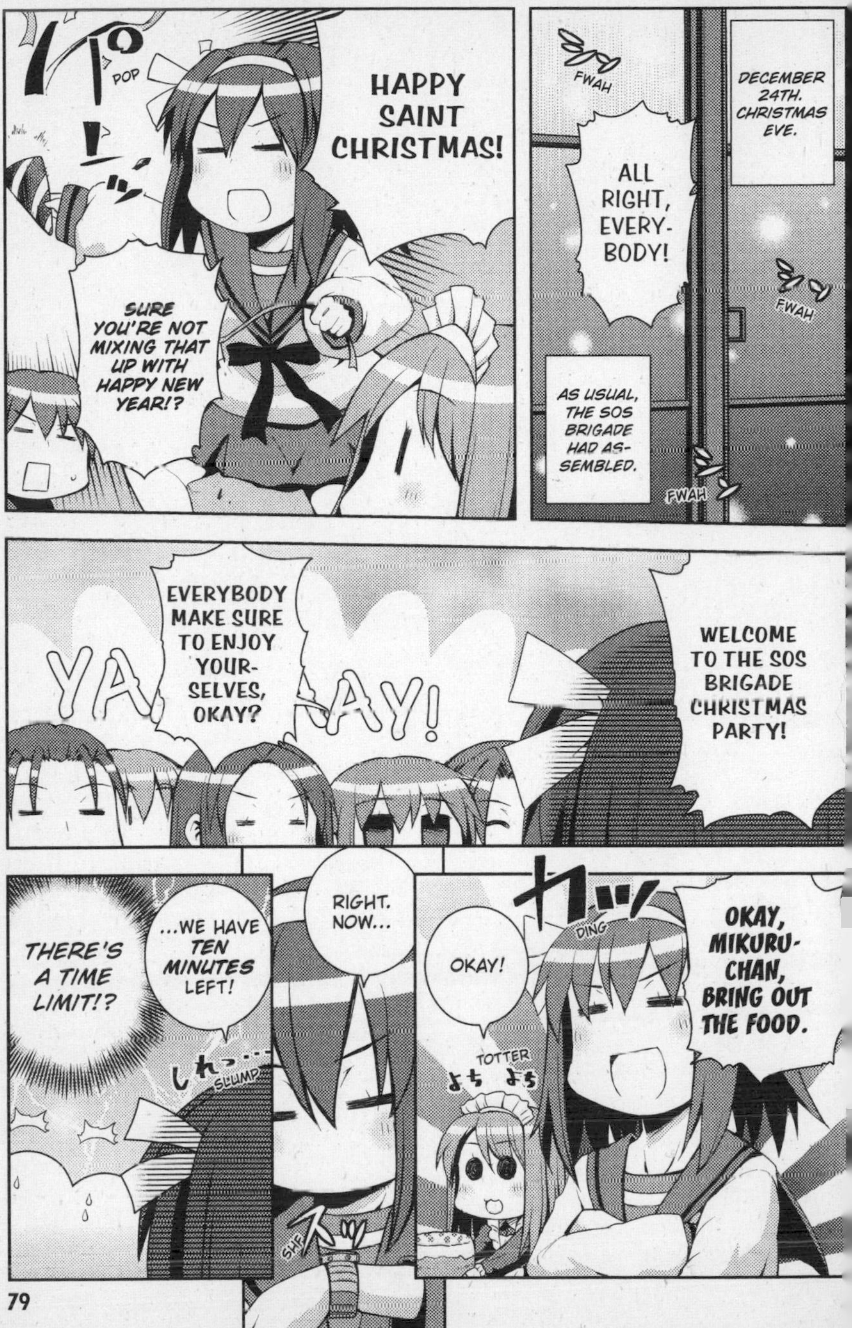
FWAH
DECEMBER 24TH. CHRISTMAS EVE.
ALL RIGHT, EVERYBODY!
FWAH
AS USUAL, THE SOS BRIGADE HAD ASSEMBLED.
FWAH
HAPPY SAINT CHRISTMAS!
POP
SURE YOU'RE NOT MIXING THAT UP WITH HAPPY NEW YEAR!?
WELCOME TO THE SOS BRIGADE CHRISTMAS PARTY!
EVERYBODY MAKE SURE TO ENJOY YOURSELVES, OKAY?
YA AY!
DING
OKAY, MIKURU-CHAN, BRING OUT THE FOOD.
OKAY!
よち よち
TOTTER
RIGHT. NOW...
SHF
...WE HAVE TEN MINUTES LEFT!
THERE'S A TIME LIMIT!?
しれっ
SLUMP

MAIN EVENT

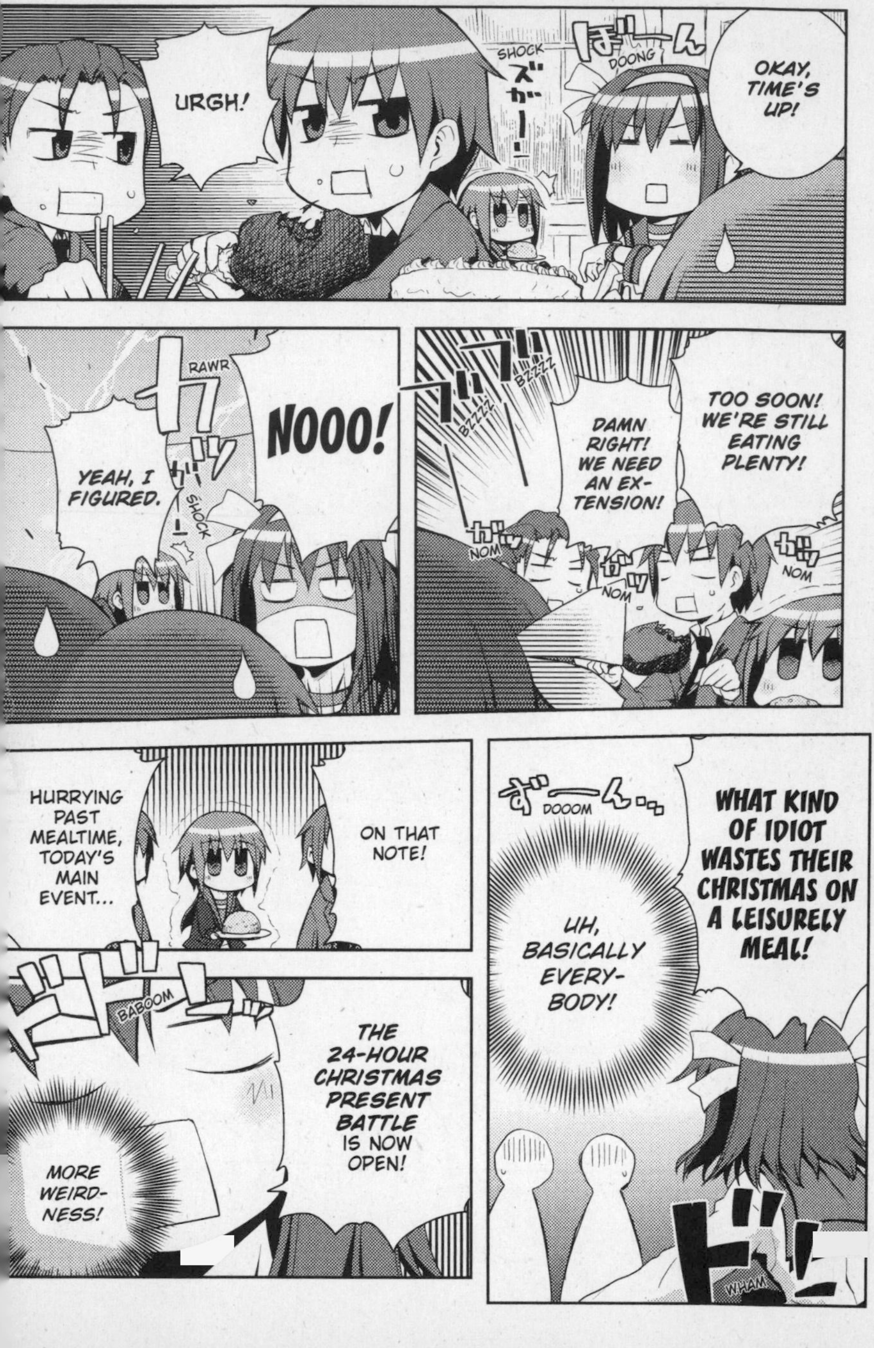
OKAY, TIME'S UP!
DOONG
SHOCK
URGH!
TOO SOON! WE'RE STILL EATING PLENTY!
DAMN RIGHT! WE NEED AN EXTENSION!
BZZZZ
BZZZZ
NOM
NOM
NOM
NOOO!
RAWR
SHOCK
YEAH, I FIGURED.
WHAT KIND OF IDIOT WASTES THEIR CHRISTMAS ON A LEISURELY MEAL!
DOOOM
UH, BASICALLY EVERY-BODY!
WHAM
ON THAT NOTE!
HURRYING PAST MEALTIME, TODAY'S MAIN EVENT...
THE 24-HOUR CHRISTMAS PRESENT BATTLE IS NOW OPEN!
BABOOM
MORE WEIRD-NESS!

RULES

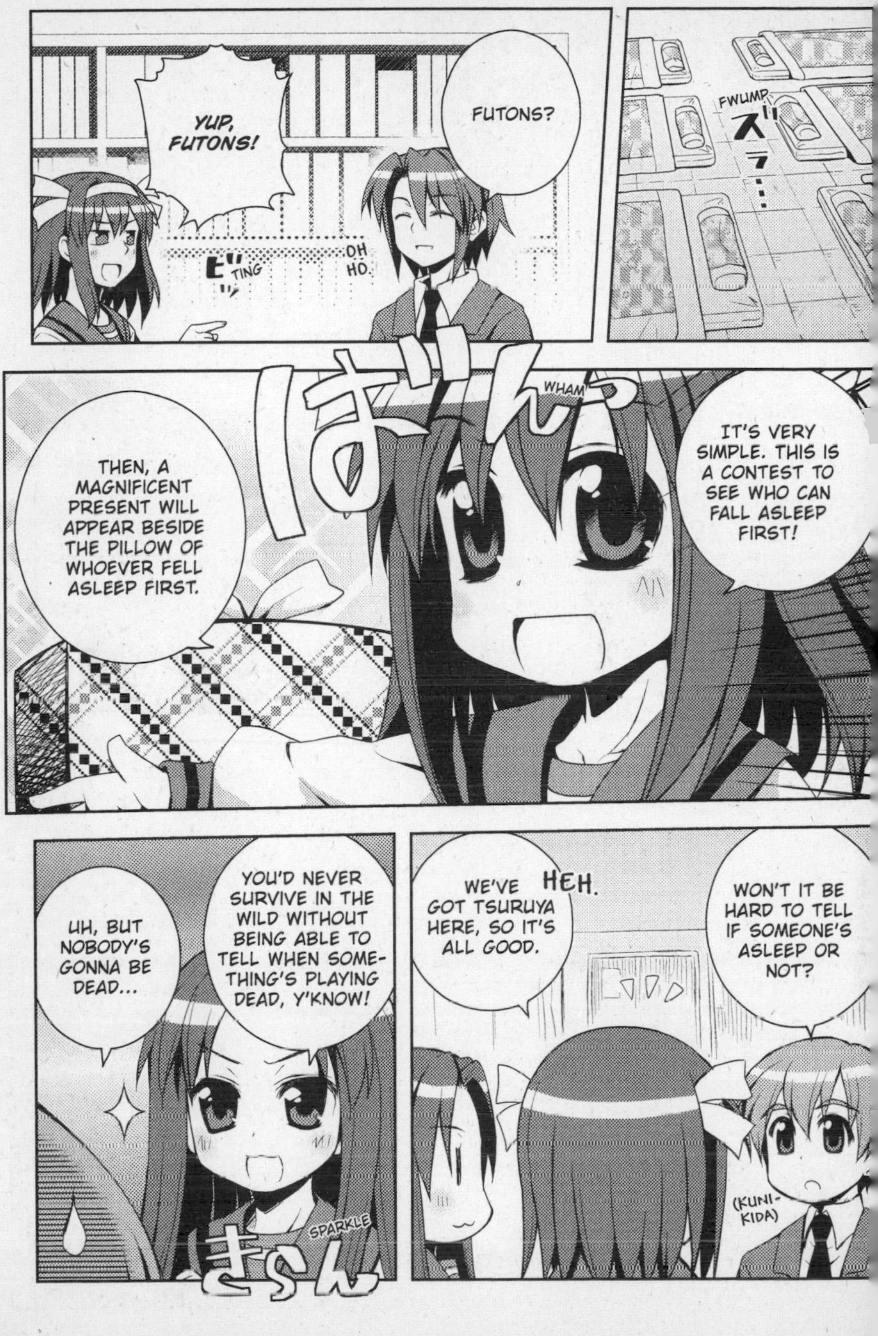
FWUMP
FUTONS?
YUP, FUTONS!
OH HO.
TING
IT'S VERY SIMPLE. THIS IS A CONTEST TO SEE WHO CAN FALL ASLEEP FIRST!
WHAM
THEN, A MAGNIFICENT PRESENT WILL APPEAR BESIDE THE PILLOW OF WHOEVER FELL ASLEEP FIRST.
WON'T IT BE HARD TO TELL IF SOMEONE'S ASLEEP OR NOT?
(KUNI-KIDA)
HEH.
WE'VE GOT TSURUYA HERE, SO IT'S ALL GOOD.
YOU'D NEVER SURVIVE IN THE WILD WITHOUT BEING ABLE TO TELL WHEN SOME-THING'S PLAYING DEAD, Y'KNOW!
UH, BUT NOBODY'S GONNA BE DEAD...
SPARKLE

A SENSITIVE MAN

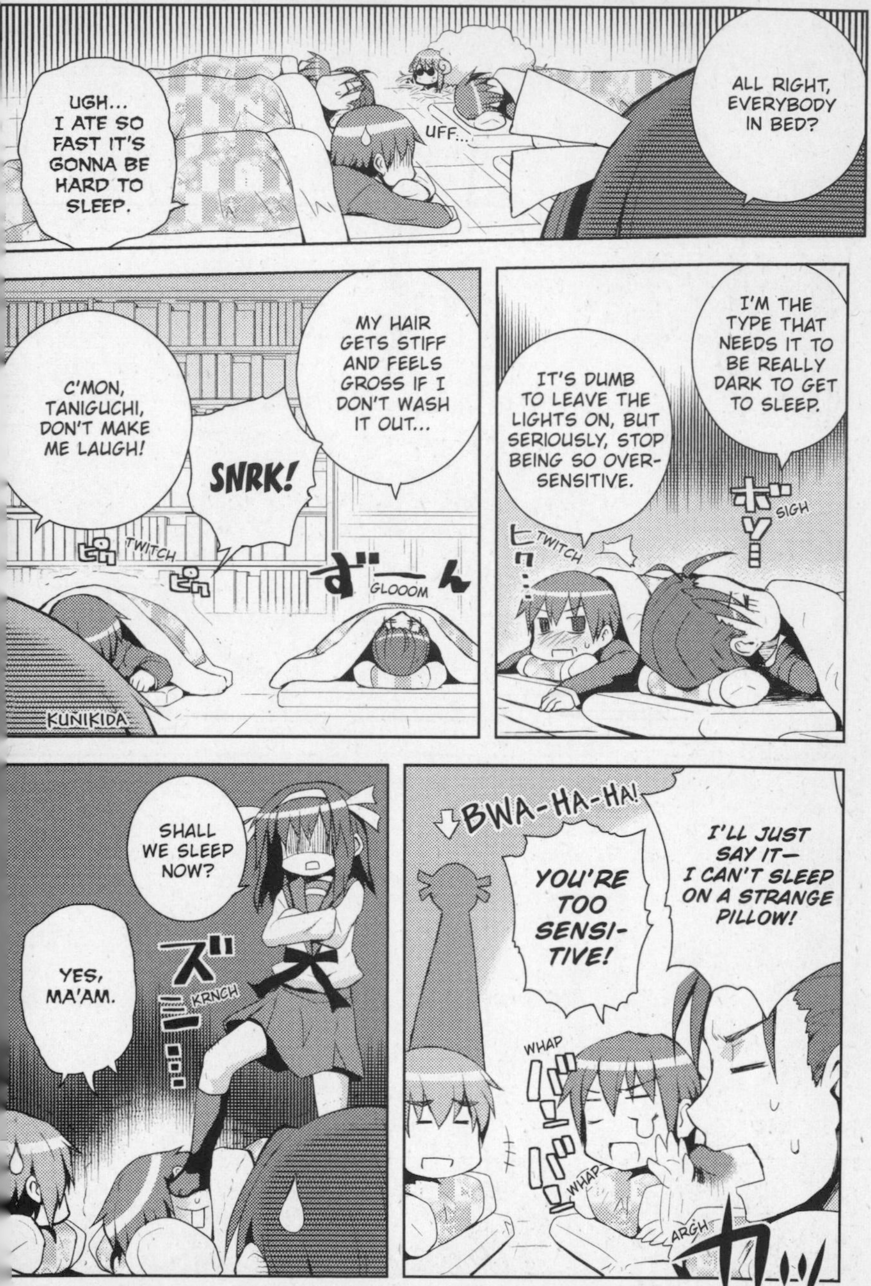
ALL RIGHT, EVERYBODY IN BED?
UFF...
UGH... I ATE SO FAST IT'S GONNA BE HARD TO SLEEP.
I'M THE TYPE THAT NEEDS IT TO BE REALLY DARK TO GET TO SLEEP.
SIGH
IT'S DUMB TO LEAVE THE LIGHTS ON, BUT SERIOUSLY, STOP BEING SO OVER-SENSITIVE.
TWITCH
MY HAIR GETS STIFF AND FEELS GROSS IF I DON'T WASH IT OUT...
SNRK!
C'MON, TANIGUCHI, DON'T MAKE ME LAUGH!
GLOOOM
TWITCH
KUNIKIDA
I'LL JUST SAY IT— I CAN'T SLEEP ON A STRANGE PILLOW!
BWA-HA-HA!
YOU'RE TOO SENSITIVE!
WHAP
WHAP
ARGH
SHALL WE SLEEP NOW?
KRNCH
YES, MA'AM.

GESTURES

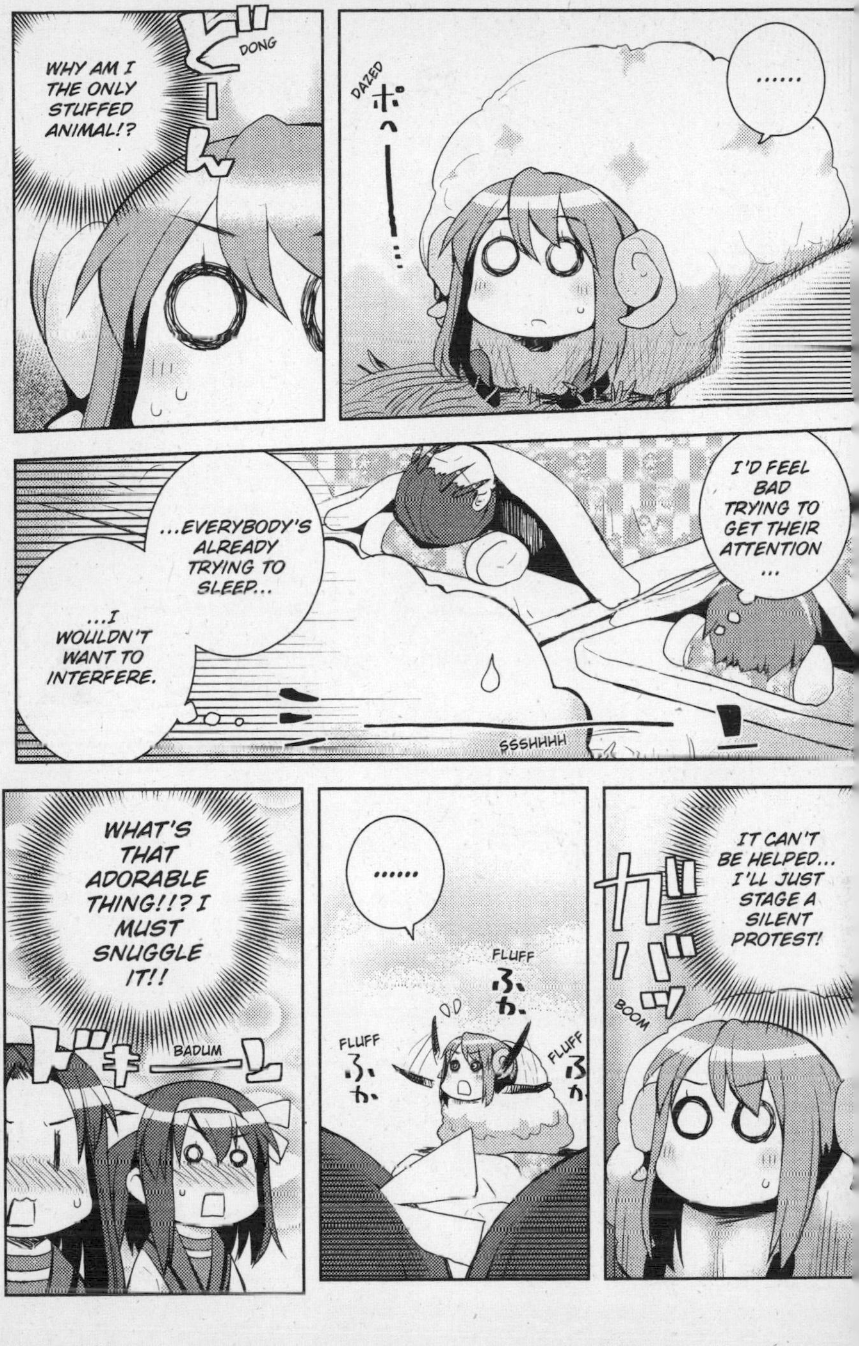
......
DAZED
ポへー
WHY AM I THE ONLY STUFFED ANIMAL!?
DONG
I'D FEEL BAD TRYING TO GET THEIR ATTENTION ...
...EVERYBODY'S ALREADY TRYING TO SLEEP...
...I WOULDN'T WANT TO INTERFERE.
SSSHHHH
IT CAN'T BE HELPED... I'LL JUST STAGE A SILENT PROTEST!
BOOM
......
FLUFF
ふか
FLUFF
ふか
FLUFF
ふか
WHAT'S THAT ADORABLE THING!!? I MUST SNUGGLE IT!!
BADUM

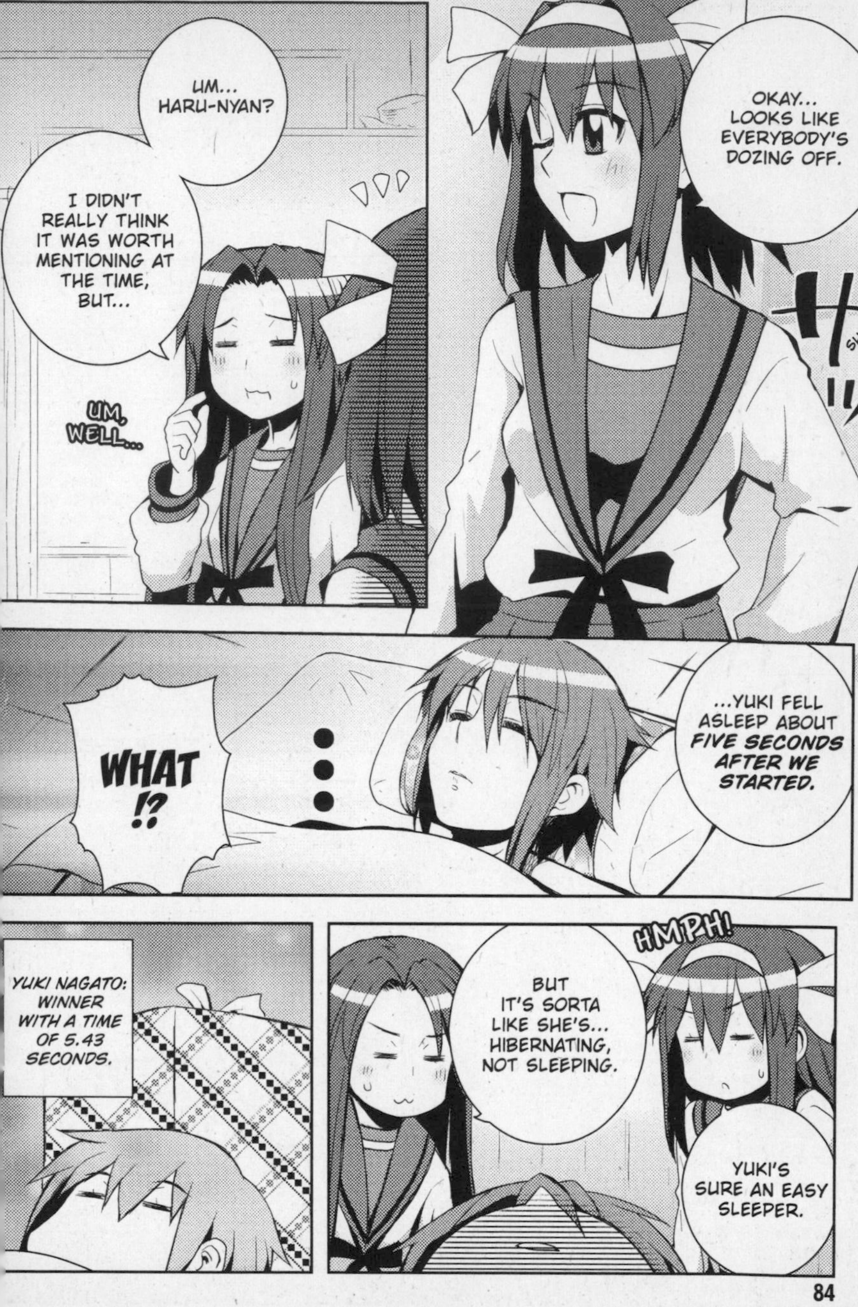
OKAY... LOOKS LIKE EVERYBODY'S DOZING OFF.
SHUP
UM... HARU-NYAN?
I DIDN'T REALLY THINK IT WAS WORTH MENTIONING AT THE TIME, BUT...
UM, WELL...
...YUKI FELL ASLEEP ABOUT *FIVE SECONDS AFTER WE STARTED.*
...
WHAT !?
HMPH!
BUT IT'S SORTA LIKE SHE'S... HIBERNATING, NOT SLEEPING.
YUKI'S SURE AN EASY SLEEPER.
YUKI NAGATO: WINNER WITH A TIME OF 5.43 SECONDS.

LOSERS

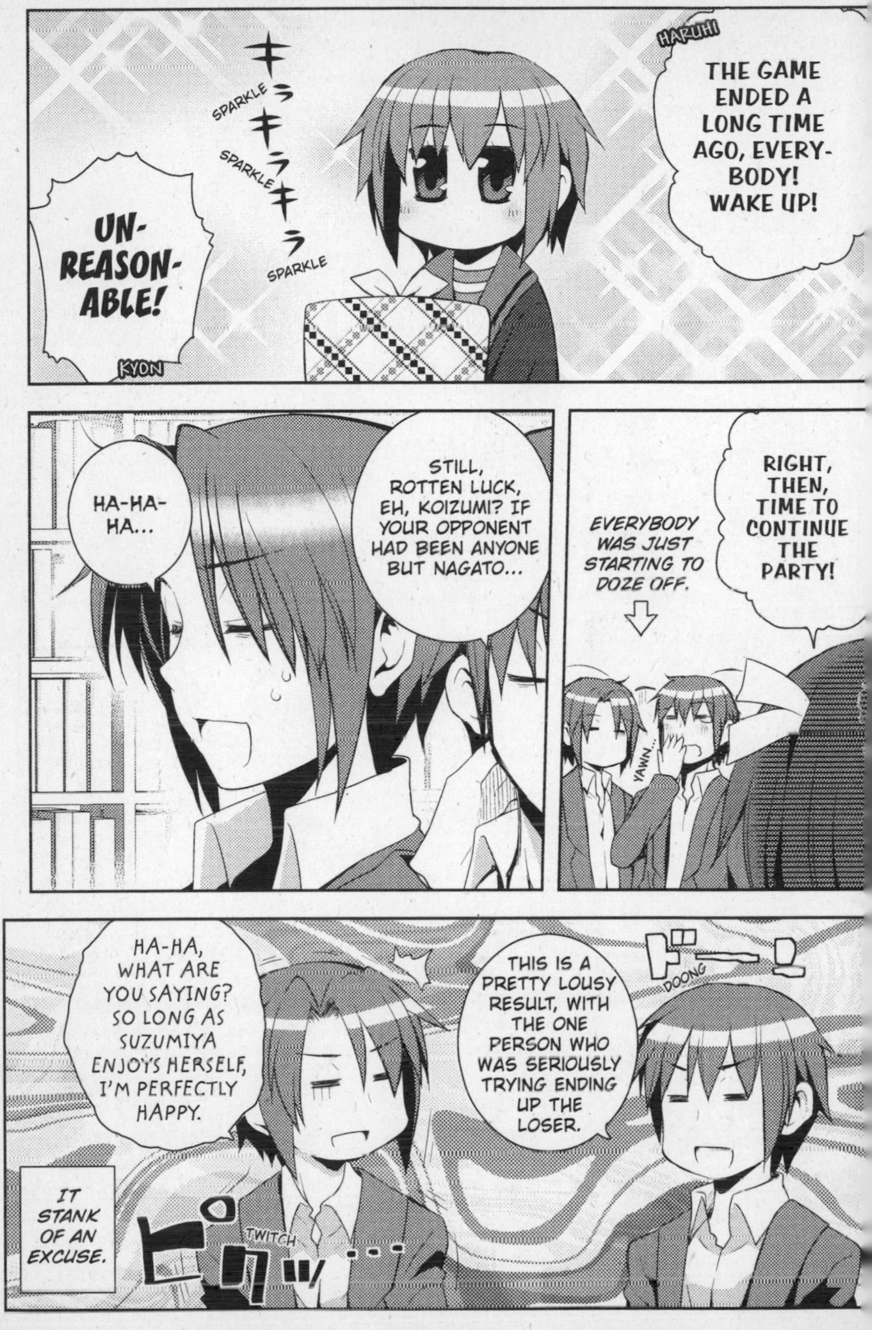
HARUHI
THE GAME ENDED A LONG TIME AGO, EVERY-BODY! WAKE UP!
SPARKLE SPARKLE SPARKLE SPARKLE
UN-REASON-ABLE!
KYON
RIGHT, THEN, TIME TO CONTINUE THE PARTY!
EVERYBODY WAS JUST STARTING TO DOZE OFF.
YAWN...
STILL, ROTTEN LUCK, EH, KOIZUMI? IF YOUR OPPONENT HAD BEEN ANYONE BUT NAGATO...
HA-HA-HA...
DOONG
THIS IS A PRETTY LOUSY RESULT, WITH THE ONE PERSON WHO WAS SERIOUSLY TRYING ENDING UP THE LOSER.
HA-HA, WHAT ARE YOU SAYING? SO LONG AS SUZUMIYA ENJOYS HERSELF, I'M PERFECTLY HAPPY.
TWITCH
IT STANK OF AN EXCUSE.

ALL NIGHT LONG

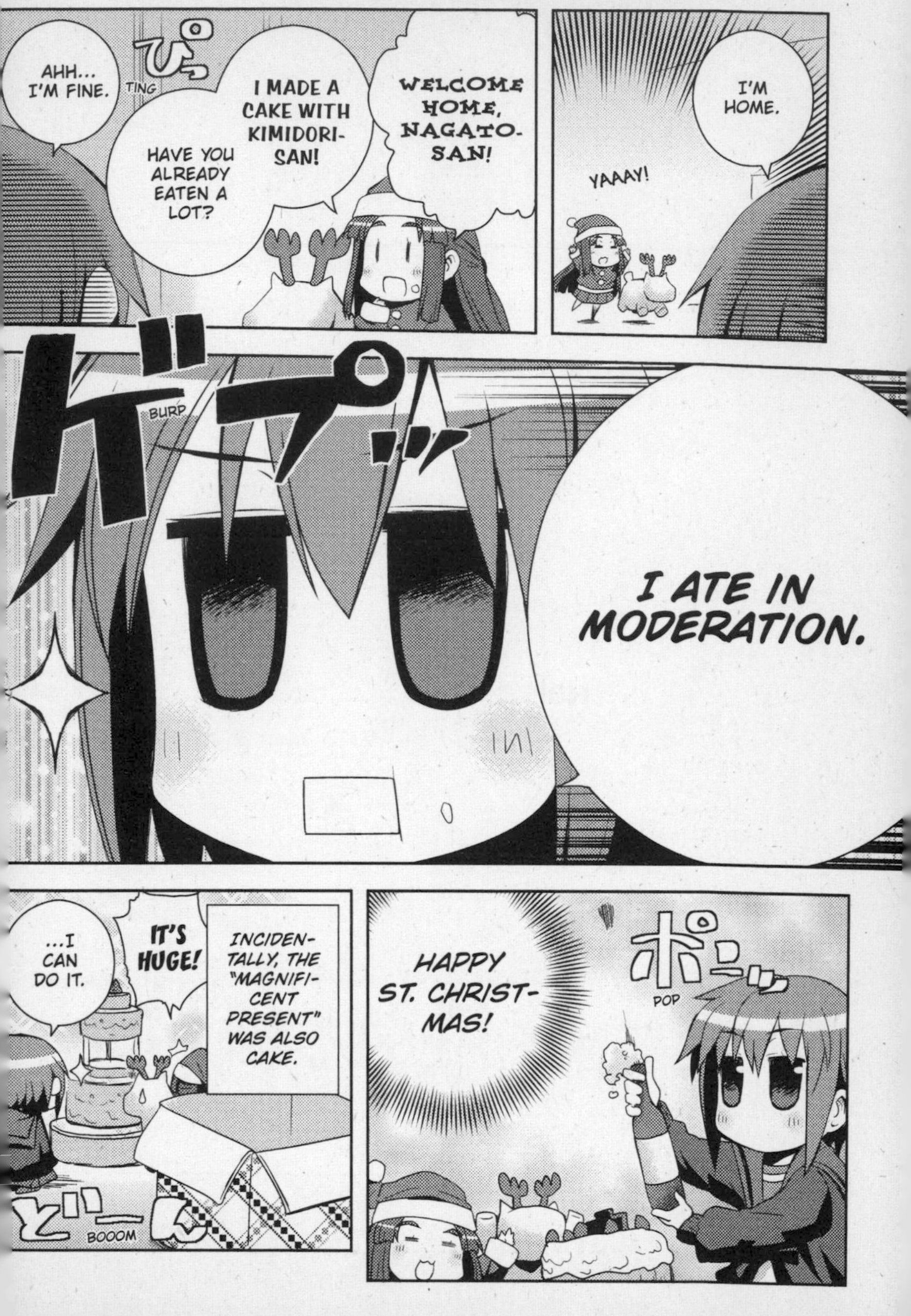
I'M HOME.
YAAAY!
WELCOME HOME, NAGATO-SAN!
I MADE A CAKE WITH KIMIDORI-SAN!
HAVE YOU ALREADY EATEN A LOT?
TING
AHH... I'M FINE.
I ATE IN MODERATION.
BURP
POP
HAPPY ST. CHRIST-MAS!
INCIDEN-TALLY, THE "MAGNIFI-CENT PRESENT" WAS ALSO CAKE.
IT'S HUGE!
...I CAN DO IT.
BOOOM

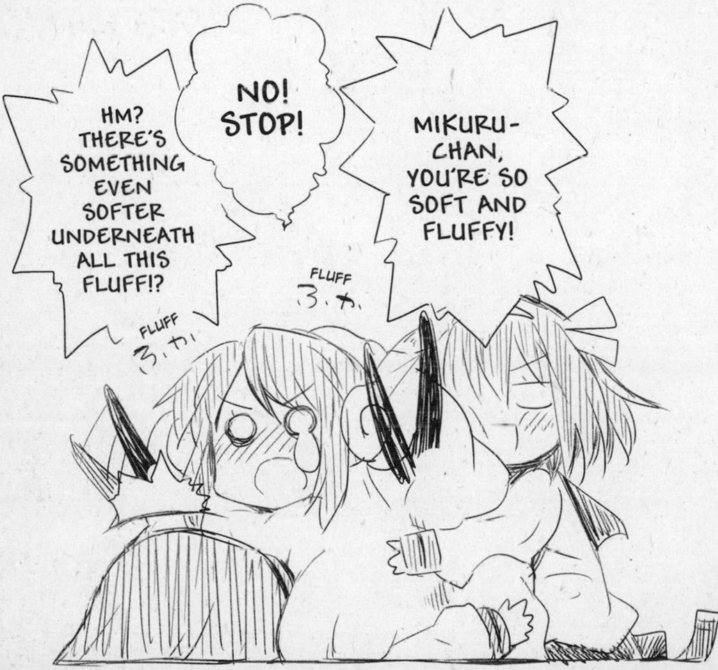
MIKURU-CHAN, YOU'RE SO SOFT AND FLUFFY!
NO! STOP!
HM? THERE'S SOMETHING EVEN SOFTER UNDERNEATH ALL THIS FLUFF!?
FLUFF
FLUFF

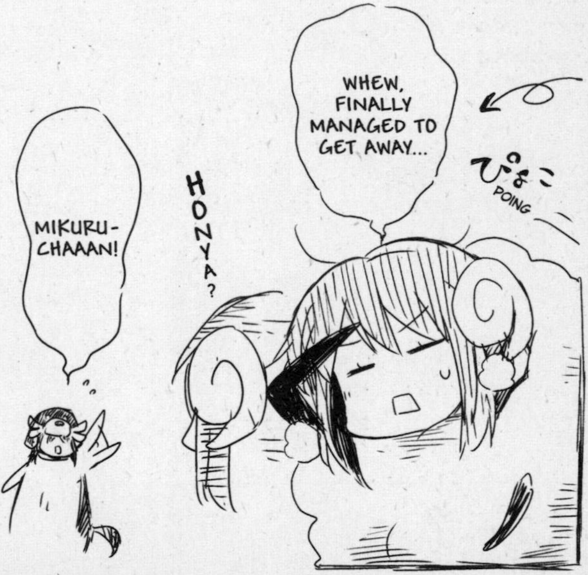
WHEW, FINALLY MANAGED TO GET AWAY...
ぴょこ
POING
HONYA?
MIKURU-CHAAAN!

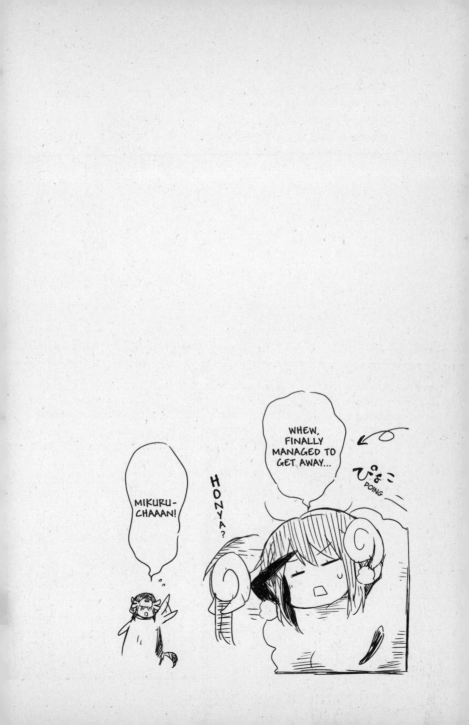

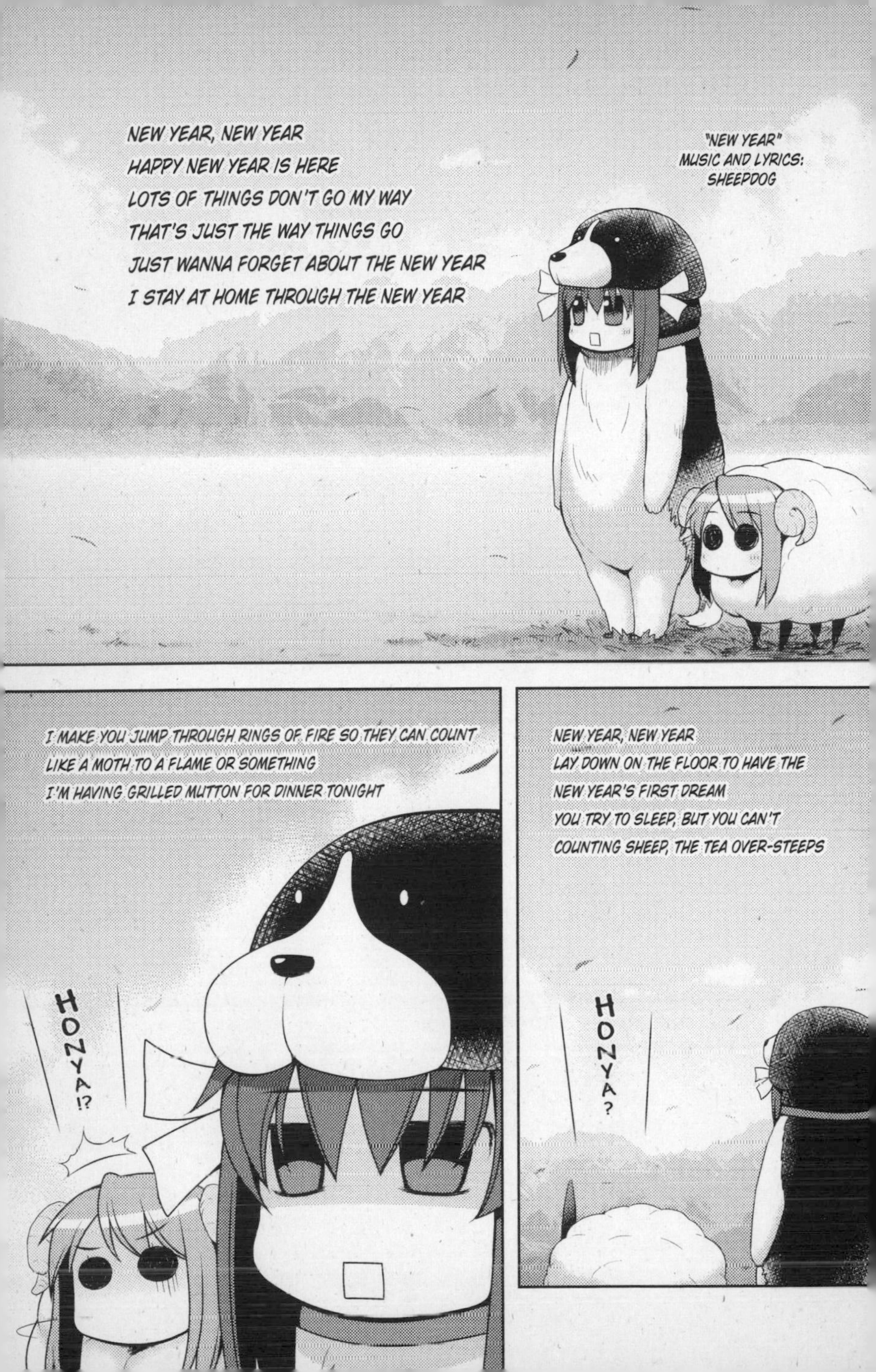
"NEW YEAR"
MUSIC AND LYRICS:
SHEEPDOG
NEW YEAR, NEW YEAR
HAPPY NEW YEAR IS HERE
LOTS OF THINGS DON'T GO MY WAY
THAT'S JUST THE WAY THINGS GO
JUST WANNA FORGET ABOUT THE NEW YEAR
I STAY AT HOME THROUGH THE NEW YEAR
NEW YEAR, NEW YEAR
LAY DOWN ON THE FLOOR TO HAVE THE
NEW YEAR'S FIRST DREAM
YOU TRY TO SLEEP, BUT YOU CAN'T
COUNTING SHEEP, THE TEA OVER-STEEPS
HONYA?
I MAKE YOU JUMP THROUGH RINGS OF FIRE SO THEY CAN COUNT
LIKE A MOTH TO A FLAME OR SOMETHING
I'M HAVING GRILLED MUTTON FOR DINNER TONIGHT
HONYA!?

SUZUMIYA HARUHI-CHAN'S FIRST DREAM OF THE YEAR

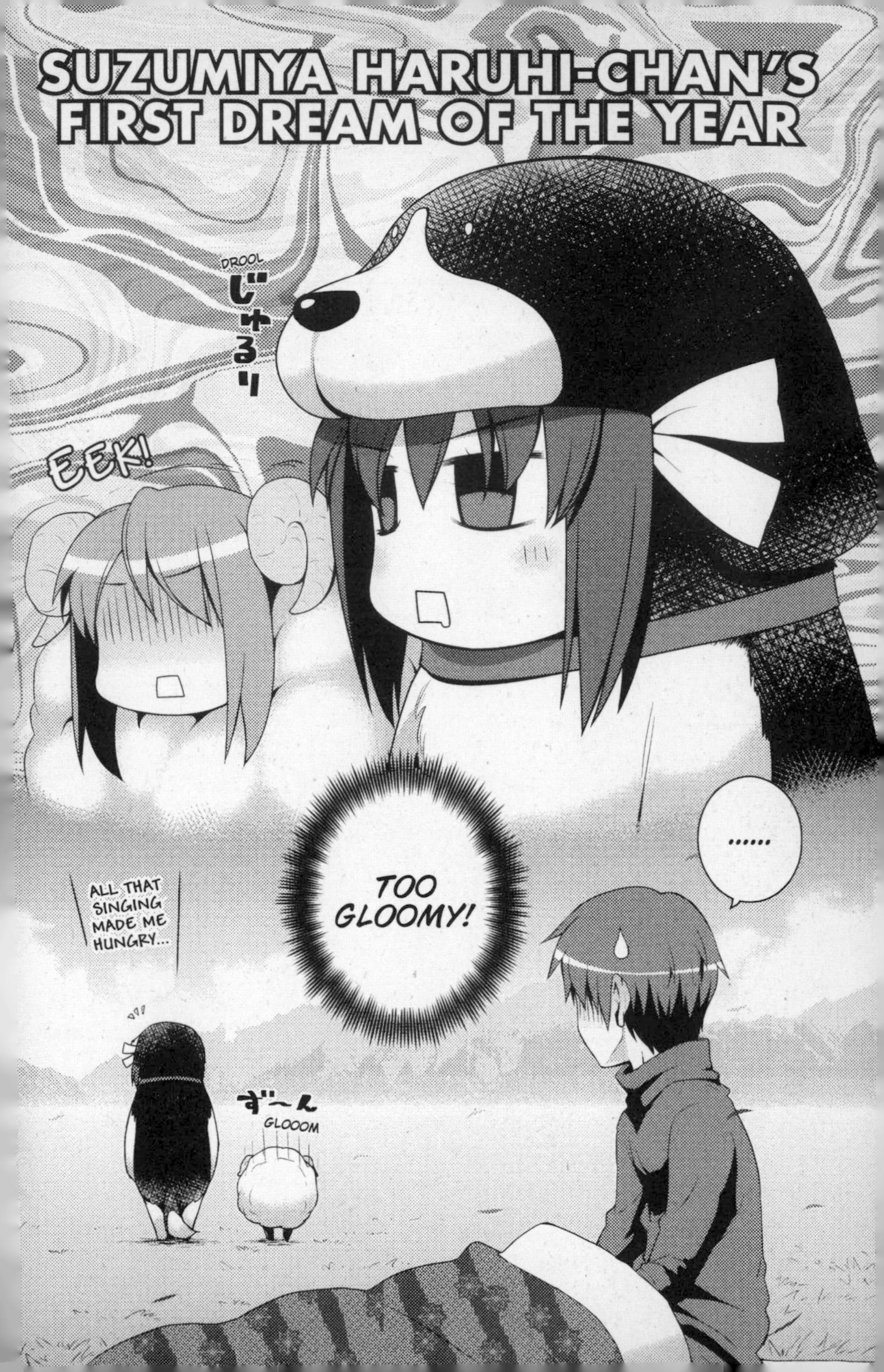

DROOL
じゅるり
EEK!
......
TOO GLOOMY!
ALL THAT SINGING MADE ME HUNGRY...
ず~ん
GLOOOM

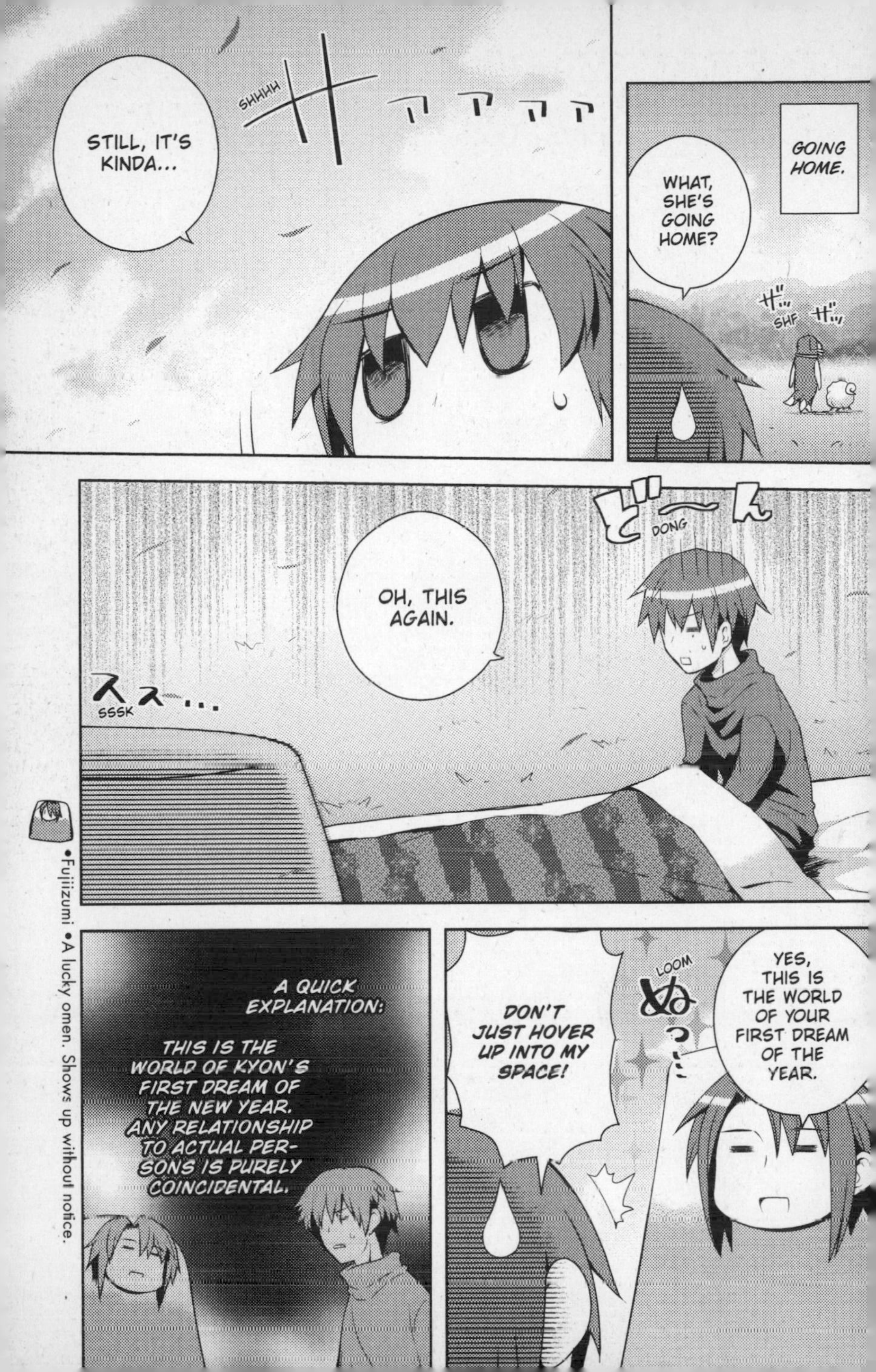
GOING HOME.
WHAT, SHE'S GOING HOME?
SHF
SHHHH
STILL, IT'S KINDA...
DONG
OH, THIS AGAIN.
SSSK
YES, THIS IS THE WORLD OF YOUR FIRST DREAM OF THE YEAR.
LOOM
DON'T JUST HOVER UP INTO MY SPACE!
A QUICK EXPLANATION:
THIS IS THE WORLD OF KYON'S FIRST DREAM OF THE NEW YEAR. ANY RELATIONSHIP TO ACTUAL PERSONS IS PURELY COINCIDENTAL.

•Fujiizumi •A lucky omen. Shows up without notice.

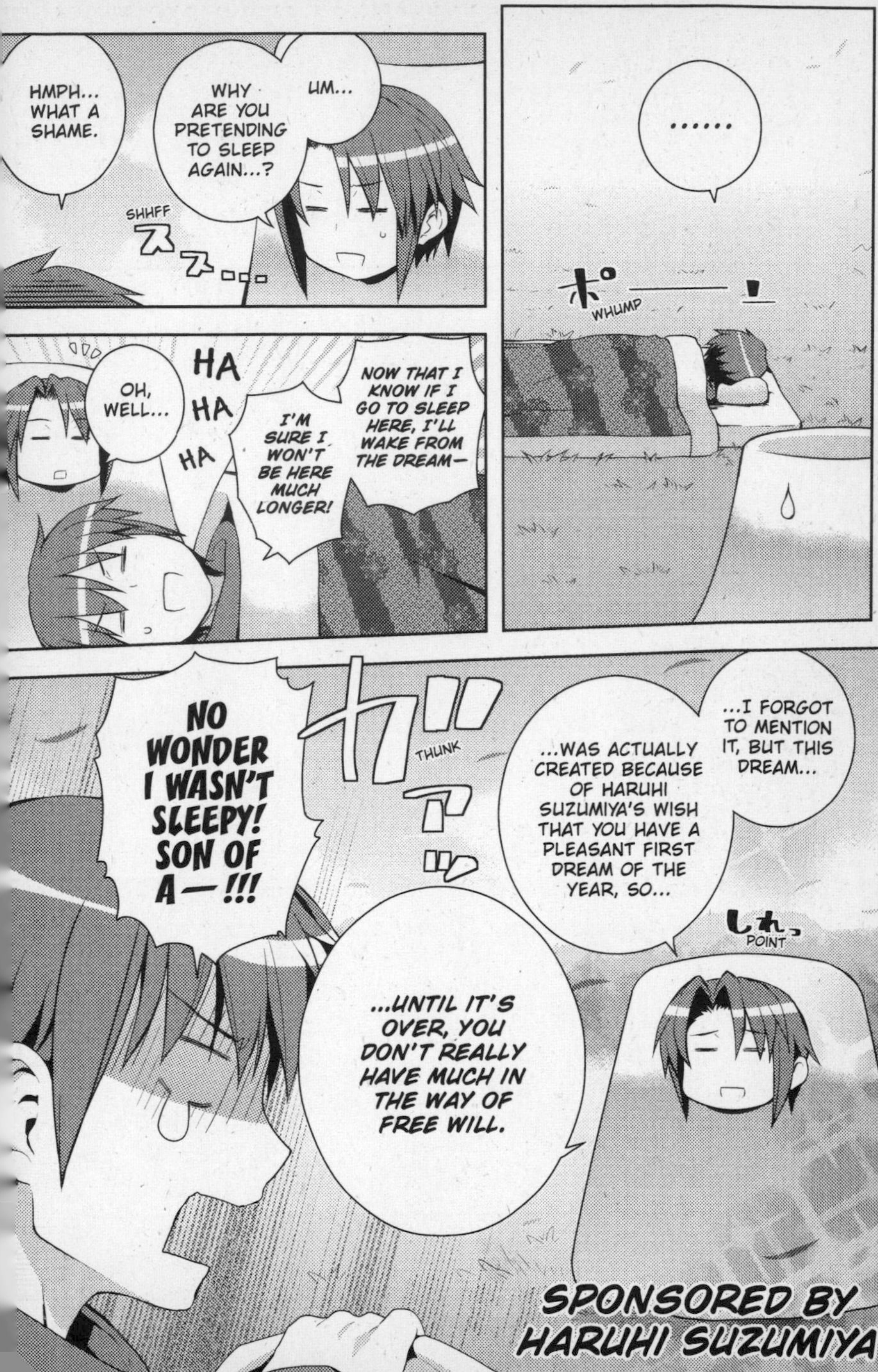
......
ポ——!
WHUMP
UM...
WHY ARE YOU PRETENDING TO SLEEP AGAIN...?
HMPH... WHAT A SHAME.
SHHFF
スス...
NOW THAT I KNOW IF I GO TO SLEEP HERE, I'LL WAKE FROM THE DREAM—
I'M SURE I WON'T BE HERE MUCH LONGER!
HA HA HA
OH, WELL...
...I FORGOT TO MENTION IT, BUT THIS DREAM...
...WAS ACTUALLY CREATED BECAUSE OF HARUHI SUZUMIYA'S WISH THAT YOU HAVE A PLEASANT FIRST DREAM OF THE YEAR, SO...
しれっ
POINT
...UNTIL IT'S OVER, YOU DON'T REALLY HAVE MUCH IN THE WAY OF FREE WILL.
THUNK
NO WONDER I WASN'T SLEEPY! SON OF A—!!!
SPONSORED BY HARUHI SUZUMIYA

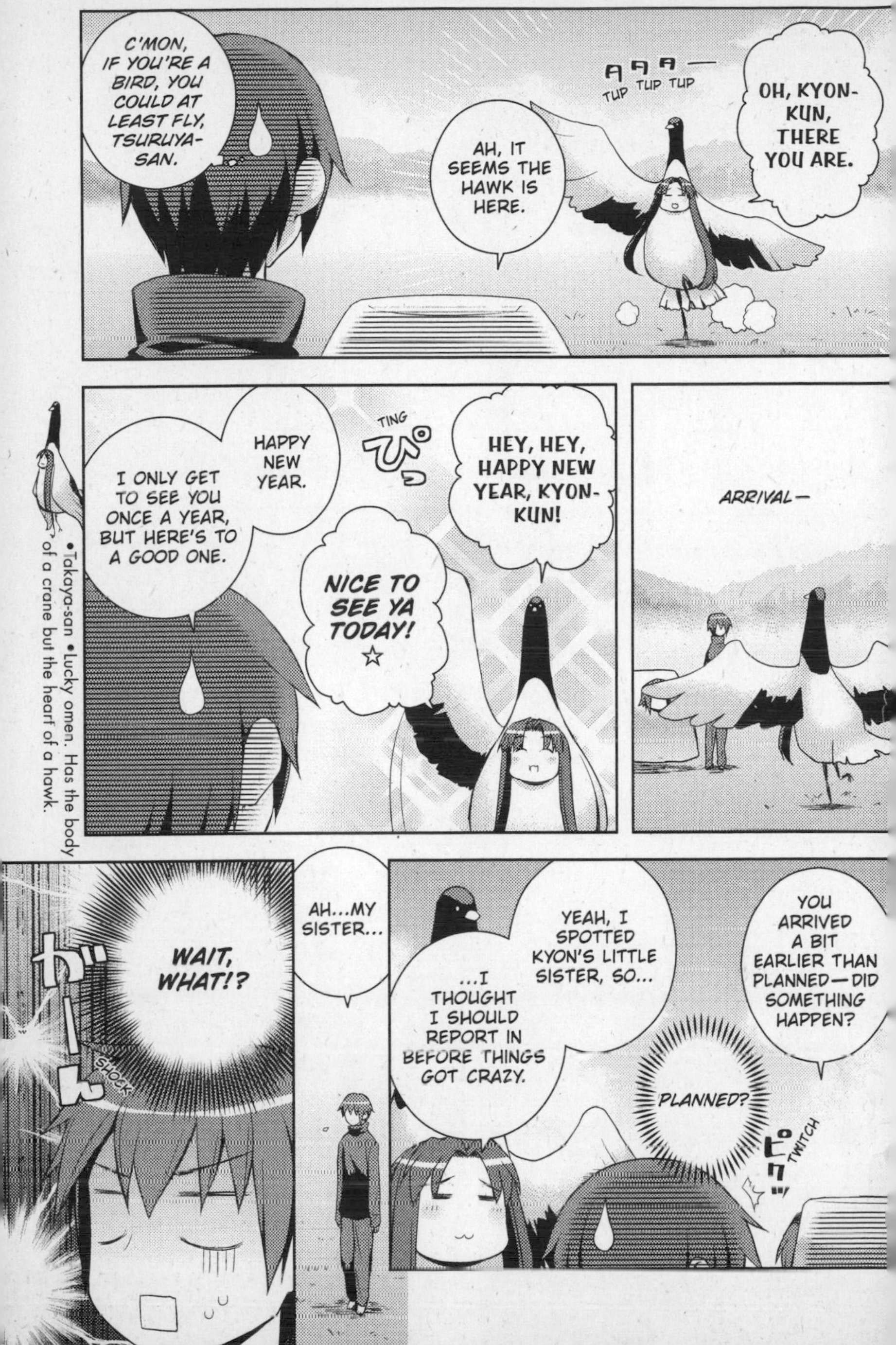
TUP TUP TUP
OH, KYON-KUN, THERE YOU ARE.
AH, IT SEEMS THE HAWK IS HERE.
C'MON, IF YOU'RE A BIRD, YOU COULD AT LEAST FLY, TSURUYA-SAN.
ARRIVAL—
HEY, HEY, HAPPY NEW YEAR, KYON-KUN!
TING
NICE TO SEE YA TODAY! ☆
HAPPY NEW YEAR.
I ONLY GET TO SEE YOU ONCE A YEAR, BUT HERE'S TO A GOOD ONE.
•Takaya-san •Lucky omen. Has the body of a crane but the heart of a hawk.
YOU ARRIVED A BIT EARLIER THAN PLANNED—DID SOMETHING HAPPEN?
PLANNED?
TWITCH
YEAH, I SPOTTED KYON'S LITTLE SISTER, SO...
...I THOUGHT I SHOULD REPORT IN BEFORE THINGS GOT CRAZY.
AH...MY SISTER...
WAIT, WHAT!?
SHOCK

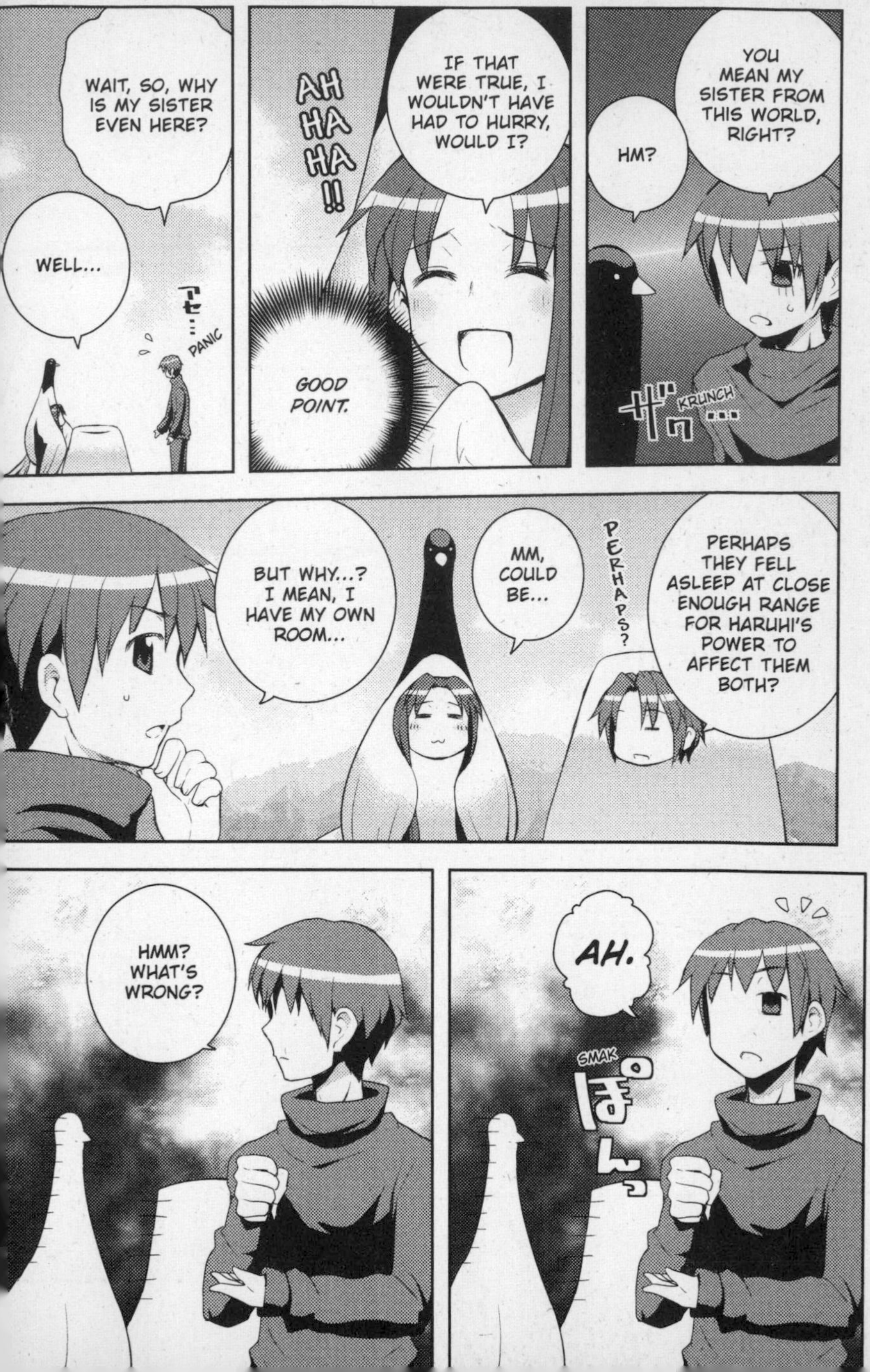
YOU MEAN MY SISTER FROM THIS WORLD, RIGHT?
HM?
ザクッ…
KRUNCH
IF THAT WERE TRUE, I WOULDN'T HAVE HAD TO HURRY, WOULD I?
AH HA HA!!
GOOD POINT.
WAIT, SO, WHY IS MY SISTER EVEN HERE?
アセ…
PANIC
WELL...
PERHAPS THEY FELL ASLEEP AT CLOSE ENOUGH RANGE FOR HARUHI'S POWER TO AFFECT THEM BOTH?
PERHAPS?
MM, COULD BE...
BUT WHY...? I MEAN, I HAVE MY OWN ROOM...
AH.
SMAK
ぽんっ
HMM? WHAT'S WRONG?

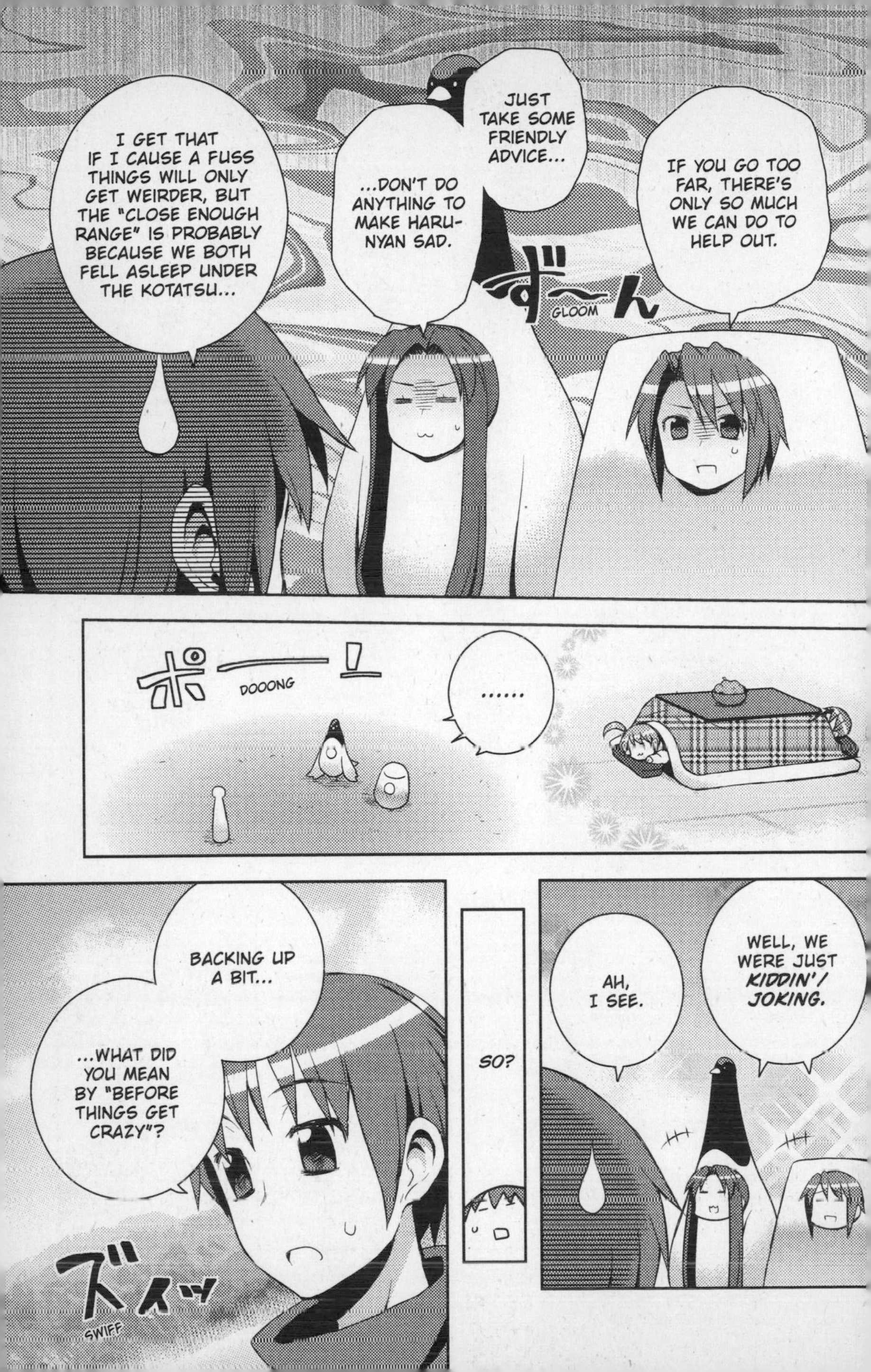
JUST TAKE SOME FRIENDLY ADVICE...
...DON'T DO ANYTHING TO MAKE HARU-NYAN SAD.
IF YOU GO TOO FAR, THERE'S ONLY SO MUCH WE CAN DO TO HELP OUT.
ず～ん
GLOOM
I GET THAT IF I CAUSE A FUSS THINGS WILL ONLY GET WEIRDER, BUT THE "CLOSE ENOUGH RANGE" IS PROBABLY BECAUSE WE BOTH FELL ASLEEP UNDER THE KOTATSU...
......
ポーーー！
DOOONG
WELL, WE WERE JUST *KIDDIN'/ JOKING.*
AH, I SEE.
SO?
BACKING UP A BIT...
...WHAT DID YOU MEAN BY "BEFORE THINGS GET CRAZY"?
ズイッ
SWIFF

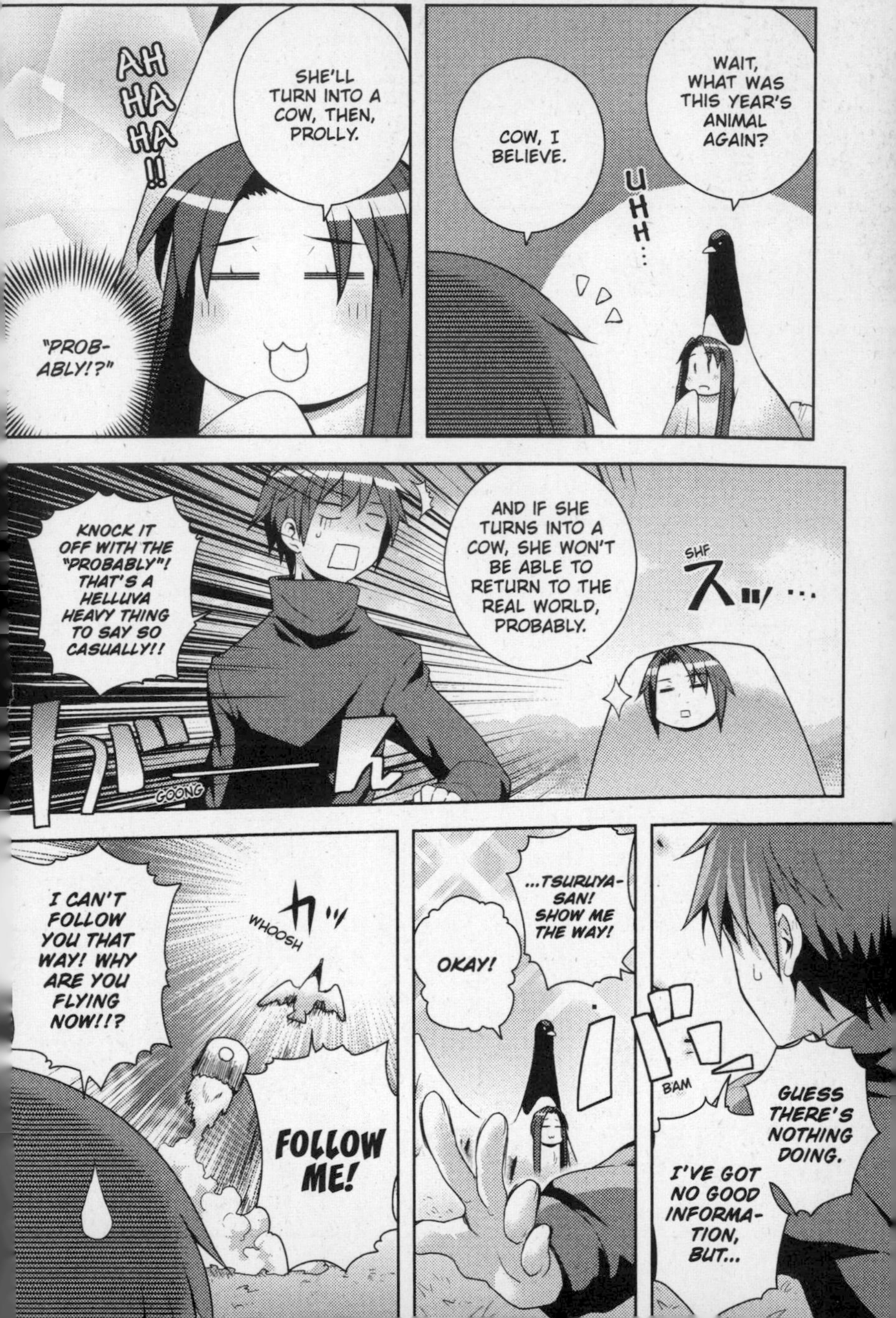
WAIT, WHAT WAS THIS YEAR'S ANIMAL AGAIN?
COW, I BELIEVE.
UHH...
SHE'LL TURN INTO A COW, THEN, PROLLY.
AH HA HA!!
"PROBABLY!?"
SHF
AND IF SHE TURNS INTO A COW, SHE WON'T BE ABLE TO RETURN TO THE REAL WORLD, PROBABLY.
KNOCK IT OFF WITH THE "PROBABLY"! THAT'S A HELLUVA HEAVY THING TO SAY SO CASUALLY!!
GOONG
GUESS THERE'S NOTHING DOING.
I'VE GOT NO GOOD INFORMATION, BUT...
BAM
...TSURUYA-SAN! SHOW ME THE WAY!
OKAY!
WHOOSH
I CAN'T FOLLOW YOU THAT WAY! WHY ARE YOU FLYING NOW!!?
FOLLOW ME!

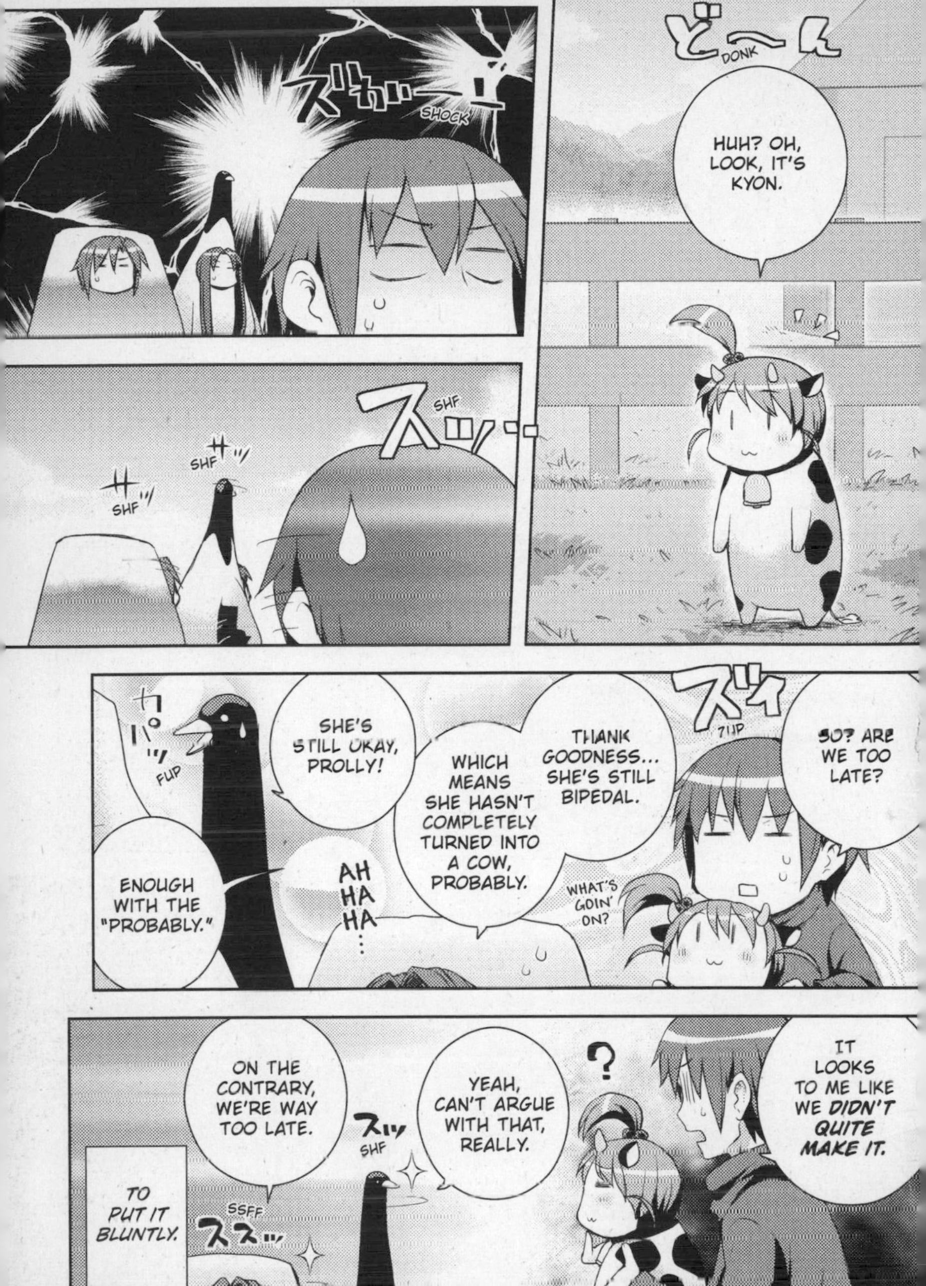
DONK
HUH? OH, LOOK, IT'S KYON.
SHOCK
SHF
SHF
SHF
SO? ARE WE TOO LATE?
ZIP
THANK GOODNESS... SHE'S STILL BIPEDAL.
WHAT'S GOIN' ON?
WHICH MEANS SHE HASN'T COMPLETELY TURNED INTO A COW, PROBABLY.
SHE'S STILL OKAY, PROLLY!
AH HA HA...
FUP
ENOUGH WITH THE "PROBABLY."
IT LOOKS TO ME LIKE WE *DIDN'T QUITE MAKE IT.*
?
YEAH, CAN'T ARGUE WITH THAT, REALLY.
SHF
ON THE CONTRARY, WE'RE WAY TOO LATE.
SSFF
TO PUT IT BLUNTLY.

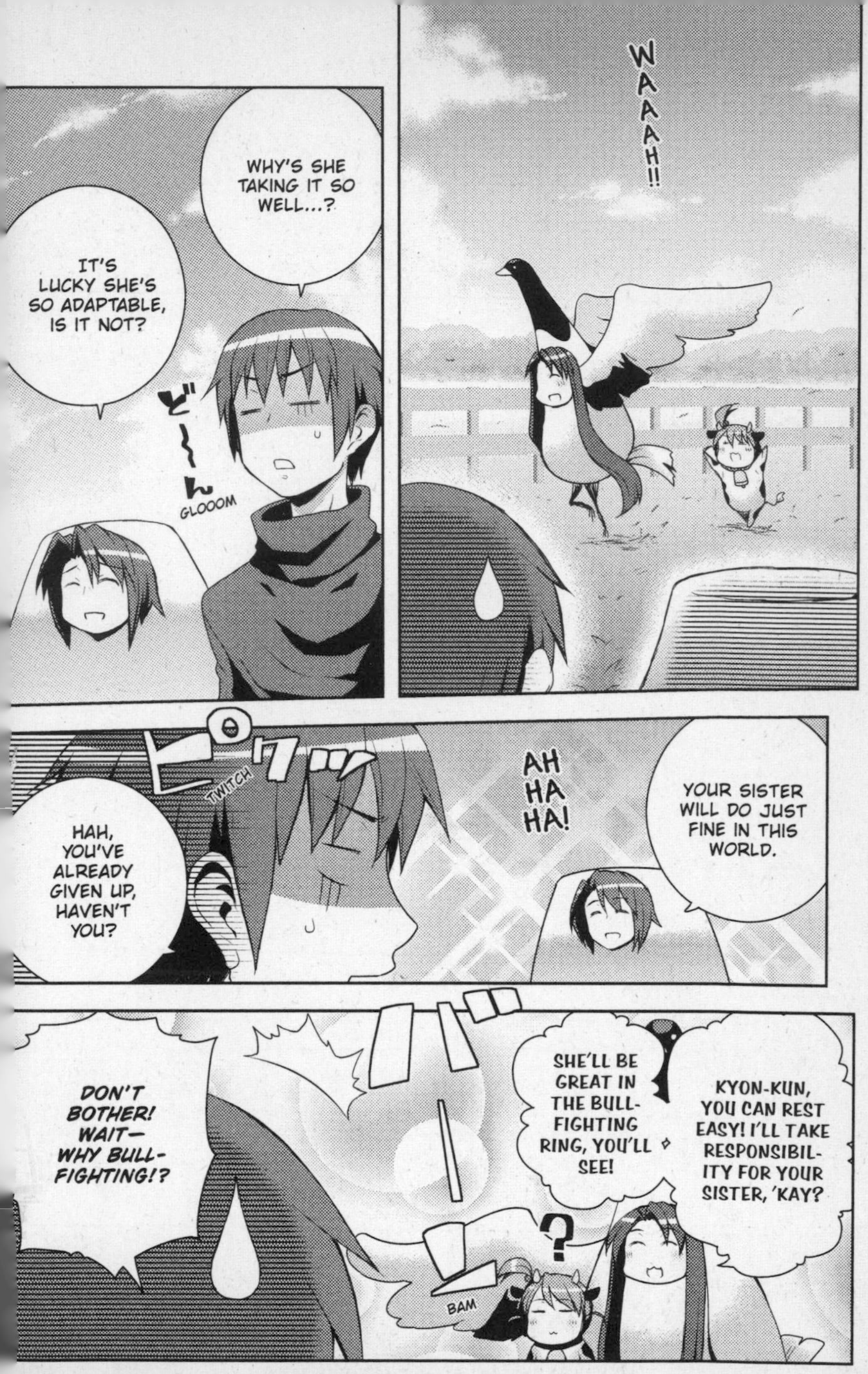
WAAAAH!!
WHY'S SHE TAKING IT SO WELL...?
IT'S LUCKY SHE'S SO ADAPTABLE, IS IT NOT?
ど〜ん
GLOOOM
YOUR SISTER WILL DO JUST FINE IN THIS WORLD.
AH HA HA!
ピクッ
TWITCH
HAH, YOU'VE ALREADY GIVEN UP, HAVEN'T YOU?
KYON-KUN, YOU CAN REST EASY! I'LL TAKE RESPONSIBILITY FOR YOUR SISTER, 'KAY?
SHE'LL BE GREAT IN THE BULL-FIGHTING RING, YOU'LL SEE! ◇
?
バッ
BAM
DON'T BOTHER! WAIT— WHY BULL-FIGHTING!?

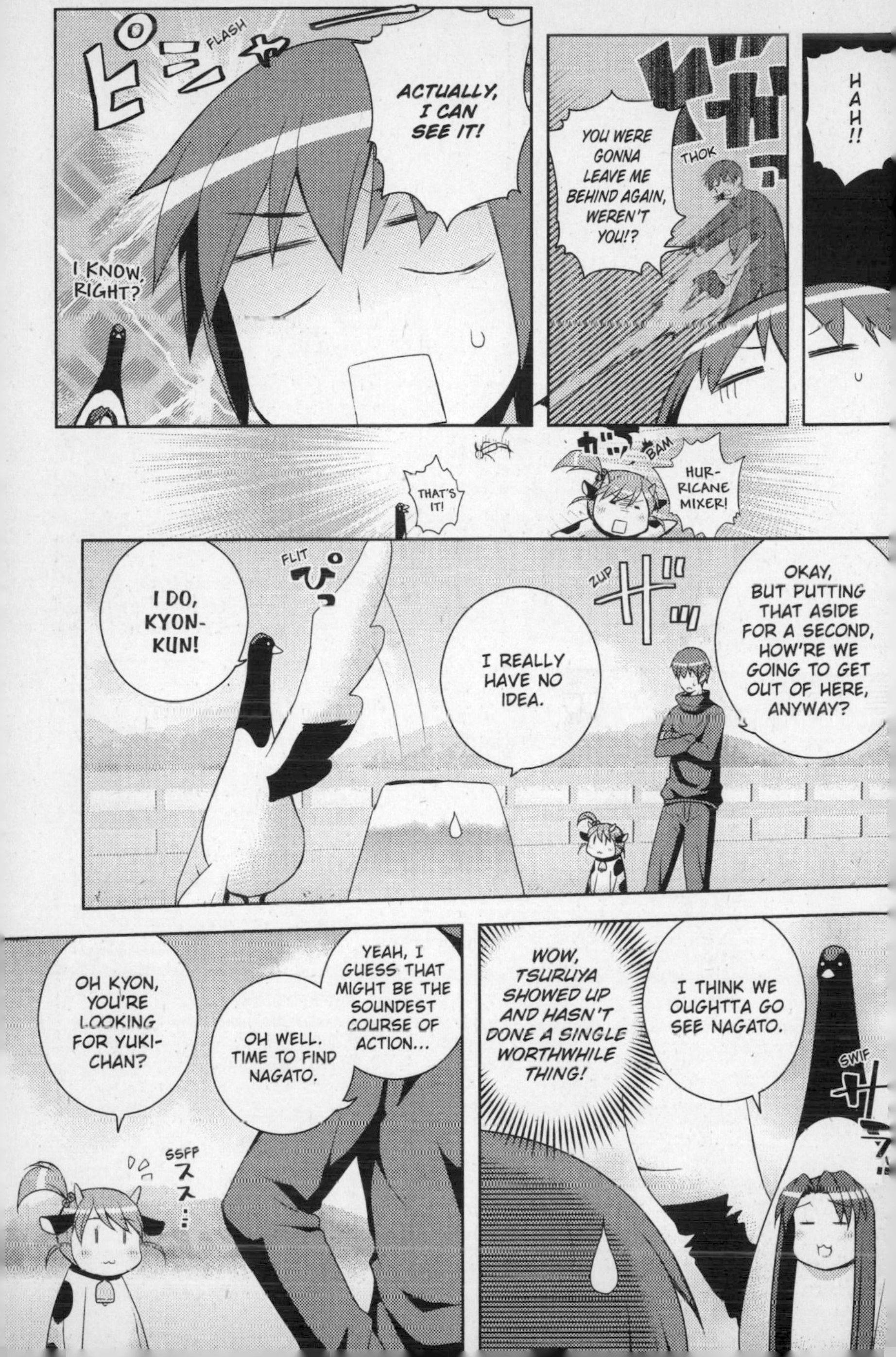
HAH!!
THOK
YOU WERE GONNA LEAVE ME BEHIND AGAIN, WEREN'T YOU!?
FLASH
ACTUALLY, I CAN SEE IT!
I KNOW, RIGHT?
BAM
HURRICANE MIXER!
THAT'S IT!
OKAY, BUT PUTTING THAT ASIDE FOR A SECOND, HOW'RE WE GOING TO GET OUT OF HERE, ANYWAY?
ZUP
I REALLY HAVE NO IDEA.
FLIT
I DO, KYON-KUN!
I THINK WE OUGHTTA GO SEE NAGATO.
SWIF
WOW, TSURUYA SHOWED UP AND HASN'T DONE A SINGLE WORTHWHILE THING!
YEAH, I GUESS THAT MIGHT BE THE SOUNDEST COURSE OF ACTION...
OH WELL. TIME TO FIND NAGATO.
OH KYON, YOU'RE LOOKING FOR YUKI-CHAN?
SSFF

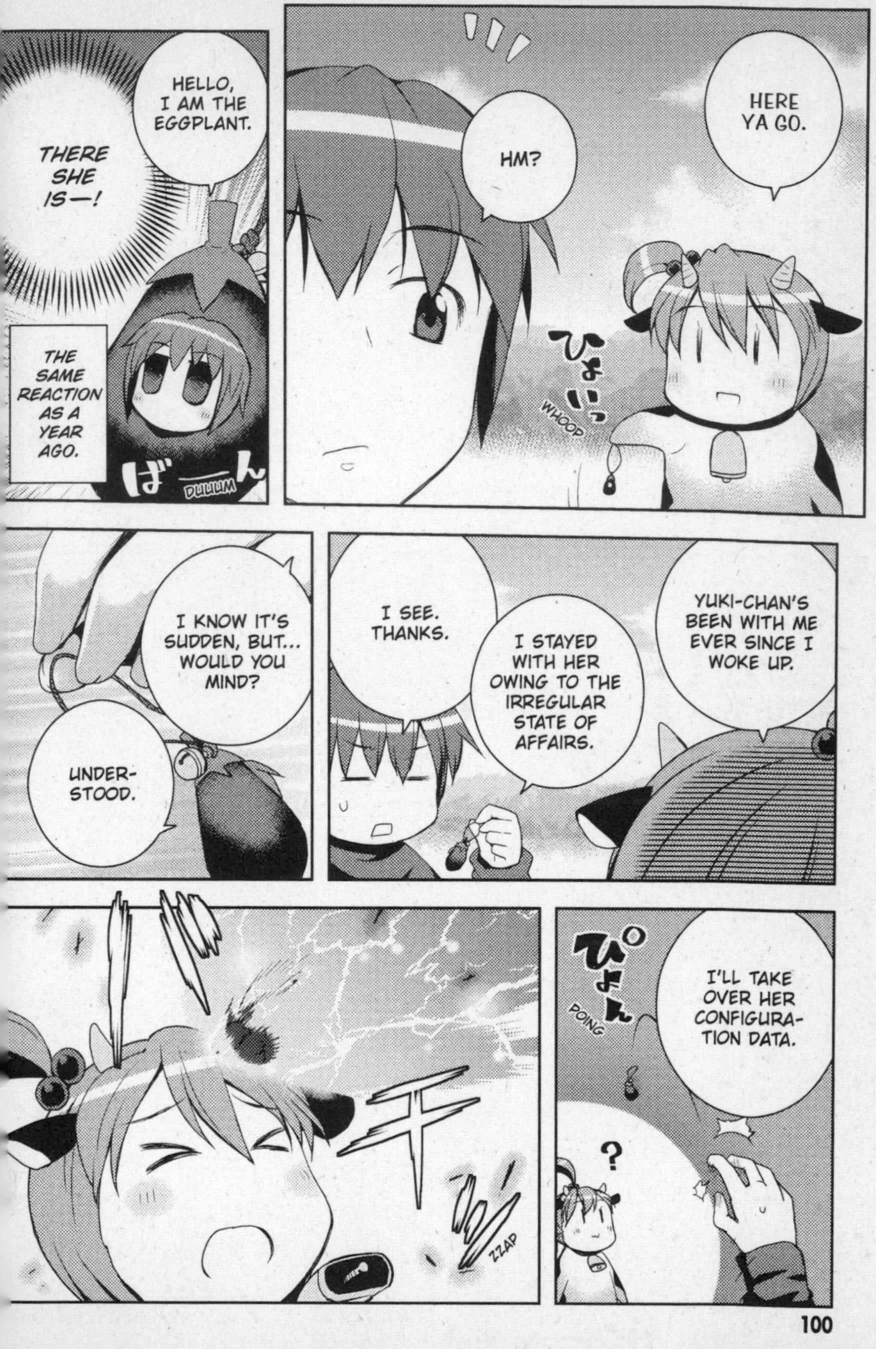
HERE YA GO.
HM?
ぴょいっ
WHOOP
HELLO, I AM THE EGGPLANT.
THERE SHE IS—!
THE SAME REACTION AS A YEAR AGO.
ばーん
DUUUM
YUKI-CHAN'S BEEN WITH ME EVER SINCE I WOKE UP.
I STAYED WITH HER OWING TO THE IRREGULAR STATE OF AFFAIRS.
I SEE. THANKS.
I KNOW IT'S SUDDEN, BUT... WOULD YOU MIND?
UNDER-STOOD.
ぴょん
POING
I'LL TAKE OVER HER CONFIGURA-TION DATA.
?
ZZAP

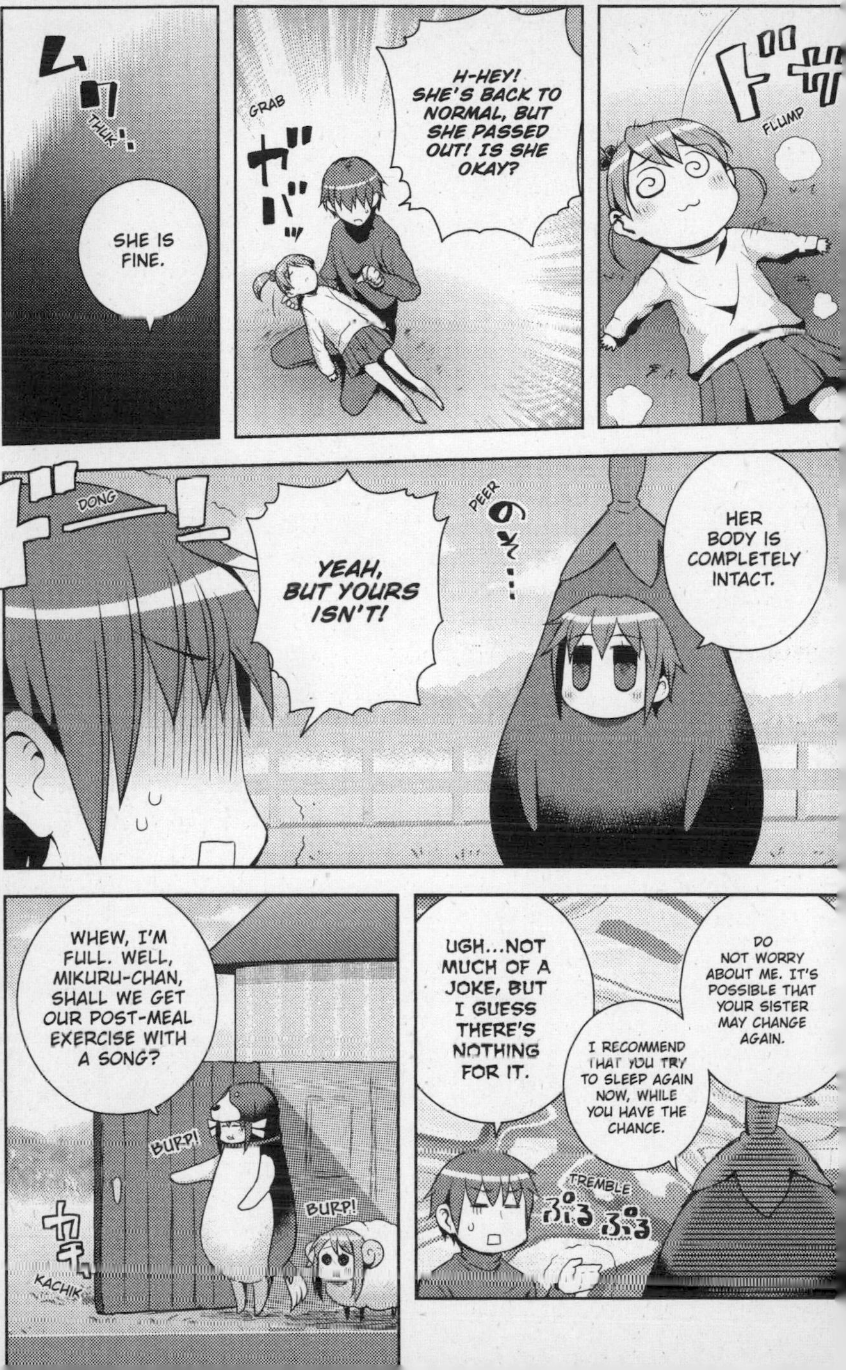
FLUMP
H-HEY! SHE'S BACK TO NORMAL, BUT SHE PASSED OUT! IS SHE OKAY?
GRAB
THUK
SHE IS FINE.
HER BODY IS COMPLETELY INTACT.
PEER
YEAH, BUT YOURS ISN'T!
DONG
DO NOT WORRY ABOUT ME. IT'S POSSIBLE THAT YOUR SISTER MAY CHANGE AGAIN.
I RECOMMEND THAT YOU TRY TO SLEEP AGAIN NOW, WHILE YOU HAVE THE CHANCE.
UGH...NOT MUCH OF A JOKE, BUT I GUESS THERE'S NOTHING FOR IT.
TREMBLE
ぷるぷる
WHEW, I'M FULL. WELL, MIKURU-CHAN, SHALL WE GET OUR POST-MEAL EXERCISE WITH A SONG?
BURP!
BURP!
KACHIK

•Eggplant Nagato [Ripe] •Lucky omen. Matured from the Nasu Strap form.

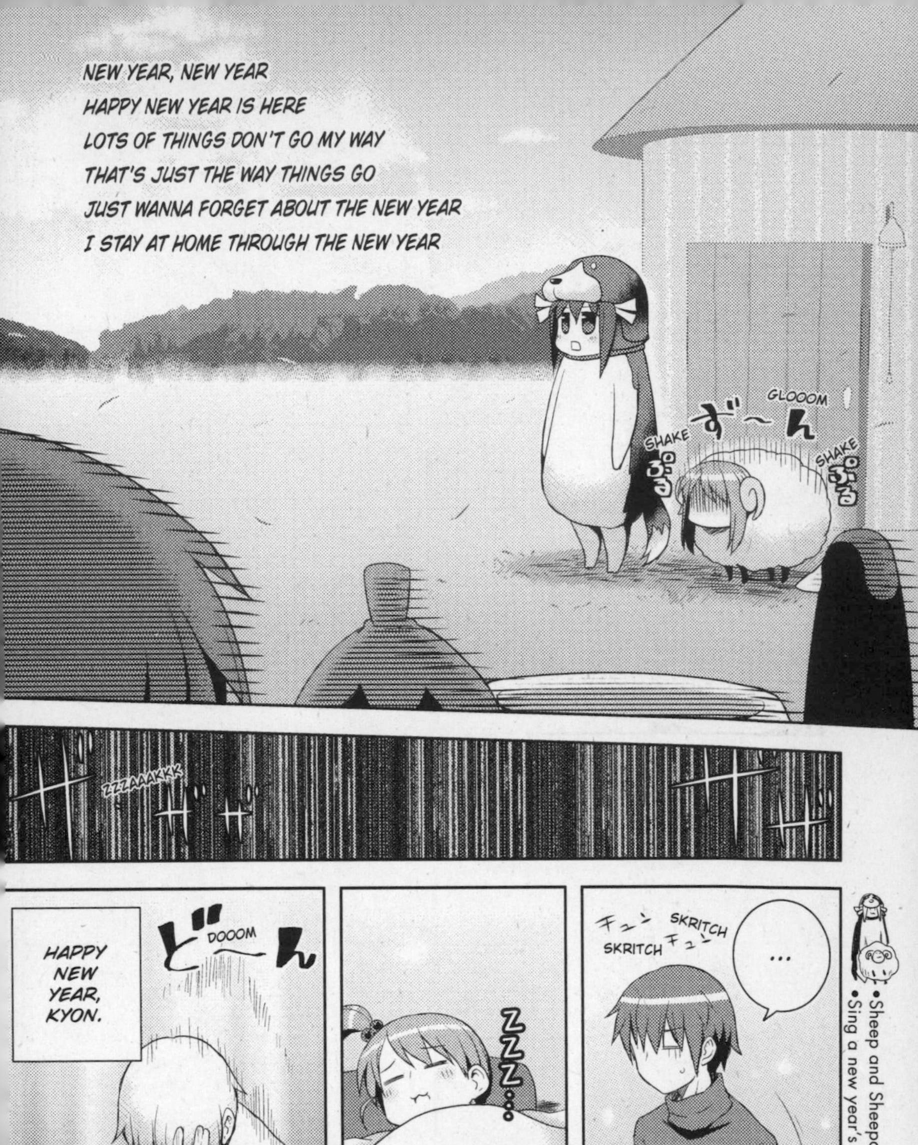
NEW YEAR, NEW YEAR
HAPPY NEW YEAR IS HERE
LOTS OF THINGS DON'T GO MY WAY
THAT'S JUST THE WAY THINGS GO
JUST WANNA FORGET ABOUT THE NEW YEAR
I STAY AT HOME THROUGH THE NEW YEAR
ず〜ん GLOOOM
SHAKE ぷる
SHAKE ぷる
ZZZAAAKKK
チュン SKRITCH
チュン SKRITCH
...
Z Z Z...
......
HAPPY NEW YEAR, KYON.
ど〜ん DOOOM

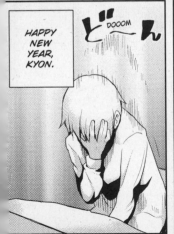

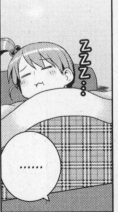

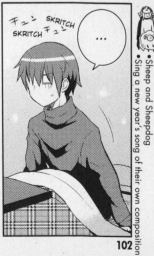

JAPANESE BADMINTON

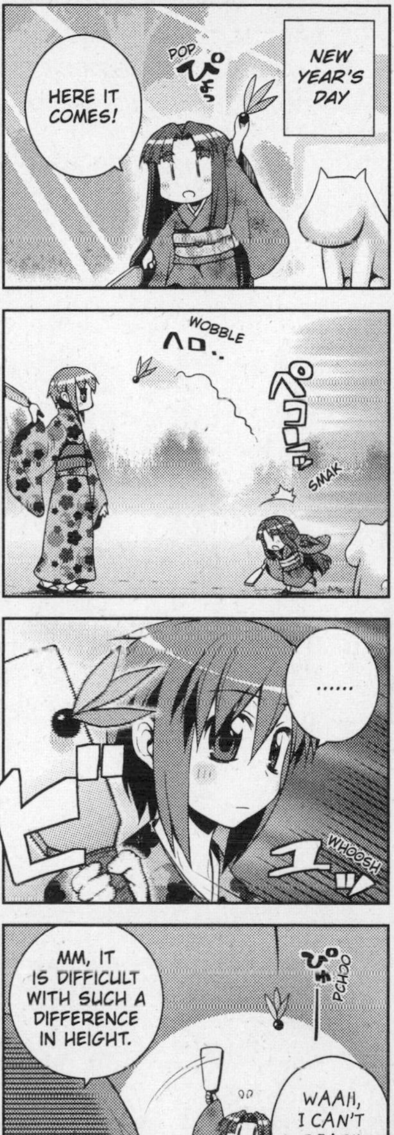
NEW YEAR'S DAY
POP
HERE IT COMES!
WOBBLE
SMAK
......
WHOOSH
PCHOO
MM, IT IS DIFFICULT WITH SUCH A DIFFERENCE IN HEIGHT.
WAAH, I CAN'T REACH IT!

STAND-IN

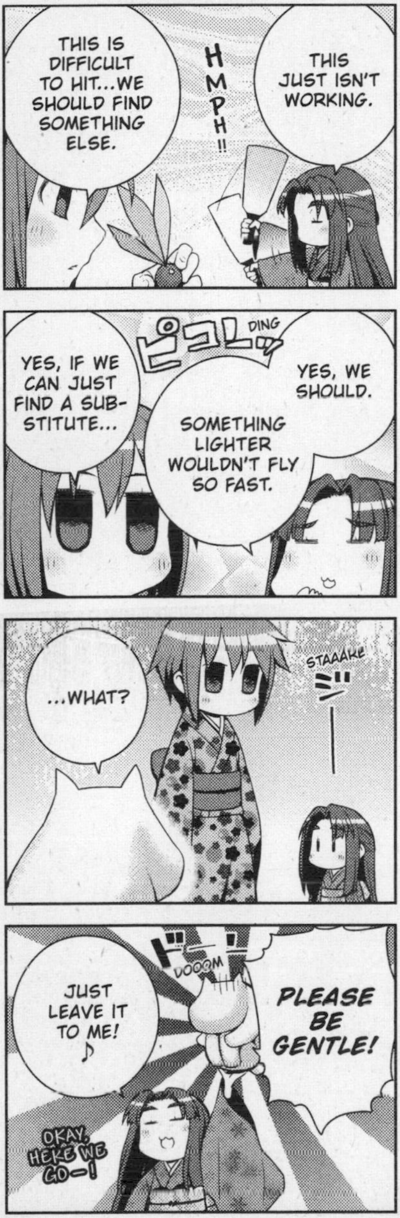
THIS JUST ISN'T WORKING.
HMPH!!
THIS IS DIFFICULT TO HIT...WE SHOULD FIND SOMETHING ELSE.
DING
YES, WE SHOULD.
SOMETHING LIGHTER WOULDN'T FLY SO FAST.
YES, IF WE CAN JUST FIND A SUB-STITUTE...
STAAAKE
...WHAT?
DOOOM
PLEASE BE GENTLE!
JUST LEAVE IT TO ME! ♪
OKAY, HEKE WE GO—!

EMA

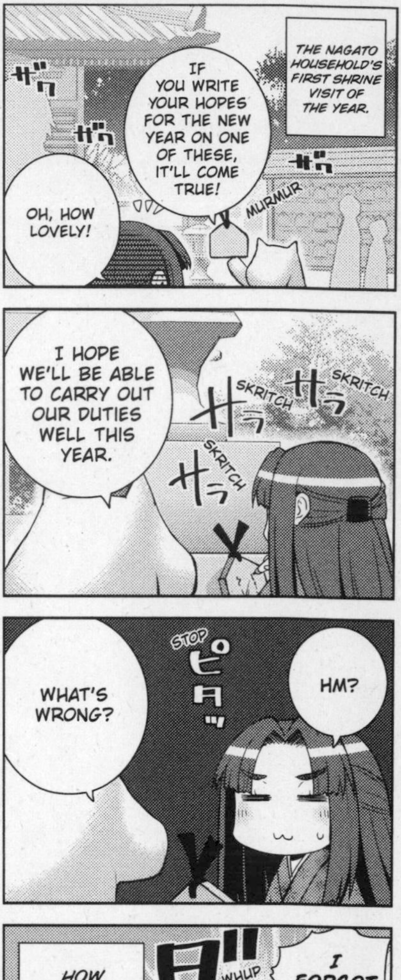
THE NAGATO HOUSEHOLD'S FIRST SHRINE VISIT OF THE YEAR.
IF YOU WRITE YOUR HOPES FOR THE NEW YEAR ON ONE OF THESE, IT'LL COME TRUE!
MURMUR
OH, HOW LOVELY!
SKRITCH
SKRITCH
SKRITCH
I HOPE WE'LL BE ABLE TO CARRY OUT OUR DUTIES WELL THIS YEAR.
HM?
STOP
WHAT'S WRONG?
I FORGOT SOME-THING!
WHUP
HOW SOON WE FORGET OUR DUTIES.
OUSEHOLD SAFETY

*AN EMA IS A WOODEN PLAQUE ON WHICH SHINTO SHRINE VISITORS WRITE THEIR WISHES BEFORE HANGING THEM IN THE SHRINE.

WISHES

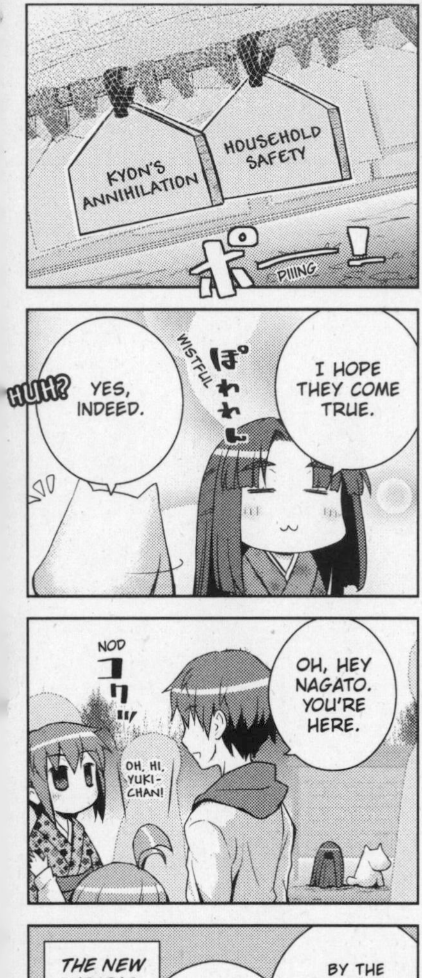
HOUSEHOLD SAFETY
KYON'S ANNIHILATION
PIIING
I HOPE THEY COME TRUE.
WISTFUL
YES, INDEED.
HUH?
OH, HEY NAGATO. YOU'RE HERE.
NOD
OH, HI, YUKI-CHAN!
BY THE WAY, WHO IS THAT "KYON-KUN" YOU WANT TO ANNIHILATE?
OH, THAT'S RIGHT, YOU'VE NEVER MET HIM.
THE NEW YEAR'S NEAR MISSES CONTINUE...
BYE-BYE! SEE YA!

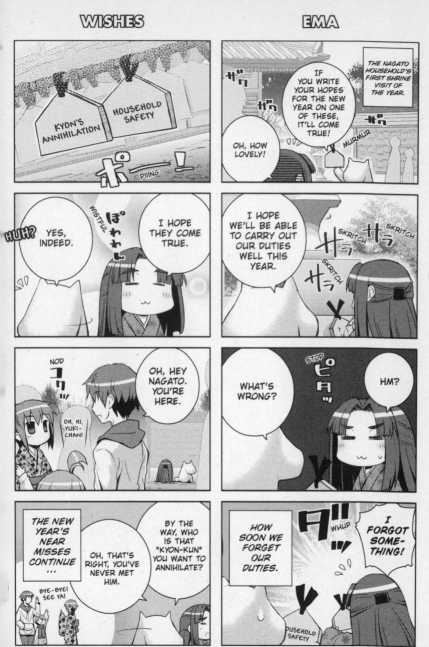

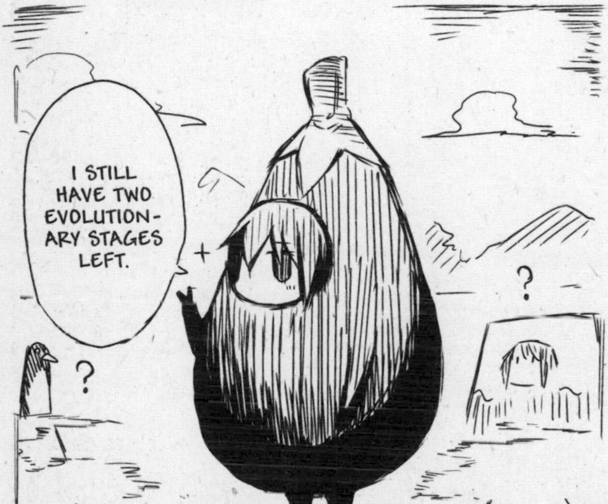
I STILL HAVE TWO EVOLUTION-ARY STAGES LEFT.
?
?

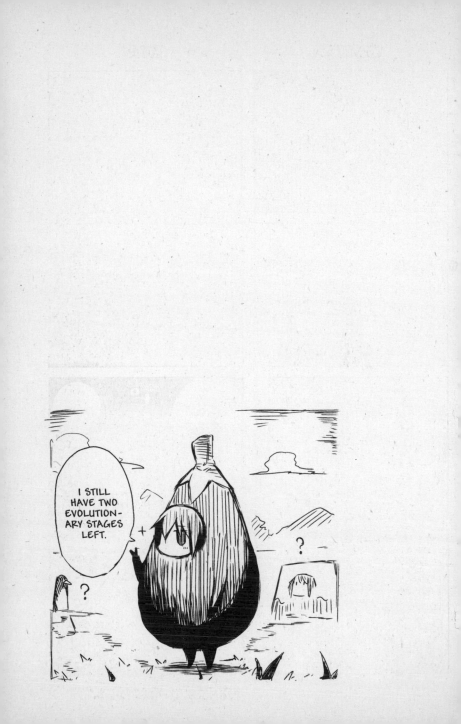

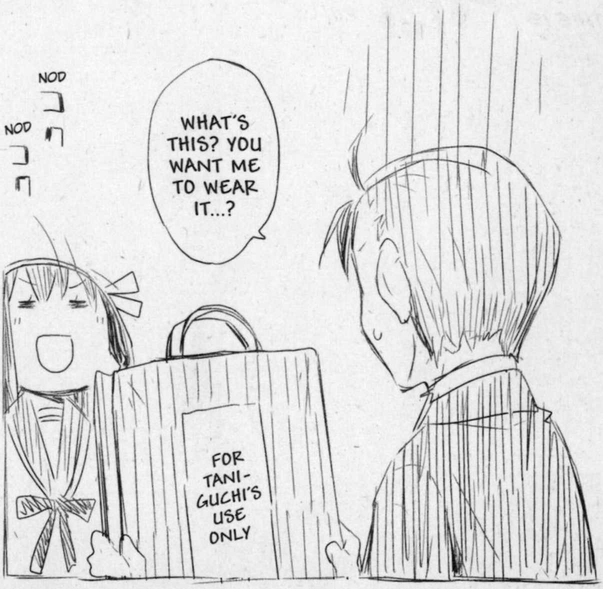
WHAT'S THIS? YOU WANT ME TO WEAR IT...?
NOD
NOD
FOR TANI-GUCHI'S USE ONLY

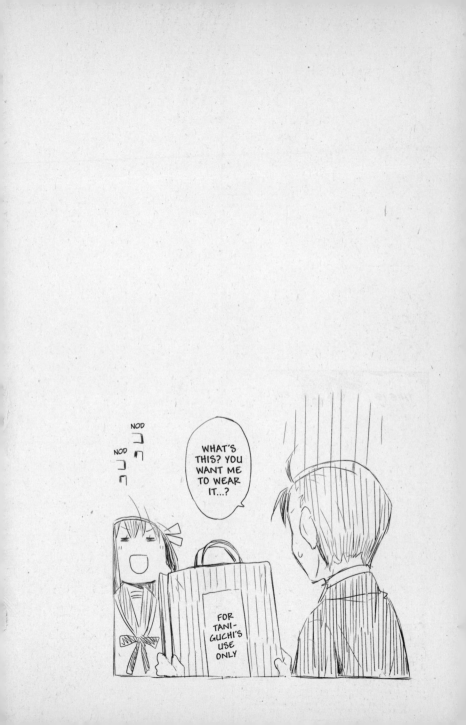

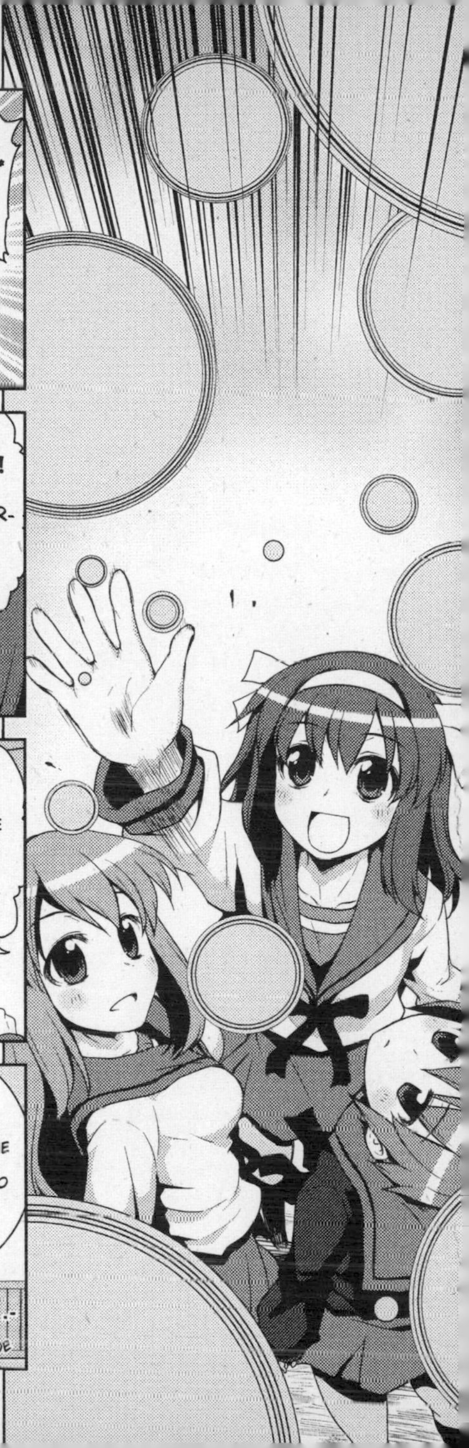

FEBRUARY 3RD

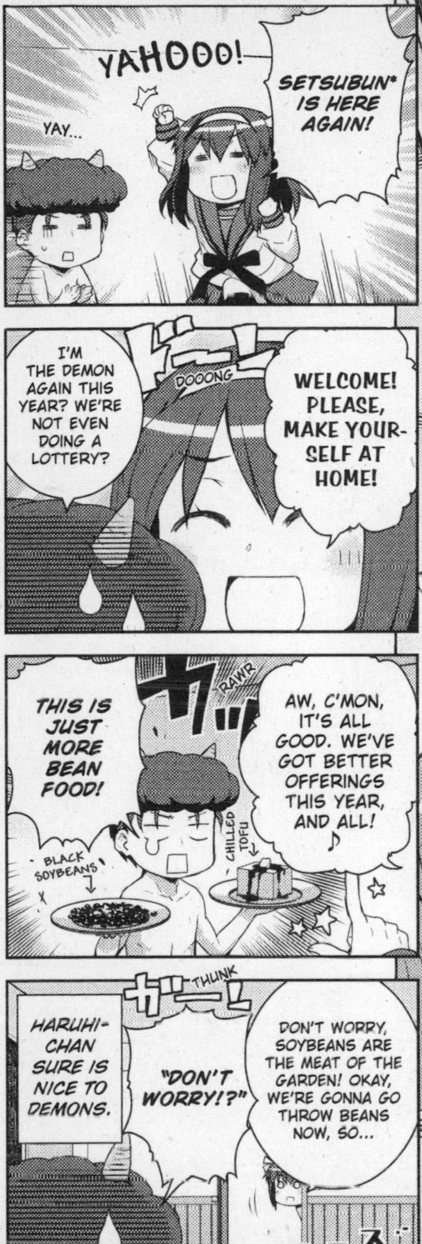

YAHOOO!
SETSUBUN* IS HERE AGAIN!
YAY...
WELCOME! PLEASE, MAKE YOURSELF AT HOME!
DOOONG
I'M THE DEMON AGAIN THIS YEAR? WE'RE NOT EVEN DOING A LOTTERY?
RAWR
AW, C'MON, IT'S ALL GOOD. WE'VE GOT BETTER OFFERINGS THIS YEAR, AND ALL! ♪
THIS IS JUST MORE BEAN FOOD!
CHILLED TOFU
BLACK SOYBEANS
THUNK
DON'T WORRY, SOYBEANS ARE THE MEAT OF THE GARDEN! OKAY, WE'RE GONNA GO THROW BEANS NOW, SO...
"DON'T WORRY!?"
HARUHI-CHAN SURE IS NICE TO DEMONS.
SLIDE

*SETSUBUN IS CONSIDERED THE FIRST HOLIDAY OF SPRING. IN ORDER TO SECURE GOOD FORTUNE FOR THE YEAR, SOMEONE DRESSES UP AS A DEMON WHILE THE REST THROW BEANS AT THEM AND SHOUT "DEMONS OUT, LUCK IN."

•Haruhi-chan •Shows kindness to demons, but her mannerisms are those of an unforgiving hunter.

•Kyon •The main character of this story. He's skilled at comebacks but is often the butt of unreasonable jokes.

•Koizumi •He's been in this volume a little more, so his introduction was a bit earlier.

RESTRAINT

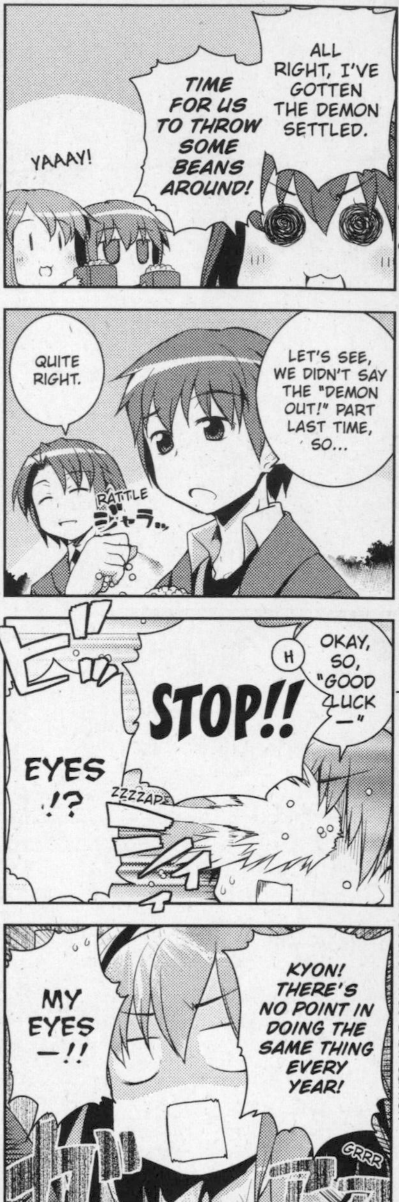
ALL RIGHT, I'VE GOTTEN THE DEMON SETTLED.
TIME FOR US TO THROW SOME BEANS AROUND!
YAAAY!
LET'S SEE, WE DIDN'T SAY THE "DEMON OUT!" PART LAST TIME, SO...
QUITE RIGHT.
RATTLE
ジャラ
OKAY, SO, "GOOD LUCK—"
H
STOP!!
EYES !?
ZZZZAP
KYON! THERE'S NO POINT IN DOING THE SAME THING EVERY YEAR!
MY EYES—!!
GRRR

BAD THINGS

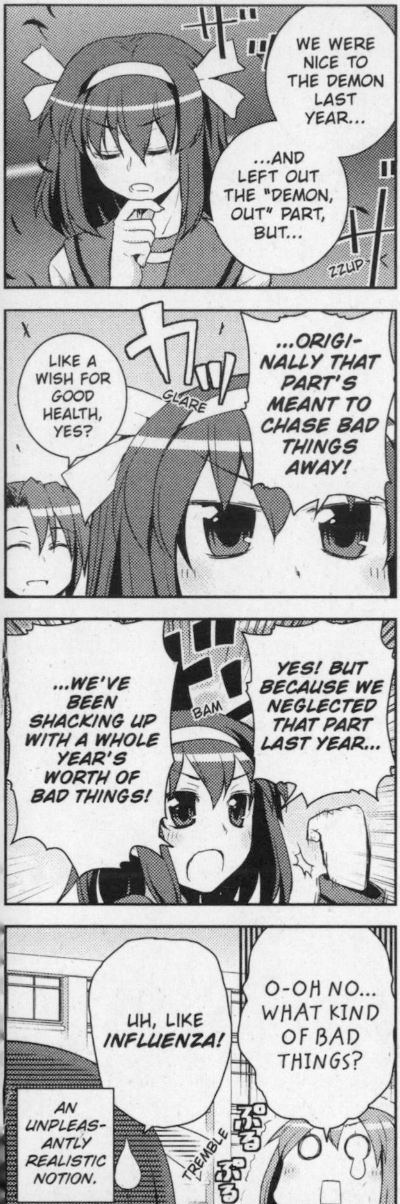
WE WERE NICE TO THE DEMON LAST YEAR...
...AND LEFT OUT THE "DEMON, OUT" PART, BUT...
ZZUP
...ORIGINALLY THAT PART'S MEANT TO CHASE BAD THINGS AWAY!
GLARE
LIKE A WISH FOR GOOD HEALTH, YES?
YES! BUT BECAUSE WE NEGLECTED THAT PART LAST YEAR...
BAM
...WE'VE BEEN SHACKING UP WITH A WHOLE YEAR'S WORTH OF BAD THINGS!
O-OH NO... WHAT KIND OF BAD THINGS?
UH, LIKE INFLUENZA!
TREMBLE
ぷるぷる
AN UNPLEASANTLY REALISTIC NOTION.

A WHOLE YEAR'S WORTH

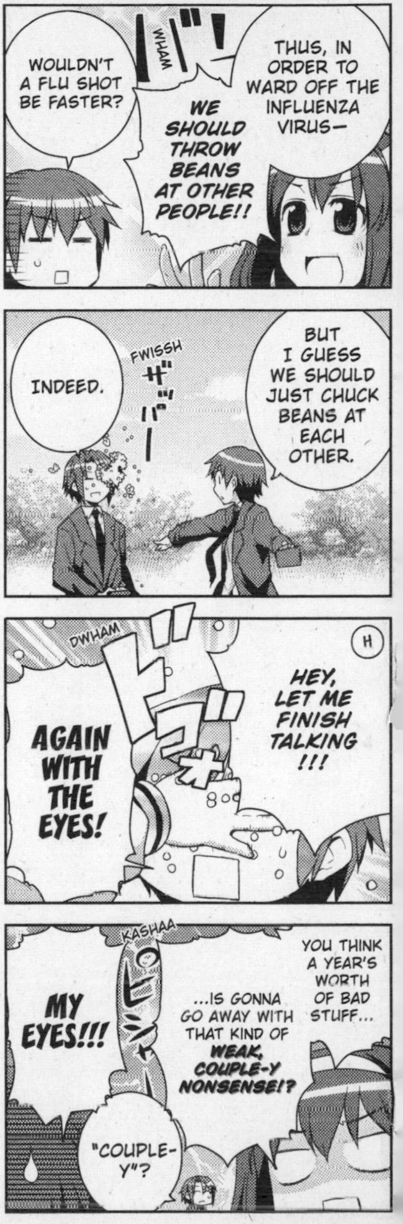
THUS, IN ORDER TO WARD OFF THE INFLUENZA VIRUS—
WE SHOULD THROW BEANS AT OTHER PEOPLE!!
WHAM
WOULDN'T A FLU SHOT BE FASTER?
BUT I GUESS WE SHOULD JUST CHUCK BEANS AT EACH OTHER.
FWISSH
INDEED.
HEY, LET ME FINISH TALKING!!!
DWHAM
AGAIN WITH THE EYES!
YOU THINK A YEAR'S WORTH OF BAD STUFF...
...IS GONNA GO AWAY WITH THAT KIND OF WEAK, COUPLE-Y NONSENSE!?
KASHAA
MY EYES!!!
"COUPLE-Y"?

SPECIALISTS

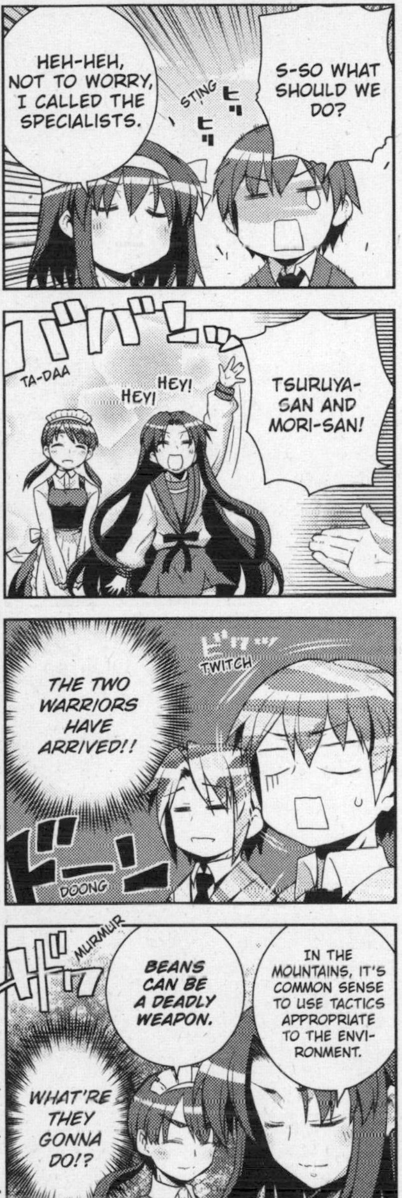
S-SO WHAT SHOULD WE DO?
STING
HEH-HEH, NOT TO WORRY, I CALLED THE SPECIALISTS.
TSURUYA-SAN AND MORI-SAN!
HEY!
HEY!
TA-DAA
TWITCH
THE TWO WARRIORS HAVE ARRIVED!!
DOONG
IN THE MOUNTAINS, IT'S COMMON SENSE TO USE TACTICS APPROPRIATE TO THE ENVI-RONMENT.
BEANS CAN BE A DEADLY WEAPON.
MURMUR
WHAT'RE THEY GONNA DO!?

•Mikuru-chan •The acorable idol of the SOS Brigade. Also, st'angely, the oldest.

•Nagato •Her alien powers make her skiled at analysis. Has a weakness for tasty foods and snacks.

•Oniguchi •Taniguchi in demon form. Ever since cppearing in volume one, seems to be turning into a regular character?

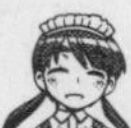

•Mori-san •One of the martial characters in Haruhi-chan. Gets along well with fellow fighter Tsuruya-san?

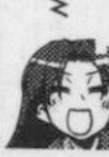

•Tsuruya-san •Has evidently mastered environmental tactics in addition to martial arts.

TEST THROW

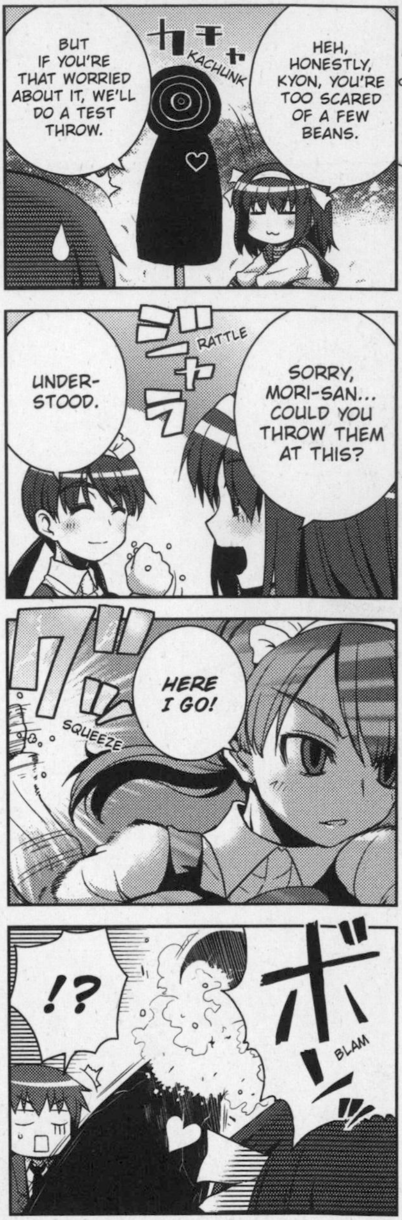

HEH, HONESTLY, KYON, YOU'RE TOO SCARED OF A FEW BEANS.
KACHUNK
BUT IF YOU'RE THAT WORRIED ABOUT IT, WE'LL DO A TEST THROW.
SORRY, MORI-SAN... COULD YOU THROW THEM AT THIS?
RATTLE
UNDER-STOOD.
HERE I GO!
SQUEEZE
BLAM
!?

PERSUASION

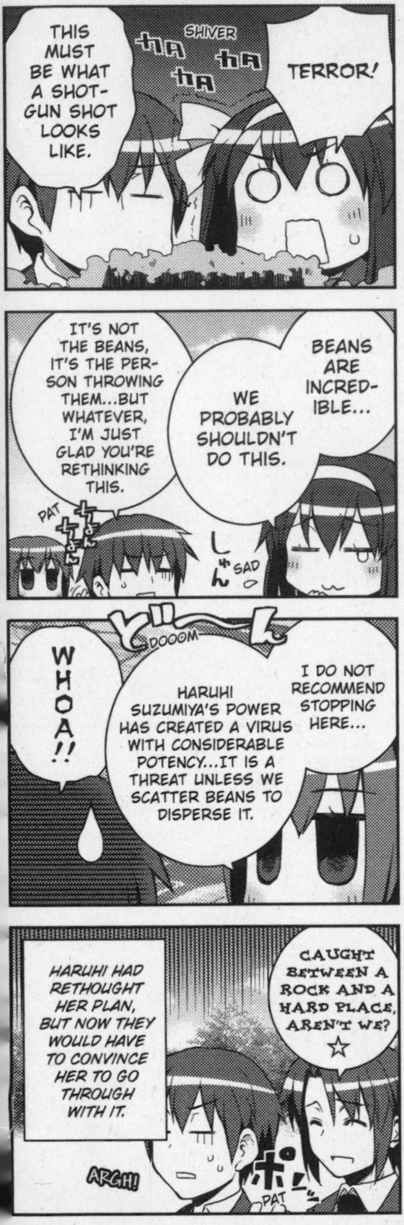

TERROR!
SHIVER
THIS MUST BE WHAT A SHOT-GUN SHOT LOOKS LIKE.
BEANS ARE INCRED-IBLE...
WE PROBABLY SHOULDN'T DO THIS.
SAD
IT'S NOT THE BEANS, IT'S THE PER-SON THROWING THEM...BUT WHATEVER, I'M JUST GLAD YOU'RE RETHINKING THIS.
PAT
DOOOM
I DO NOT RECOMMEND STOPPING HERE...
HARUHI SUZUMIYA'S POWER HAS CREATED A VIRUS WITH CONSIDERABLE POTENCY...IT IS A THREAT UNLESS WE SCATTER BEANS TO DISPERSE IT.
WHOA!!
CAUGHT BETWEEN A ROCK AND A HARD PLACE, AREN'T WE? ☆
HARUHI HAD RETHOUGHT HER PLAN, BUT NOW THEY WOULD HAVE TO CONVINCE HER TO GO THROUGH WITH IT.
PAT
ARGH!

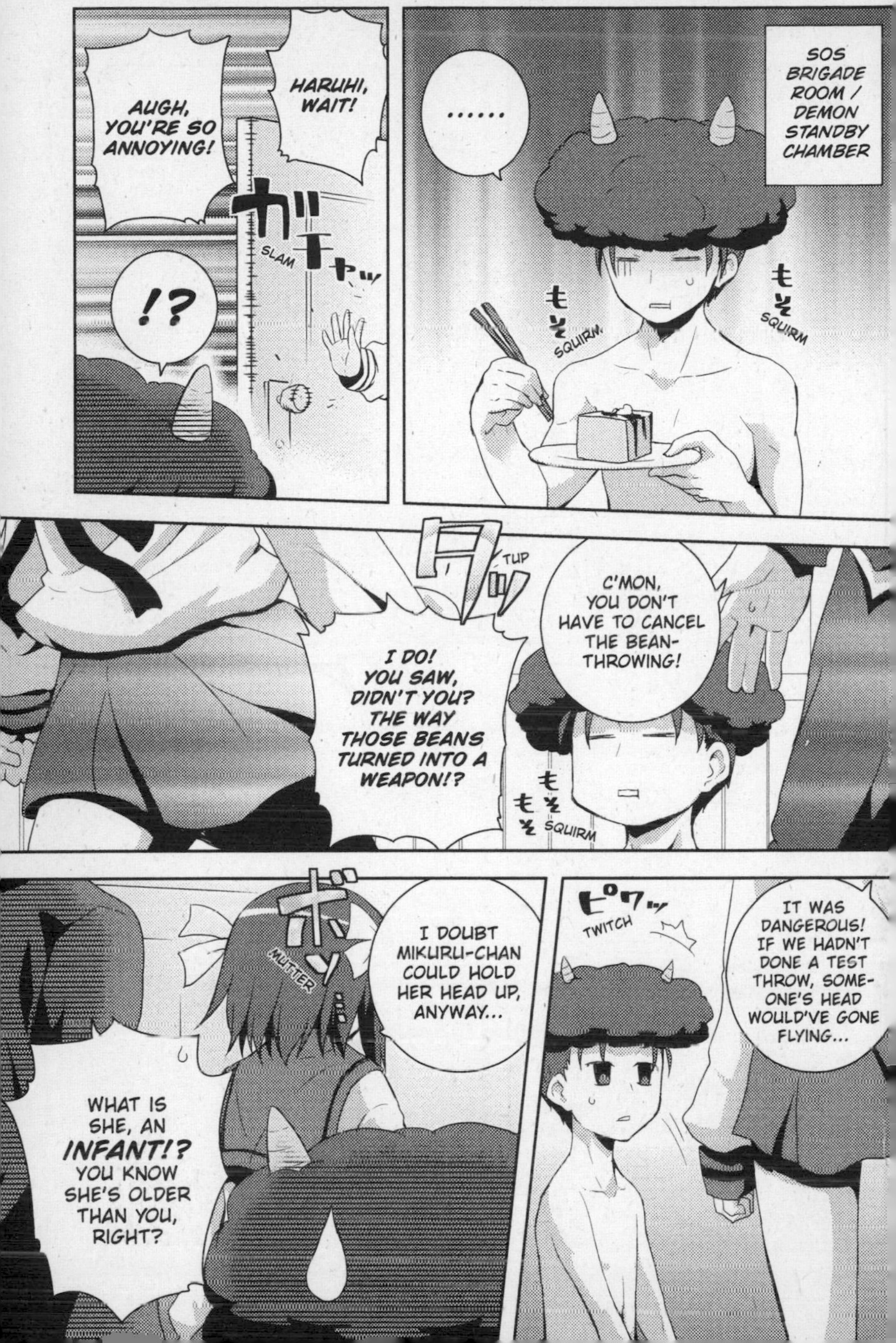
SOS BRIGADE ROOM / DEMON STANDBY CHAMBER
......
SQUIRM
SQUIRM
HARUHI, WAIT!
AUGH, YOU'RE SO ANNOYING!
SLAM
!?
C'MON, YOU DON'T HAVE TO CANCEL THE BEAN-THROWING!
TUP
I DO! YOU SAW, DIDN'T YOU? THE WAY THOSE BEANS TURNED INTO A WEAPON!?
SQUIRM
IT WAS DANGEROUS! IF WE HADN'T DONE A TEST THROW, SOMEONE'S HEAD WOULD'VE GONE FLYING...
TWITCH
I DOUBT MIKURU-CHAN COULD HOLD HER HEAD UP, ANYWAY...
MUTTER
WHAT IS SHE, AN INFANT!? YOU KNOW SHE'S OLDER THAN YOU, RIGHT?

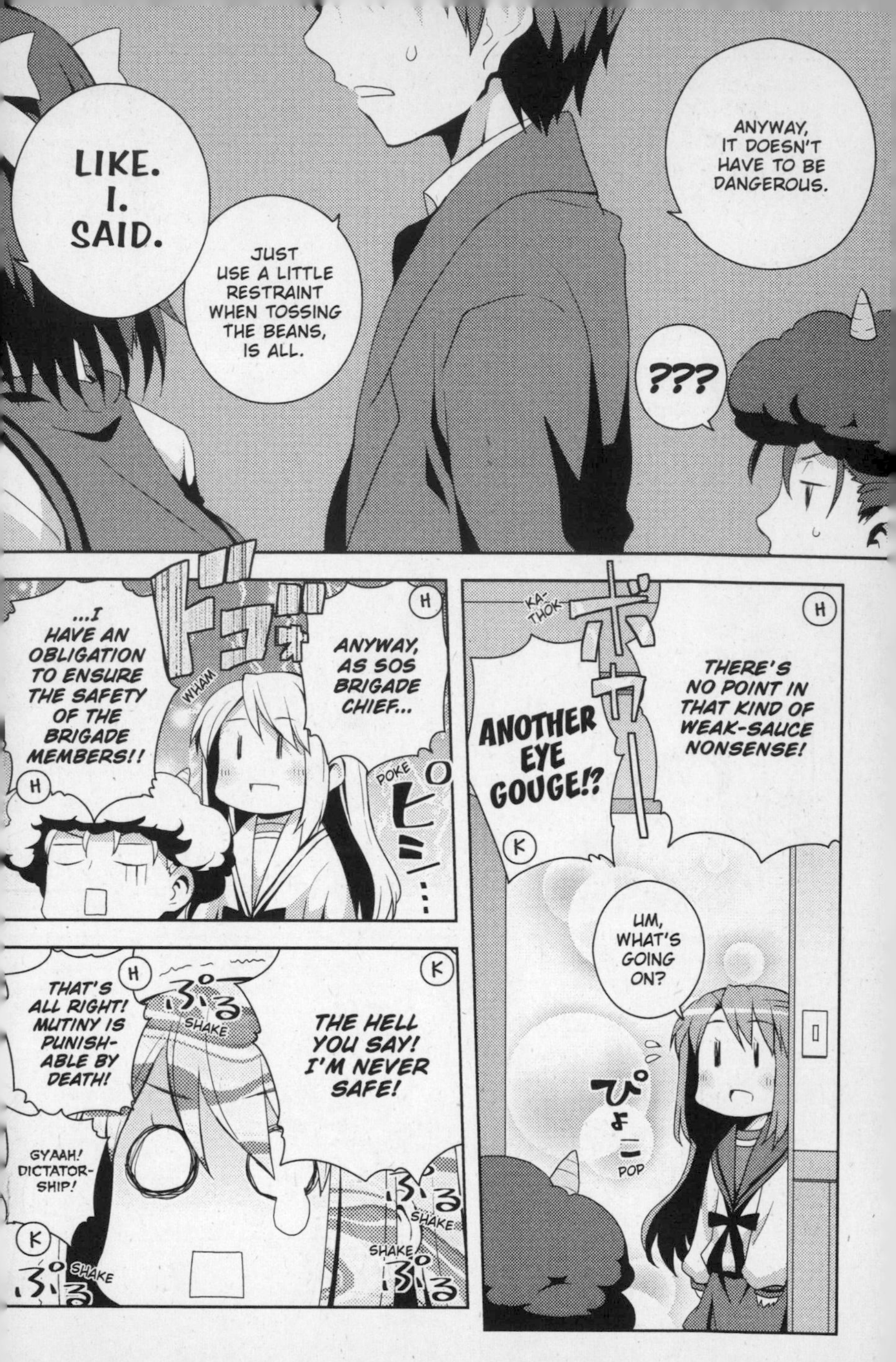
ANYWAY, IT DOESN'T HAVE TO BE DANGEROUS.
???
JUST USE A LITTLE RESTRAINT WHEN TOSSING THE BEANS, IS ALL.
LIKE. I. SAID.
KA-THOK
THERE'S NO POINT IN THAT KIND OF WEAK-SAUCE NONSENSE!
ANOTHER EYE GOUGE!?
UM, WHAT'S GOING ON?
POP
WHAM
ANYWAY, AS SOS BRIGADE CHIEF...
...I HAVE AN OBLIGATION TO ENSURE THE SAFETY OF THE BRIGADE MEMBERS!!
POKE
THE HELL YOU SAY! I'M NEVER SAFE!
THAT'S ALL RIGHT! MUTINY IS PUNISH-ABLE BY DEATH!
SHAKE
GYAAH! DICTATOR-SHIP!
SHAKE
SHAKE
SHAKE

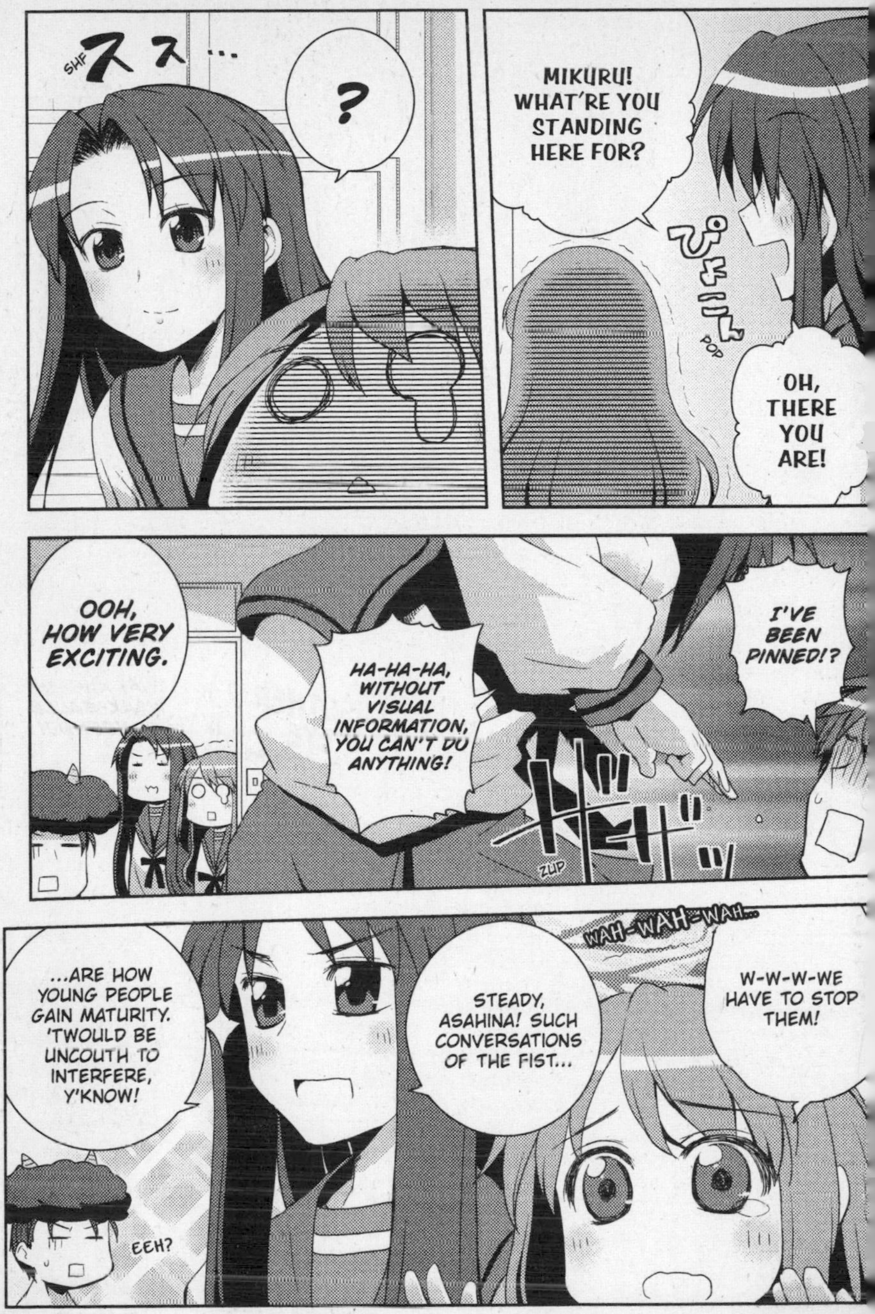
MIKURU! WHAT'RE YOU STANDING HERE FOR?
ぴょこん
POP
OH, THERE YOU ARE!
SHF
スス...
?
I'VE BEEN PINNED!?
ZUP
HA-HA-HA, WITHOUT VISUAL INFORMATION, YOU CAN'T DO ANYTHING!
OOH, HOW VERY EXCITING.
W-W-W-WE HAVE TO STOP THEM!
WAH-WAH-WAH...
STEADY, ASAHINA! SUCH CONVERSATIONS OF THE FIST...
...ARE HOW YOUNG PEOPLE GAIN MATURITY. 'TWOULD BE UNCOUTH TO INTERFERE, Y'KNOW!
EEH?

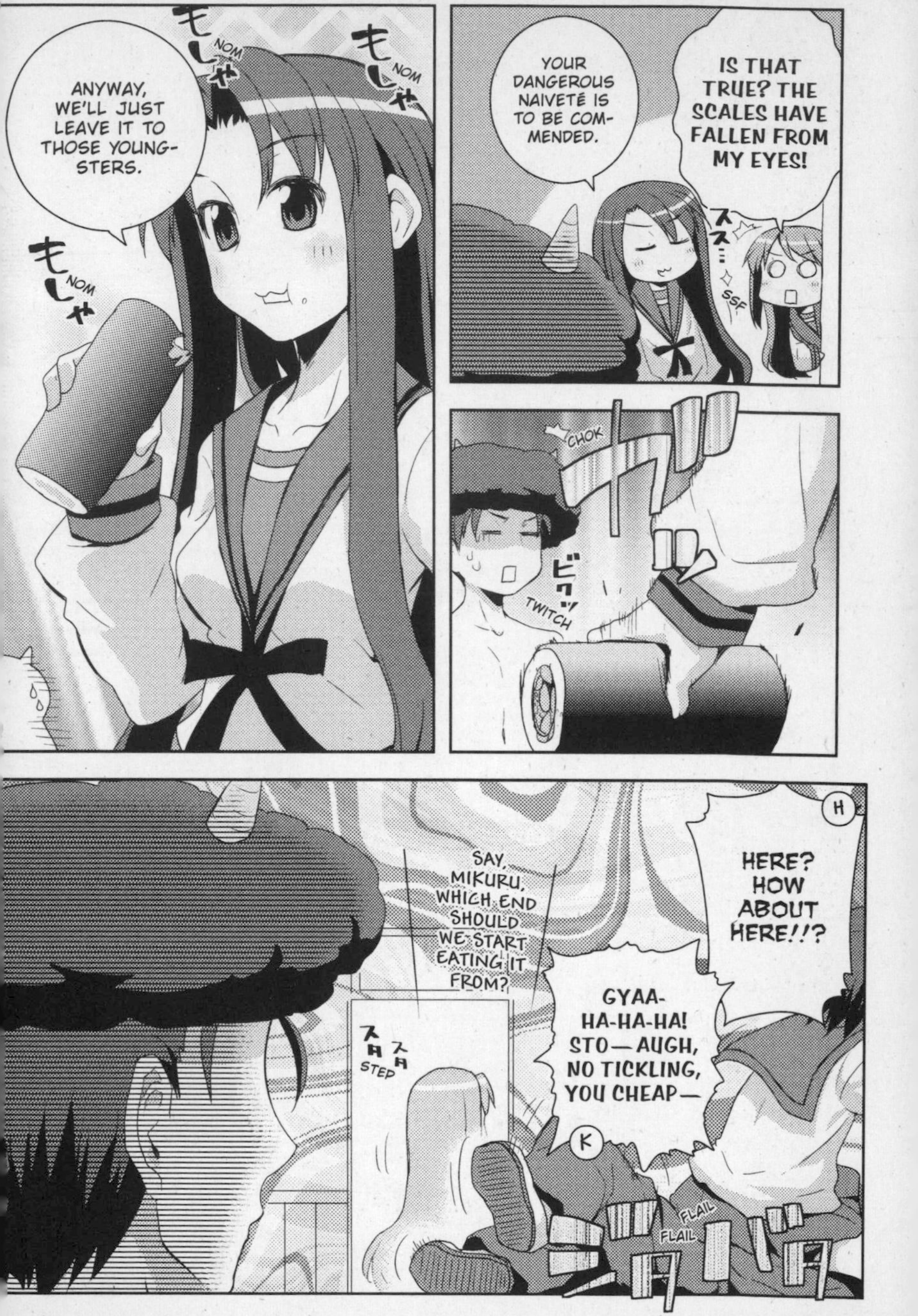
IS THAT TRUE? THE SCALES HAVE FALLEN FROM MY EYES!
YOUR DANGEROUS NAIVETÉ IS TO BE COMMENDED.
ススッ
SSF
CHOK
ビクッ
TWITCH
もしゃ
NOM
もしゃ
NOM
ANYWAY, WE'LL JUST LEAVE IT TO THOSE YOUNGSTERS.
もしゃ
NOM
H
HERE? HOW ABOUT HERE!!?
GYAA-HA-HA-HA! STO—AUGH, NO TICKLING, YOU CHEAP—
K
FLAIL
FLAIL
SAY, MIKURU, WHICH END SHOULD WE START EATING IT FROM?
スタスタ
STEP

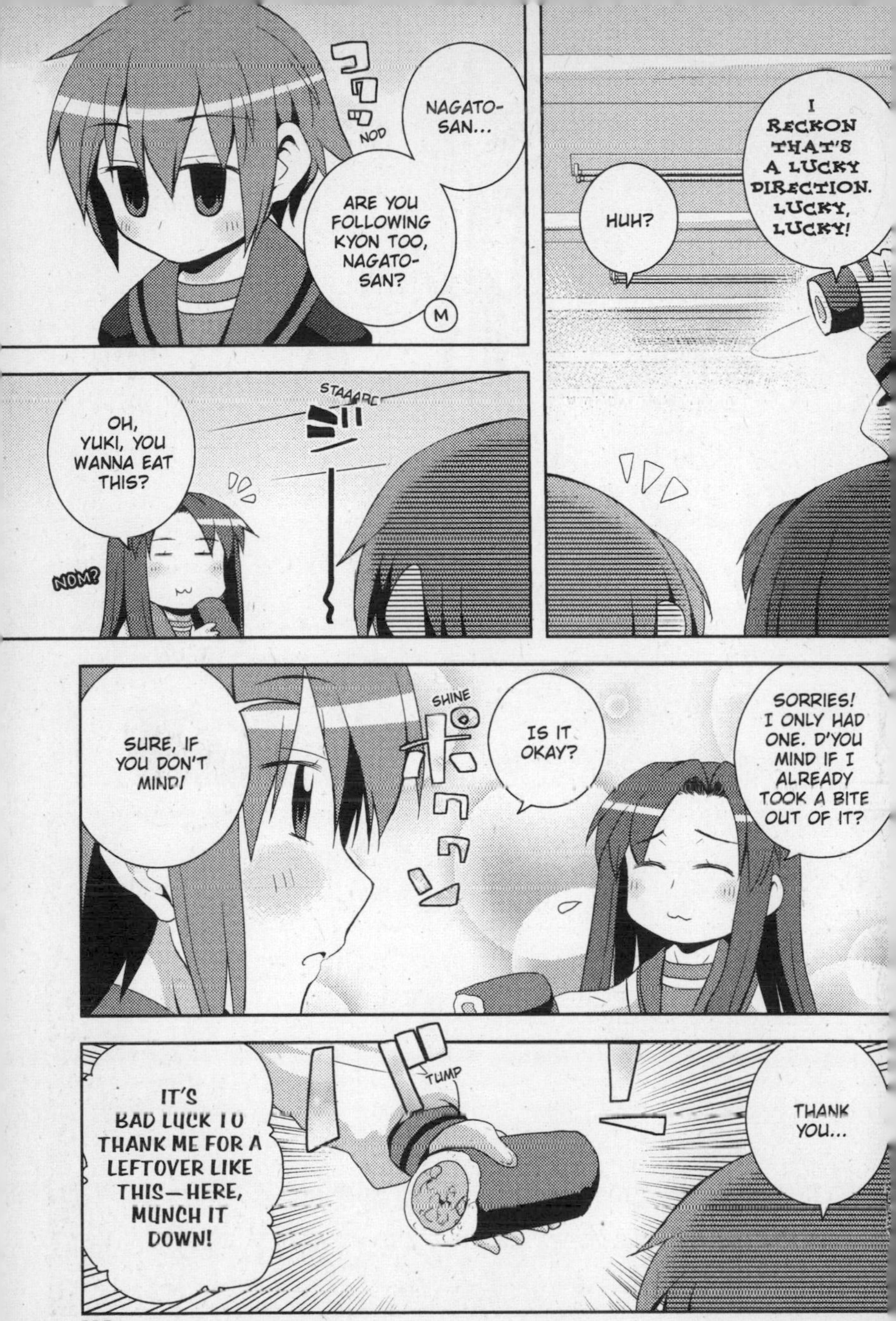
I RECKON THAT'S A LUCKY DIRECTION. LUCKY, LUCKY!
HUH?
NAGATO-SAN...
NOD
ARE YOU FOLLOWING KYON TOO, NAGATO-SAN?
M
STAAARE
OH, YUKI, YOU WANNA EAT THIS?
NOM?
SORRIES! I ONLY HAD ONE. D'YOU MIND IF I ALREADY TOOK A BITE OUT OF IT?
IS IT OKAY?
SHINE
SURE, IF YOU DON'T MIND!
THANK YOU...
TUMP
IT'S BAD LUCK TO THANK ME FOR A LEFTOVER LIKE THIS—HERE, MUNCH IT DOWN!

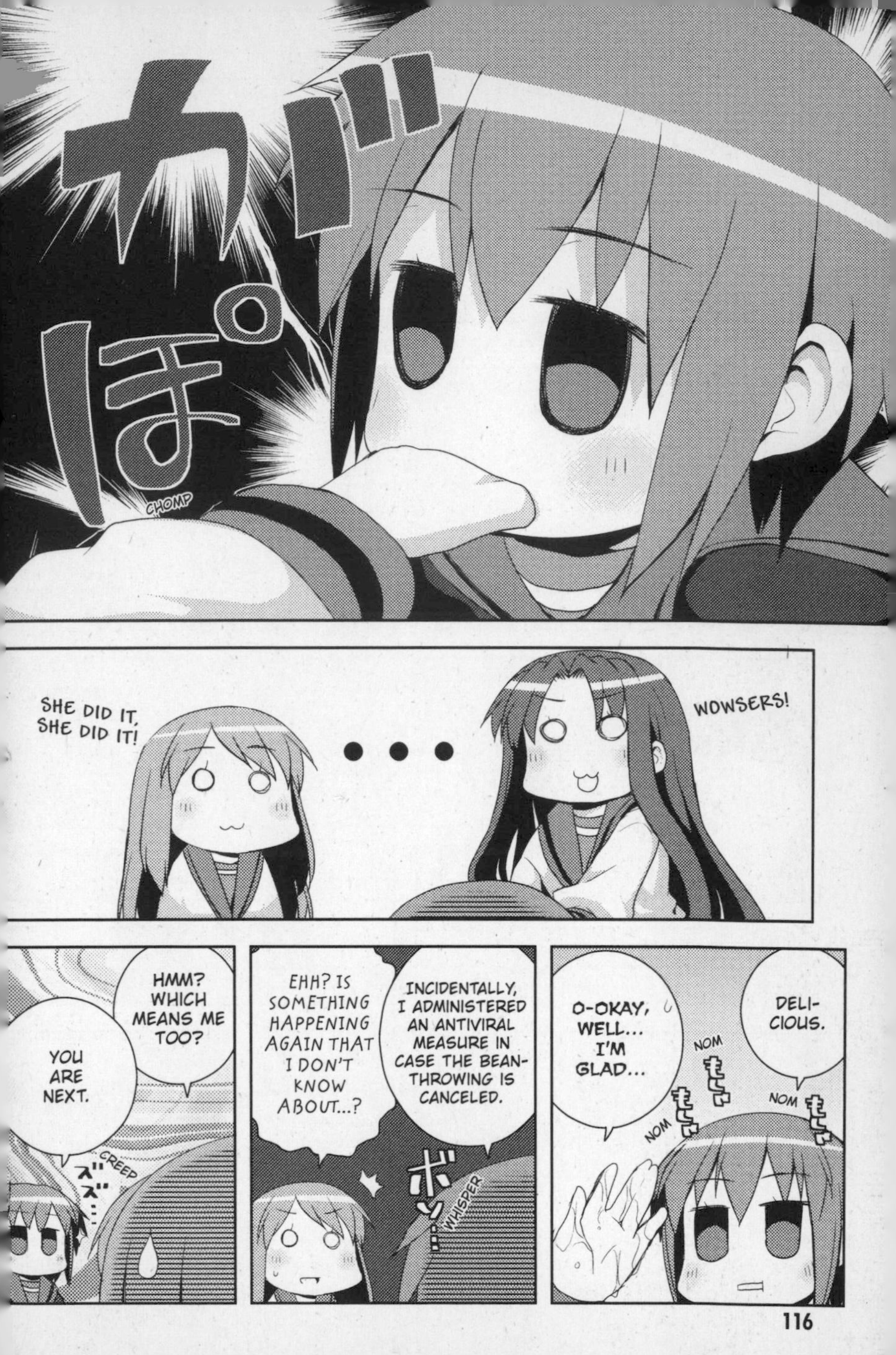
CHOMP
WOWSERS!
• • •
SHE DID IT, SHE DID IT!
DELI- CIOUS.
NOM
NOM
NOM
O-OKAY, WELL... I'M GLAD...
INCIDENTALLY, I ADMINISTERED AN ANTIVIRAL MEASURE IN CASE THE BEAN-THROWING IS CANCELED.
WHISPER
EHH? IS SOMETHING HAPPENING AGAIN THAT I DON'T KNOW ABOUT...?
HMM? WHICH MEANS ME TOO?
YOU ARE NEXT.
CREEP

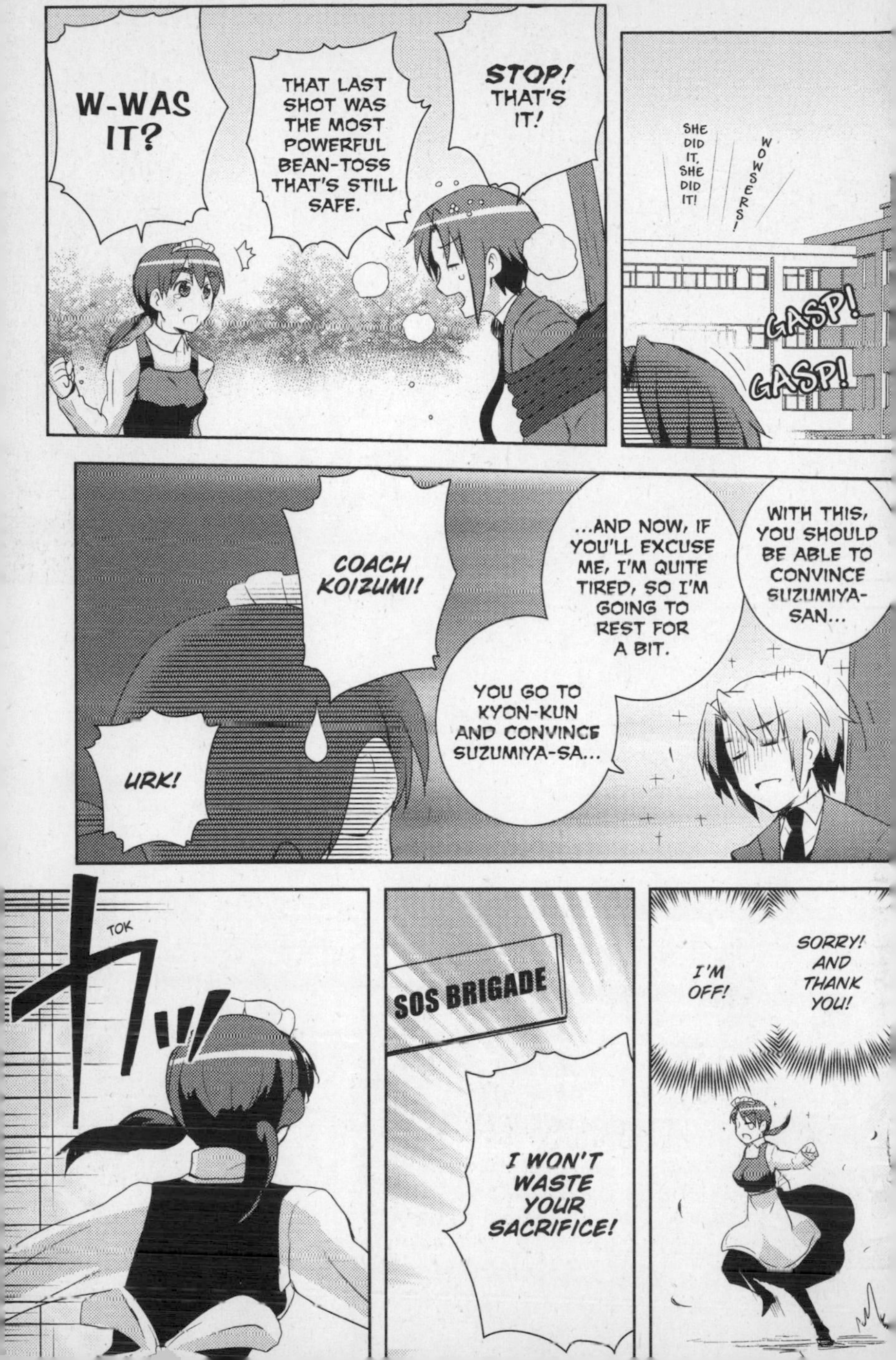
SHE DID IT, SHE DID IT!
WOWSERS!
GASP!
GASP!
STOP! THAT'S IT!
THAT LAST SHOT WAS THE MOST POWERFUL BEAN-TOSS THAT'S STILL SAFE.
W-WAS IT?
WITH THIS, YOU SHOULD BE ABLE TO CONVINCE SUZUMIYA-SAN...
...AND NOW, IF YOU'LL EXCUSE ME, I'M QUITE TIRED, SO I'M GOING TO REST FOR A BIT.
YOU GO TO KYON-KUN AND CONVINCE SUZUMIYA-SA...
COACH KOIZUMI!
URK!
SORRY! AND THANK YOU!
I'M OFF!
SOS BRIGADE
I WON'T WASTE YOUR SACRIFICE!
TOK

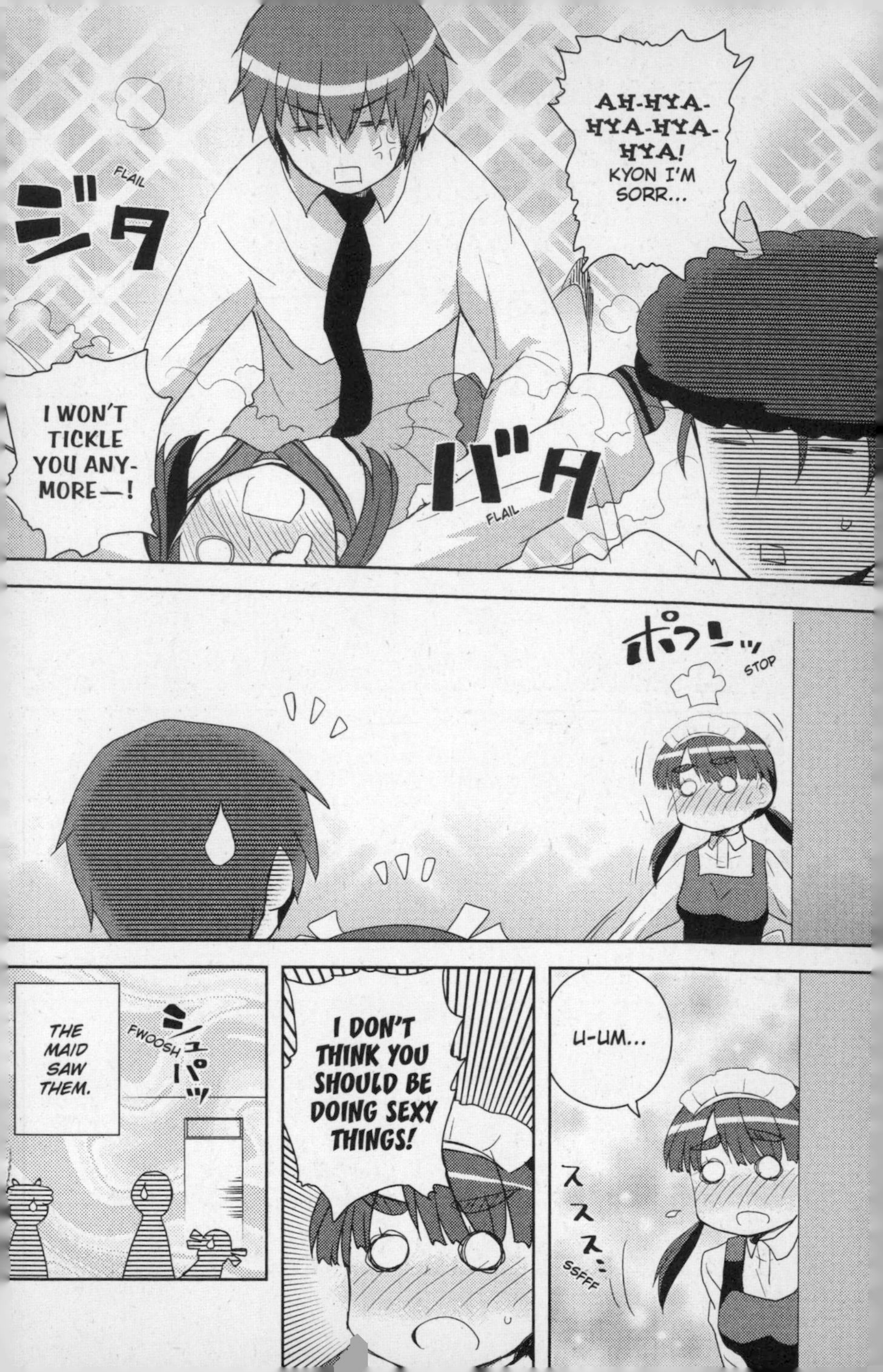
AH-HYA-HYA-HYA-HYA! KYON I'M SORR...
ジタ
FLAIL
バタ
FLAIL
I WON'T TICKLE YOU ANY-MORE—!
ポフーッ
STOP
U-UM...
ススス
SSFFF
I DON'T THINK YOU SHOULD BE DOING SEXY THINGS!
シュパッ
FWOOSH
THE MAID SAW THEM.

VALENTINE

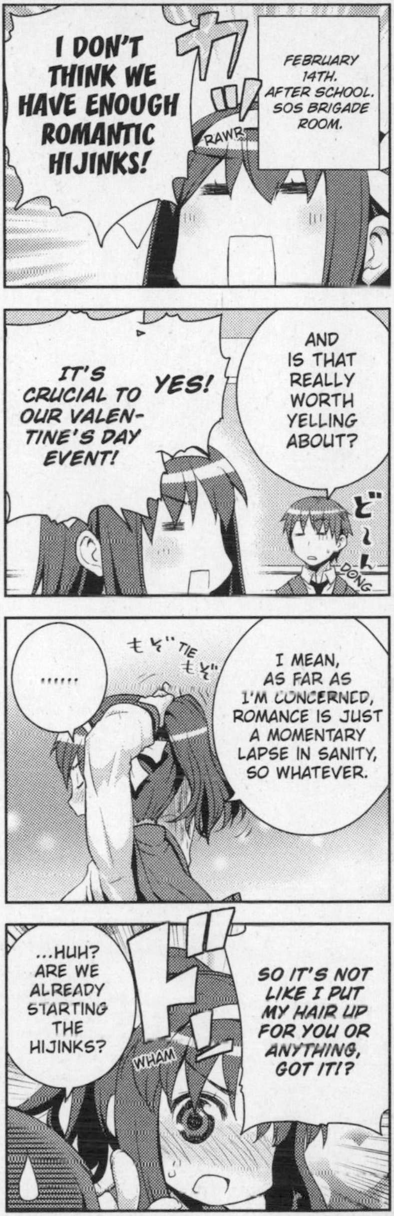
FEBRUARY 14TH. AFTER SCHOOL. SOS BRIGADE ROOM.
RAWR
I DON'T THINK WE HAVE ENOUGH ROMANTIC HIJINKS!
AND IS THAT REALLY WORTH YELLING ABOUT?
DONG
YES!
IT'S CRUCIAL TO OUR VALENTINE'S DAY EVENT!
I MEAN, AS FAR AS I'M CONCERNED, ROMANCE IS JUST A MOMENTARY LAPSE IN SANITY, SO WHATEVER.
TIE
......
SO IT'S NOT LIKE I PUT MY HAIR UP FOR YOU OR ANYTHING, GOT IT!?
WHAM
...HUH? ARE WE ALREADY STARTING THE HIJINKS?

TSUNDERE PLUS KLUTZ

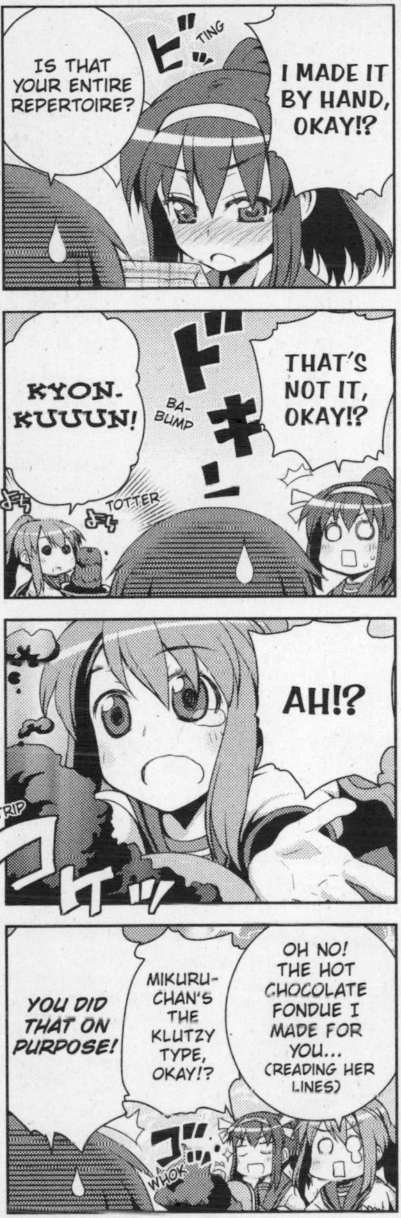
I MADE IT BY HAND, OKAY!?
TING
IS THAT YOUR ENTIRE REPERTOIRE?
THAT'S NOT IT, OKAY!?
BA-BUMP
KYON-KUUUN!
TOTTER
AH!?
TRIP
OH NO! THE HOT CHOCOLATE FONDUE I MADE FOR YOU... (READING HER LINES)
MIKURU-CHAN'S THE KLUTZY TYPE, OKAY!?
WHOK
YOU DID THAT ON PURPOSE!

THE MYSTERIOUS GIRL

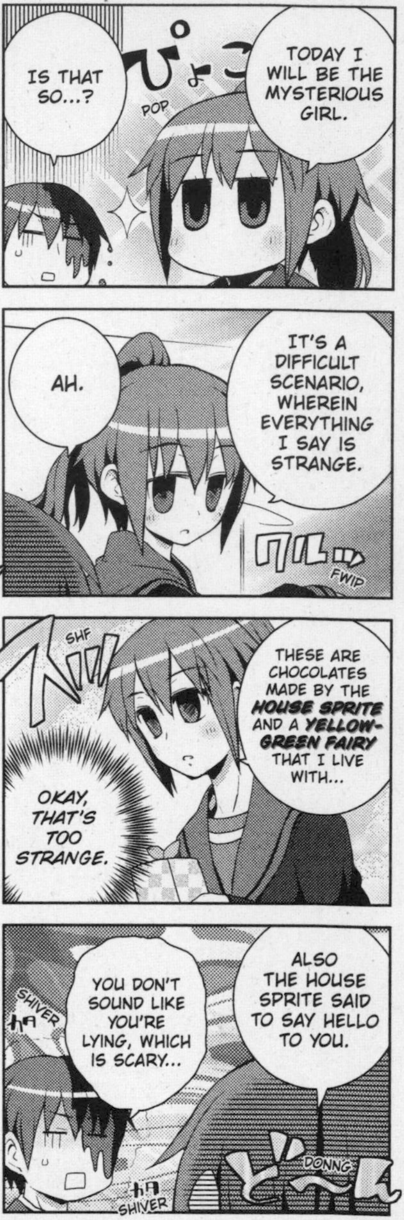
TODAY I WILL BE THE MYSTERIOUS GIRL.
POP
IS THAT SO...?
IT'S A DIFFICULT SCENARIO, WHEREIN EVERYTHING I SAY IS STRANGE.
AH.
FWIP
SHF
THESE ARE CHOCOLATES MADE BY THE HOUSE SPRITE AND A YELLOW-GREEN FAIRY THAT I LIVE WITH...
OKAY, THAT'S TOO STRANGE.
ALSO THE HOUSE SPRITE SAID TO SAY HELLO TO YOU.
YOU DON'T SOUND LIKE YOU'RE LYING, WHICH IS SCARY...
SHIVER
DONNG
SHIVER

NECESSITY

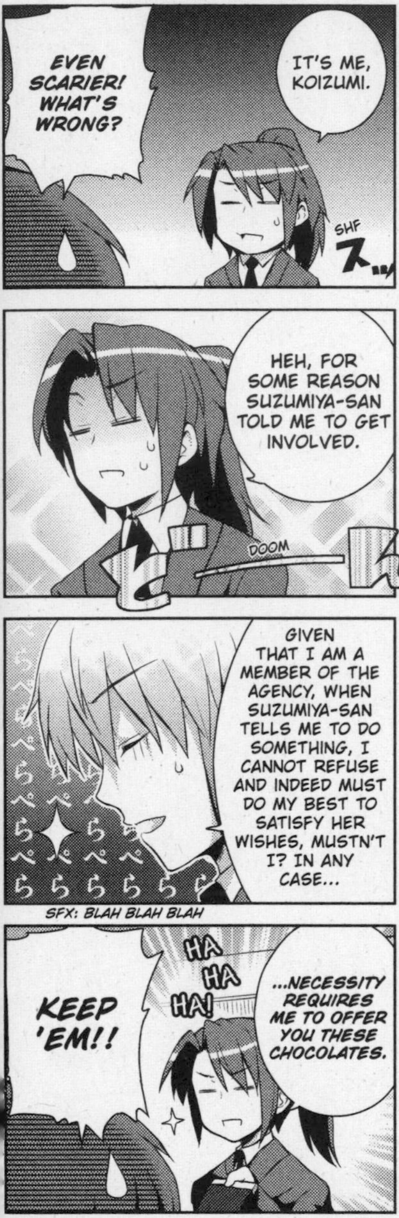
IT'S ME, KOIZUMI.
EVEN SCARIER! WHAT'S WRONG?
SHF
HEH, FOR SOME REASON SUZUMIYA-SAN TOLD ME TO GET INVOLVED.
DOOM
GIVEN THAT I AM A MEMBER OF THE AGENCY, WHEN SUZUMIYA-SAN TELLS ME TO DO SOMETHING, I CANNOT REFUSE AND INDEED MUST DO MY BEST TO SATISFY HER WISHES, MUSTN'T I? IN ANY CASE...
SFX: BLAH BLAH BLAH
...NECESSITY REQUIRES ME TO OFFER YOU THESE CHOCOLATES.
HA HA HA!
KEEP 'EM!!

BRAINS

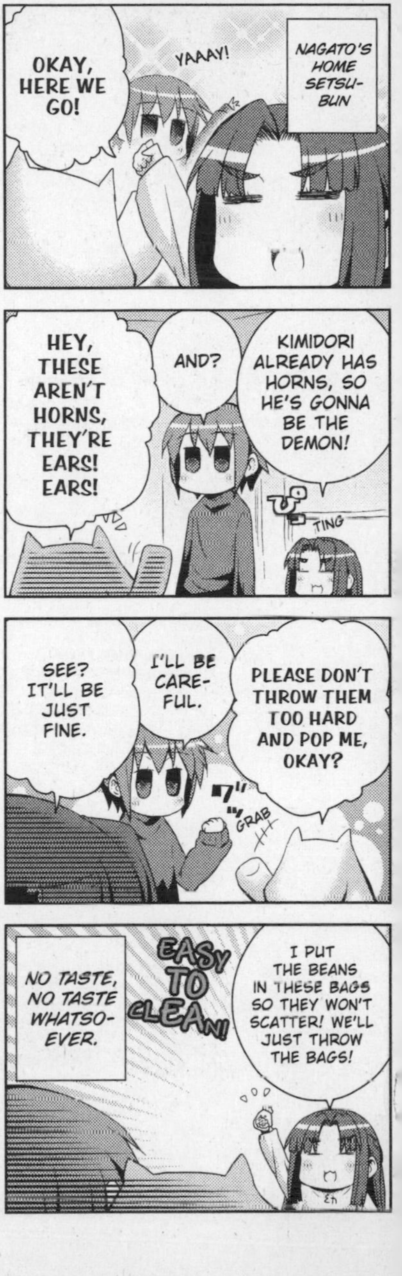
NAGATO'S HOME SETSU-BUN
YAAAY!
OKAY, HERE WE GO!
KIMIDORI ALREADY HAS HORNS, SO HE'S GONNA BE THE DEMON!
TING
AND?
HEY, THESE AREN'T HORNS, THEY'RE EARS! EARS!
PLEASE DON'T THROW THEM TOO HARD AND POP ME, OKAY?
GRAB
I'LL BE CARE-FUL.
SEE? IT'LL BE JUST FINE.
I PUT THE BEANS IN THESE BAGS SO THEY WON'T SCATTER! WE'LL JUST THROW THE BAGS!
EASY TO CLEAN!
NO TASTE, NO TASTE WHATSO-EVER.

AGE

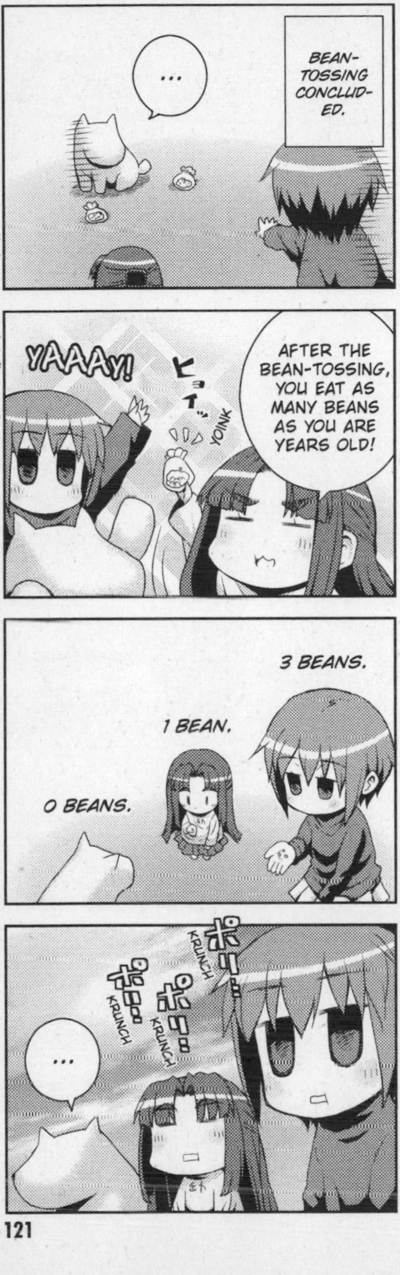
BEAN-TOSSING CONCLUD-ED.
...
AFTER THE BEAN-TOSSING, YOU EAT AS MANY BEANS AS YOU ARE YEARS OLD!
YOINK
YAAAy!
3 BEANS.
1 BEAN.
0 BEANS.
KRUNCH
KRUNCH
KRUNCH
...

•Achakura-san •Small, but once she flips into housewife mode, she's the most dependable member of the Nagato household.

•Kimidori-san •A balloon life-form that often teams up with Nagato to trifle with Achakura-san.

FEARLESS

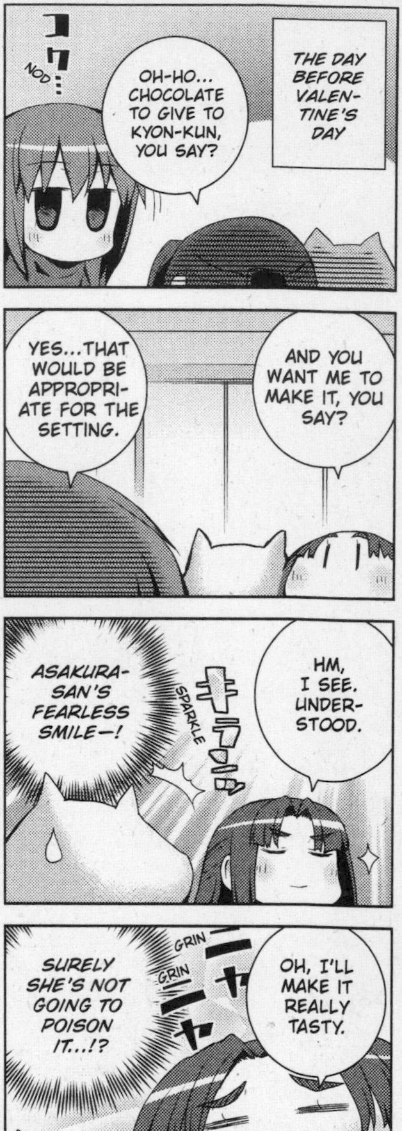
THE DAY BEFORE VALENTINE'S DAY
OH-HO... CHOCOLATE TO GIVE TO KYON-KUN, YOU SAY?
NOD
AND YOU WANT ME TO MAKE IT, YOU SAY?
YES...THAT WOULD BE APPROPRIATE FOR THE SETTING.
HM, I SEE. UNDERSTOOD.
SPARKLE
ASAKURA-SAN'S FEARLESS SMILE—!
OH, I'LL MAKE IT REALLY TASTY.
GRIN GRIN
SURELY SHE'S NOT GOING TO POISON IT...!?

THE MESSAGE'S PATH

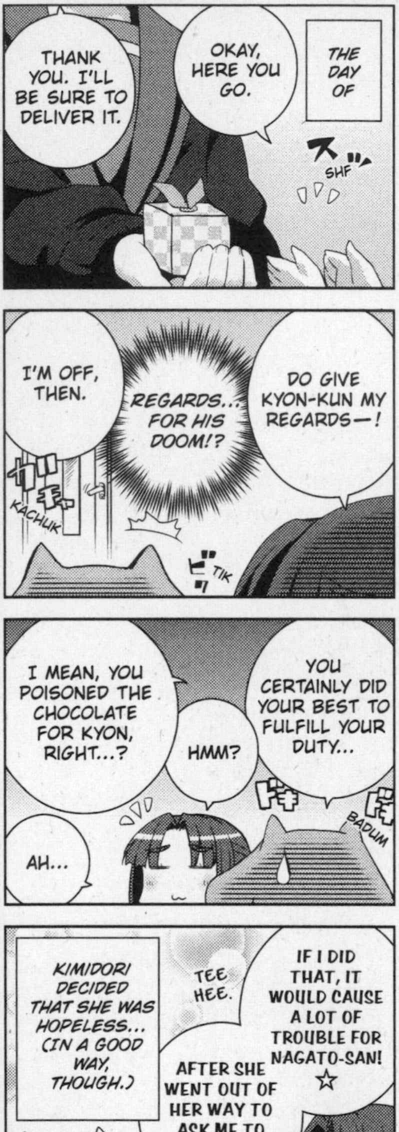
THE DAY OF
OKAY, HERE YOU GO.
SHF
THANK YOU. I'LL BE SURE TO DELIVER IT.
DO GIVE KYON-KUN MY REGARDS—!
REGARDS... FOR HIS DOOM!?
I'M OFF, THEN.
TIK
KACHUK
YOU CERTAINLY DID YOUR BEST TO FULFILL YOUR DUTY...
BADUM
HMM?
I MEAN, YOU POISONED THE CHOCOLATE FOR KYON, RIGHT...?
AH...
IF I DID THAT, IT WOULD CAUSE A LOT OF TROUBLE FOR NAGATO-SAN! ☆
TEE HEE.
AFTER SHE WENT OUT OF HER WAY TO ASK ME TO HELP HER TOO!
KIMIDORI DECIDED THAT SHE WAS HOPELESS... (IN A GOOD WAY, THOUGH.)

MORI-SAN
IN A PONYTAIL

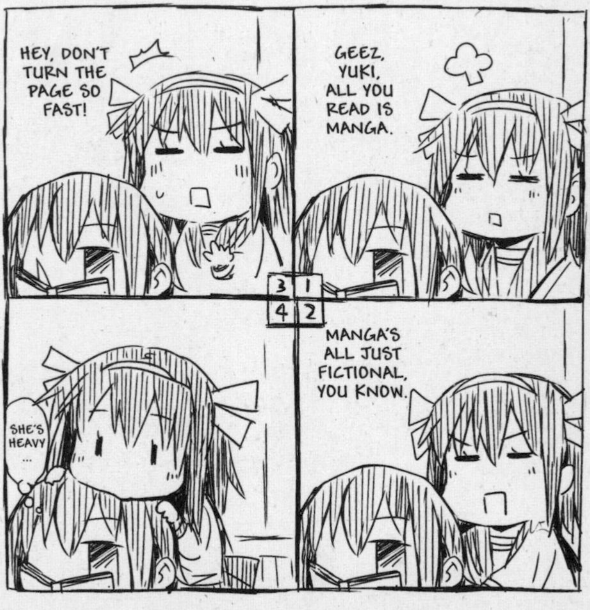
GEEZ, YUKI, ALL YOU READ IS MANGA.
MANGA'S ALL JUST FICTIONAL, YOU KNOW.
HEY, DON'T TURN THE PAGE SO FAST!
SHE'S HEAVY ...

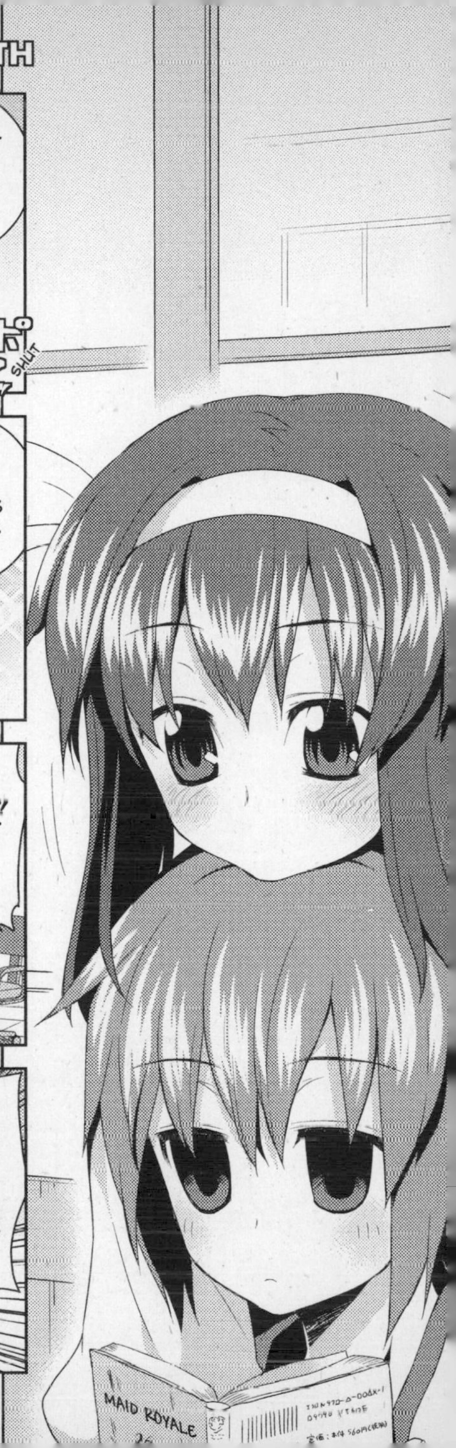
MAID ROYALE

JOB TITLE OF THE MONTH

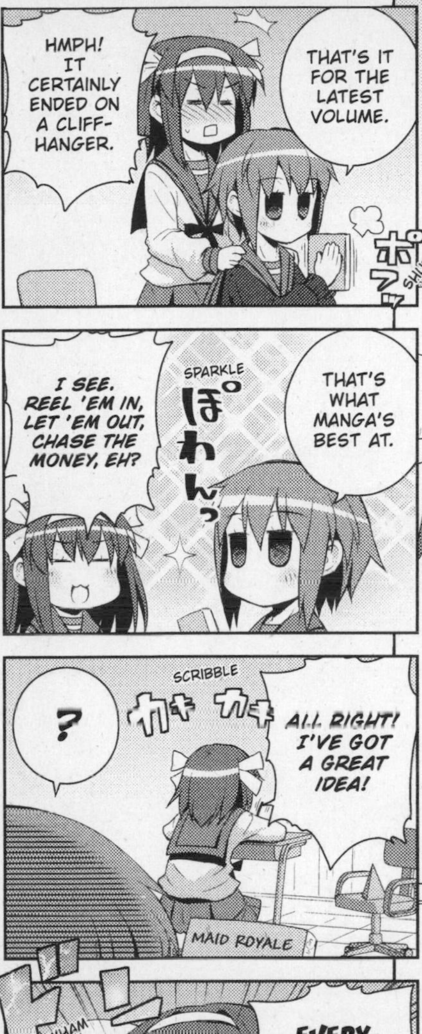
THAT'S IT FOR THE LATEST VOLUME.
ポフッ
SHUT
HMPH! IT CERTAINLY ENDED ON A CLIFF-HANGER.
THAT'S WHAT MANGA'S BEST AT.
SPARKLE
ぽわんっ
I SEE. REEL 'EM IN, LET 'EM OUT, CHASE THE MONEY, EH?
ALL RIGHT! I'VE GOT A GREAT IDEA!
SCRIBBLE
カキ カキ
?
MAID ROYALE
EVERY-BODY, WE'RE DOING A MANGA!
QUEEN OF MANGA
WHAM

QUEEN OF MANGA

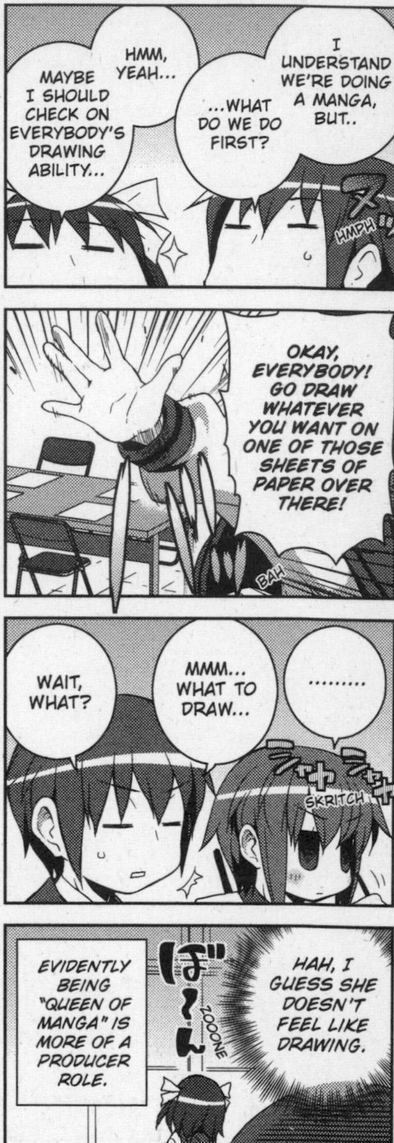
I UNDERSTAND WE'RE DOING A MANGA, BUT..
...WHAT DO WE DO FIRST?
HMM, YEAH...
MAYBE I SHOULD CHECK ON EVERYBODY'S DRAWING ABILITY...
HMPH
OKAY, EVERYBODY! GO DRAW WHATEVER YOU WANT ON ONE OF THOSE SHEETS OF PAPER OVER THERE!
BAH
....
MMM... WHAT TO DRAW...
WAIT, WHAT?
SKRITCH
HAH, I GUESS SHE DOESN'T FEEL LIKE DRAWING.
ZOOONE
EVIDENTLY BEING "QUEEN OF MANGA" IS MORE OF A PRODUCER ROLE.

DRAWING ABILITY

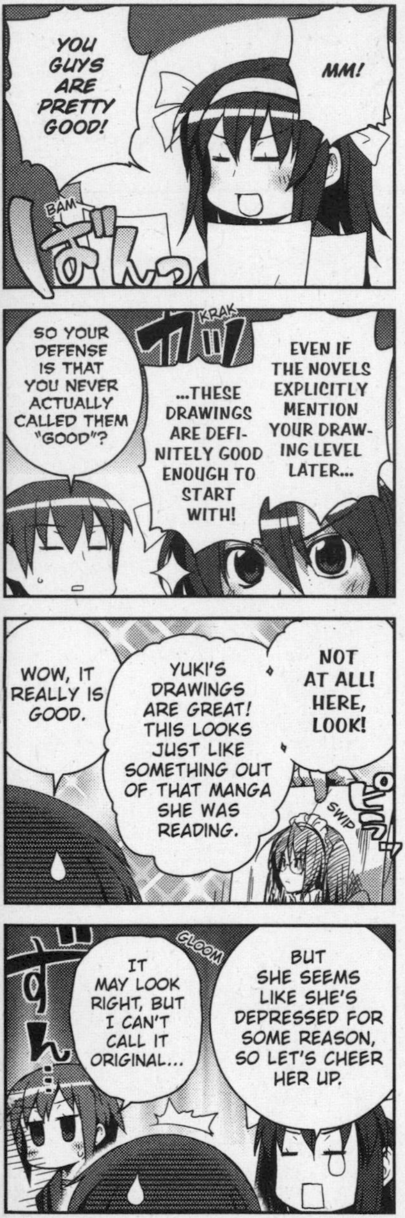
MM!
YOU GUYS ARE PRETTY GOOD!
BAM
EVEN IF THE NOVELS EXPLICITLY MENTION YOUR DRAWING LEVEL LATER...
...THESE DRAWINGS ARE DEFINITELY GOOD ENOUGH TO START WITH!
KRAK
SO YOUR DEFENSE IS THAT YOU NEVER ACTUALLY CALLED THEM "GOOD"?
NOT AT ALL! HERE, LOOK!
SWIP
YUKI'S DRAWINGS ARE GREAT! THIS LOOKS JUST LIKE SOMETHING OUT OF THAT MANGA SHE WAS READING.
WOW, IT REALLY IS GOOD.
BUT SHE SEEMS LIKE SHE'S DEPRESSED FOR SOME REASON, SO LET'S CHEER HER UP.
IT MAY LOOK RIGHT, BUT I CAN'T CALL IT ORIGINAL...
GLOOM

•Haruhi-chan •SOS Brigade brigade chief. Current title: Queen of Manga, but she's more like the Queen of Editors.

• Nagato •Alien. Enjoys reading, but as an otaku, her knowledge of manga and video games is deep.

•Kyon•The main character of this story. Given his wide repertoire of snappy comebacks, he seems to have some otaku knowledge.

STORY

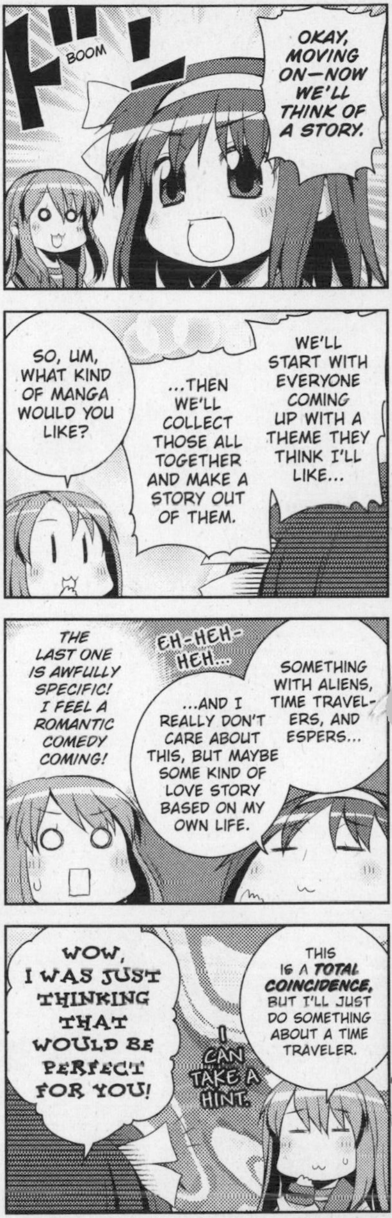
OKAY, MOVING ON—NOW WE'LL THINK OF A STORY.
BOOM
WE'LL START WITH EVERYONE COMING UP WITH A THEME THEY THINK I'LL LIKE...
...THEN WE'LL COLLECT THOSE ALL TOGETHER AND MAKE A STORY OUT OF THEM.
SO, UM, WHAT KIND OF MANGA WOULD YOU LIKE?
SOMETHING WITH ALIENS, TIME TRAVEL-ERS, AND ESPERS...
EH-HEH-HEH...
...AND I REALLY DON'T CARE ABOUT THIS, BUT MAYBE SOME KIND OF LOVE STORY BASED ON MY OWN LIFE.
THE LAST ONE IS AWFULLY SPECIFIC! I FEEL A ROMANTIC COMEDY COMING!
THIS IS A TOTAL COINCIDENCE, BUT I'LL JUST DO SOMETHING ABOUT A TIME TRAVELER.
I CAN TAKE A HINT.
WOW, I WAS JUST THINKING THAT WOULD BE PERFECT FOR YOU!

SCRIPT

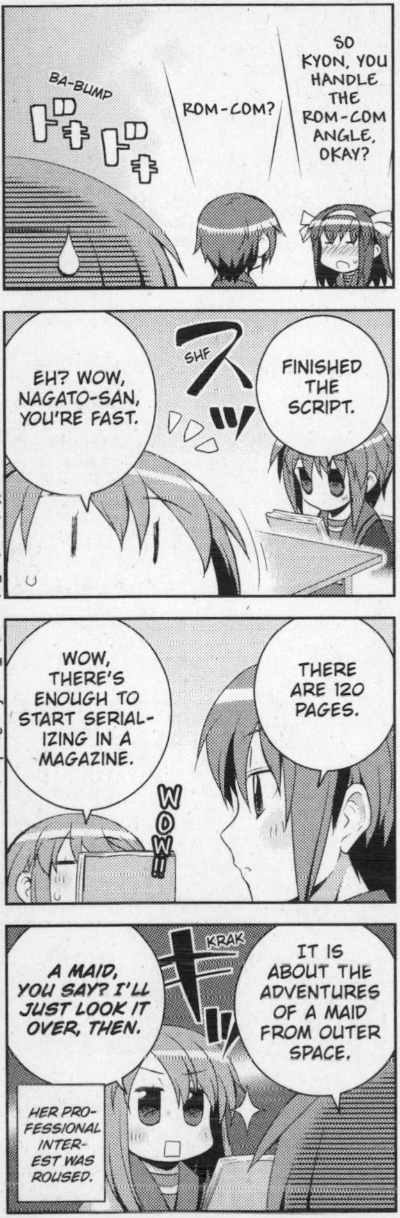
SO KYON, YOU HANDLE THE ROM-COM ANGLE, OKAY?
ROM-COM?
BA-BUMP
FINISHED THE SCRIPT.
SHF
EH? WOW, NAGATO-SAN, YOU'RE FAST.
THERE ARE 120 PAGES.
WOW, THERE'S ENOUGH TO START SERIAL-IZING IN A MAGAZINE.
WOW!!
IT IS ABOUT THE ADVENTURES OF A MAID FROM OUTER SPACE.
KRAK
A MAID, YOU SAY? I'LL JUST LOOK IT OVER, THEN.
HER PRO-FESSIONAL INTER-EST WAS ROUSED.

• Mikuru-chan •Time traveler. Barely knows about the "A" in "Anime."

•Koizumi •Enigmatic Transfer Student of Flame, also an esper. Still active within a team of similar espers.

•Chief Maid •Chief Maid made her mircculous comeback in vol. 26 of Maid Royale.

TOOLS

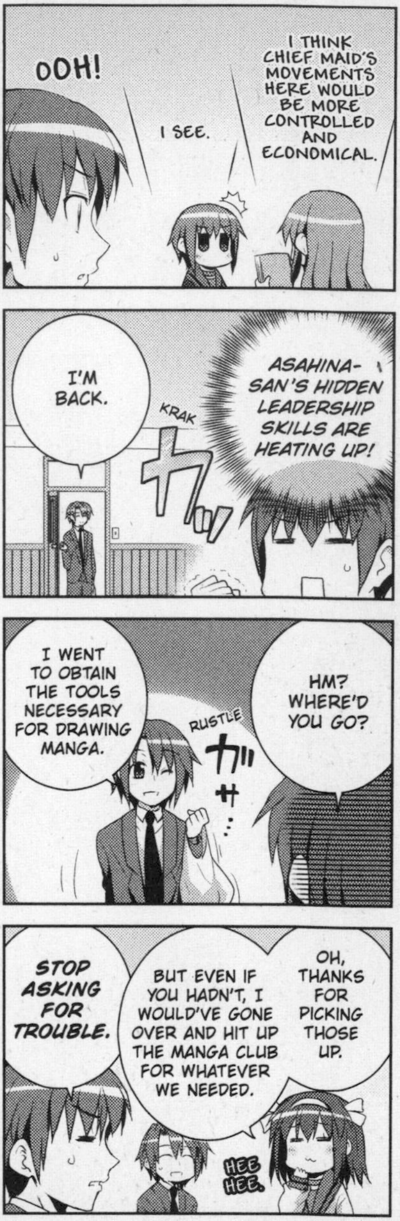
I THINK CHIEF MAID'S MOVEMENTS HERE WOULD BE MORE CONTROLLED AND ECONOMICAL.
I SEE.
OOH!
ASAHINA-SAN'S HIDDEN LEADERSHIP SKILLS ARE HEATING UP!
KRAK
I'M BACK.
HM? WHERE'D YOU GO?
RUSTLE
I WENT TO OBTAIN THE TOOLS NECESSARY FOR DRAWING MANGA.
OH, THANKS FOR PICKING THOSE UP.
BUT EVEN IF YOU HADN'T, I WOULD'VE GONE OVER AND HIT UP THE MANGA CLUB FOR WHATEVER WE NEEDED.
HEE HEE.
STOP ASKING FOR TROUBLE.

PEN NIB

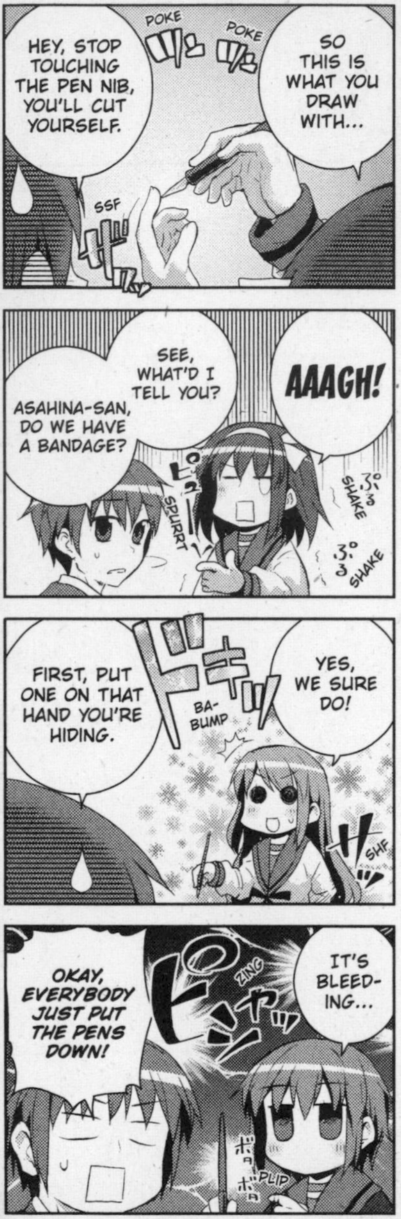
SO THIS IS WHAT YOU DRAW WITH...
POKE
POKE
HEY, STOP TOUCHING THE PEN NIB, YOU'LL CUT YOURSELF.
SSF
AAAGH!
SHAKE
SHAKE
SEE, WHAT'D I TELL YOU?
SPURRT
ASAHINA-SAN, DO WE HAVE A BANDAGE?
YES, WE SURE DO!
BA-BUMP
SHF
FIRST, PUT ONE ON THAT HAND YOU'RE HIDING.
IT'S BLEEDING...
ZING
PLIP
OKAY, EVERYBODY JUST PUT THE PENS DOWN!

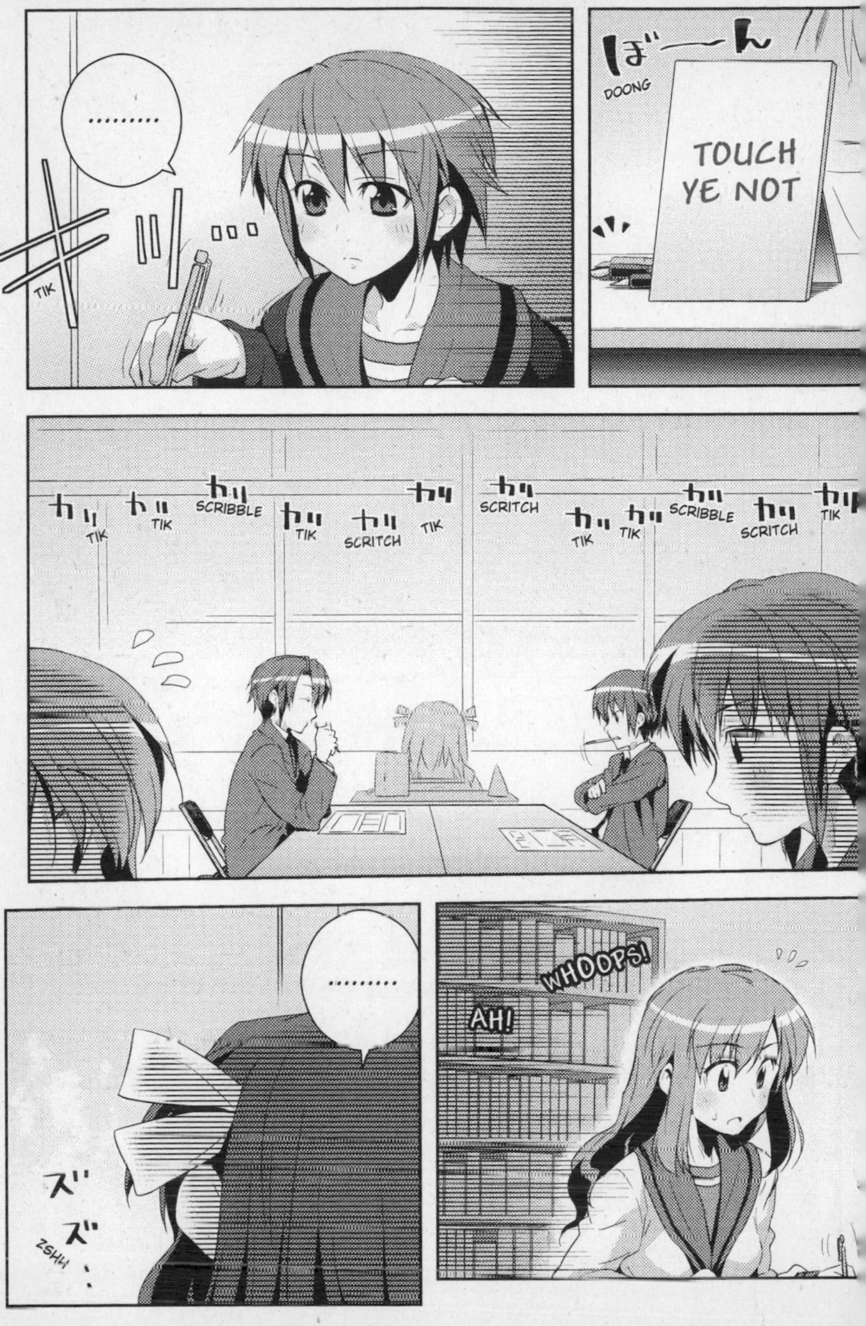
ぼーーん
DOONG
TOUCH YE NOT
....
TIK
カリ
TIK
カリ
SCRITCH
カリ
SCRIBBLE
カリ
TIK
カリ
TIK
カリ
SCRITCH
カリ
TIK
カリ
TIK
カリ
SCRIBBLE
カリ
TIK
カリ
TIK
WHOOPS!
AH!
....
ズズ…
ZSHH

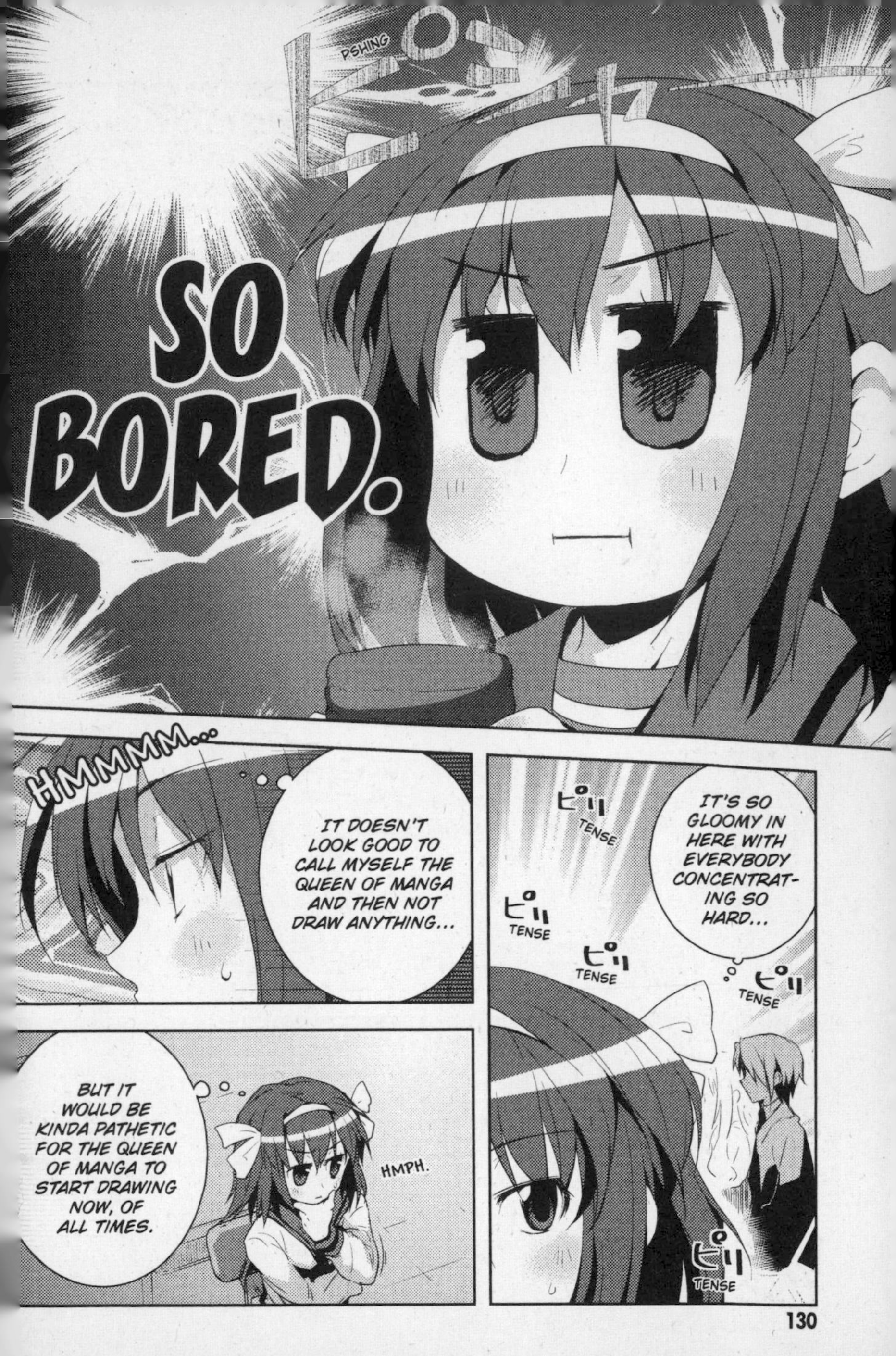
PSHING
SO BORED.
TENSE
TENSE
TENSE
TENSE
IT'S SO GLOOMY IN HERE WITH EVERYBODY CONCENTRAT-ING SO HARD...
TENSE
HMMMM...
IT DOESN'T LOOK GOOD TO CALL MYSELF THE QUEEN OF MANGA AND THEN NOT DRAW ANYTHING...
BUT IT WOULD BE KINDA PATHETIC FOR THE QUEEN OF MANGA TO START DRAWING NOW, OF ALL TIMES.
HMPH.

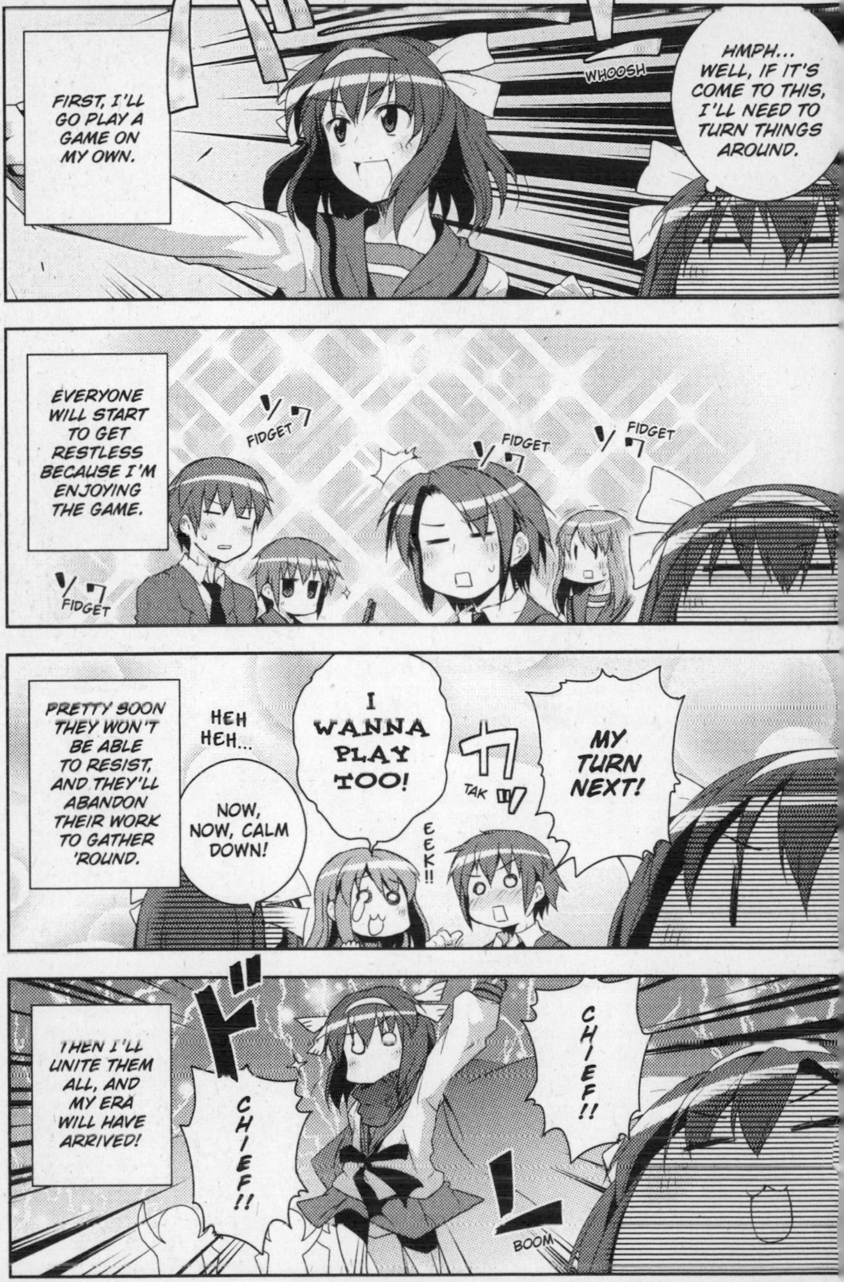
HMPH... WELL, IF IT'S COME TO THIS, I'LL NEED TO TURN THINGS AROUND.
WHOOSH
FIRST, I'LL GO PLAY A GAME ON MY OWN.
FIDGET
FIDGET
FIDGET
EVERYONE WILL START TO GET RESTLESS BECAUSE I'M ENJOYING THE GAME.
FIDGET
MY TURN NEXT!
TAK
I WANNA PLAY TOO!
EEK!!
HEH HEH...
NOW, NOW, CALM DOWN!
PRETTY SOON THEY WON'T BE ABLE TO RESIST, AND THEY'LL ABANDON THEIR WORK TO GATHER 'ROUND.
CHIEF!!
BOOM
CHIEF!!
THEN I'LL UNITE THEM ALL, AND MY ERA WILL HAVE ARRIVED!

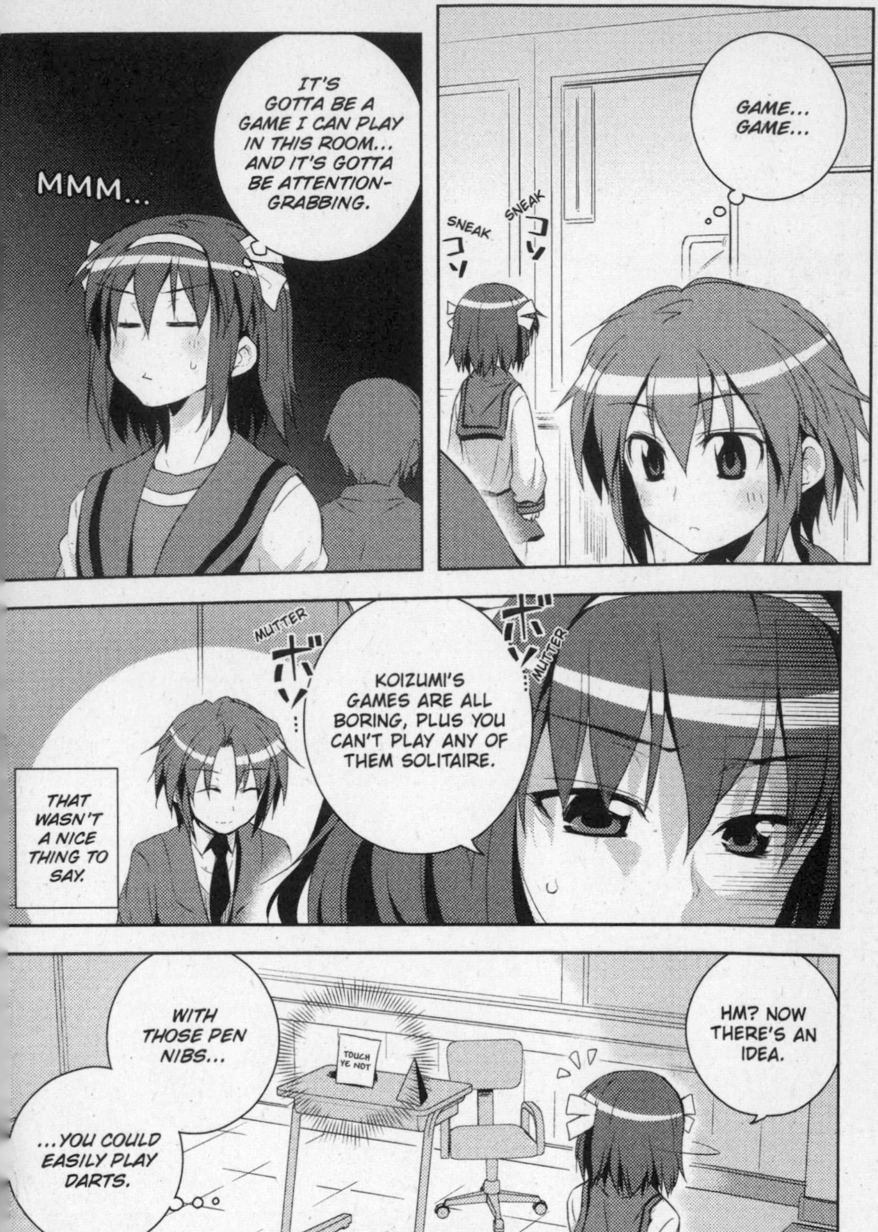
GAME... GAME...
SNEAK
SNEAK
IT'S GOTTA BE A GAME I CAN PLAY IN THIS ROOM... AND IT'S GOTTA BE ATTENTION-GRABBING.
MMM...
MUTTER
KOIZUMI'S GAMES ARE ALL BORING, PLUS YOU CAN'T PLAY ANY OF THEM SOLITAIRE.
MUTTER
THAT WASN'T A NICE THING TO SAY.
HM? NOW THERE'S AN IDEA.
TOUCH YE NOT
WITH THOSE PEN NIBS...
...YOU COULD EASILY PLAY DARTS.

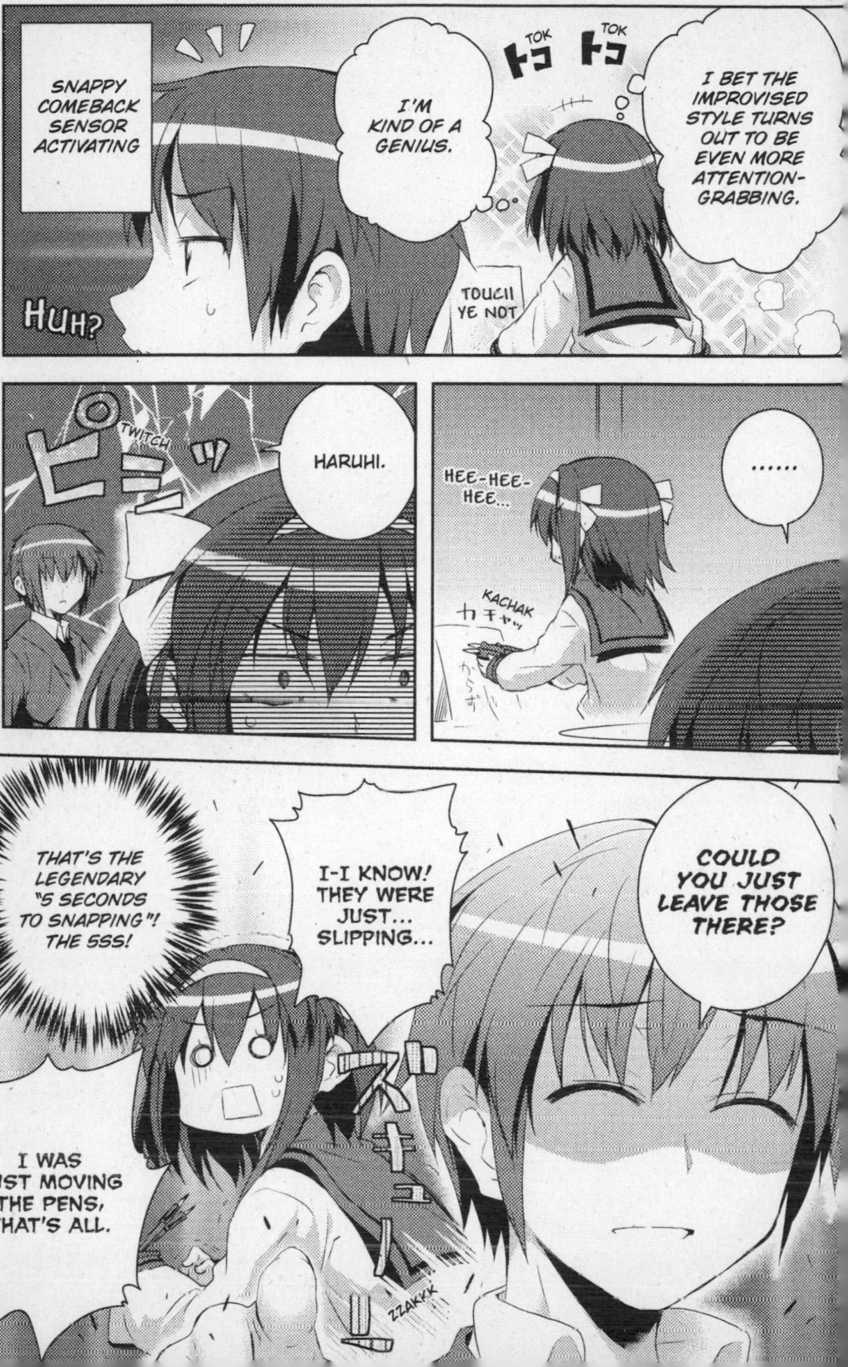
I BET THE IMPROVISED STYLE TURNS OUT TO BE EVEN MORE ATTENTION-GRABBING.
TOK TOK
TOUCII YE NOT
I'M KIND OF A GENIUS.
SNAPPY COMEBACK SENSOR ACTIVATING
HUH?
......
HEE-HEE-HEE...
KACHAK
HARUHI.
TWITCH
COULD YOU JUST LEAVE THOSE THERE?
I-I KNOW! THEY WERE JUST... SLIPPING...
THAT'S THE LEGENDARY "5 SECONDS TO SNAPPING"! THE 5SS!
I WAS JUST MOVING THE PENS, THAT'S ALL.
ZZAKKK

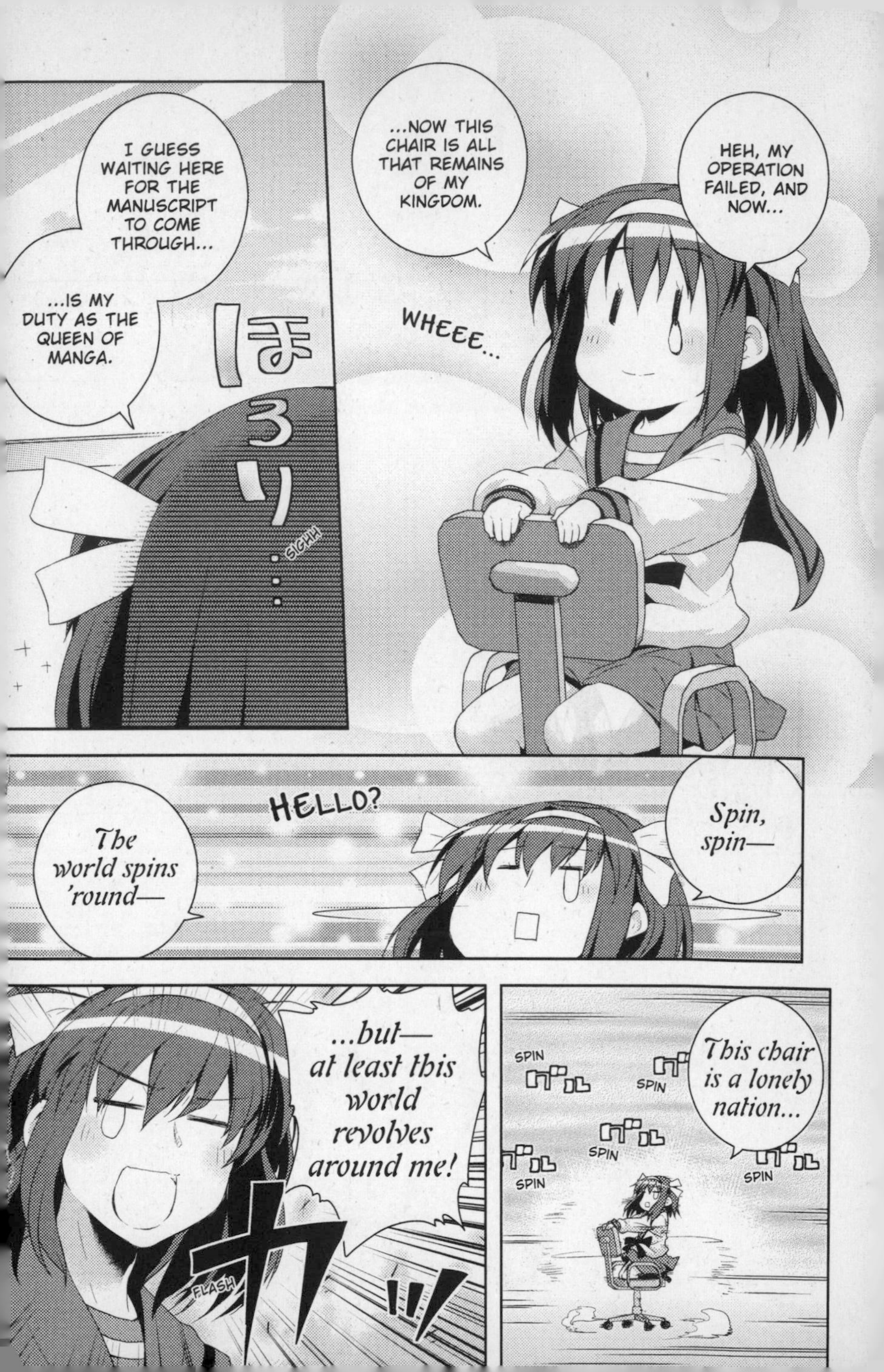
HEH, MY OPERATION FAILED, AND NOW...
...NOW THIS CHAIR IS ALL THAT REMAINS OF MY KINGDOM.
WHEEE...
I GUESS WAITING HERE FOR THE MANUSCRIPT TO COME THROUGH...
...IS MY DUTY AS THE QUEEN OF MANGA.
SIGHH
Spin, spin—
HELLO?
The world spins 'round—
This chair is a lonely nation...
SPIN
SPIN
SPIN
SPIN
SPIN
...but— at least this world revolves around me!
FLASH

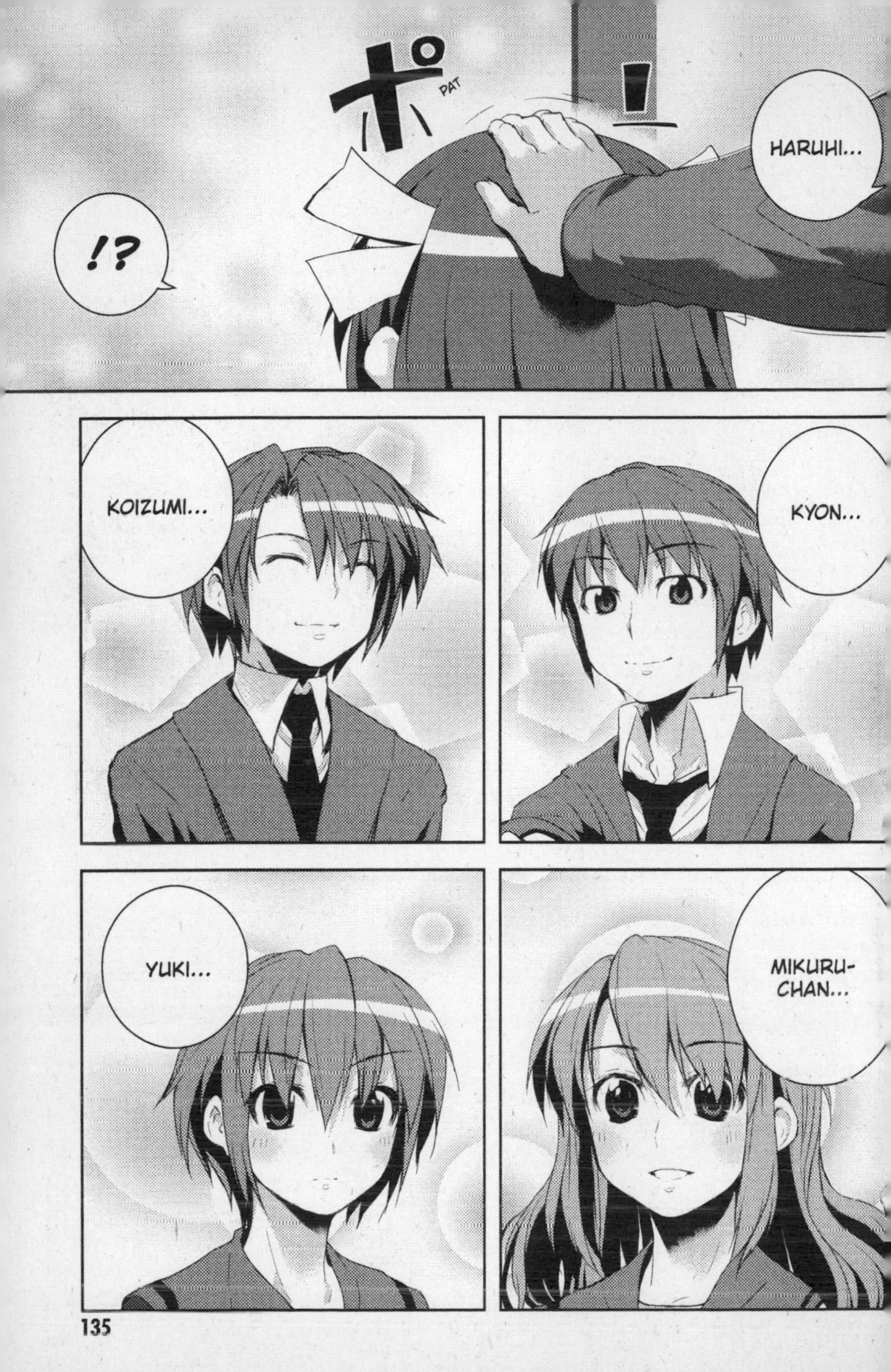
HARUHI...
ポ
PAT
!?
KYON...
KOIZUMI...
MIKURU-
CHAN...
YUKI...

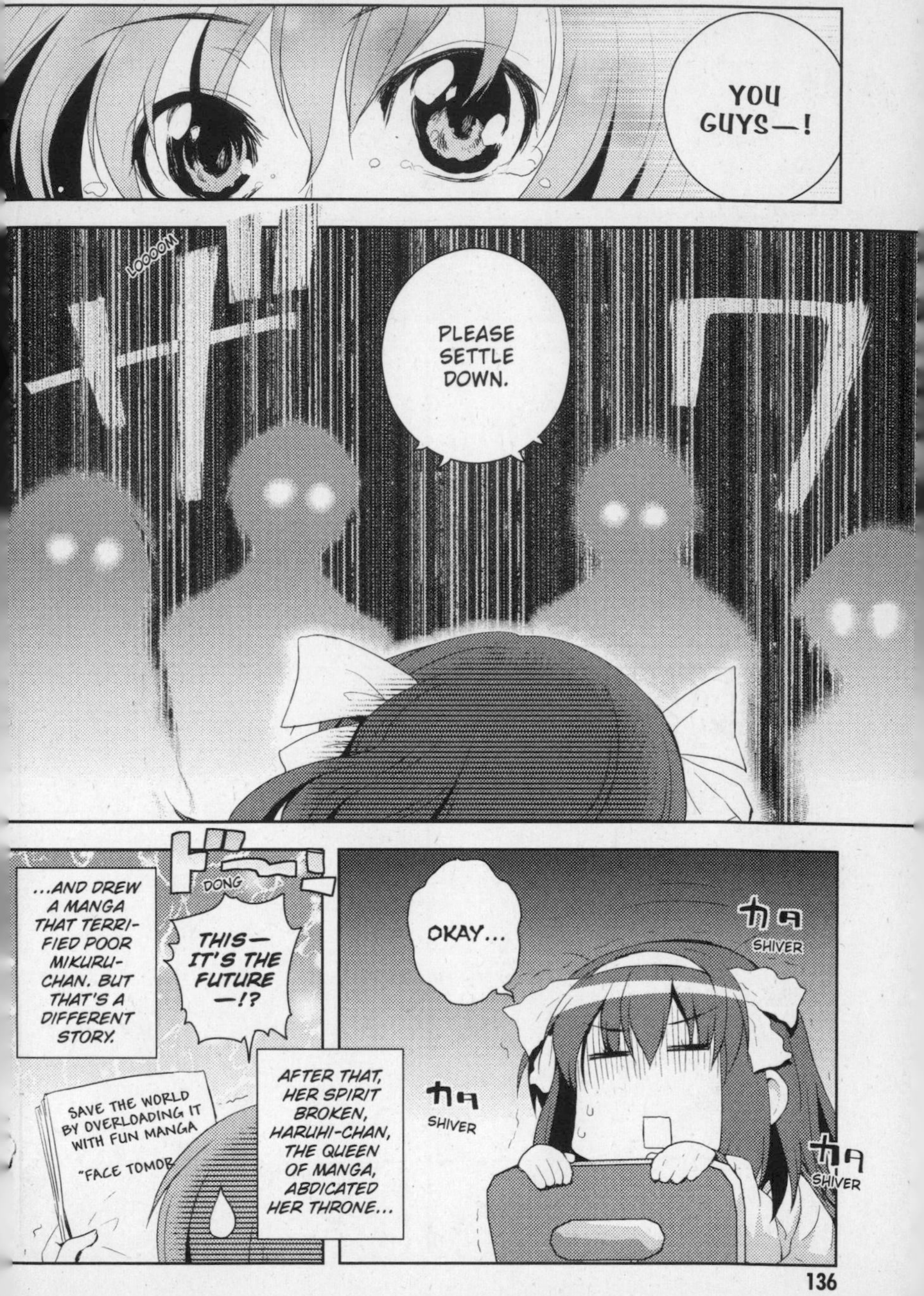

YOU GUYS—!
LOOOOM
PLEASE SETTLE DOWN.
OKAY...
カタ
SHIVER
カタ
SHIVER
カタ
SHIVER
ドーン
DONG
...AND DREW A MANGA THAT TERRIFIED POOR MIKURU-CHAN. BUT THAT'S A DIFFERENT STORY.
THIS— IT'S THE FUTURE —!?
AFTER THAT, HER SPIRIT BROKEN, HARUHI-CHAN, THE QUEEN OF MANGA, ABDICATED HER THRONE...
SAVE THE WORLD BY OVERLOADING IT WITH FUN MANGA
"FACE TOMOR

A WINDY DAY

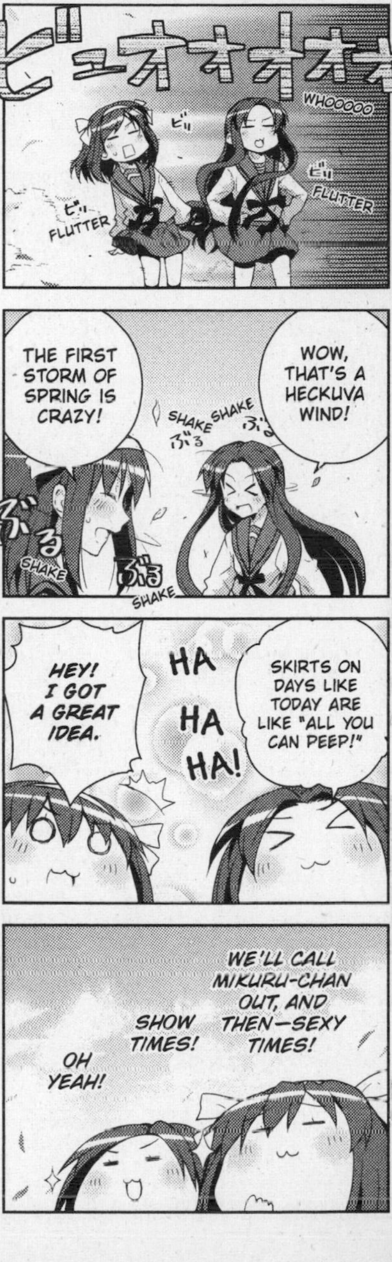
ビュオオオオオ
WHOOOOO
ビゥ
ビゥ
FLUTTER
ビゥ
FLUTTER
WOW, THAT'S A HECKUVA WIND!
SHAKE
SHAKE
THE FIRST STORM OF SPRING IS CRAZY!
SHAKE
SHAKE
SKIRTS ON DAYS LIKE TODAY ARE LIKE "ALL YOU CAN PEEP!"
HA HA HA!
HEY! I GOT A GREAT IDEA.
WE'LL CALL MIKURU-CHAN OUT, AND THEN—SEXY TIMES!
SHOW TIMES!
OH YEAH!

EXECUTION

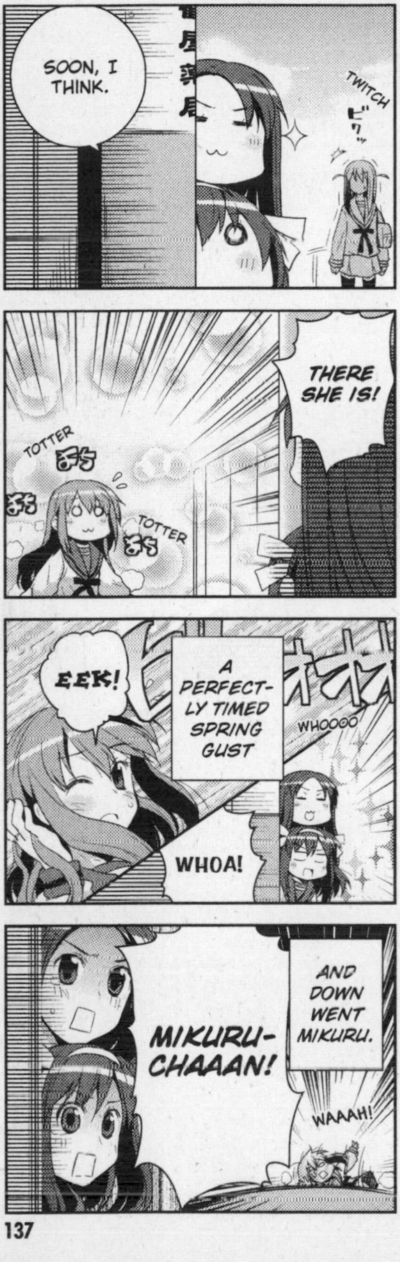
TWITCH
SOON, I THINK.
THERE SHE IS!
TOTTER
TOTTER
A PERFECTLY TIMED SPRING GUST
WHOOOO
EEK!
WHOA!
AND DOWN WENT MIKURU.
MIKURU-CHAAAN!
WAAAH!

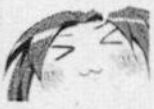

•Tsuruya-san •Rich girl. Haruhi's co-conspirator in fawning over Mikuru-chan.

A WINDY DAY 2

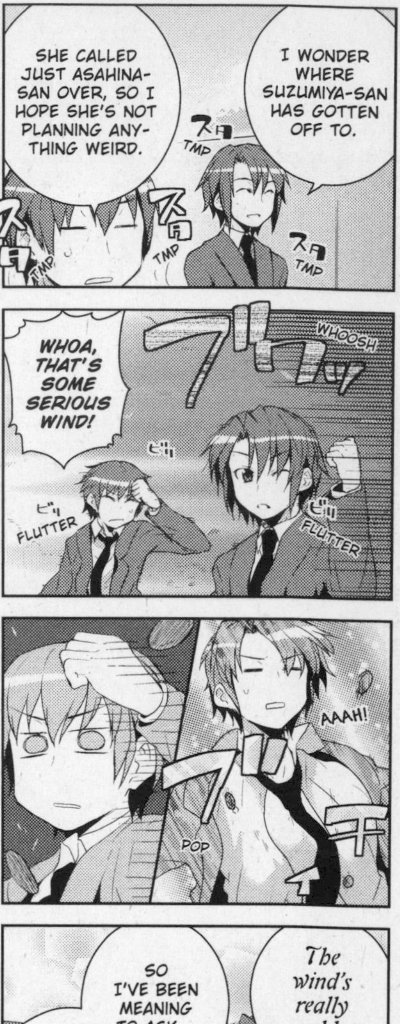
I WONDER WHERE SUZUMIYA-SAN HAS GOTTEN OFF TO.
SHE CALLED JUST ASAHINA-SAN OVER, SO I HOPE SHE'S NOT PLANNING ANY-THING WEIRD.
TMP
TMP
TMP
TMP
WHOOSH
WHOA, THAT'S SOME SERIOUS WIND!
FLUTTER
FLUTTER
AAAH!
POP
The wind's really cold.
SO I'VE BEEN MEANING TO ASK...
...DO THE BUTTONS ON YOUR CLOTHES JUST COME UNDONE REALLY EASILY, OR WHAT?
WHEW!

SEXY TIMES

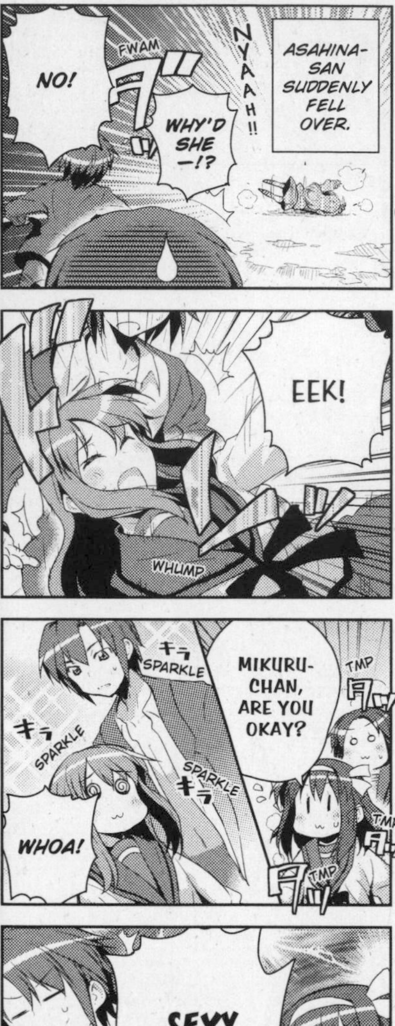
ASAHINA-SAN SUDDENLY FELL OVER.
NYAAAH!!
WHY'D SHE—!?
FWAM
NO!
EEK!
WHUMP
TMP
MIKURU-CHAN, ARE YOU OKAY?
SPARKLE
SPARKLE
SPARKLE
TMP
TMP
WHOA!
SEXY TIMES!
TWITCH
BAM

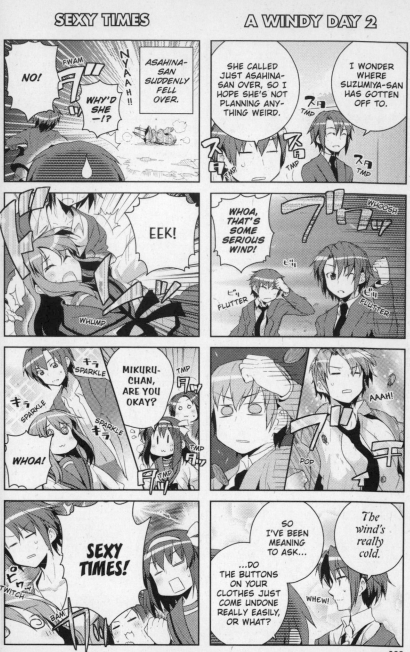

SAKURA

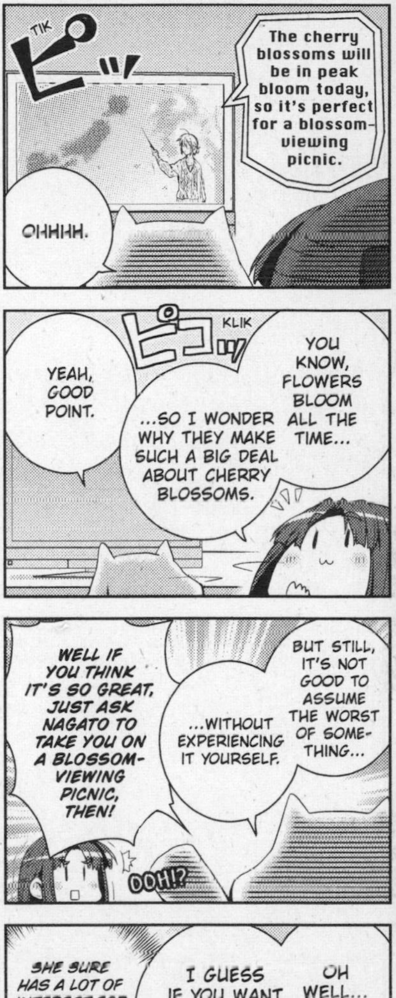
TIK
The cherry blossoms will be in peak bloom today, so it's perfect for a blossom-viewing picnic.
OHHHH.
KLIK
YOU KNOW, FLOWERS BLOOM ALL THE TIME...
...SO I WONDER WHY THEY MAKE SUCH A BIG DEAL ABOUT CHERRY BLOSSOMS.
YEAH, GOOD POINT.
BUT STILL, IT'S NOT GOOD TO ASSUME THE WORST OF SOME-THING...
...WITHOUT EXPERIENCING IT YOURSELF.
WELL IF YOU THINK IT'S SO GREAT, JUST ASK NAGATO TO TAKE YOU ON A BLOSSOM-VIEWING PICNIC, THEN!
DOH!?
OH WELL...
I GUESS IF YOU WANT TO GO THAT BADLY, I'LL GO WITH YOU.
SHE SURE HAS A LOT OF INTEREST FOR SOMEONE WHO CLAIMS NOT TO CARE.
EH-HEH-HEH.

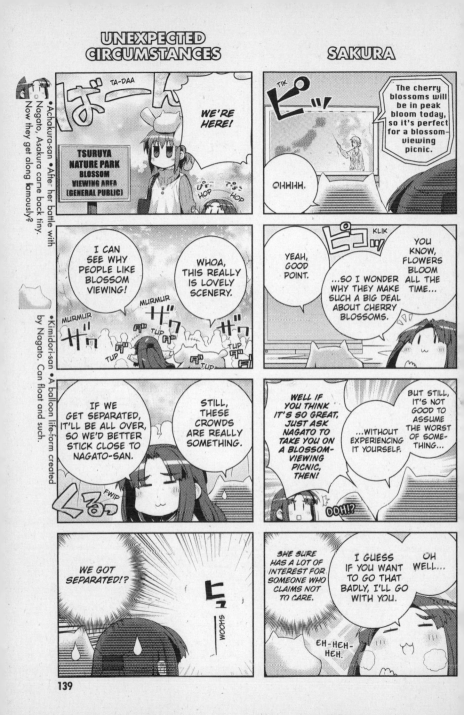

UNEXPECTED CIRCUMSTANCES

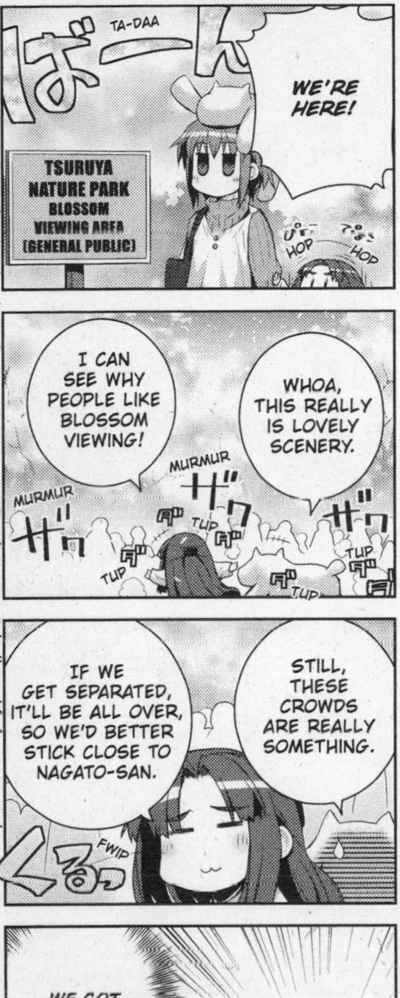
TA-DAA
WE'RE HERE!
TSURUYA NATURE PARK BLOSSOM VIEWING AREA (GENERAL PUBLIC)
HOP
HOP
WHOA, THIS REALLY IS LOVELY SCENERY.
I CAN SEE WHY PEOPLE LIKE BLOSSOM VIEWING!
MURMUR
MURMUR
TUP
TUP
TUP
TUP
STILL, THESE CROWDS ARE REALLY SOMETHING.
IF WE GET SEPARATED, IT'LL BE ALL OVER, SO WE'D BETTER STICK CLOSE TO NAGATO-SAN.
FWIP
WE GOT SEPARATED!?

•Achakura-san •After her battle with Nagato, Asakura came back tiny. Now they get along famously?

•Kimidori-san •A balloon life-form created by Nagato. Can float and such.

LOST CHILD

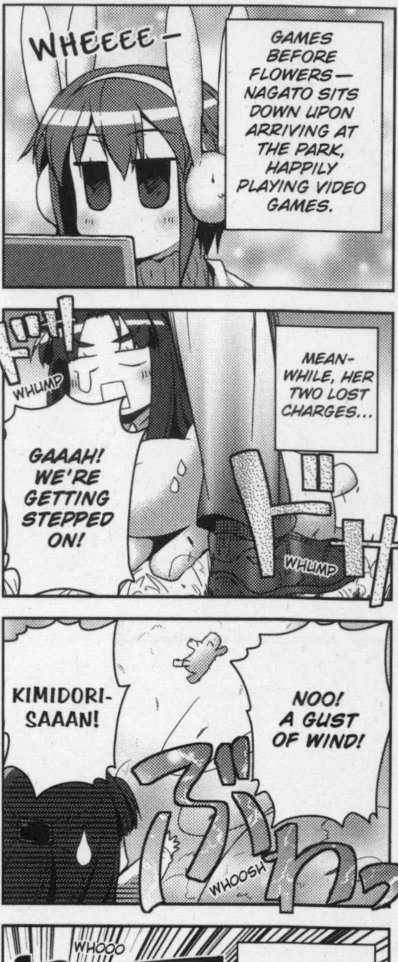
GAMES BEFORE FLOWERS—NAGATO SITS DOWN UPON ARRIVING AT THE PARK, HAPPILY PLAYING VIDEO GAMES.
WHEEEE—
MEAN-WHILE, HER TWO LOST CHARGES...
WHUMP
GAAAH! WE'RE GETTING STEPPED ON!
WHUMP
NOO! A GUST OF WIND!
KIMIDORI-SAAAN!
WHOOSH
AND NOW, FINALLY, SHE REALIZES SHE'S TWO BODIES SHORT.
WHOOO
ヒュー

REUNION

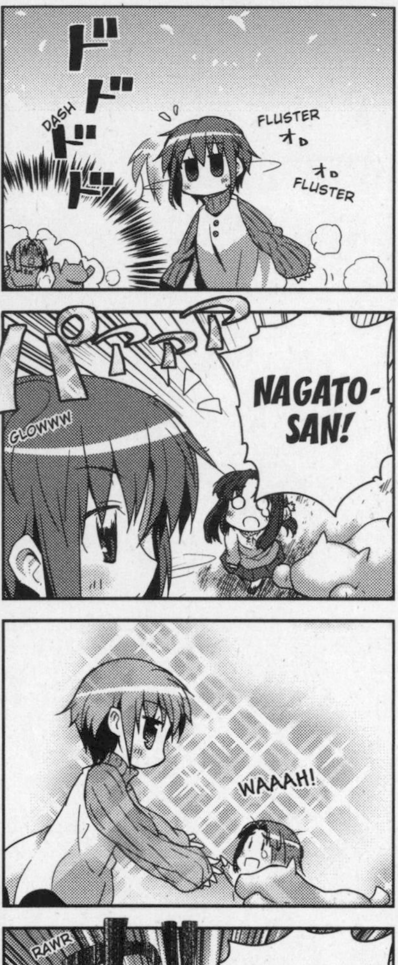
FLUSTER
オロ
オロ
FLUSTER
DASH
NAGATO-SAN!
GLOWWW
WAAAH!
WHERE'D YOU GO!?
RAWR
THEY WERE FURIOUS.

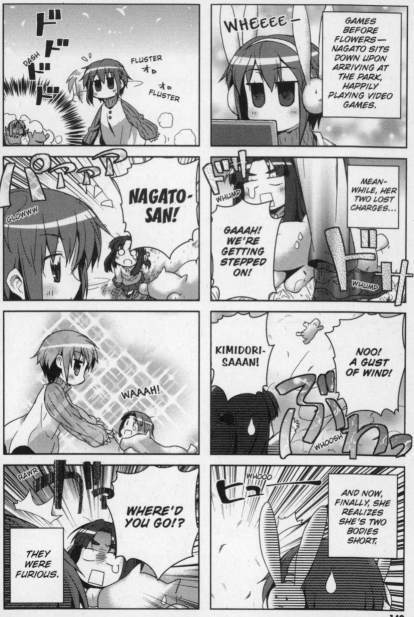

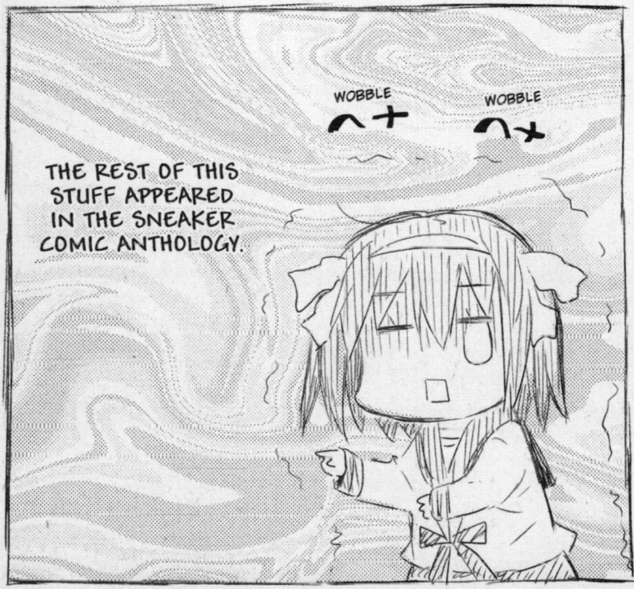
WOBBLE
WOBBLE
THE REST OF THIS STUFF APPEARED IN THE SNEAKER COMIC ANTHOLOGY.

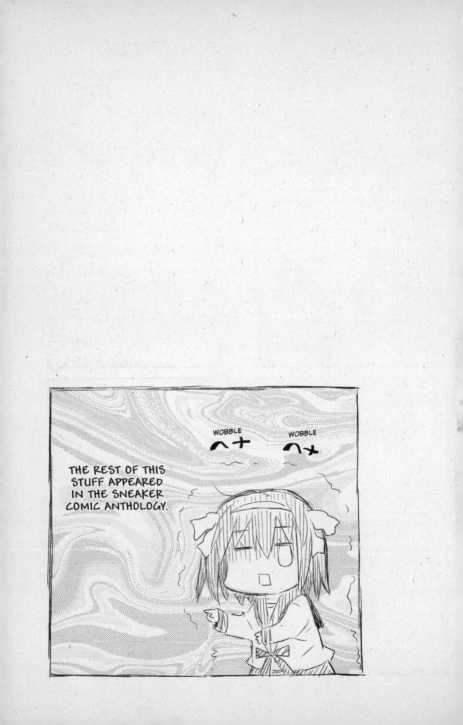

OPENING

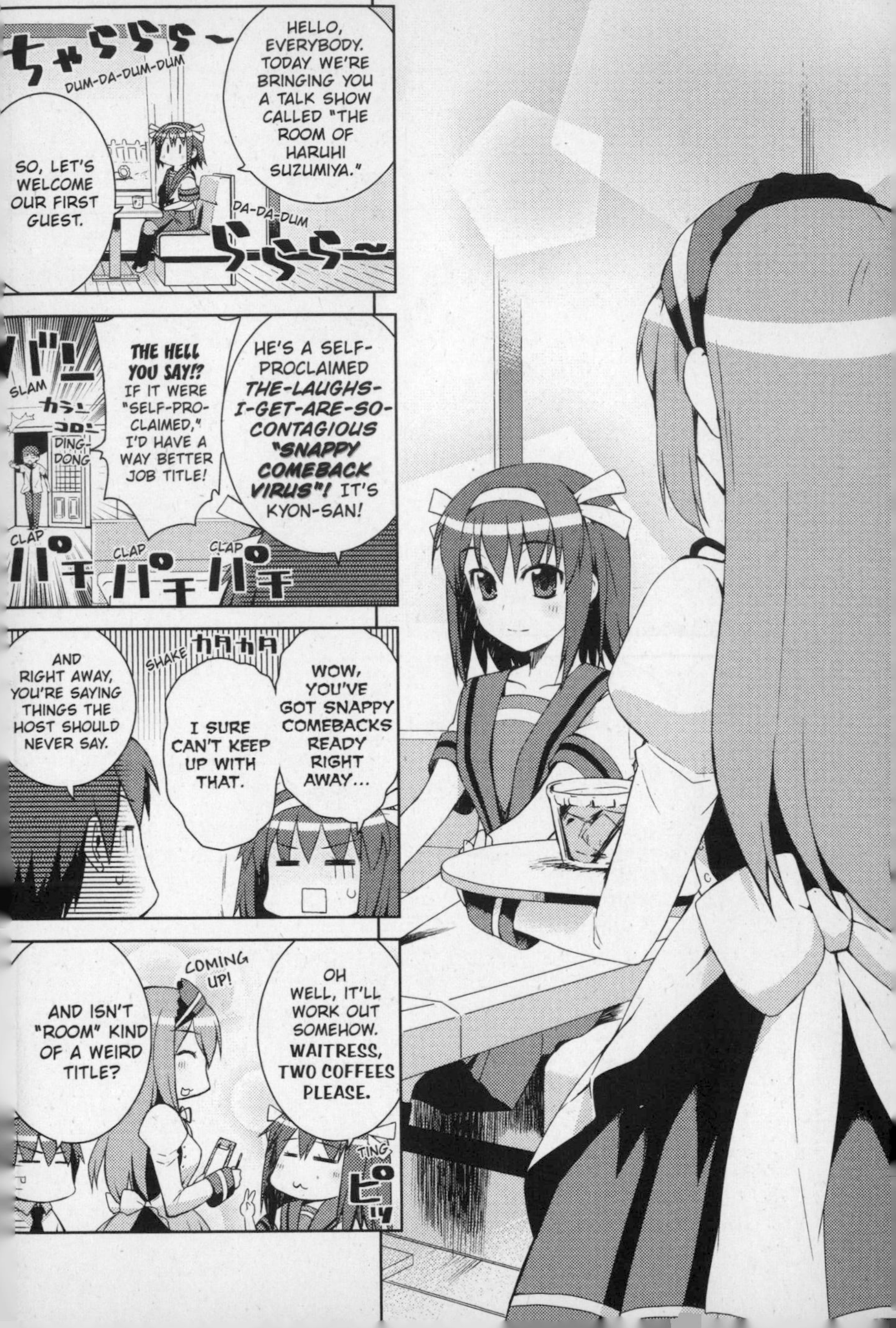
ちゃらら～
DUM-DA-DUM-DUM
HELLO, EVERYBODY. TODAY WE'RE BRINGING YOU A TALK SHOW CALLED "THE ROOM OF HARUHI SUZUMIYA."
SO, LET'S WELCOME OUR FIRST GUEST.
DA-DA-DUM
ら-ら-ら～
HE'S A SELF-PROCLAIMED THE-LAUGHS-I-GET-ARE-SO-CONTAGIOUS "SNAPPY COMEBACK VIRUS"! IT'S KYON-SAN!
THE HELL YOU SAY!? IF IT WERE "SELF-PROCLAIMED," I'D HAVE A WAY BETTER JOB TITLE!
SLAM
DING-DONG
CLAP
CLAP
CLAP
SHAKE
WOW, YOU'VE GOT SNAPPY COMEBACKS READY RIGHT AWAY...
I SURE CAN'T KEEP UP WITH THAT.
AND RIGHT AWAY, YOU'RE SAYING THINGS THE HOST SHOULD NEVER SAY.
OH WELL, IT'LL WORK OUT SOMEHOW. WAITRESS, TWO COFFEES PLEASE.
COMING UP!
AND ISN'T "ROOM" KIND OF A WEIRD TITLE?
TING

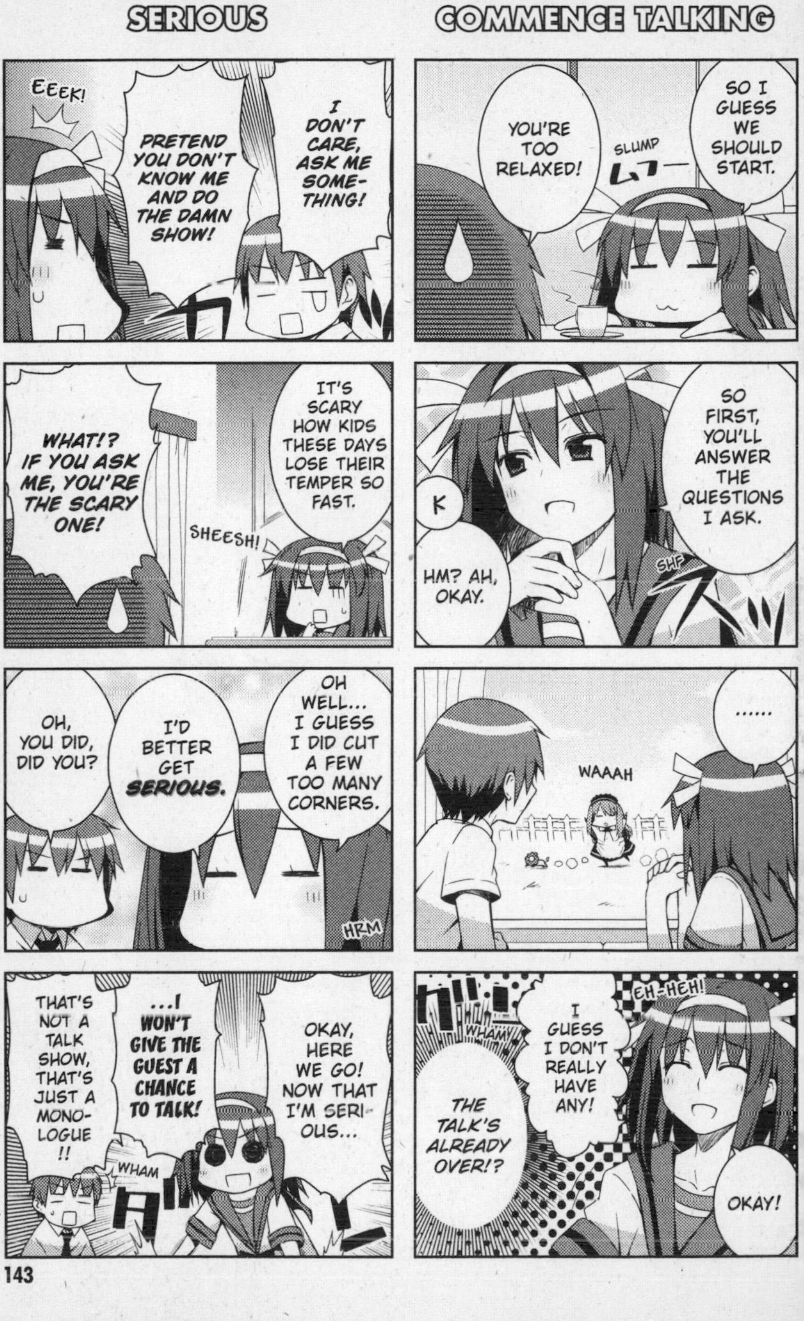
COMMENCE TALKING
SO I GUESS WE SHOULD START.
SLUMP
YOU'RE TOO RELAXED!
SO FIRST, YOU'LL ANSWER THE QUESTIONS I ASK.
SHF
K
HM? AH, OKAY.
......
WAAAH
EH-HEH!
I GUESS I DON'T REALLY HAVE ANY!
OKAY!
WHAM
THE TALK'S ALREADY OVER!?
SERIOUS
I DON'T CARE, ASK ME SOMETHING!
PRETEND YOU DON'T KNOW ME AND DO THE DAMN SHOW!
EEEK!
IT'S SCARY HOW KIDS THESE DAYS LOSE THEIR TEMPER SO FAST.
SHEESH!
WHAT!? IF YOU ASK ME, YOU'RE THE SCARY ONE!
OH WELL... I GUESS I DID CUT A FEW TOO MANY CORNERS.
I'D BETTER GET SERIOUS.
HRM
OH, YOU DID, DID YOU?
OKAY, HERE WE GO! NOW THAT I'M SERIOUS...
...I WON'T GIVE THE GUEST A CHANCE TO TALK!
WHAM
THAT'S NOT A TALK SHOW, THAT'S JUST A MONOLOGUE!!

•Haruhi-chan •SOS Brigade Chief. Lately interested in television production.

•Mikuru-chan •Time traveler. Acts very much like a small animal, especially when she plays with Infy.

•Kyon •Supposed to be the main character of this story. A guest on Haruhi's TV show, but treated terribly.

NOT REALLY EPISODE

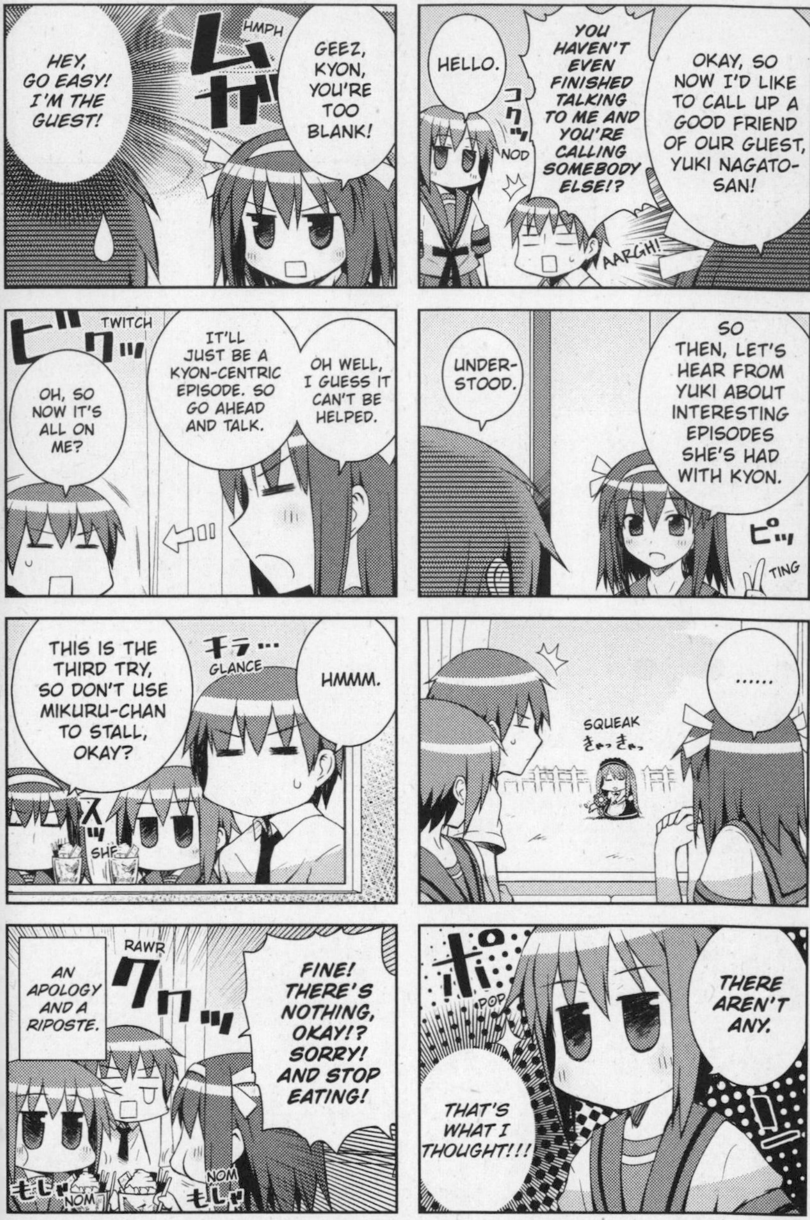
OKAY, SO NOW I'D LIKE TO CALL UP A GOOD FRIEND OF OUR GUEST, YUKI NAGATO-SAN!
AARGH!
YOU HAVEN'T EVEN FINISHED TALKING TO ME AND YOU'RE CALLING SOMEBODY ELSE!?
コクッ
NOD
HELLO.
SO THEN, LET'S HEAR FROM YUKI ABOUT INTERESTING EPISODES SHE'S HAD WITH KYON.
ピッ
TING
UNDER-STOOD.
......
SQUEAK
きゃっきゃっ
THERE AREN'T ANY.
ポ
POP
THAT'S WHAT I THOUGHT!!!
GEEZ, KYON, YOU'RE TOO BLANK!
HMPH
HEY, GO EASY! I'M THE GUEST!
OH WELL, I GUESS IT CAN'T BE HELPED.
IT'LL JUST BE A KYON-CENTRIC EPISODE. SO GO AHEAD AND TALK.
TWITCH
OH, SO NOW IT'S ALL ON ME?
HMMM.
チラ…
GLANCE
THIS IS THE THIRD TRY, SO DON'T USE MIKURU-CHAN TO STALL, OKAY?
スッ
SHF
FINE! THERE'S NOTHING, OKAY!? SORRY! AND STOP EATING!
RAWR
AN APOLOGY AND A RIPOSTE.
NOM
NOM

•Nagato •Actually an alien gamer. Enjoys snacks. Really puts 'em away.

•Koizumi •Enigmatic transfer student and esper. It doesn't appear on-screen, but he's dressed as a handsome waiter.

•Infinity Lion •Space creature that Mikuru keeps as a pet. Lives in a teapot.

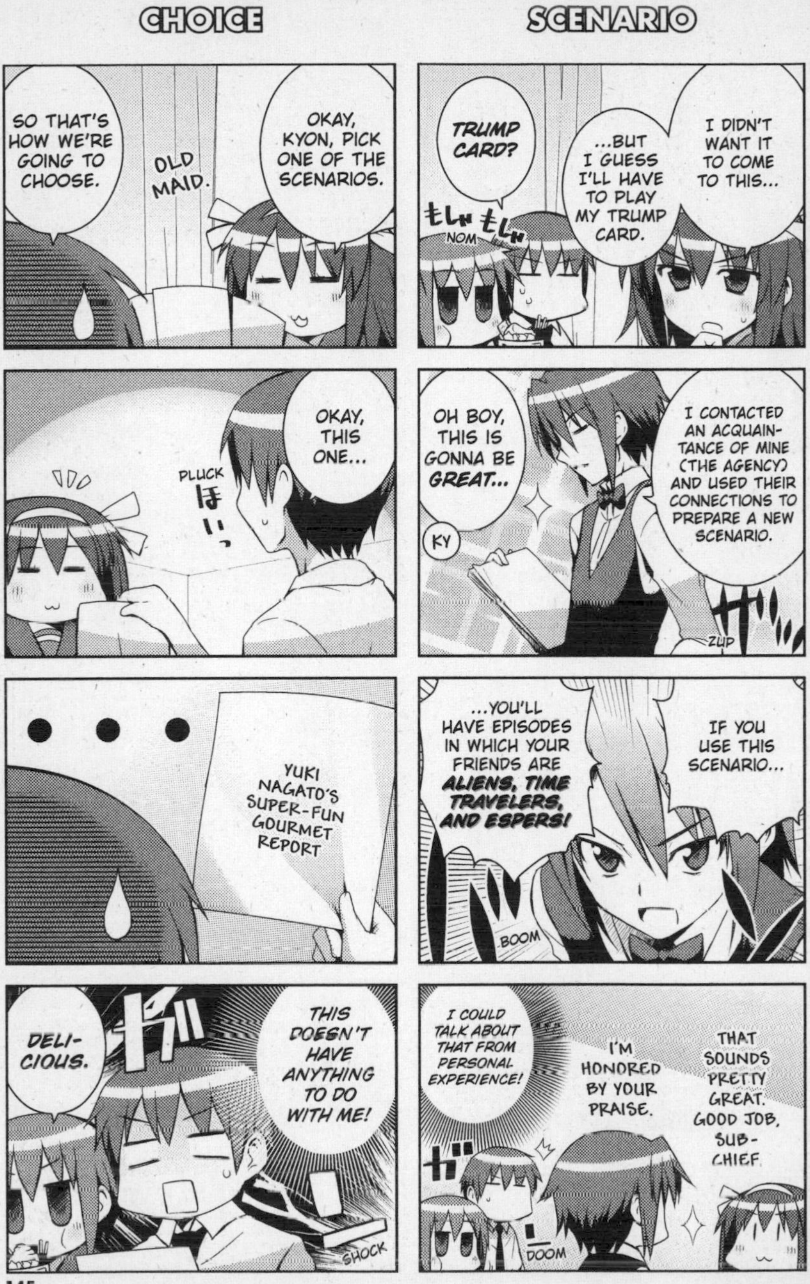
SCENARIO
I DIDN'T WANT IT TO COME TO THIS...
...BUT I GUESS I'LL HAVE TO PLAY MY TRUMP CARD.
TRUMP CARD?
もしゃ もしゃ
NOM
I CONTACTED AN ACQUAINTANCE OF MINE (THE AGENCY) AND USED THEIR CONNECTIONS TO PREPARE A NEW SCENARIO.
OH BOY, THIS IS GONNA BE GREAT...
KY
ZUP
IF YOU USE THIS SCENARIO...
...YOU'LL HAVE EPISODES IN WHICH YOUR FRIENDS ARE ALIENS, TIME TRAVELERS, AND ESPERS!
BOOM
THAT SOUNDS PRETTY GREAT. GOOD JOB, SUB-CHIEF.
I'M HONORED BY YOUR PRAISE.
I COULD TALK ABOUT THAT FROM PERSONAL EXPERIENCE!
ガ
DOOM
CHOICE
OKAY, KYON, PICK ONE OF THE SCENARIOS.
OLD MAID.
SO THAT'S HOW WE'RE GOING TO CHOOSE.
OKAY, THIS ONE...
ほいっ
PLUCK
YUKI NAGATO'S SUPER-FUN GOURMET REPORT
• • •
THIS DOESN'T HAVE ANYTHING TO DO WITH ME!
DELI-CIOUS.
SHOCK

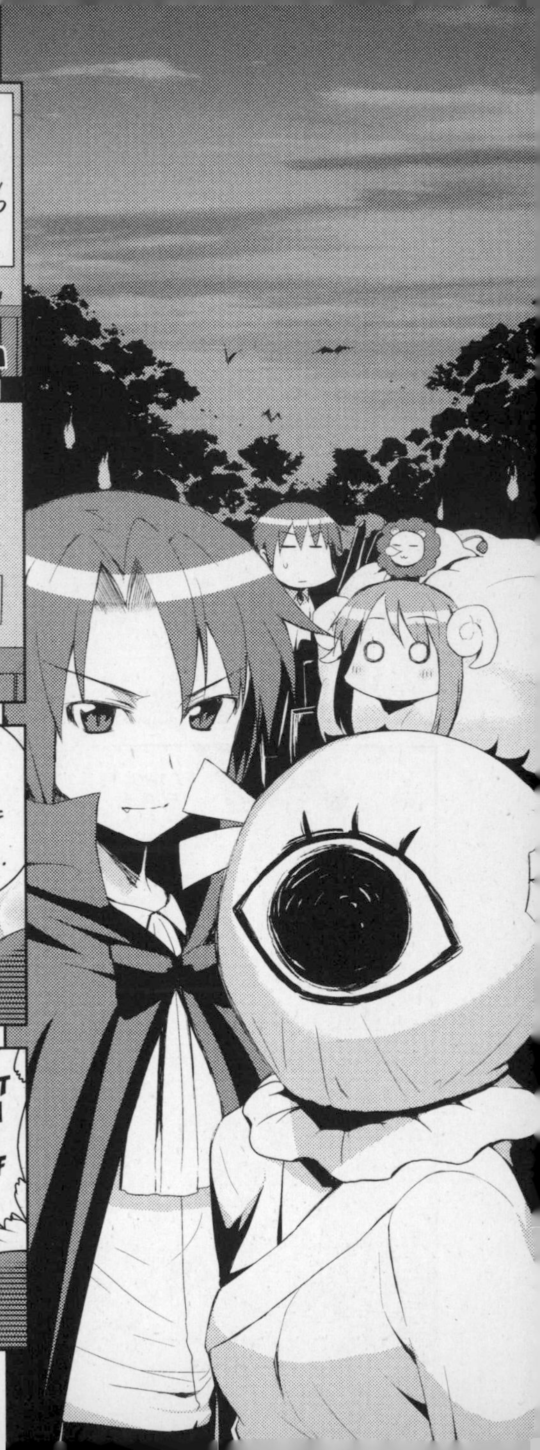

HAUNTED HOUSE

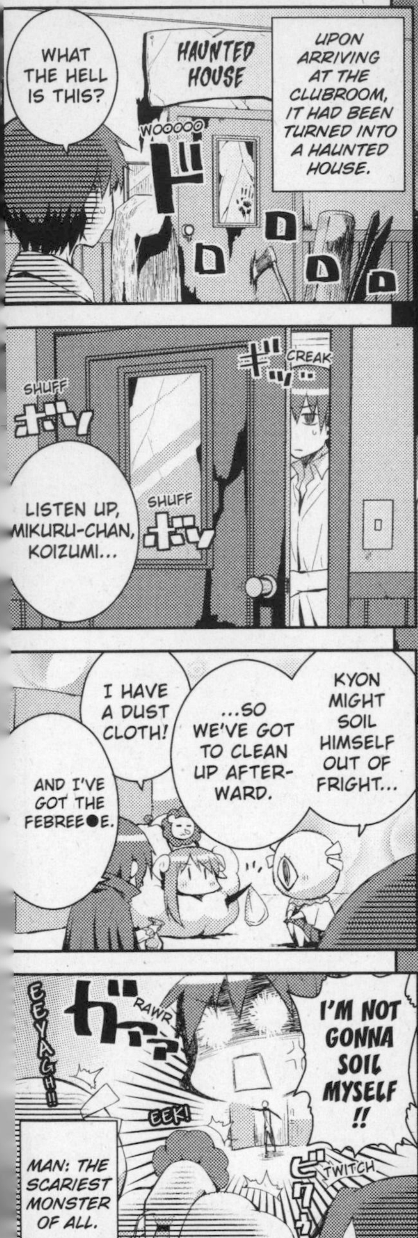
UPON ARRIVING AT THE CLUBROOM, IT HAD BEEN TURNED INTO A HAUNTED HOUSE.
HAUNTED HOUSE
WHAT THE HELL IS THIS?
WOOOOO
CREAK
SHUFF
SHUFF
LISTEN UP, MIKURU-CHAN, KOIZUMI...
KYON MIGHT SOIL HIMSELF OUT OF FRIGHT...
...SO WE'VE GOT TO CLEAN UP AFTER-WARD.
I HAVE A DUST CLOTH!
AND I'VE GOT THE FEBREE●E.
I'M NOT GONNA SOIL MYSELF!!
TWITCH
RAWR
EEK!
EEYAGH!!
MAN: THE SCARIEST MONSTER OF ALL.

HOW CONSIDERATE

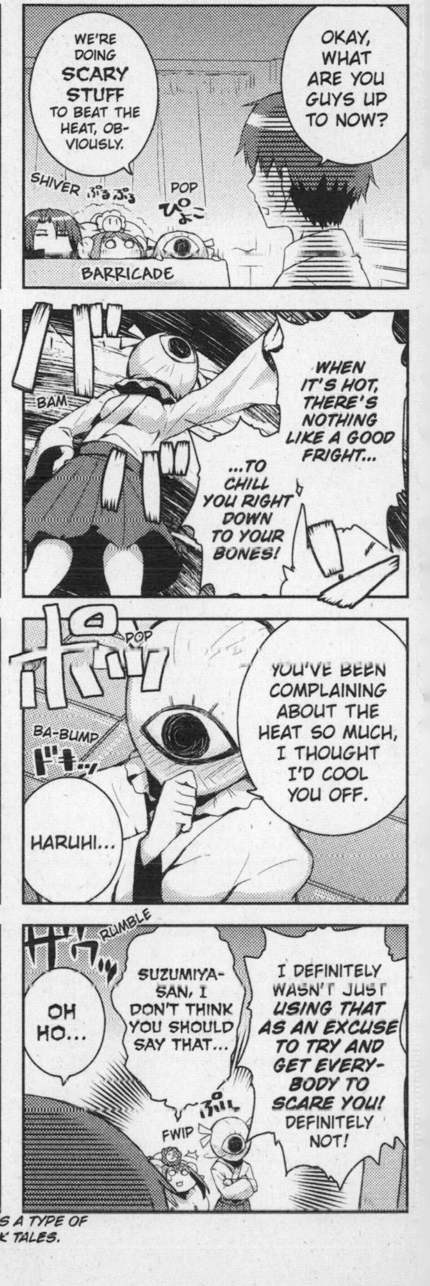
OKAY, WHAT ARE YOU GUYS UP TO NOW?
WE'RE DOING SCARY STUFF TO BEAT THE HEAT, OBVIOUSLY.
SHIVER ぷるぷる
POP ぴよこ
BARRICADE
BAM
WHEN IT'S HOT, THERE'S NOTHING LIKE A GOOD FRIGHT...
...TO CHILL YOU RIGHT DOWN TO YOUR BONES!
POP
YOU'VE BEEN COMPLAINING ABOUT THE HEAT SO MUCH, I THOUGHT I'D COOL YOU OFF.
BA-BUMP
HARUHI...
RUMBLE
I DEFINITELY WASN'T JUST USING THAT AS AN EXCUSE TO TRY AND GET EVERYBODY TO SCARE YOU! DEFINITELY NOT!
SUZUMIYA-SAN, I DON'T THINK YOU SHOULD SAY THAT...
OH HO...
FWIP

DEFORM-EYE-TY

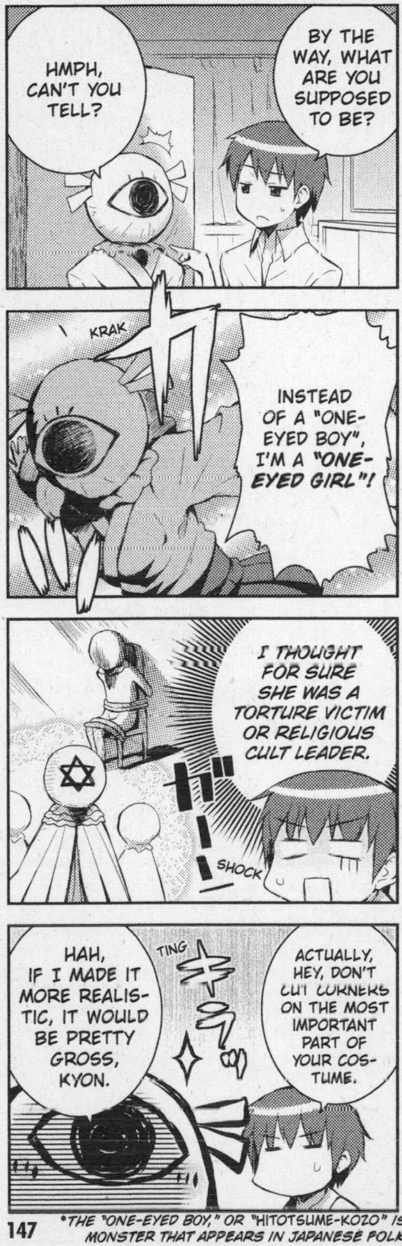
BY THE WAY, WHAT ARE YOU SUPPOSED TO BE?
HMPH, CAN'T YOU TELL?
KRAK
INSTEAD OF A "ONE-EYED BOY", I'M A "ONE-EYED GIRL"!
I THOUGHT FOR SURE SHE WAS A TORTURE VICTIM OR RELIGIOUS CULT LEADER.
SHOCK
ACTUALLY, HEY, DON'T CUT CORNERS ON THE MOST IMPORTANT PART OF YOUR COSTUME.
TING
HAH, IF I MADE IT MORE REALISTIC, IT WOULD BE PRETTY GROSS, KYON.

THE "ONE-EYED BOY," OR "HITOTSUME-KOZO" IS A TYPE OF MONSTER THAT APPEARS IN JAPANESE FOLK TALES.

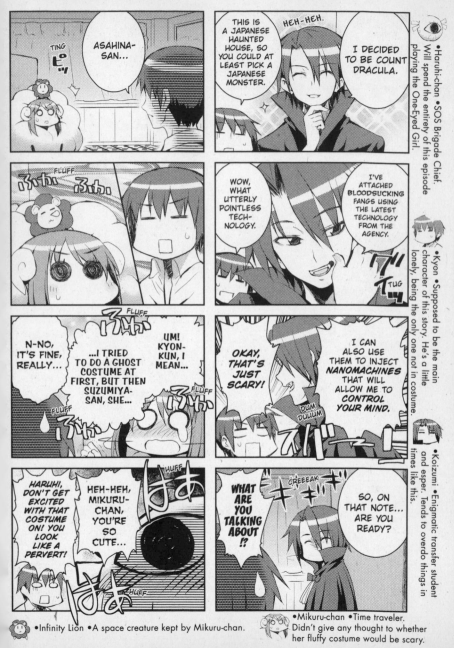

READY

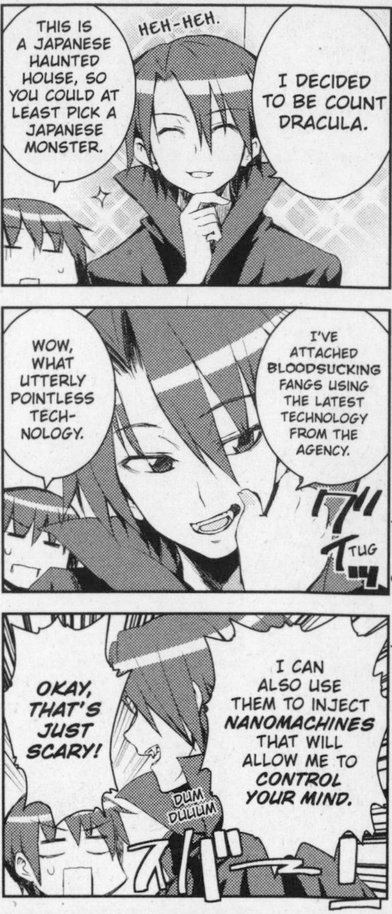
HEH-HEH.
I DECIDED TO BE COUNT DRACULA.
THIS IS A JAPANESE HAUNTED HOUSE, SO YOU COULD AT LEAST PICK A JAPANESE MONSTER.
I'VE ATTACHED BLOODSUCKING FANGS USING THE LATEST TECHNOLOGY FROM THE AGENCY.
WOW, WHAT UTTERLY POINTLESS TECH-NOLOGY.
TUG
I CAN ALSO USE THEM TO INJECT NANOMACHINES THAT WILL ALLOW ME TO CONTROL YOUR MIND.
OKAY, THAT'S JUST SCARY!
DUM DUUUM
GREEEAK
SO, ON THAT NOTE... ARE YOU READY?
WHAT ARE YOU TALKING ABOUT!?

FLUFFY MONSTER

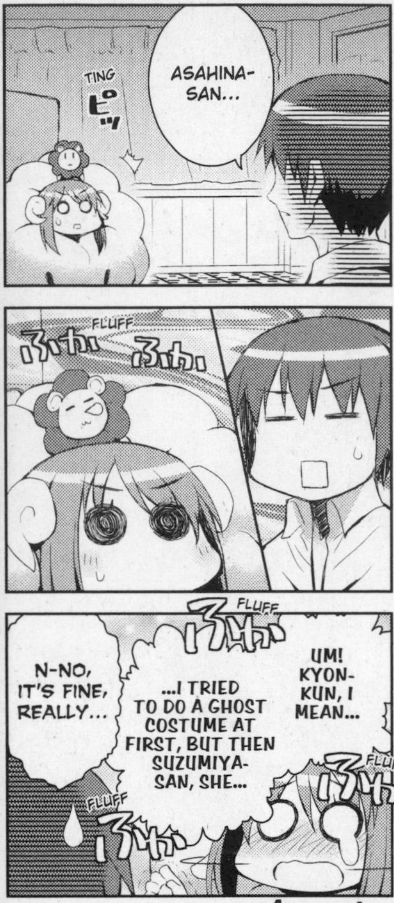
ASAHINA-SAN...
TING
ピッ
FLUFF
ふわ ふわ
FLUFF
UM! KYON-KUN, I MEAN...
...I TRIED TO DO A GHOST COSTUME AT FIRST, BUT THEN SUZUMIYA-SAN, SHE...
N-NO, IT'S FINE, REALLY...
FLUFF
FLUFF
HUFF
はぁ
HEH-HEH, MIKURU-CHAN, YOU'RE SO CUTE...
HARUHI, DON'T GET EXCITED WITH THAT COSTUME ON! YOU LOOK LIKE A PERVERT!
HUFF
はぁ

•Haruhi-chan •SOS Brigade Chief. Will spend the entirety of this episode playing the One-Eyed Girl.

•Kyon •Supposed to be the main character of this story. He's a little lonely, being the only one not in costume.

•Koizumi •Enigmatic transfer student and esper. Tends to overdo things in times like this.

•Mikuru-chan •Time traveler. Didn't give any thought to whether her fluffy costume would be scary.

•Infinity Lion •A space creature kept by Mikuru-chan.

AN INSTANT

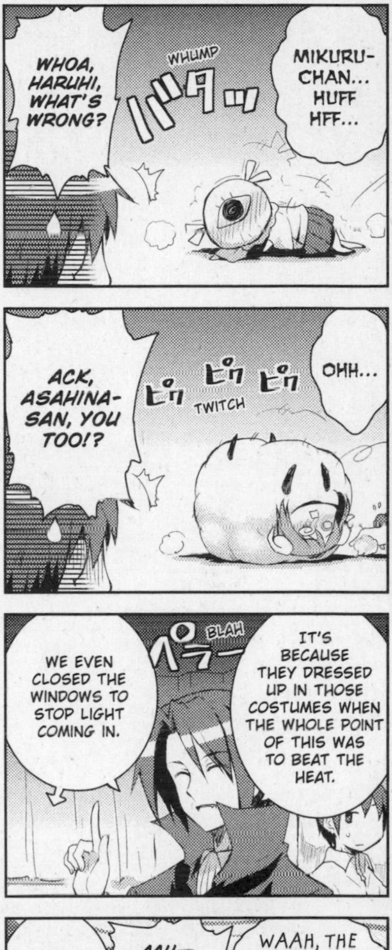
MIKURU-CHAN... HUFF HFF...
WHUMP
WHOA, HARUHI, WHAT'S WRONG?
OHH...
TWITCH
ACK, ASAHINA-SAN, YOU TOO!?
IT'S BECAUSE THEY DRESSED UP IN THOSE COSTUMES WHEN THE WHOLE POINT OF THIS WAS TO BEAT THE HEAT.
BLAH
WE EVEN CLOSED THE WINDOWS TO STOP LIGHT COMING IN.
WAAH, THE PINK PIGGY IS FLYING... KYON, WE'RE HAVING SUKIYAKI TODAY...
AAH— WE DON'T HAVE A MOMENT TO LOSE! KOIZUMI, VENTILA-TION!
UNDER-STOOD.
GASP
GASP

NAGATO-SAN

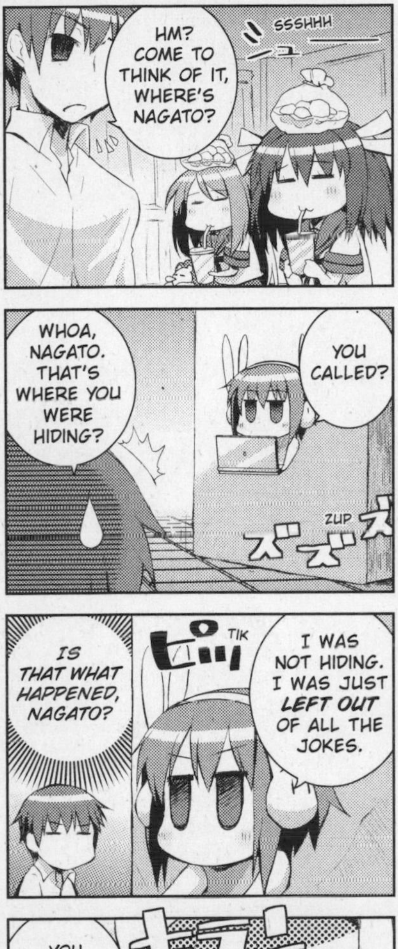
SSSHHH
HM? COME TO THINK OF IT, WHERE'S NAGATO?
YOU CALLED?
WHOA, NAGATO. THAT'S WHERE YOU WERE HIDING?
ZUP
I WAS NOT HIDING. I WAS JUST LEFT OUT OF ALL THE JOKES.
TIK
IS THAT WHAT HAPPENED, NAGATO?
AND I WAS PLAYING VIDEO GAMES UNTIL JUST THIS MOMENT.
SPARKLE
YOU PROBABLY SHOULDN'T SAY THAT, YUKI.

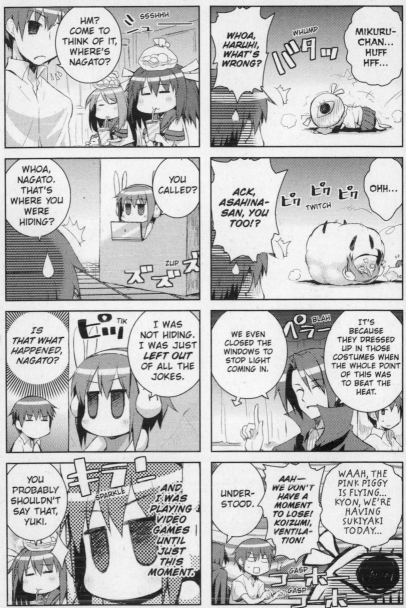

COFFEE

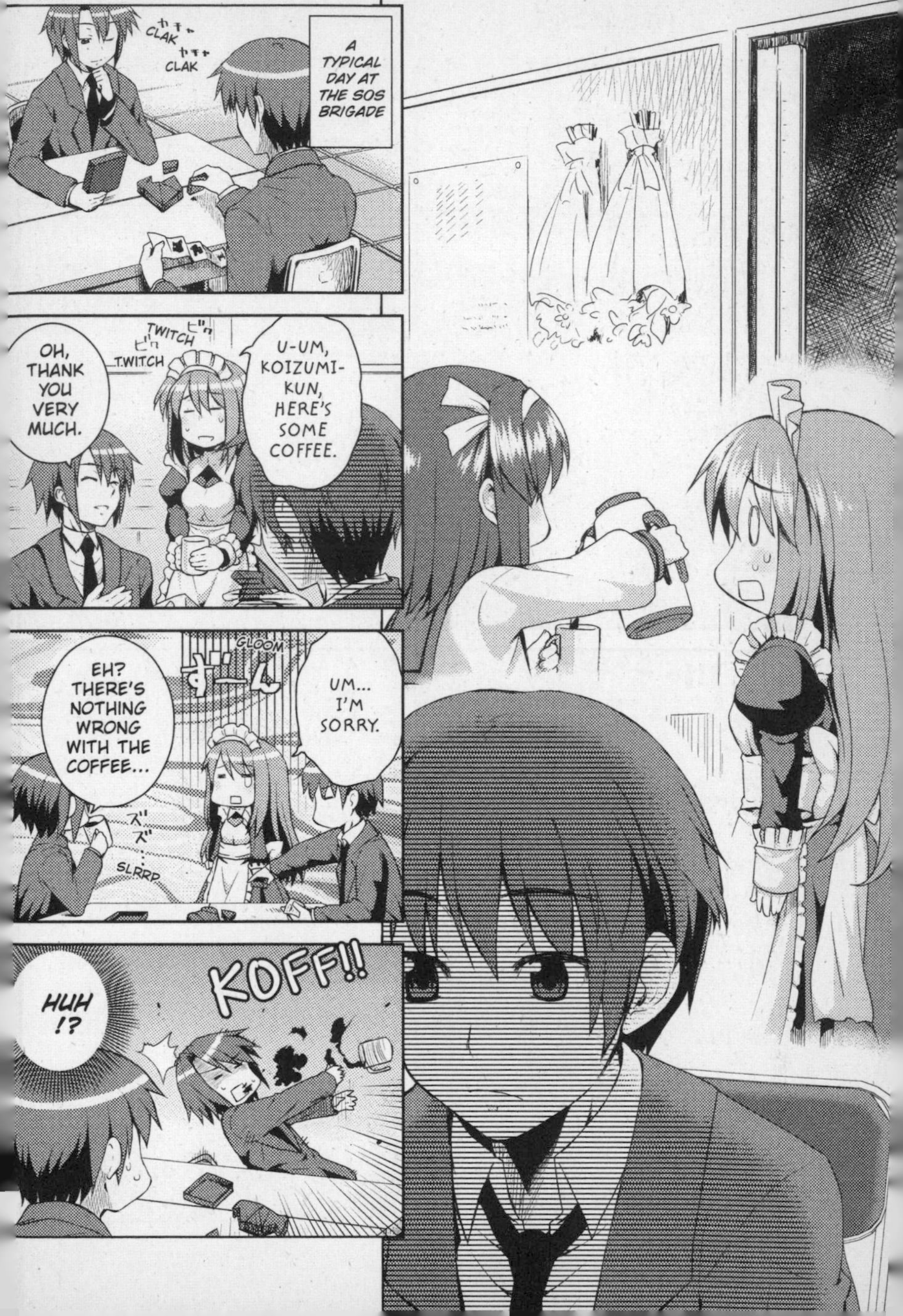

A TYPICAL DAY AT THE SOS BRIGADE
CLAK
CLAK
U-UM, KOIZUMI-KUN, HERE'S SOME COFFEE.
TWITCH
TWITCH
OH, THANK YOU VERY MUCH.
UM... I'M SORRY.
GLOOM
EH? THERE'S NOTHING WRONG WITH THE COFFEE...
SLRRP
KOFF!!
HUH!?

HIDDEN FLAVOR

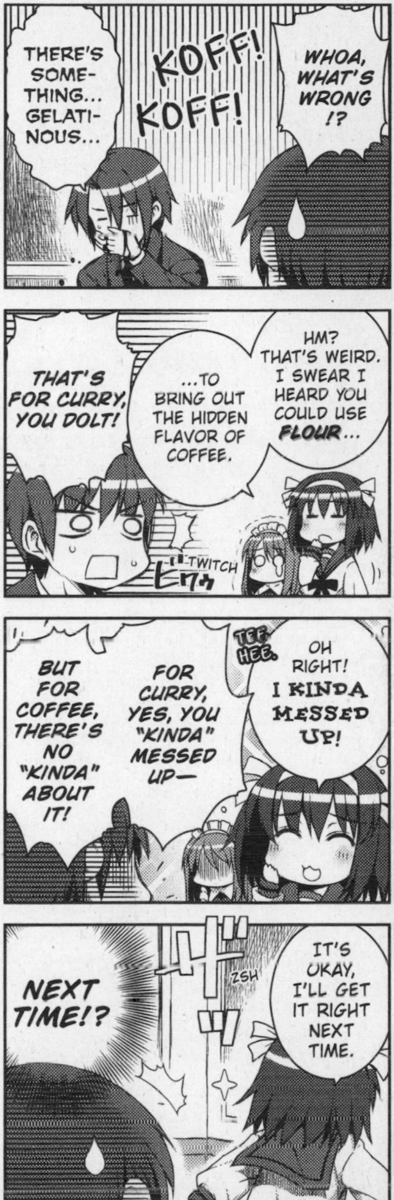
WHOA, WHAT'S WRONG!?
KOFF! KOFF!
THERE'S SOMETHING... GELATINOUS...
HM? THAT'S WEIRD. I SWEAR I HEARD YOU COULD USE FLOUR...
...TO BRING OUT THE HIDDEN FLAVOR OF COFFEE.
THAT'S FOR CURRY, YOU DOLT!
TWITCH
TEE HEE.
OH RIGHT! I KINDA MESSED UP!
FOR CURRY, YES, YOU "KINDA" MESSED UP—
BUT FOR COFFEE, THERE'S NO "KINDA" ABOUT IT!
IT'S OKAY, I'LL GET IT RIGHT NEXT TIME.
ZSH
NEXT TIME!?

DAMAGE

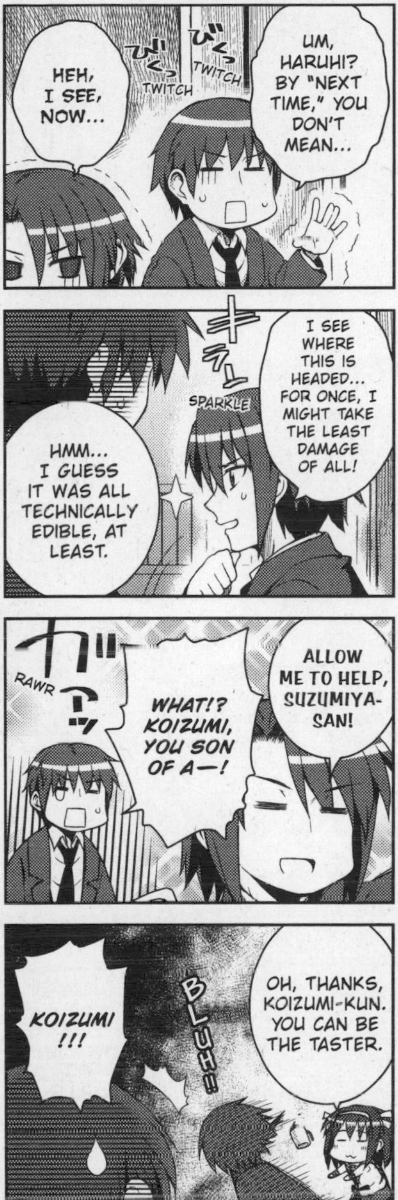
UM, HARUHI? BY "NEXT TIME," YOU DON'T MEAN...
TWITCH
TWITCH
HEH, I SEE, NOW...
I SEE WHERE THIS IS HEADED... FOR ONCE, I MIGHT TAKE THE LEAST DAMAGE OF ALL!
SPARKLE
HMM... I GUESS IT WAS ALL TECHNICALLY EDIBLE, AT LEAST.
ALLOW ME TO HELP, SUZUMIYA-SAN!
WHAT!? KOIZUMI, YOU SON OF A—!
RAWR
OH, THANKS, KOIZUMI-KUN. YOU CAN BE THE TASTER.
BLUH!!
KOIZUMI!!!

SUCCESSOR

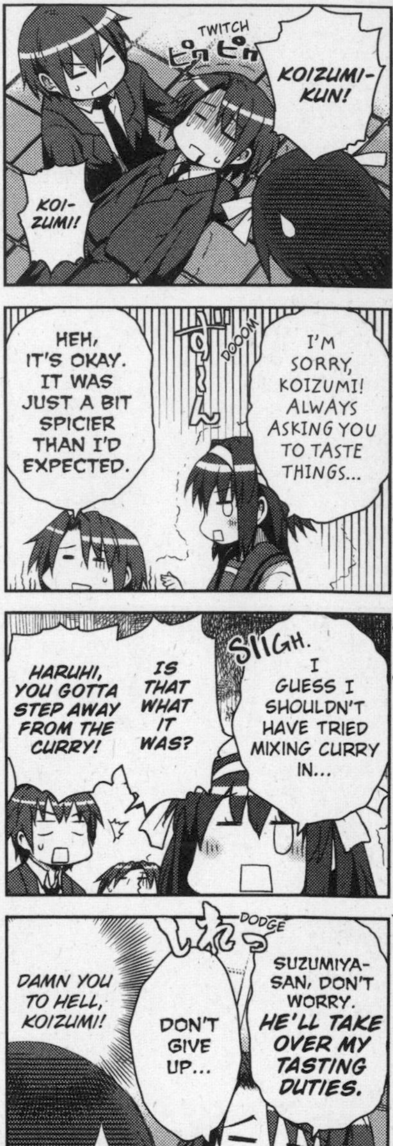
KOIZUMI-KUN!
TWITCH
KOI-ZUMI!
I'M SORRY, KOIZUMI! ALWAYS ASKING YOU TO TASTE THINGS...
DOOOM
HEH, IT'S OKAY. IT WAS JUST A BIT SPICIER THAN I'D EXPECTED.
SIIGH.
I GUESS I SHOULDN'T HAVE TRIED MIXING CURRY IN...
IS THAT WHAT IT WAS?
HARUHI, YOU GOTTA STEP AWAY FROM THE CURRY!
DODGE
SUZUMIYA-SAN, DON'T WORRY. HE'LL TAKE OVER MY TASTING DUTIES.
DON'T GIVE UP...
DAMN YOU TO HELL, KOIZUMI!

THE KNACK

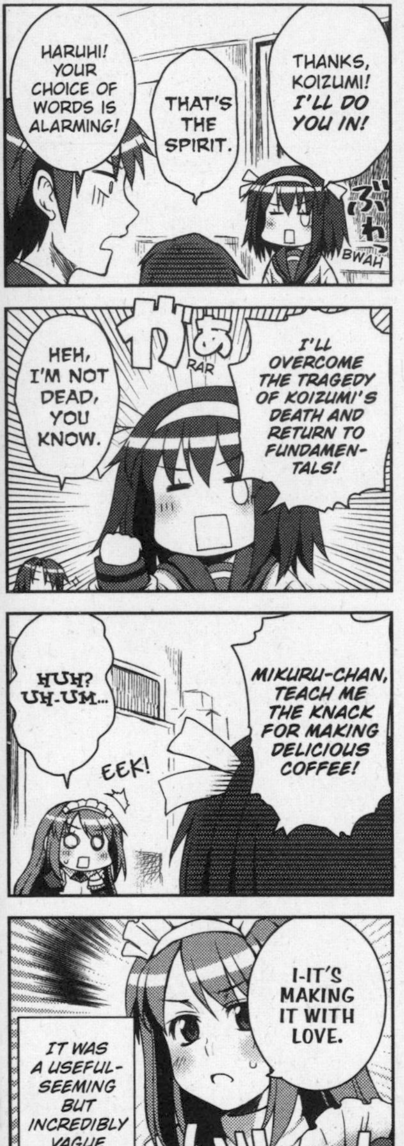
THANKS, KOIZUMI! I'LL DO YOU IN!
THAT'S THE SPIRIT.
HARUHI! YOUR CHOICE OF WORDS IS ALARMING!
BWAH
I'LL OVERCOME THE TRAGEDY OF KOIZUMI'S DEATH AND RETURN TO FUNDAMENTALS!
RAR
HEH, I'M NOT DEAD, YOU KNOW.
MIKURU-CHAN, TEACH ME THE KNACK FOR MAKING DELICIOUS COFFEE!
HUH? UH-UM...
EEK!
I-IT'S MAKING IT WITH LOVE.
IT WAS A USEFUL-SEEMING BUT INCREDIBLY VAGUE ANSWER.
BA-BUM

•Haruhi-chan •SOS Brigade brigade chief. A high school girl whose heart and body cannot be separated from curry.

•Kyon •Supposed to be the main character of this story. His potential as a straight man is beginning to blossom.

•Koizumi •Enigmatic transfer student and esper. Always manages to saunter away, but what about this time...?

• Nagato •Actually an alien gamer. Has a variety of alien powers, but often just sticks to the sidelines.

• Mikuru-chan •Time traveler. The brigade idol, she has a large vocabulary of nonsensical reaction sounds.

LOVE MIXING

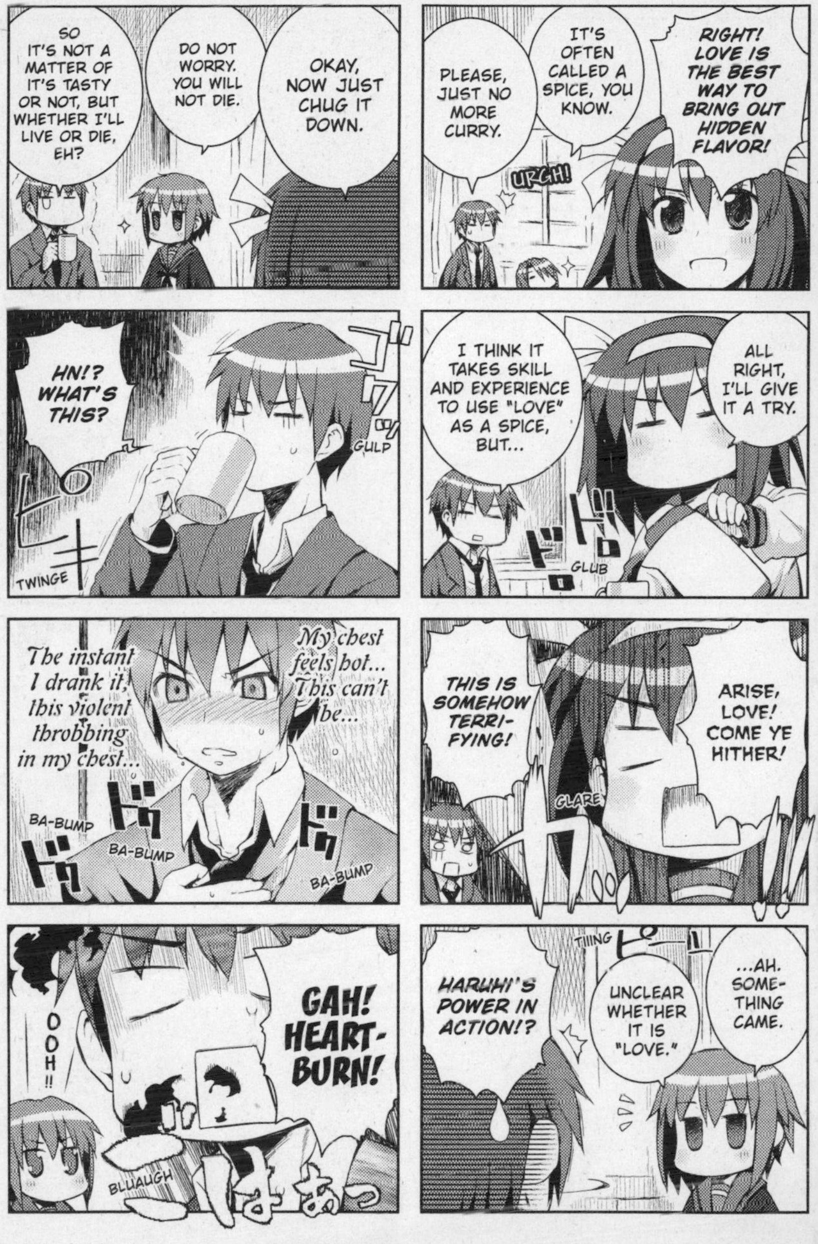
RIGHT! LOVE IS THE BEST WAY TO BRING OUT HIDDEN FLAVOR!
IT'S OFTEN CALLED A SPICE, YOU KNOW.
PLEASE, JUST NO MORE CURRY.
URGH!
ALL RIGHT, I'LL GIVE IT A TRY.
I THINK IT TAKES SKILL AND EXPERIENCE TO USE "LOVE" AS A SPICE, BUT...
GLUB
ARISE, LOVE! COME YE HITHER!
THIS IS SOMEHOW TERRIFYING!
GLARE
...AH. SOMETHING CAME.
TIING
UNCLEAR WHETHER IT IS "LOVE."
HARUHI'S POWER IN ACTION!?
OKAY, NOW JUST CHUG IT DOWN.
DO NOT WORRY. YOU WILL NOT DIE.
SO IT'S NOT A MATTER OF IT'S TASTY OR NOT, BUT WHETHER I'LL LIVE OR DIE, EH?
GULP
HN!? WHAT'S THIS?
TWINGE
My chest feels hot... This can't be...
The instant I drank it, this violent throbbing in my chest...
BA-BUMP
BA-BUMP
BA-BUMP
GAH! HEART-BURN!
OOH!!
BLUAUGH

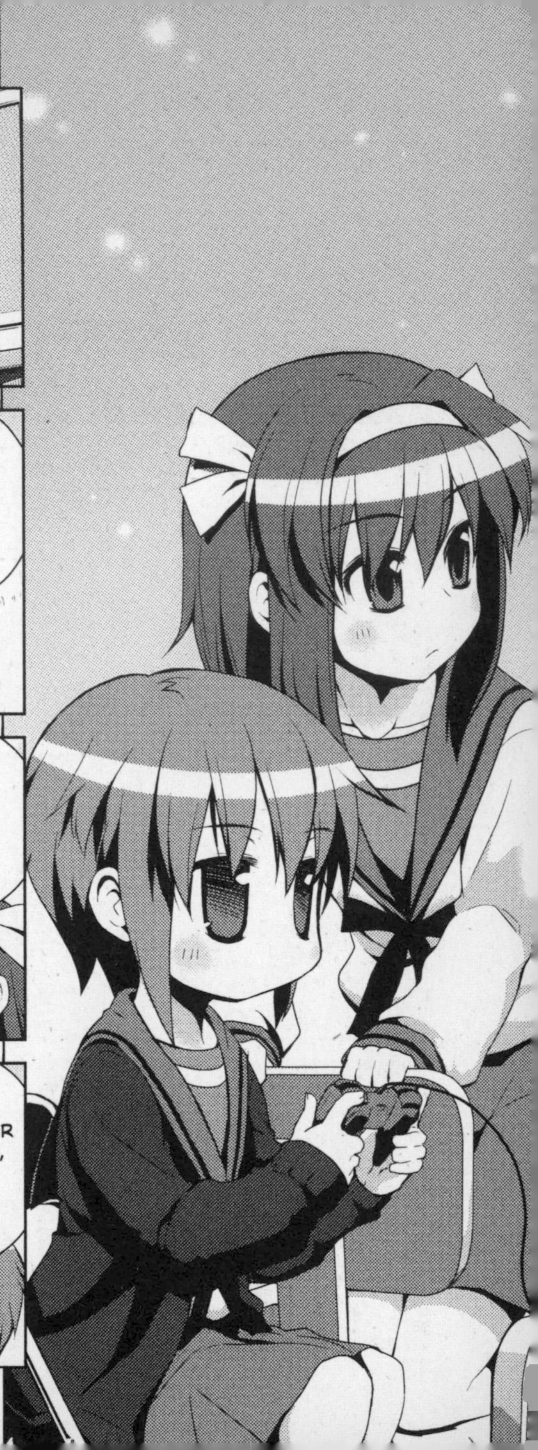

UNRIVALED ONE

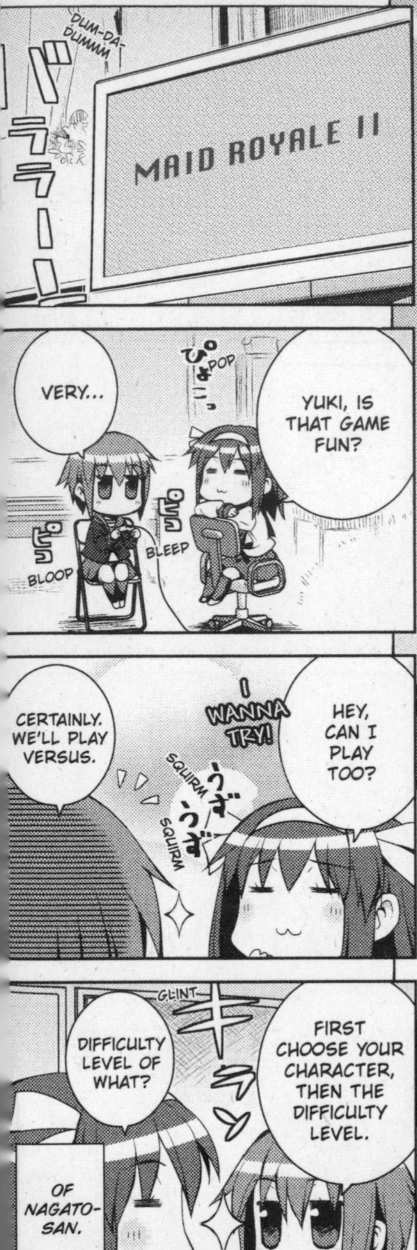
DUM-DA-DUMMM
MAID ROYALE II
YUKI, IS THAT GAME FUN?
POP
BLEEP
BLOOP
VERY...
HEY, CAN I PLAY TOO?
I WANNA TRY!
SQUIRM
SQUIRM
CERTAINLY. WE'LL PLAY VERSUS.
FIRST CHOOSE YOUR CHARACTER, THEN THE DIFFICULTY LEVEL.
GLINT
DIFFICULTY LEVEL OF WHAT?
OF NAGATO-SAN.

FULL STRENGTH

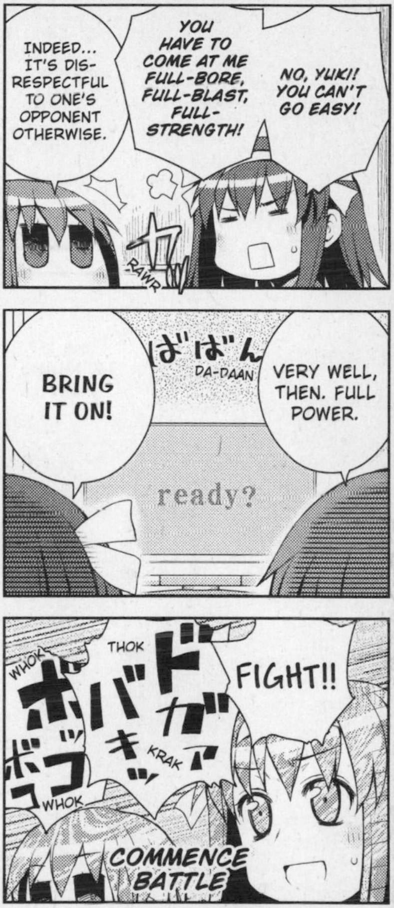
NO, YUKI! YOU CAN'T GO EASY!
YOU HAVE TO COME AT ME FULL-BORE, FULL-BLAST, FULL-STRENGTH!
INDEED... IT'S DIS-RESPECTFUL TO ONE'S OPPONENT OTHERWISE.
RAWR
VERY WELL, THEN. FULL POWER.
ばばん
DA-DAAN
BRING IT ON!
ready?
FIGHT!!
THOK
WHOK
KRAK
WHOK
COMMENCE BATTLE
KO
DONG
SHE GOT ME WHILE I WAS STILL IN MID-AIR—!
INSTA-KILL COMBO.

EASY TO UNDERSTAND

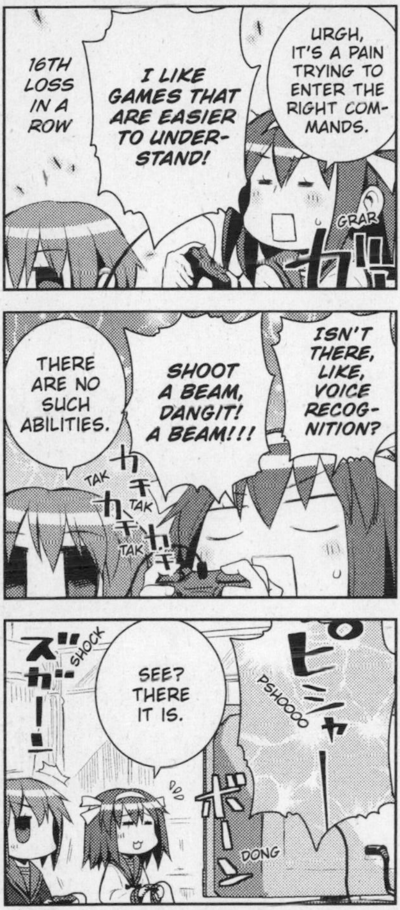
URGH, IT'S A PAIN TRYING TO ENTER THE RIGHT COM-MANDS.
GRAR
I LIKE GAMES THAT ARE EASIER TO UNDER-STAND!
16TH LOSS IN A ROW
ISN'T THERE, LIKE, VOICE RECOG-NITION?
SHOOT A BEAM, DANGIT! A BEAM!!!
THERE ARE NO SUCH ABILITIES.
TAK
TAK
TAK
PSHOOOO
SEE? THERE IT IS.
SHOCK
DONG
HA HA HA!
OKAY, YUKI! THE REAL CHALLENGE STARTS NOW!
HARUHI'S POWER STRUCK AGAIN.
DOOM

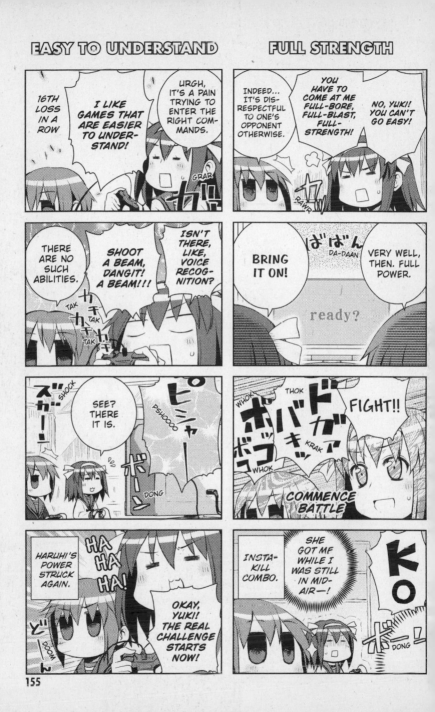

A MATTER OF DIGNITY

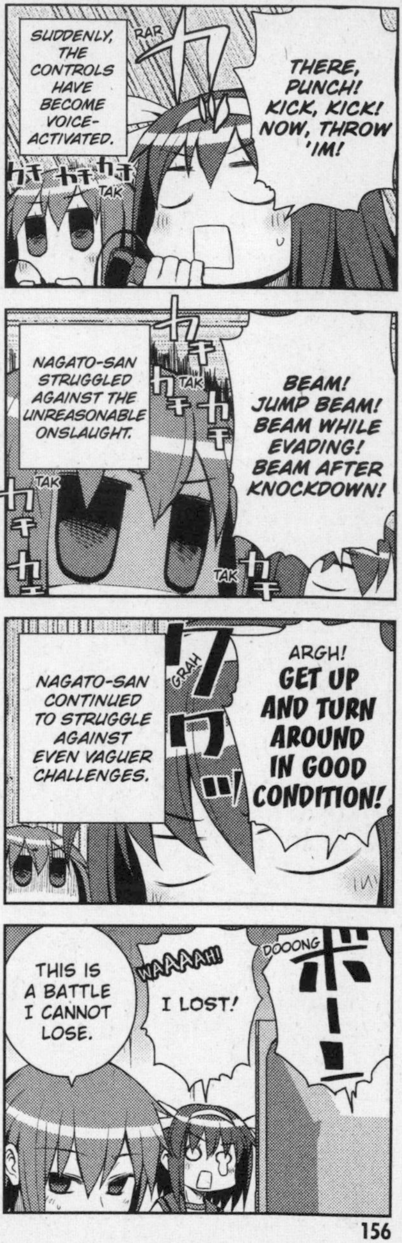
THERE, PUNCH! KICK, KICK! NOW, THROW 'IM!
RAR
SUDDENLY, THE CONTROLS HAVE BECOME VOICE-ACTIVATED.
TAK
BEAM! JUMP BEAM! BEAM WHILE EVADING! BEAM AFTER KNOCKDOWN!
NAGATO-SAN STRUGGLED AGAINST THE UNREASONABLE ONSLAUGHT.
TAK
TAK
TAK
ARGH! GET UP AND TURN AROUND IN GOOD CONDITION!
GRAH
NAGATO-SAN CONTINUED TO STRUGGLE AGAINST EVEN VAGUER CHALLENGES.
DOOONG
I LOST!
WAAAAH!
THIS IS A BATTLE I CANNOT LOSE.

CHANGE OF OPPONENTS

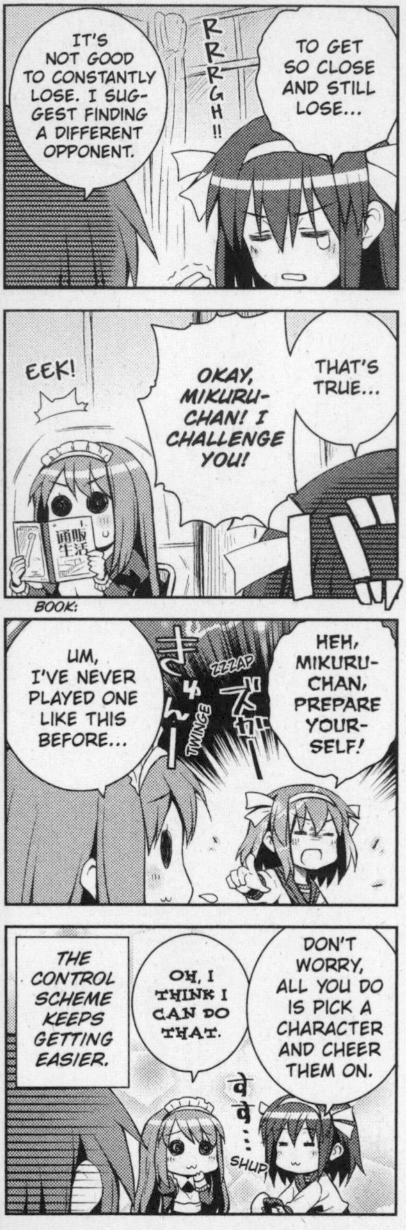
TO GET SO CLOSE AND STILL LOSE...
RRRGH!!
IT'S NOT GOOD TO CONSTANTLY LOSE. I SUGGEST FINDING A DIFFERENT OPPONENT.
THAT'S TRUE...
OKAY, MIKURU-CHAN! I CHALLENGE YOU!
EEK!
通販生活
BOOK:
HEH, MIKURU-CHAN, PREPARE YOURSELF!
ZZZAP
TWINGE
UM, I'VE NEVER PLAYED ONE LIKE THIS BEFORE...
DON'T WORRY, ALL YOU DO IS PICK A CHARACTER AND CHEER THEM ON.
OH, I THINK I CAN DO THAT.
SHUP
THE CONTROL SCHEME KEEPS GETTING EASIER.

CHEER BATTLE

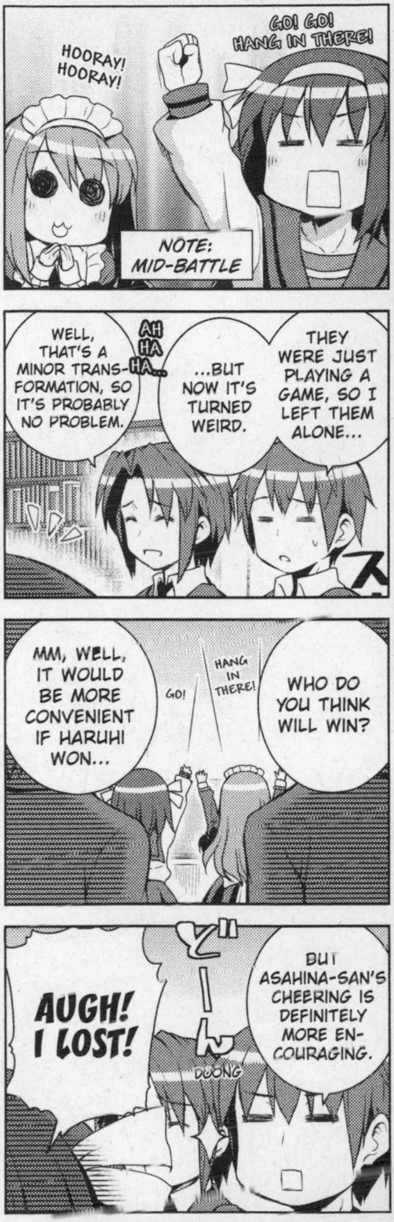
GO! GO! HANG IN THERE!
HOORAY! HOORAY!
NOTE: MID-BATTLE
THEY WERE JUST PLAYING A GAME, SO I LEFT THEM ALONE...
...BUT NOW IT'S TURNED WEIRD.
AH HA HA...
WELL, THAT'S A MINOR TRANS-FORMATION, SO IT'S PROBABLY NO PROBLEM.
WHO DO YOU THINK WILL WIN?
HANG IN THERE!
GO!
MM, WELL, IT WOULD BE MORE CONVENIENT IF HARUHI WON...
BUT ASAHINA-SAN'S CHEERING IS DEFINITELY MORE EN-COURAGING.
どーん
DOONG
AUGH! I LOST!

THE SAVIOR

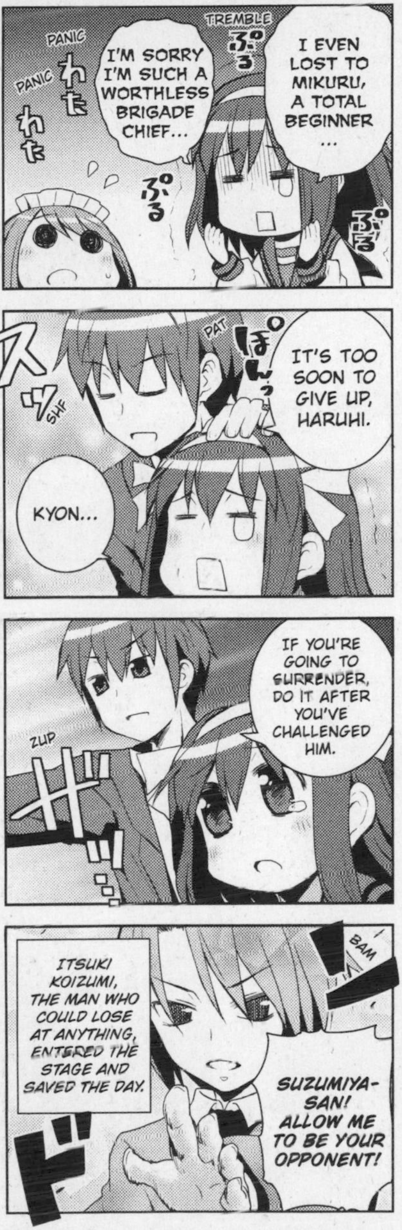
I EVEN LOST TO MIKURU, A TOTAL BEGINNER ...
TREMBLE
I'M SORRY I'M SUCH A WORTHLESS BRIGADE CHIEF...
PANIC
PANIC
IT'S TOO SOON TO GIVE UP, HARUHI.
PAT
SHF
KYON...
IF YOU'RE GOING TO SURRENDER, DO IT AFTER YOU'VE CHALLENGED HIM.
ZUP
BAM
SUZUMIYA-SAN! ALLOW ME TO BE YOUR OPPONENT!
ITSUKI KOIZUMI, THE MAN WHO COULD LOSE AT ANYTHING, ENTERED THE STAGE AND SAVED THE DAY.

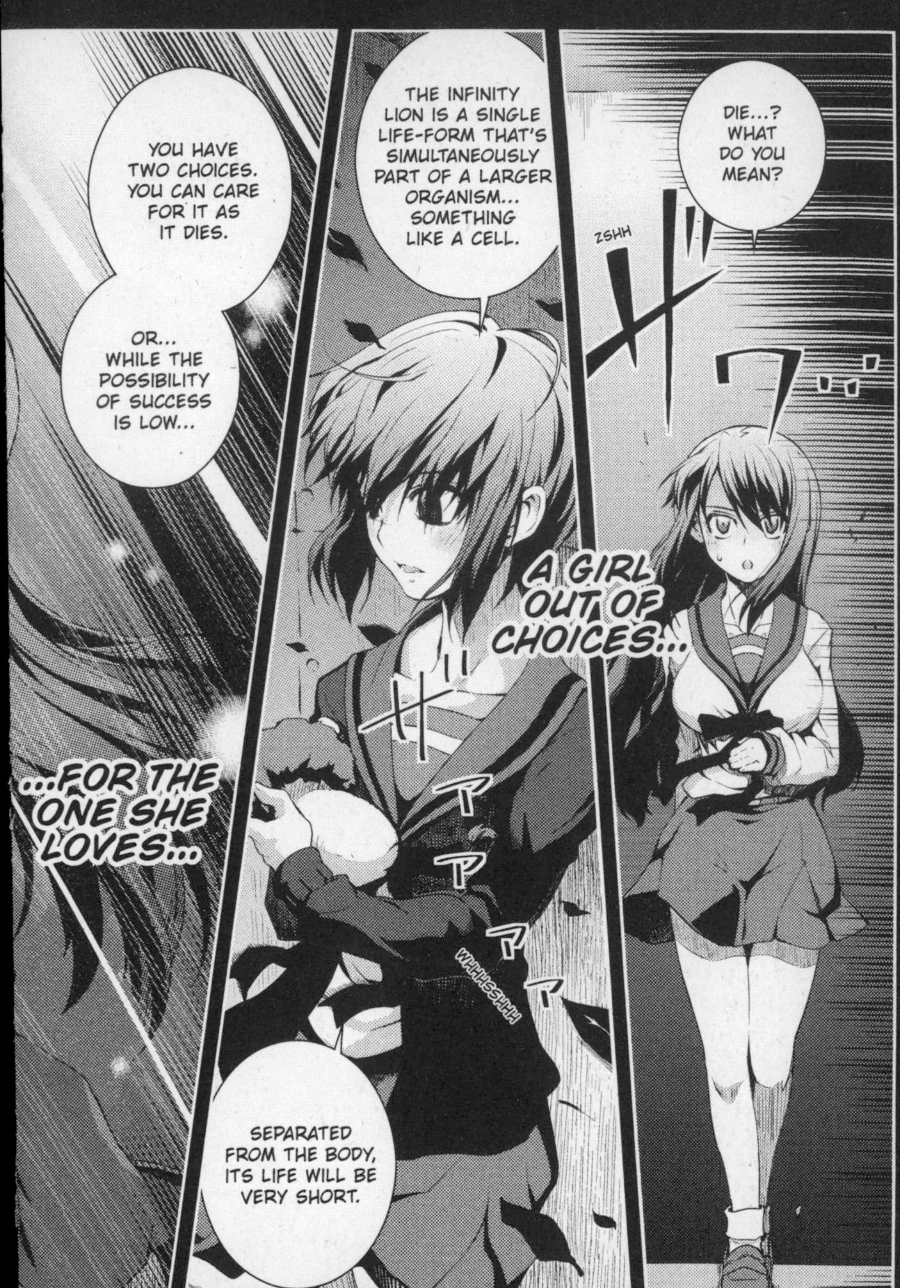

DIE...? WHAT DO YOU MEAN?
ZSHH
A GIRL OUT OF CHOICES...
THE INFINITY LION IS A SINGLE LIFE-FORM THAT'S SIMULTANEOUSLY PART OF A LARGER ORGANISM... SOMETHING LIKE A CELL.
WHHHSSHHH
SEPARATED FROM THE BODY, ITS LIFE WILL BE VERY SHORT.
YOU HAVE TWO CHOICES. YOU CAN CARE FOR IT AS IT DIES.
OR... WHILE THE POSSIBILITY OF SUCCESS IS LOW...
...FOR THE ONE SHE LOVES...

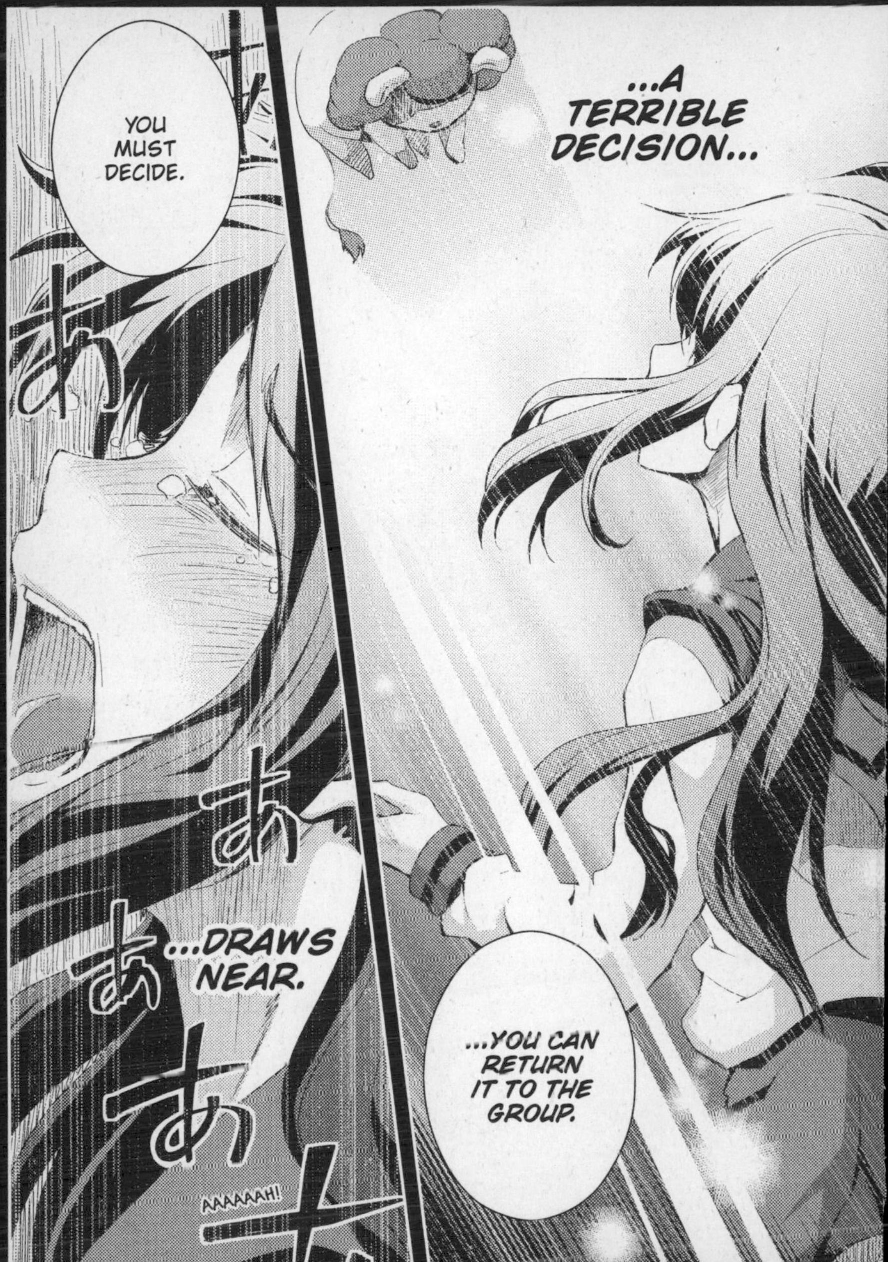
...A TERRIBLE DECISION...
...YOU CAN RETURN IT TO THE GROUP.
YOU MUST DECIDE.
あ あ あ あ
...DRAWS NEAR.
AAAAAAH!

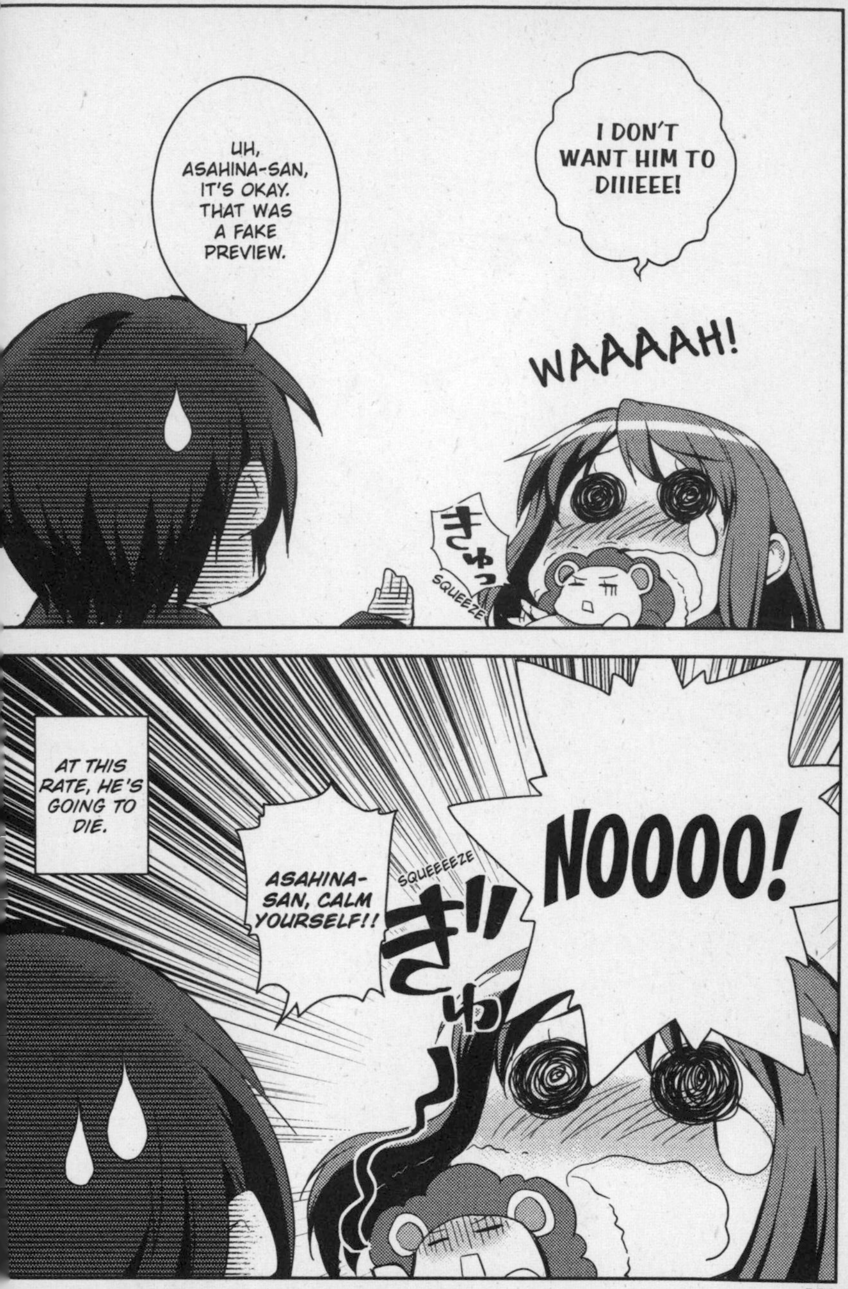
I DON'T WANT HIM TO DIIIEEE!
UH, ASAHINA-SAN, IT'S OKAY. THAT WAS A FAKE PREVIEW.
WAAAAH!
きゅっ
SQUEEZE
NOOOO!
ぎゅ～
SQUEEEEZE
ASAHINA-SAN, CALM YOURSELF!!
AT THIS RATE, HE'S GOING TO DIE.

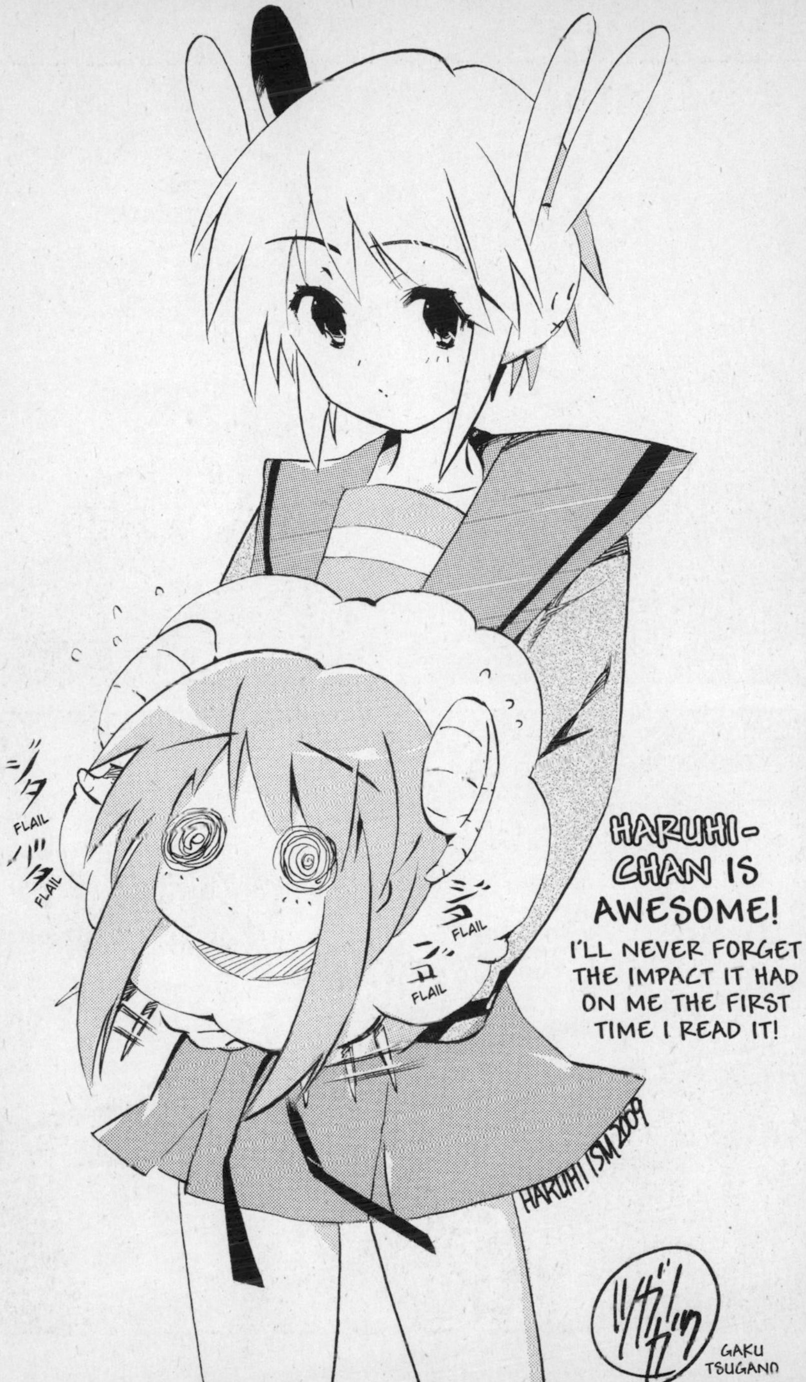
ジタ
FLAIL
バタ
FLAIL
ジ
FLAIL
タ
FLAIL
HARUHI-CHAN IS AWESOME!
I'LL NEVER FORGET THE IMPACT IT HAD ON ME THE FIRST TIME I READ IT!
HARUHI ISM 2009
GAKU TSUGANO

THE MELANCHOLY OF SUZUMIYA
HARUHI-CHAN
❸

Original Story: Nagaru Tanigawa
Manga: PUYO
Character Design: Noizi Ito

Translation: Paul Starr
Lettering: Hope Donovan

The Melancholy of Suzumiya Haruhi-chan Volume 3
© Nagaru TANIGAWA • Noizi ITO 2009 © PUYO 2009. First published in Japan in 2009
by KADOKAWA SHOTEN Co., Ltd., Tokyo. English translation rights arranged with
KADOKAWA SHOTEN Co., Ltd., Tokyo through TUTTLE-MORI AGENCY, INC., Tokyo.

English translation © 2011 by Hachette Book Group, Inc.

Yen Press
Hachette Book Group
237 Park Avenue, New York, NY 10017

www.HachetteBookGroup.com
www.YenPress.com

Yen Press is an imprint of Hachette Book Group, Inc.
The Yen Press name and logo are trademarks of Hachette Book Group, Inc.

First Yen Press Edition: August 2011

ISBN: 978-0-316-18763-3

10 9 8 7 6 5 4 3 2 1

BVG

Printed in the United States of America